Fund Monitor 1998

CANACCORD
C A P I T A L

PETER CHE B.A.Sc.
INVESTMENT ADVISOR

CANACCORD CAPITAL CORPORATION
P.O. BOX 10337 PACIFIC CENTRE
2200-609 GRANVILLE STREET VANCOUVER BC CANADA V7Y 1H2
TEL: 604 643.7029 FAX: 604 601.5940
E-MAIL: peter_che@canaccord.com

Prentice Hall Canada Inc.
Scarborough, Ontario

Canadian Cataloguing in Publication Data

Annual.
1998-
"An expert's guide to building the best mutual fund portfolio."
By Duff Young.
ISSN 1482-7492
ISBN 0-13-674482-6 (1998 ed.)

1. Mutual funds - Canada. I. Young, Duff, 1967-

HG5154.5.M64   332.63'27   C97-900994-4

 © 1997 Duff Young
Prentice Hall Canada Inc., Scarborough, Ontario
A Division of Simon & Schuster/A Viacom Company

Prentice-Hall, Inc., Upper Saddle River, New Jersey
Prentice-Hall International (UK) Limited, London
Prentice-Hall of Australia, Pty. Limited, Sydney
Prentice-Hall Hispanoamericana, S.A., Mexico City
Prentice-Hall of India Private Limited, New Delhi
Prentice-Hall of Japan, Inc., Tokyo
Simon & Schuster Southeast Asia Private Limited, Singapore
Editora Prentice-Hall do Brasil, Ltda., Rio de Janeiro

ISBN 0-13-674482-6

Acquisitions Editor: Robert Harris
Editor: Kimberley Love
Copy Editor: Dianne Broad
Editorial Assistant: Joan Whitman
Production Coordinator: Julie Preston
Art Director: Mary Opper
Cover and Interior Design: Alex Li
Cover Photograph: Ray Boudreau
Illustrations: Dave Klug
Page Layout: Arlene Edgar

2 3 4 5   TC   01 00 99 98

Printed and bound in Canada

Visit the Prentice Hall Canada Web site! Send us your comments,
browse our catalogues, and more. **www.phcanada.com**
For mutual fund updates, visit **www.fundmonitor.com**

Although every effort has been taken to make certain the information contained in this
book is thorough and reliable, the author and publisher assume no responsibility for
any inaccuracies or omissions in the book. The author and publisher are not engaged
in rendering any professional services in this publication. Readers should consult a
competent professional for advice applying to their particular circumstances.

Dedication

I dedicate this special new book to my wife, Jennifer, and our little girl, Courtney, for their enduring patience and endless support.

Table of Contents

Foreword

A telling little axiom is often repeated with real conviction in the mutual fund industry: "Mutual funds aren't bought, they're sold!" That axiom is the reason I'm writing *FundMonitor 1998*.

The mutual fund industry drives me crazy. Everyone is trying to sell you a great fund — but the simple truth is that most funds just aren't great. In fact, most funds aren't even good! And real gems are very rare.

That's an abbreviated summary of what I've learned about mutual funds after seven years of rigorous fund research. Like the average Canadian mutual fund investor, I share a healthy cynicism about the industry. The industry that has grown eightfold in eight years. The industry in which I make my living.

What I've learned is that most people take the wrong approach to mutual fund investing. They focus on the micro-level — which fund should I buy? When should I buy that fund? Is this another good fund to add to the other 17 funds I already have? Wait! Shouldn't I buy the one that returned 89 percent last year?

The truth is that success in mutual funds has little to do with which funds we choose or which funds we've sold. It is, instead, about simpler things. Like investing systematically over time. Like having a balanced portfolio. Like working with a good financial advisor who can help keep us on track. Mutual funds are just one part of our financial lives: a means to an end.

Since my expertise lies in mutual fund research, this is — of course — a book about mutual fund research. I think it presents the most forward-thinking, common-sense research ever presented in Canada. And while

I am not an expert financial planner, in this book I will offer a new context to my research: an approach to developing a strategy that makes sense for your overall financial life, as well as a way to find the best funds. I will remind you of simple things that you already know — such as the importance of an RRSP — and I'll suggest some effective ways to save money for your kids' future.

This book, I hope, will challenge you to think about your own financial situation. Chapter 1 contains an important section for many readers: getting out of debt. I'll also offer candid advice on whether you should pay down your mortgage or invest extra cash in a mutual fund. (Hint: I won't be recommending a fund.)

Although this big stuff consumes only a little space in the book, I have placed it before the fund research to help you see its priority in your financial life.

And really, I hope that you'll come away from the book with a sense that sound management of your personal financial life is within your grasp, and that mutual funds — the best funds — really can help you achieve your financial goals.

I've presented my research here in a concise, candid, and colourful way. You don't need to work in the financial industry to understand the analysis and observations.

The preparation of this book has converged with an exciting time for me, professionally. The purpose in my career — as I'm learning it — is really about how to identify new, common-sense approaches to evaluating mutual funds and then convey them without all the nonsense, in a way that's easy to understand, even for the average investor.

I hope that this book will be — of all of the mutual fund books — the easiest to understand and use. Furthermore, I hope it's the one that uses the most rigorous fund research, the most legitimate evaluation criteria, and the most credible top picks.

Use the book as a reference. Or feel free to just browse. Respond to a quiz, or look up a fund. This book really isn't intended to be read from cover to cover so much as it's meant to be used as a reference guide on your shelf. I hope it will be an important addition to the work that you're already doing with your financial advisor.

This book should be a living book for us all to use, because it's designed to be used in conjunction with my special Web site — www.FundMonitor.com — which also happens to be the name of my business. And while the figures in this book won't become stale-dated like others, updating will help to keep you in touch with what's happening in the mutual fund marketplace. Valuable updates are available on the Web site.

One of the shocking new pieces of research to come out in this book is the startling news that some investors aren't doing that well in mutual funds. It's not because the funds don't do well, but because people make systematic mistakes in investing in funds. The challenge of my work as a mutual fund analyst is to help people overcome those systematic investing mistakes with mutual funds.

The road to financial independence is one filled with both opportunity and risk. You've probably already recognized that mutual funds can play an integral role in that journey.

This book — I hope — will become your guide.

Duff Young, CFA
November, 1997

Acknowledgments

This new book was a herculean effort made easy by the dedicated, talented team I've been lucky enough to work with for some time. For weeks, Glen Priestley, our senior analyst, and Joe Latouf, our systems chief, worked full time on this book. A special thanks is owed, as well, to Kim Love, my editor, and to Mel O'Neill, who does administrative work for our firm. I would also like to acknowledge the contributions made by countless editors, readers, proofreaders, artists, and designers — including Karen Alliston, Marc Marzotto, Dave Klug, and Alex Li. Finally, I'd like to thank Robert Harris — who was a leader in getting this project started for Prentice Hall and who ignited my vision of what this book could be.

Putting Mutual Funds into Perspective

MUTUAL FUNDS ARE MY AREA OF EXPERTISE, the topic of this book, and the subject of microscopic focus by the media. At RRSP time, the attention becomes almost obsessive. If you want a reliable topic of conversation for your next cocktail party, brush up on your mutual fund trivia.

But don't let this focus on the details of various mutual funds divert you from the fact that the process of actually choosing the best funds is one of the last steps in getting your financial house in order. Before you even begin to fall in love with a particular fund or before you become a fund expert (too many people are), you must get the foundation of your financial security in place. Now.

In fact, if we think about that metaphor of a financial "house," we could say that your mutual fund purchases are somewhere up near the roofline. To begin, you need a solid foundation and sturdy walls. The various components of your financial plan depend on one another; but together, they provide you with a solid and secure financial future.

Risk Management — The Foundations of Your Financial Security

The focus of this book is mutual fund analysis — which funds are good at the moment, which ones are reliably good, and which ones aren't worth your attention. But nothing I tell you in the FundMonitor Profiles is as important as the basic principles described in this chapter. If after reading this chapter you discover that you don't have the foundation of your financial plan in place, go and look after the basics right away. In fact, do it before you read Chapter 2.

for more information

I'm no expert on this financial planning stuff. But I'm smart enough to know that you need to find someone who is. I urge you to read an excellent book on the subject — *The Money Coach,* by my old friend Riley Moynes.

The first cornerstone of your financial plan is insurance. If you have other people who depend on you — family members, for example — you need insurance. In terms of life insurance, basic term insurance will suffice. I say purchase it at the lowest price you can find, but make sure that you get adequate coverage. And don't forget long-term disability coverage. After all, you are considerably less likely to die between now and age 65 than you are to develop a disability. And if you become permanently disabled, it could be more expensive for your family than if you had died.

The second cornerstone of your financial foundation is your emergency fund. This fund is a nice chunk of money that you have tucked away for any little surprises that could wreak havoc on your household cash flow. Few people make this emergency fund a priority. But if you're faced with a huge dental bill, a flooded basement, or if you lose your job, you'll need an emergency fund. Without one, you're faced with some unappealing options such as borrowing money at a high rate of interest on a credit card or borrowing from a family member. How large should your fund be? Some people suggest as much as three months' salary should be available to you in an emergency fund.

Third, and related to the point above, get a line of credit — even if you don't need it right now. Lines of credit come in two varieties: secured and unsecured. Secured lines of credit offer larger credit limits and better interest rates. The way I accomplished this was through a "collateral mortgage" against my house. Some paperwork and expense are involved in setting this up, but it allows me a large line of credit at attractive interest rates if I ever need it. For me — as I embark on my own business — it's a wonderful financial tool! It's also good if you ever lose your job; you'll find that you have access to low-rate cash that is repayable on attractive terms. When you need the money, you don't have to apply for it — you just write a cheque. If you're not carrying a balance, there's no cost to having a line of credit. That's another reason to consider a line of credit as a third cornerstone in the foundation of your financial security.

Zooming in

Where Mutual Funds Fit in Your Financial Security Structure

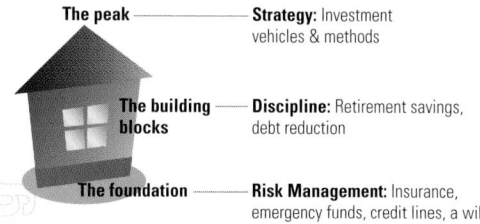

The peak ———— **Strategy:** Investment vehicles & methods

The building blocks ———— **Discipline:** Retirement savings, debt reduction

The foundation ———— **Risk Management:** Insurance, emergency funds, credit lines, a will

Mutual funds offer you access to professional money management, which, over time, or can extend the margin and possibilities of your financial security. Your mutual fund strategy rests on more fundamental aspects of financial security that include various forms of risk management and the disciplines of retirement savings and debt reduction.

The final cornerstone involves having a will. Honestly, no one in Canada would want to die without one. Things can become very messy very quickly. If you're like me — with one wife and one child — you won't believe what could happen upon your death. For example, in my case, the Province of Ontario children's guardian would be responsible for administering the money that would go to my two-year-old daughter, which would be half of everything over $200 000. Clearly, that's not my wish. (No one I know would want the government looking after his or her money.) But in the absence of a valid, up-to-date will, your wishes aren't even relevant in determining how to divide your money and how to manage your family's affairs in your absence. And that's a scary thought.

Taken together, these four cornerstones provide a basic level of security — by managing the major financial risks. Most working families can afford them. Few can afford to be without them.

Discipline: Retirement Savings and Reducing Debt — The Building Blocks of Financial Security

If the foundation of financial security calls for putting risk management tools and decisions in place, the building blocks of financial security call for a regular discipline of saving for retirement and reducing debt.

Most working Canadians need to tackle these two tasks at the same time because our tax and registered retirement savings plan (RRSP) rules make it sensible to begin saving for retirement long before mortgages and other debts are cleared off. Handling both tasks at the same time can feel like a tough slog. But the time-honoured wisdom on this subject says that a regular approach — such as making RRSP contributions from each pay cheque and shortening the amortization on your mortgage by paying more than the minimum each month — can help you achieve financial security.

Registered Savings Plans

Canada's RRSP program is one of the most generous programs of its kind anywhere in the world. That's why it's so disappointing that only 22 percent of working Canadians made their maximum allowable contributions in 1996.

for more information

Recommended
Reading:

*A Piece of the Action:
How the Middle Class
Joined the Money Class,*
by Joseph Nocera.

If you have any RRSP room available from prior years, find a way to backfill those contributions. Some people become stalled by deciding how they will actually invest that money once it's in an RRSP. The key move, however, is just making the contribution. You could just open an RRSP account at a bank and invest the money in a 30-day term deposit while you do some homework and talk to a professional about how to get the money invested properly for the long term.

Pay Down Your Mortgage or Buy Funds?

Outside of your RRSP, the surest investment you can make is reducing debt.

Think About It | Would you buy a mutual fund with a guaranteed double-digit rate of return? One that you could get cash out of (if you needed it later) without any penalty? Well, that's exactly what you get when you make lump-sum mortgage payments.

Assuming that you've already | maximized your RRSP contributions and you've still got some extra cash to invest (in a bank account or an investment account earning taxable income), one of the smartest decisions is to take that cash and (if there is no penalty for doing so) make a lump-sum payment against your mortgage. That way you'll save the interest costs on that debt. The interest savings, of course, are equivalent to the interest rate on your mortgage, but since your mortgage isn't tax deductible, paying off your mortgage with a rate of seven percent is like earning seven percent after-tax guaranteed. No mutual fund in Canada

⌠ *Action!*

Are You Too Deep in Debt?

Here's a quiz from the editors of *Money Magazine* to tell if you are.

1. Do your monthly credit card and loan payments exceed 20 percent of your after-tax pay? (Exclude mortgages and car loans here.)

2. Have you ever borrowed from one lender to pay another?

3. Have you ever been forced to ask a friend or relative to co-sign a loan for you?

4. Do you hold more than just a basic charge card or do you hold store credit cards and gas credit cards — the ones with the highest rates of interest?

5. Do you make only minimum monthly payments? Or are you unable to say how much money you owe?

If you answered "Yes" to any of these questions, you've probably got a debt problem, but you are not alone. I recommend that you tackle this immediately. I know because I've been there.

Here's my tip list for helping you to get the information you need to help you get out of debt faster.

● When you've got some money available, pay off your highest rate debt first.

● If you're having trouble paying down your debts and believe that it has become a problem, contact a non-profit credit counselling service.

● Request a copy of your credit report. Call Equifax at 1-800-937-4093.

● Consolidate. For instance, if you own your home, a home equity loan with a flexible repayment schedule could consolidate all of your bills at high interest rates into one low monthly bill at a lower rate of interest.

Action!

Three Things You Can Do Right Now!

This is a test — a big test — of your resolve. Think of three things that you could do now to improve your financial situation.

For some people, a simple move would be to pay down their credit cards by spending the cash in their bank account. For others it would be a consolidation of high-rate credit-card debt with a low-rate line of credit. Other people will have cash sitting around that they should move into an RRSP right now — even if it's not February. Some people might say that they could improve their situation right now by putting their will in order or getting some quotes on cheap term insurance.

No matter what, writing out an action plan with three basic moves that you can make right now to improve your situation is a key way of becoming more psychologically committed to those actions. So write them out now and make a commitment to act on these things soon.

1. _____

_____

_____

_____

2. _____

_____

_____

_____

3. _____

_____

_____

_____

can offer anything like seven percent after-tax guaranteed. In fact, let me repeat that. As a mutual fund analyst, I can attest that *no* mutual fund in Canada can offer anything like seven percent after-tax guaranteed.

The second benefit to paying down that mortgage — in addition to making a great investment — is that you'll boost your home equity. That equity is a resource you could tap in the future if you're ever strapped for cash due to an emergency. Some mortgages will allow for lump-sum repayments that allow you to skip payments later. This could be a nice little security blanket during some tough times down the road.

Eliminating "Consumer" Debt

Consumer debt is generally connected with credit cards. It may be obvious that credit cards are an expensive way to borrow money. Still, in the United States, 70 percent of credit-card holders carry a balance from month-to-month at rates of interest that average 18 percent. For those who maintain a practice of paying the minimum monthly payment, big-ticket items such as a $1500 television or stereo system will take 13 years to pay off — and cost twice as much as the initial cost of the item!

Two out of five Americans under age 35 have such bad credit that they have been turned down for more. The discipline of getting out of credit-card debt, and other high-cost consumer debt vehicles, should be another building block in your financial security program.

Getting your financial house in order is the first step in achieving financial independence.

Now let's talk about mutual funds — and the role they can play in helping you to achieve that independence.

Mutual Funds:
The Basics

ANYONE WANT TO GUESS HOW MANY MUTUAL funds are expected to be available to Canadians for the 1998 RRSP season? Although I don't know the exact number — you'd have to do a recount almost daily to keep up — it's around 1600.

What accounts for the spectacular growth of this industry in the past decade? I believe that it is the result of a convergence of two trends: a recognition by average Canadians that they will need to take their retirement planning into their own hands, coupled with an increasingly complex and globalized marketplace, which has experienced the longest bull run in history. Faced with the need to invest, and the complexity of the task, Canadians have turned to "managed money" — and especially to mutual funds.

Demographers remind us that baby boomers are moving from their spending years (on the house and the kids) into their savings years (the house is paid and the kids are gone). Retirement looms ahead, and boomers are saving their money.

This demographic group is educated and confident, and they like what they see in mutual funds. Most recognize that they are no longer restricted to their parents' traditional investment choices — whole-life insurance policies, Guaranteed Investment Certificates (GICs), Canada Savings Bonds (CSBs), treasury bills, or term deposits. On the other hand, they clearly welcome an alternative to direct stock market investment.

The growth of the mutual fund industry has also been fuelled by the recognition that even an extra single-percentage-point return, when compounded over the long term, can yield significantly more accumulated wealth — and a full-time professional will almost always achieve better investment results than a part-time amateur will.

All of these events have contributed to phenomenal growth in the mutual fund industry in Canada, as shown below.

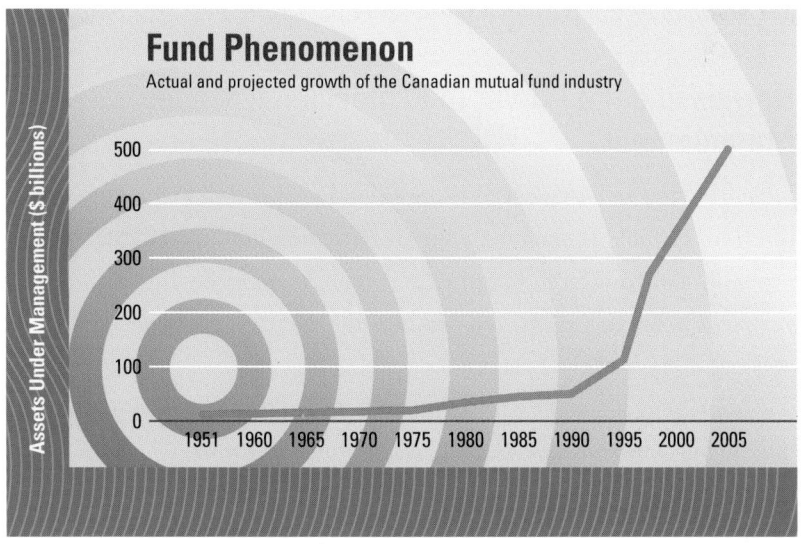

Fund Phenomenon

Actual and projected growth of the Canadian mutual fund industry

In this sea of choices — and opportunities — my FundMonitor mutual fund research can help you make sense of your options.

If you've been around the block a few times as a mutual fund investor, you may want to skip ahead to my fund reviews — the research analysis that is the main purpose of this book. But if you're new to mutual funds, or you'd like a recap, let's first look at the basics.

What Is a Mutual Fund?

A mutual fund is a "pool" of money composed of the investments of many individuals — sometimes thousands or even hundreds of thousands of people. A professional money manager invests the pool of money in a selected, predetermined range of investments. A mutual fund must be sold by prospectus, and this document provides the basic information about the fund: its investment objective, the investment style of its manager, and the types of investments that the fund is mandated to participate in.

Stripped to the bare asset classes, there are only three types of investments: cash (generally in the form of treasury bills), bonds (usually very secure government or corporate bonds), and equities (the shares of Canadian or international corporations).

Harnessing the Power of Professional Money Management

Face it. If you're like most working Canadians, you probably don't have the time or tools to oversee your investments effectively. And you're probably not trained to be an expert money manager. But with an investment in mutual funds, you can benefit from the experience and skills of some of the world's best money managers.

Your fund manager works full time to capture the best opportunities for the fund. A manager's tasks include scrutinizing national and international news, and staying abreast of any economic, political or demographic trends. In the case of an international fund, you can expect your manager to be closely connected with the markets in which the fund invests. Many even take up a home base in their international market.

Ultimately, the goal of a fund manager is to produce superior, solid, long-term growth for the fund. Your most important job is to choose your mutual funds carefully. I recommend that you use a financial advisor for this task — and then let the money manager do his or her best possible work over the long term.

One of the most successful mutual funds ever is the **Templeton Growth Fund.** This fund was managed by Sir John Templeton until 1988, when the current manager, Mark Holowesko, stepped into the lead role in one of the world's most famous funds. If you had invested $10 000 in this fund when it began in 1954, you would have seen your investment grow to $4.8 million by 1997. That's an average annual compounded growth rate of over 15.5 percent!

Diversifying with Mutual Funds

When you were growing up, your mother probably warned you not to put all your eggs in one basket. That sage advice also applies to investing. The problem is that the average investor isn't wealthy enough to diversify his or her investment effectively. If you wanted a well-diversified portfolio of stocks, you would need to buy many shares in several different companies — both in Canada and abroad.

Thanks to the economies of scale provided by the mutual fund "pool" (which often totals millions or even billions of dollars), even a small investment is well diversified. Your mutual fund holding represents a vast array of stocks, bonds, and/or other investments. In fact, I don't know of any better way to diversify your investments than through carefully selected mutual funds.

A World of Investment Choice with Mutual Funds

The good news is that, no matter what your investment needs or your financial situation, there really is a mutual fund for everyone. In fact, there are many mutual funds that suit your unique needs.

Maybe RRSP savings are your key investment priority, and a portfolio of mutual funds is a way to achieve your retirement goals. Perhaps you're a very aggressive investor looking for maximum growth, and willing to weather some dramatic ups and downs to get there. Or maybe the ups and downs make you seasick, and you'd prefer a slower, steadier path to growth.

You may want to invest in equities, or real estate funds, or mortgage funds. Or you may have an interest in a specialty fund, such as gold, or a particular market, like Japan or Europe.

A wealth of choices is open to you. You can use this book to explore some of the best funds in every category. And, as always, you should discuss your preferences with your financial advisor.

Zooming in

A Mutual Fund Does Not Equal a Stock Market Investment

I've heard people exclaim that they'd never buy a mutual fund because they don't want to "play the stock market." Obviously there's a misconception that a mutual fund equals a stock market investment. This is not necessarily the case.

Many mutual funds are based on equities — that is, stocks in publicly traded companies. But not all mutual funds are equity funds. As you can see by the way I've categorized my fund research, many mutual funds are based on bonds or are "money market" funds, based on treasury bills, or very liquid investments. Others are based on mortgages, or gold, or real estate, to name a few.

Types of Mutual Funds

The vast array of mutual fund choices can leave investors paralyzed. With around 1600 mutual funds to choose from, it's hard to find the right one for your needs and preferences.

A terrific first step is to identify the type of fund you would like to invest in. I've described each major type of fund and then offered some subgroupings that you may find helpful. Equity funds, in particular, can be extremely varied. You'll see here that, for example, I've categorized Canadian equity funds by the size of the companies they usually invest in.

A Range of Options

The wide range of mutual funds available today provides something for virtually every type of investor.

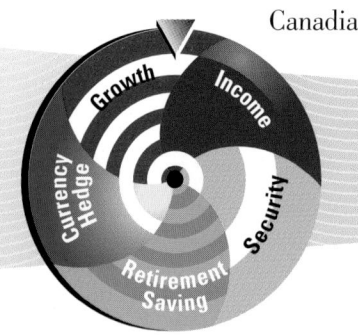

For simplicity, I've grouped the major fund types into four categories: money market, fixed income, equity, and balanced.

1. Money Market Funds: Canadian and U.S. Funds

While a money market fund should provide you with a return that beats the average savings account, it is not designed for superior returns, and is usually not a particularly attractive long-term investment.

A money market fund can provide an important "cash" component in a balanced portfolio, but it is most often viewed as a place to "park" investment money temporarily.

Money market funds generally invest in very safe, short-term debt securities. They invest in government treasury bills, or bank-guaranteed deposits, with the purpose of providing current income where necessary without taking any risks with the capital.

As a category, money market funds have the lowest level of risk among mutual funds. (The corollary, of course, is the lowest potential return.) Not surprisingly, money market funds are very popular when interest rates are high, and investors lose interest as interest rates drop.

Canadian money market funds | are fully RRSP-eligible, since they are invested in a range of Canadian short-term investments: like federal or provincial government guaranteed treasury bills (T-bills), for example.

You might ask, why not just buy T-bills on your own? Well, the fund buys enormous quantities (that "strength-in-numbers" feature again) of T-bills, so they can be purchased at a significantly lower price than average investors could purchase them. The cheaper price improves your chances of a better return. And besides, you don't have to roll over your maturing T-bill every few months, because the manager does it for you.

Money market funds also invest in GICs, short-term promissory notes issued by major corporations (called "corporate paper"), and bankers' acceptances, which are promissory notes issued by corporations and guaranteed by a bank that the amount of the note will be paid in full on the date specified.

Duff's Tips

How not to explain the bond market to your spouse

Opportunities for big capital gains! No risk! (Because everything's guaranteed.) The volatility in interest rates makes for big opportunities in bonds!

While true, all of these things are likely to scare your partner about bonds and bond funds. The truth about bond funds is far more simple. When interest rates go up, bonds and bond-like instruments, including bond funds, are negatively affected. That's because somebody would be less eager to buy your old 8 percent bond if a new one were suddenly available that paid 9 percent every year for years to come.

Duff's Tips

If you spend a lot of time or money in the U.S. on a regular basis, keeping some of your funds denominated in U.S. dollars is a good idea.

As with T-bills, all of these are short-term and highly liquid investments that are usually issued in amounts of several hundred thousand dollars, so most individual investors only have access to these vehicles through a mutual fund.

Many fund companies also offer U.S. money market funds. These funds work the same way as their Canadian counterparts, but offer a better return when U.S. rates are higher than those in Canada (as they are at the moment). An investment in a U.S. money market fund is a good choice for investors who are looking for a hedge in the event that the Canadian dollar falls. They're also good for investors who frequently need access to U.S. currency.

2. Fixed-Income Funds: Bond, Mortgage, and Dividend Funds

Many types of fixed-income funds are available. The term generally refers to mutual funds based on any asset that pays a fixed rate of return: bonds and mortgages, or preferred stocks that pay dividends. These are all relatively secure investments, and they provide a steady source of income. This feature makes them especially popular with conservative investors and retirees alike.

If long-term interest rates decline, you may earn a capital gain — a bonus on top of your interest. Still, the main objective of these funds is generally to achieve maximum income while preserving invested capital and minimizing risk.

Fixed-income funds are an especially good choice during times of declining interest rates, but may actually lose value when rates rise. As a result, these funds are riskier than money market funds. On the other hand, they have the potential to provide higher returns than money market funds.

Bond Funds

Bond funds generally invest in very secure government (federal, provincial or municipal) or corporate bonds. The focus of a bond fund is typically to maximize income. If the fund also manages to make a capital gain, it's considered a very nice bonus.

Canadian bond funds | had a terrible year in 1994 (the worst in three decades) but have bounced back since then. Though the bond markets have suffered some nerve-racking highs and lows, bond funds as a category have had a healthy run well into 1997.

When Interest Rates Rise: Winners and Losers

In 1994, Dan Richards, president of Marketing Solutions, surveyed over 5000 people and asked them whether they believed that the value of their investments would increase with rising interest rates. Surprisingly, 30 percent of respondents believed that yes, their investments would increase in value. Sorry, folks — guess again.

In fact, higher interest rates have a negative impact on all fixed-income investments except cash (that is, money market funds).

Stocks, too, often fall in value when interest rates rise. This occurs because companies that are big borrowers will face higher interest rate charges (and less profits) when rates rise.

Guaranteed investment certificates can also fall in value, but their prices are generally not listed daily, so you don't notice the change. In fact, there would be little point in tracking the value of a GIC, since you probably couldn't sell it anyway. Your money is generally locked in. Do GICs offer a higher return to compensate for this lack of liquidity and lack of pricing? Not usually. Government bonds often yield higher rates of return, are liquid, and have higher credit quality, generally speaking, than bank GICs, which offer only limited deposit insurance.

International bond funds | have been out of the limelight, as the Canadian market takes the spotlight. But they offer an excellent opportunity for diversification. These funds should pick up as investors jump back into international investment opportunities in general.

These funds hold bonds denominated in foreign currencies, including the pound sterling, Deutschemarks, U.S. dollars, French francs, and so on.

If you're looking for an international bond market, seek out an economy that's suffering through a recession. If interest rates are declining, bond prices should rise — and that will translate into returns for your fund.

Think about your diversification strategy; a fixed-income component is important to any well-balanced portfolio, and an international bond fund can diversify your portfolio two ways.

International bond funds with a European tilt continue to offer the best opportunities today.

Mortgage Funds

Mortgage funds are just what you might expect them to be: they invest in residential first mortgages, like the one I've got in my filing cabinet at home.

If you've ever applied for a mortgage, you'll know this is a fairly secure investment for the lenders. Generally, mortgage funds are based on "conventional" mortgages, where the loan does not exceed 75 percent of the appraised value of the home. However, they may also include "insured" mortgages, in which the loan may exceed 75 percent of the appraised value, but is insured against default by Canada Mortgage and Housing Corporation (CMHC). Some mortgage funds also hold commercial mortgages. A prospectus can provide such details.

These funds are generally very conservative and offer comparatively little risk. Returns are mostly in the form of interest income.

Dividend Funds

Scan the list of investments for a dividend fund and you'll often find a list of familiar names: the big, steady "blue-chip" companies, as they're called. Dividend funds invest in high-quality, preferred shares (which pay fixed dividends) of taxable Canadian corporations. They may also invest in the common shares of banks and utilities, which also pay regular dividends.

A dividend fund has an important tax advantage: dividend income is taxed at a much lower rate than interest income. If you must claim income, this is the best kind. Dividends represent the lowest-taxed form of income in every province except Quebec.

Because of this, of course, it makes sense to hold your dividend fund in a non-registered account. A dividend fund in an RRSP is a lost tax-savings opportunity.

3. Equity Funds

Growth is the main reason to own an equity fund; you're looking for the best possible gains in the value of your investment over a period of time. That gain, incidentally, is a capital gain.

Equity funds are the riskiest category of investment in the short term. But if you have several years to invest, you should remember that — over the longer term — equity funds have left the other fund categories in the dust.

Think of it this way: whereas money market and fixed-income investors are "loaners," equity investors are "owners." Equity funds have one thing in common: they all hold stocks. The type and nationality of those stocks will depend on the fund's objective and investment mandate. A huge variety of equity funds are available to Canadians.

Let's look at some of the main equity fund categories;

(**for more information**

Labour funds still a "buy"

The joke about labour-sponsored investment funds is that they're supposed to be for the "rich or desperate." If you're rich, you can handle the risk, benefit from the diversification, and reinvest your big credits. If you're desperate, you can get a bank loan for an RRSP purchase — and your total rebates can pay off up to 83% of the loan.

I buy the maximum allowable every year, and I'll do it again, even though those fat tax benefits have been trimmed by new legislation. Maximum investment is now $3500 per person, tax credits max out at 30%, and you have to hold for eight years.

Canadians have pumped more than $2 billion into labour funds, and I don't think these funds are ready to grind to a halt yet. They're still a great deal, and they're also getting some deserved praise for their role in the economy and for (surprise!) the returns they're achieving for investors. In fact, I think that labour funds are one of the few categories where professional management still adds value and where return potential is still good — even when interest rates are low. (Try to say that about an income fund!)

Check these out in our Ultimate Fund Tables:

- Capital Alliance Ventures
- Canadian Medical Discoveries
- C.I. Covington
- Vengrowth
- Triax Growth Fund

Canadian Equity Funds

Canadian equity funds invest in the common shares of Canadian corporations. Most are eligible for RRSP investments.

But not all of these funds are alike. Look for other clues about investment styles. Is the fund a "large-cap" fund? If so, it specializes in the big, "blue-chip" corporations, and you'll recognize many of the names. If the fund specializes in "small caps," it will be more aggressive in its investment style — seeking out the best small Canadian companies.

Sometimes a fund will have a "top-down" sector approach. It presumes, for example, that medical technology will be hot, and invests in a range of companies in that sector. These are called "sector funds."

Some funds take a "value" approach to choosing stocks. They look for companies that are cheap; that is, they represent a bargain stock price, considering their assets and sales. The fund buys at a bargain price, then waits for the stock price to rise.

A "growth" fund, on the other hand, doesn't look for bargains, but seeks out stocks of companies that are growing. Some of the most aggressive growth funds are invested in stocks that already appear overvalued, but are continuing to soar.

Recently, there's been a proliferation of "ethical funds" — those funds that invest only in companies that meet certain moral or ethical standards. These funds would typically avoid manufacturers of armaments, tobacco, or alcohol, or those companies that (directly or indirectly) carry on business in countries with oppressive or discriminatory political regimes.

U.S. Equity Funds

These funds are similarly varied in their styles and objectives, but invest almost exclusively in the United States — the world's largest market. As a caution, though, I'll observe that — after 15 years of extraordinary growth — these funds seem unlikely to maintain their current pace for much longer.

International Equity Funds

International equity funds invest in the stocks of companies in several countries, and many roam the world looking for the "best of the best." Some limit themselves to investing in certain geographic areas (the Pacific Rim, Latin America, Europe), while others restrict themselves to investing in a specific country. Latin America has been one of this year's international success stories.

Precious Metals Funds

You guessed it — these funds fed the Bre-X gold fever. You'll find lots of gold in most precious metals funds. The fund invests either by purchasing bullion directly or by investing in the shares of gold mining companies. Some funds also hold other precious metals such as platinum and silver, and can invest worldwide. If you think we'll see a jump in inflation, a precious metals fund is a good way to hedge your savings from that risk.

Real Estate Funds/Real Estate Investment Trusts (REITs)

These funds invest in income-generating commercial and industrial property. They make their money three ways: through the income generated by the property, through the capital gains earned when the property is sold, and through the interest on short-term deposits, which the fund holds in preparation for upcoming opportunities.

If you've been around for a few years, you'll remember that real estate — especially commercial real estate — took a serious punch in the last recession. As a result, these funds have been largely redesigned; most real estate funds are closed-end funds that now trade on stock exchanges.

4. Balanced Funds

A good balanced fund is a great foundation for an investment portfolio of less than $10 000. These "one-decision" funds spread your assets between equities and cash or fixed-income investments. The result is a smoother ride on your overall returns from year to year, and a hedge against a sudden drop in either equities or bonds.

Managers of a balanced fund will generally hold different weightings of asset types, depending on current or anticipated economic developments. A balanced fund will often work within some constraints: no more than 60 percent, or less than 40 percent, in equities or fixed income at any given time, for example.

Balanced funds are a very successful fund category. They make sense to average investors, and have become one of the popular foundation buys for an investment portfolio. More than 200 balanced funds are available in Canada.

Counting the Cost

Since there's a lot of anxious talk about the cost of owning a mutual fund, it makes sense to clarify this issue.

First, two costs are involved in your mutual fund purchase: the sales charge (or load) and the ongoing annual management fees. Both of these costs can affect your final return.

It's ironic that many investors believe that they are beating the system by buying a no-load fund, yet fail to realize that the management expenses to hold that fund year after year may actually be higher than those for the "load" fund they were considering.

Let's take a look.

The Big Panic: Sales Charges, or "Loads"

If the fund has a sales charge (many do), you have two choices. You can either pay a front-end load — in which the fund company claims a small percentage of your investment right away — or you can choose a back-end load, in which you might have to pay later if you remove your money from the fund within the first five or six years.

These rear-load funds' redemption charges decline each year you hold the fund — eventually reaching zero after about six years. If you're not sure what type of fund you own, look at your statement. If it says "DSC" (Deferred Sales Charge) beside the fund name, then it's a rear-load fund.

Front-End Loads

In the earlier years of mutual fund investing, sales charges of up to nine percent were levied on investments. Today, you shouldn't pay more than five percent on even a small investment. (If, for example, your sales charge was 4% on a $10 000 purchase, the actual amount invested will be ($10 000 – 4%=) $9600.) If you are investing a large amount, most advisors will negotiate a lower rate.

If, however, you are purchasing through a discount broker, you will be restricted in your negotiating; loads are pretty well fixed. One popular discount broker advertises a rate of 2.5 percent on mutual fund investments under $5000, two percent on orders from $5000 to $25 000, and one percent on orders larger than $25 000.

A final caution on front-end loads. Since you will lose some of your investment potential right off the top, you will have less money going to work for you.

Back-End Loads

With back-end loads all of your money goes to work for you right away. This option was first offered in 1987, and has become very popular. People are very resistant to upfront costs. More than 90 percent of load-fund sales in recent years have been of the back-end load variety.

Here's how it works. If you redeem these units before a certain period (usually about six years or so) has elapsed, you'll be required to pay a fee based on the value of your investment. This percentage declines over time.

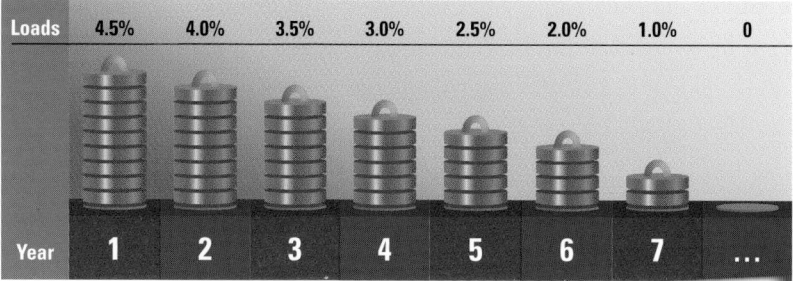

Loads	4.5%	4.0%	3.5%	3.0%	2.5%	2.0%	1.0%	0
Year	1	2	3	4	5	6	7	...

Redemption Charges

Here's the way several of the larger fund companies currently handle their redemption charges:

Redemption Policy	Acquisition Cost	Redemption Value	Redemption Policy	Acquisition Cost	Redemption Value
AGF	●		Investors		●
Canadian International	●		Mackenzie		●
Dynamic		●	Templeton	●	
Fidelity		●	Trimark	●	
Global Strategy	●		Spectrum United	●	
Guardian	●		BPI	●	

Some companies charge the redemption fee on the original amount invested; a few, however, charge on the market value of funds when you cash them. In most cases, the first option is preferable.

Due to the popularity of back-end load funds, many funds that used to charge only a front-end load can now be purchased either way. In fact, Trimark set up the "Select" group of DSC funds to mirror their successful front-load funds such as the **Trimark Fund** (the DSC clone is **Trimark Select Growth**) and the **Trimark Canadian Fund** (the DSC clone is **Trimark Select Canadian Growth Fund**).

Before I completely sell you on the back-end load approach, you must also factor some additional fees into your decision.

Management Fees | If you manage to avoid the front-end sales charges, fund companies will get you anyway with management fees — which can sometimes be higher for funds purchased on a back-end load basis. **Trimark**, for example, charges as much as 0.8 percent more annually for their back-end load funds. Therefore, if you're buying a Trimark fund, I'd advise you to choose the front-load option.

Do your homework on your fund costs. They directly affect the bottom line, and the differences between the options can be significant over time. Based on how long you will be invested in the fund, ask how much it is going to cost you. Put your advisor on the spot before you put your money on the table.

The No-Load Option

No-load funds have been popular with the banks and trust companies — and of course with Altamira, the best-known no-load seller.

When you deal with a direct seller, however, remember that typically you will not be discussing your financial plans with an independent financial advisor. The salaried employees who manage the phones can only provide information about the funds offered by their company.

Still, Canadians are gradually warming to the idea of no-load funds. Nothing is deducted on purchase, and there are no redemption charges. No-loads are very popular in the United States, and Canadian fund companies are now waking up to the message.

What You Don't See: Management Expenses

Investors must recognize that all mutual funds — even no-load funds — charge these fees. After all, this is how money is generated to pay the fund managers, and to support the advertising and education efforts for the fund. You've gone looking for the best manager in the country; someone has to pay her.

Management expenses generally range between 1 and 2.5 percent of the total assets in the fund. Not surprisingly, some of the biggest funds have the lowest management fees, since the cost of the management team, the research facilities, and all the other necessities are spread over more unitholders. Although the percentage of management fees may decline as a fund grows in size, this is not always the case.

Fees are determined by the type of assets managed by the fund. Obviously, more infrastructure is needed to support an equity fund (which requires lots of company and industry research) than to manage a cash fund, which really just rolls T-bills. Look for expenses of about two percent for equity-based funds, and about one percent for cash management funds.

You don't see management fees. Since they're charged directly to the fund, you never see a statement of the amount. That doesn't mean they're invisible, however; you'll see the impact on your final returns. For example, if a fund charges two percent in management expenses and earns a 20 percent return in a given year, your net return is 18 percent. The law, by the way, states that mutual fund ads must always show returns *after* expenses have been deducted.

My advice is to disregard management fees, and focus instead on the **management expense ratio**. This figure is expressed as a percentage of the fund's total assets. It's based on the total of all the management fees and other expenses, divided by the number of fund units. It includes legal, accounting, custodial, and safekeeping costs, as well as the costs of producing prospectuses and other reporting materials.

All else being equal, the higher the management expense ratio, the more money is being spent by the manager and the lower the return to the investor. As a result, examine these factors when considering any fund purchase.

Nickels and Dimes

A few other charges may apply to the fund you are considering. These include:

- **Set-Up Fees**
  This one-time fee is often charged by no-load companies. Set-up fees usually fall in the range of $40.

- **Close-Out or Transfer Fees**
  You may be charged a modest fee for closing out your account with a particular fund company. Many fund companies charge $20 on the termination or transfer out of a tax plan for an RRSP or a Registered Retirement Income Fund (RRIF). Growing numbers of financial institutions are also charging this fee.

- **Trustee Fees for RRSPs, RRIFs, or Registered Education Savings Plans (RESPs)**
  For these types of accounts, an annual trustee fee may be charged, usually about $50. Some fund companies reduce or eliminate such fees from time to time as a promotional strategy. If your mutual fund units are held in your RRSP at a brokerage or financial planning firm, you'll be charged between $100 and $200 per year.

- **Systematic Withdrawal Fees/Charges**

  A systematic withdrawal plan (SWP) allows investors to receive regular income from their fund. A few companies charge an annual fee, while others charge a fee for each withdrawal.

- **Pre-Authorized Chequing Fees**

  If you set up a regular investment program and invest monthly by pre-authorized cheque, you may have to pay a service charge. If your bank account has insufficient funds to make this monthly investment, expect to pay a fee of about $15.

- **Switching Fees**

  Almost all companies allow funds to be switched within the same family. Often the prospectus will allow for a negotiable charge of between zero and two percent. When your advisor works hard to re-build your portfolio in a way that improves your overall investment without leaving a fund family (and triggering a big fee), then he or she deserves that small (two percent or less) switching fee.

The Bigness Debate: Big Is Beautiful in Choosing the Best Funds

Investors prefer large funds. In fact, two-thirds of fund industry assets are clustered in about 100 of the 1600 funds sold in Canada.

And my research suggests that Canadians are on the right track. Indeed, the big funds are better performers. These giants consistently beat the smaller funds — sometimes by a little, sometimes by a lot.

In my 1995 study I found that global equity funds are the most striking example. Just 11 funds, which comprise a staggering 75 percent of the assets in this group, trounce the pack of 100 smaller ones with which they compete. These large funds earned 13.9 percent annually over the five years ended June 30, dwarfing the nine percent earned by the rest of the group.

You also see this pattern in Canadian bond funds. Of 129 bond funds, the 13 largest comprise 60 percent of the assets. Over the prior five years, these few big funds earned 11 percent annually, versus 10.5

percent for the small funds. An annual difference of half a percent point may not sound like much, but in the world of bonds, it's a big deal.

Jumbo U.S. equity funds sold in Canada enjoy a similar performance advantage. Their annual return is half a percentage point higher than the little guys in their group. The fact that monster funds perform better might shock investors who are fearful about bigness when it comes to equity funds. Many believe big funds won't be nimble enough to trade in and out of stocks at the best prices.

People also believe that large funds miss out on the sizzle from small-cap stocks — an area proven to offer higher returns — because their size makes a tiny small-cap position meaningless. The net asset value of a $2-billion fund won't even budge if a $1-million stock holding doubles in value. But these fears are unfounded. Lipper Analytical Services, a U.S. firm that monitors fund returns, says big-fund superiority has held stable every year since it has been breaking out performance by size. Consider the world's largest fund, Fidelity Magellan, with over US$50 billion in assets (which, unfortunately, is not sold in Canada). This huge U.S. equity fund has beaten the market and 80 percent of its peers.

Toronto-based Trimark has over $10 billion in its Canadian equity funds, holding enough stocks to make up two percent of the entire domestic stock market. But you won't find many fund groups with more consistently strong returns in Canada.

My calculations went beyond taking a simple look at how today's biggest funds did over the last five years. Naturally, today's giants would have better track records — after all, that's why they became big.

Instead, each month I looked at how the biggest funds were doing that month. By rejigging the list monthly, I crafted a composite of what the returns of the biggest funds really were at various moments in time. Why the performance gap between big and small funds? There are three key reasons, all of which relate to success breeding success.

The first is simply great fund management. Not every big fund is superbly managed, or triumphs in every market climate. But consistency wins investor loyalty and builds a fund over time. While some funds balloon because of great marketing, lasting size is usually the result of investment success.

The second reason is lower expenses. For example, consider bond funds, where expenses are so important. The average management expense ratio for the 13 largest bond funds is 1.5 percent — low, but still not low enough in my opinion — versus 1.7 percent for the rest of the pack. The economies created by size allow for a wider base across which to spread the fixed costs of managing a fund.

Mutual funds are a curious product: the highest quality is often found at the lowest price. Successful and established funds usually have lower expenses, while unproven upstarts often charge a bundle.

The third reason is trading and research economies. Bigger funds can afford more talent, whether in the form of more attention from brokerage analysts or more money for in-house analysts, and they pay even lower commissions on some trades than the already slim institutional rates.

You'd do well to stick to the big names, like most Canadians do, for most of your portfolio. But don't get me wrong. Lots of great small funds exist. Setting aside up to 20 percent of your mutual fund dollars for an undiscovered gem, especially a small-cap player, could be very rewarding.

Understanding
Performance:
Numbers May Not Tell the Whole Story

What the Advertising Says

When a mutual fund advertisement provides numbers for a fund's performance, the company is using what are known as standard performance figures. The mutual fund company doesn't have a choice in how they present them; it's the law (although you'll find that many companies are very opportunistic about when they advertise performance).

Standard performance figures are both the bait and the bane of mutual fund companies. They're designed to show a fund's results over time, based on the belief that, the longer the performance period, the more reliable the guide.

Look at any mutual fund advertisement and you are likely to find a lot of impressive numbers that attest to the fund's performance over the past six months, one year, three years, or five years — all of which make the fund appear to be a fairly attractive investment. But in the worst cases, the numbers are simply statistical hocus-pocus that's ideal for marketing funds.

Since provincial securities regulators recognize that performance figures can be deceiving, they've added their own fine print to mutual fund advertisements. At the bottom of each advertisement, a snippet of copy appears that usually reads something like this: "Past performance is not necessarily indicative of future returns...."

Granted, this is fairly obvious to most investors. No one can be certain that a fund will keep performing the way it has in the past. But that's only part of the problem. The disclaimer should actually read something like this: "This is a really dumb way to calculate past performance, but we couldn't think of anything better at the time. Buyer beware."

I think that past performance data is an extremely valuable tool in predicting future returns — but only if the performance is measured properly. The problem is that it's still very difficult to find the right kind of performance data in conventional sources.

What the Newspaper Says

You may think that the performance figures reported in most of

Duff's Tips

Star-Chasing Can Be a Losing Game

In the past few years, some star managers have left behind the funds they made famous. If this happens to your fund, should you also bail out?

Probably not. There's compelling evidence that investors should stay put, rather than chase the star.

This year I decided to examine the impact of major manager changes in Canadian equity funds over the past decade. I looked at the performance record of high-profile managers who defected to run or start a competing fund, and then I directly compared their performance in their new role with the performance of the fund they left behind. In almost every case, the "fund faithful" are rewarded for sitting tight. And where new managers outperformed the departed star, they did so by margins that ranged from modest to mammoth.

Why do departing stars so consistently underperform the funds they left behind? I believe that they are constrained by a combination of market environment and the marketing process. Combine a hot market with a hot new star (heavily promoted) and assets soar. It's tough to buy and maintain a good portfolio with tens of millions of dollars coming in every day.

So, it's not that these managers are falling stars; it's just that the very marketing machine that builds them up can also poison their performance. For the investor, the evidence is clear. Star-chasing is almost always a losing game the daily newspaper listings are likely to be more accurate and unbiased than the advertising numbers. Think again. They're the same standard performance figures, reported exactly the same way.

For the clearest picture of a fund's performance history, you will have to look beyond the advertising and beyond the usual daily listings. Why? Because they're biased. Ending-date biased, that is.

What's the Problem? Ending-Date Bias

Last year I wrote a newspaper column describing how long-term performance figures can mislead investors. In it, I described how a fund with a fairly mediocre track record became an overnight star; in a mere three months, the fund's 10-year performance leaped from a lacklustre seven percent annually to a handsome 11.8 percent annually for the 10-year period.

Can a 10-year performance figure make that kind of jump in three months? You bet.

Let's just say that column generated some heated response — with most of the heat blowing in the direction of the fund companies' marketing departments.

We've been led to believe that long-term return figures are fairly reliable. So what's the issue? Well, while the standard performance figures don't actually lie, they seldom tell the whole truth. In the case of the fund I wrote about in my column, the portfolio earned a cool 60.8 percent in the three months. Because all of the calculations for the one-, three-, five-, and 10-year rates of return are always tied to a single ending day, we could be looking at distorted returns for years to come.

The Best Solution: Average Monthly Rankings

To get a clear look at a fund's ability to perform over time, we need to eliminate the end-date bias that gives us those funhouse mirror figures.

I've developed a simple, mathematical model based on average monthly ranking of a fund's performance since inception — or to a maximum of 20 years. Each month, I measure how a fund stacks up against its peers. With this method, a mediocre fund that's been hot for three months has no place to hide.

By measuring each fund against others in their same category, I can get a good sense of how each fund manager weathers the ups and downs of the markets.

For example, each Canadian equity fund is ranked against other Canadian equity funds for as many months as the fund has been in existence. Then I average the accumulated rankings to find the cream of the fund crop.

The funds that emerge as winners in this system are the ones that perform consistently well in most periods. Funds that do spectacularly well in some periods but spectacularly poorly in others are unlikely to make the grade. Consistency generally wins — especially in the mutual fund game.

Standard performance figures are everywhere — at least for now. Use them to identify the funds you'd like to know more

Why Newbie Funds Don't Rate

This year, veteran AGF celebrates the fortieth anniversary of its American Growth Fund. Such long histories, however, are extremely rare. As you may have noticed, the Canadian mutual fund industry is exploding, and many funds are relative newcomers.

You'll find many of these newbie funds in my Ultimate Fund Tables at the back of this book, but you won't find them in my FundMonitor Profiles, which detail the very best funds available in each category.

That's not to say that some newbies aren't terrific funds. But I'm a big believer that a fund must prove its performance over time. And any fund less than three years old hasn't had time to demonstrate its ability to keep investors happy in the long term.

Mind you, I have my eye on a few of these child prodigies, and you'll be hearing more about some of them in next year's edition.

about. Develop your shortlist. Then look at real performance numbers.

Ask your advisor to help you find calendar-year returns for the fund (or watch for this special edition in *The Globe and Mail*). Look for your fund in my Ultimate Fund Tables to see what my performance analysis has turned up.

But that's enough about performance for now. In the next chapter, we'll look at how I refine my criteria to select what I think are this year's top picks for investors.

Selecting the
Best Funds:
The FundMonitor System

The "Star" Score Rewards Great Performance

Overall performance: ★ ★ ★ ★ ★

If you've read the preceding chapter's examination of fund performance, you'll already know that when I go looking for this year's best funds, I'm going beyond a summary of the past year's returns.

Every fund in my FundMonitor Profiles listing has earned its place as one of the best in its fund category. Naturally, some of these funds score higher than their peers, so I've designed a ranking system that provides more specific scoring for the individual funds. You'll notice that — like Michelin restaurant reviewers — I have used a "star" system to designate the very best performers. Each of the best funds is scored — with a maximum five stars — on their comparative monthly rankings against their peer funds.

If you are interested in a ranking for a fund that doesn't qualify as one of my FundMonitor Profiles picks, check the Ultimate Fund Tables, in which I have gathered some basic research on all of the funds.

The "star" scoring system only measures performance based on the fund's average monthly ranking. And while this provides an accurate and objective measure of performance, it's still a rather limited perspective. To make your most informed investment choice, you must supplement the star score with more qualitative data about consistency, risk, efficiency, and style.

Qualifier 1: Consistency of Performance

Consistency
Year-by-year quartile ranking of this
fund against only similar rivals

Total Return: -9.2% 6.2% 2.1% 12.5% -8.8% 13.1% 35.2% 51.5% -13.5% 3.7% 26.3% -17.8%

To qualify for my FundMonitor Profiles list, a fund must demonstrate consistency: consistent performance in good and bad markets, as well as consistency of people — that is, the people guiding the fund. The ideal, of course, would be a fund that ranked in the top "quartile" (the top 25 percent in its category) in every measurable period for the past 35 years, and whose manager and research team never changed. Although that ideal fund doesn't exist, you get the idea.

Let's examine these consistency factors:

Consistent Performance

The average monthly ranking system evaluates a fund's performance history — usually since inception. My system compensates for the fact that different funds have vastly different histories. For example, if you consider that the past several years have represented the longest bull market in history, you can expect that some funds introduced during this time have had a pretty spectacular run of positive performances. An older fund that has weathered a few rough years in the beginning may not sport such a high compound return as does a younger fund.

I overcame this unfairness by deconstructing my average monthly ranking formula — examining the performance rankings of each of my profiled funds relative to those in the same group for a given number of recent time periods. The series of horizontal bars you see illustrates how the fund performed compared to its peers — for the years 1987 to 1996, and through to September 1997.

This is shown graphically as a matrix, with each column representing a calendar year (moving chronologically from left to right), ▬▬▀▬▬ and with each row representing the "performance quartile" for the time period.

A key benefit of comparing performance over discrete (that is, non-overlapping) time periods is that it allows us to see how similar funds fared in good and bad markets.

For some very valuable insight, take a moment to compare the performance graph carefully with the consistency grid. You may see instances where the markets were down and even the performance of the fund was down, but where it still scored in the top quartile in its category. That suggests that the fund performed well in a downturn. Support for such a conclusion would come in the form of a down market grade of "A".

Look, also, for meaningful trends in a fund's performance over time. You may see that the performance of a highly ranked fund has declined over the past few years. Or you may see that an average-ranked fund has lately picked up. Either observation may influence your investment decision.

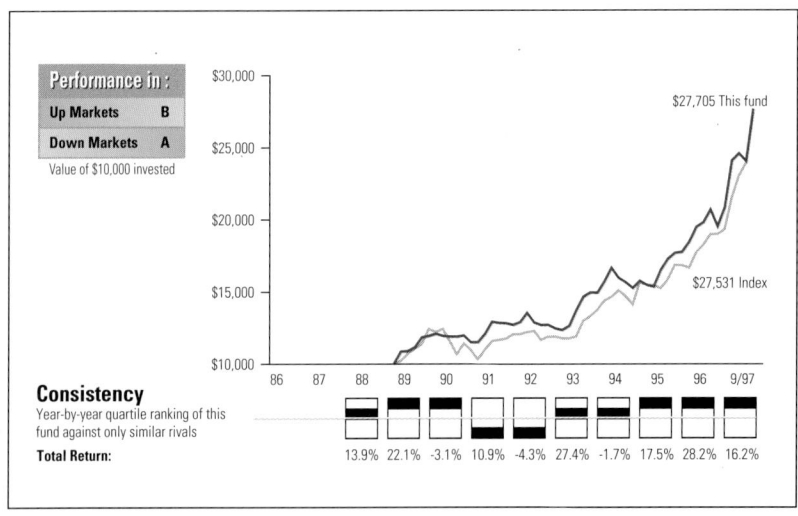

Choosing Talent

Is it talent or luck? Some fund managers make the headlines with their spectacular performances. Does that mean that we should seek out these "stars," and throw our money behind them?

Not necessarily. I'd be willing to bet that the fund manager who posted the 100 percent-plus performance last year cannot repeat that performance for the next five years.

But I do think that talent exists. I believe that some fund managers consistently outperform their counterparts in other funds. And I think that, overall, a long-term investor (and that's most of us) will do well to remain with a manager, or team, that has done well in the past.

How do you recognize talent? In general, time will tell. For example, Sir John Templeton turned $10 000 invested in the Templeton Growth Fund in 1954 into $4.8 million by 1997. Or an even more spectacular performance involved George Soros, manager of the off-shore-based Quantum Fund, who turned US$10 000 in 1969 into more than US$20 million by 1997. And for those who don't remember what the markets were doing in 1969, they were at a peak — and about to plunge into the biggest bear market in history.

The Curse of the Cover

There is a widespread belief in sports circles that the worst thing that can happen to a professional athlete is to appear on the cover of *Sports Illustrated*. Shortly after the glory, the career fades. This well-documented "curse of the cover" is also said to be true of *Time* magazine's Man or Woman of the Year cover profile, which has notoriously signalled the top of a brilliant career.

According to a study I conducted this year, the curse of the cover also exists in the Canadian mutual fund world. From 1991 to 1996, I analyzed the cover story of every issue of *The Globe and Mail*'s Report on Mutual Funds. I found that funds had big returns in the two or three years leading up to their manager's photograph on the cover. But performance in the subsequent one-year period after the publicity was considerably diminished. On average, those funds did only 70 percent as well as their prior pace. In fact, some funds plummeted in value.

Who's to blame for this phenomenon? Those famous fund managers? Hardly. Often, simple human nature is to blame — ours, not theirs. In fact, many of these funds, and their highly regarded, well-publicized managers, remain excellent long-term bets. But investors are infatuated with hot funds. A story about a high-performing fund attracts buckets of new money. And those investors, of course, are flocking to the fund at just the wrong time.

My study proves that investors systematically fall in love with hot funds — just before they're about to cool. Tomorrow's best funds are likely to be the lean, steady types today. So skip the cover story, and look at year-by-year performance, as well as annual fees, and you won't ever catch the curse.

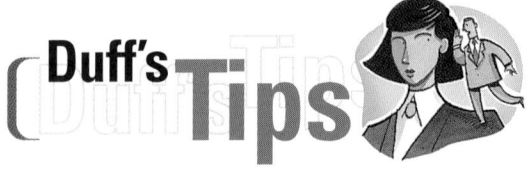

Duff's Tips

Finding the Good Managers and Avoiding the Bad

It takes some homework to find a talented manager, but it is possible to identify the consistently good ones. Talented managers have the following characteristics:

- they consistently beat the market,

- they are supported by a management team that demonstrates both talent and depth (it takes more than a "star" manager to run a successful fund),

- they make consistent use of sound research as part of the decision-making process.

   Bad managers are easier to identify. These fund companies or individuals exhibit all the opposite characteristics of the best managers — and usually in abundance. Look for these danger signs:

- fund performance that is consistently below par, compared to its peers, or performance that swings wildly between hot and cold,

- high turnover of managers or support team members. This is a reliable indicator of an unsupportive environment, poor compensation, and/or an ineffective management structure,

- funds with high fees (often a warning signal for an ineffective structure),

- an absence of a support "team," or a shortage of analysts. You can't beat first-hand research, but you need the resources to do it effectively.

That's not luck. That's a talented manager at work.

There are talented managers out there today, but it takes some homework to find them. Look for a manager who consistently beats the market — whether the market is going up or down. Look for depth of talent in the whole management team that supports the fund. And look for evidence that sound research is informing the team's decisions. Or, let me look for you. I've gone through this process for every fund and have presented my conclusions in this book.

Consistent Management

Behind every great mutual fund performance is a dedicated group of professionals. Most investors like to put a face to their fund. They want to know something about the person or team that they are entrusting with their money. They intuitively understand that their success rests on the people factor. For this reason, watch out for frequent changes, or turnover, of management teams. When people leave, your fund becomes a different entity. I identify the lead manager(s) of each of my FundMonitor choices. I also tell you how long they've been on the job to give you a sense of the management consistency of your fund.

It is also important to note that a change in management does not necessarily require a switch out of your fund. In fact, research indicates that you're better to remain with your existing fund than to follow your manager to another fund. But long-term consistency of a management team is always a good sign. If you're hunting for funds yourself, do some research. Find out how long the management team has been together and who owns a piece of the firm (and can reasonably be expected to remain). This is valuable information.

Behind Every Star Is a Management Firm

When we talk about a "fund manager," we usually think about the one person whose smiling photograph dominates advertising and fund communications. But these lead managers couldn't operate without the support of a team that works collaboratively to make investment decisions.

Are some firms better than others? Absolutely. Here are some guidelines for identifying a superior company.

Dynamic: A Look Back at Consistency in Action

Last year at this time, many people believed that Jonathan Goodman and his team at Dynamic had completely missed the gold-plated boat. In the exploration stock hysteria (with a vortex centred around Bre-X), Goodman resolutely pursued his value discipline. He passed on Bre-X and others, and the Dynamic Precious Metals Fund lagged almost all its peers. The wisdom of the Goodman team's consistent approach deserves accolades. This kind of consistent management style — and their ability to resist the tremendous temptation to stray from it — makes them a management team worth watching.

Been around the block a few times.

Look for a fund company that's been around for at least ten years. History has shown that the economy takes about that length of time to go through a full cycle of recession, recovery, and growth. (Okay, this cycle is a little longer.) If the company has survived a full cycle, it will probably be around for a while.

Lots of money under management.

Sure, there are lots of small firms with hot little funds, but you can't beat the advantages of a good asset base. Companies with lots of money in their funds can afford to hire the best managers, they can support them with the best resources, and they have the buying power to get the best deals on significant blocks of stocks, for example. When we think of "big," we're referring to total assets of $3 billion or more for bond managers, and at least $1 billion for equity managers.

Managers stick with the company.

While there's no reason to panic if your longtime fund manager suddenly leaves (see above), a revolving door of managers is a bad sign. In general, a company should not lose more than one senior investment professional every five years. Turnover both creates and reflects problems; if fund managers are jumping ship, you should be asking some pointed questions.

Managers live where they invest.

Who is likely to know more about what is happening in southeast Asia — the guy in a Bay Street office or the woman living and working in Singapore? I've heard the arguments for and against, but I believe that fund managers who buy stocks or bonds in overseas markets can get a much better feel for opportunities and threats if they are living where they invest. Look for a firm that has offices or advisors located in the markets where it is doing business.

Minimum red tape in management structure.

Granted, it is difficult for the average investor to know how the management structure of a company affects the fund managers, but I have looked at this situation fairly closely in most fund companies. I like to see a firm that gives its individual fund managers complete and immediate authority to make buy and sell transactions as they see fit (provided, of course, that they meet the fund's mandate). A bureaucratic structure is seldom a good thing for managers. When opportunity knocks suddenly, you want to answer the door without having a committee meeting first.

Qualifier 2: Appropriate Risk

Since my system for evaluating mutual funds is based on past performance, it makes sense that the highest-flying funds (the ones that took the most risk) would have the highest rates of return over time. But that doesn't make them the most appropriate funds for investors.

In this new publication, I am presenting a fresh approach to measuring risk. In the FundMonitor Profiles and Ultimate Fund Tables (a summary of all available funds), you will find more detailed information about risk than you've ever seen before. I have augmented each fund's performance with information about the risk that they have taken to achieve that performance.

One of my ways of measuring risk is simple. If we are all going to fall in love with a fund's past performance, then why not study, measure, and compare its past risk? How has it done in tough times? How much did it lose in its biggest slide? And how long did it take to recover? I've also looked at how a currency-sensitive fund — such as a foreign fund — has performed during the tough times when the Canadian dollar is appreciating against foreign currencies.

This notion of downside risk measured in a common-sense way is all too rare in Canada. It should be an essential part of not only choosing mutual funds for Canadians, but also of setting our expectations about what we can expect in future tough periods from any given fund.

I may be somewhat of an agitator, but I've been urging Canadian regulators to make mandatory disclosures about a fund's past risk. I believe that this information should be conveyed in common-sense ways such as how often a fund did worse than a simple benchmark such as the five-year GIC. Or how often a fund did worse than its benchmark index. Most fund companies don't want to publicize that information, because so few funds (even the good ones) manage to outperform the benchmark, or earn consistent, double-digit returns.

These companies would doubtless prefer if investors simply bought funds based on the long-term rates of return. But I believe that an investor who is better informed about what is likely to happen in tough times is more likely to exhibit behaviour that is congruent with good, successful, long-term results.

Qualifier 3: Efficiency

The third feature that distinguishes my FundMonitor picks is efficiency, or the total level of expenses charged by a fund. Here I am talking about the management expense ratio: a percentage figure that represents the sum of all management fees and other expenses.

I believe that the whole concept and terminology of management fees is downright misleading and shouldn't be allowed. For example, I've had money managers tell me that their fund charges only "reasonable fees" of 2.25 percent. I call their bluff and respond, "But wait, the management expense ratio is 2.6 percent! That's well above average and your fund's performance has been pretty mediocre." Their response is usually something inane like, "Yes, well, but our management *fees* are low." That's nonsense.

The management expense ratio (MER) is the only measure that includes all charges and is therefore the only one to focus on. Most importantly, the MER is the number included in most newspaper listings of performance and is always, by law, net of the management expense ratio.

Now that I've said all this, let me emphasize that I would happily recommend funds with very high expense ratios — but only when they have a very high net return

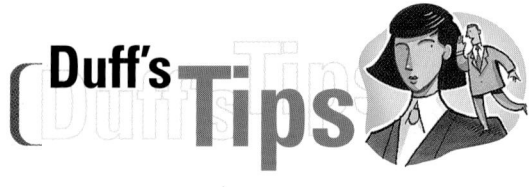

How High Annual Expenses Make Loads Pale by Comparison

Consider this. Ten years ago you made a $10 000 investment, and it's been netting 13 percent annually in a fund that charges a management expense ratio of 2.3 percent. (This is not unrealistic, by the way. Over the past 10 years, most funds have performed at about 13 percent, and 2.3 percent is the average management expense ratio.)

Your investment will have accrued and paid out something like $5000 in management expenses over that period. That's big dough!

Even though your investment has an ending value after 10 years of something over $30 000, you've paid a stunning amount of money for management expenses.

What does this tell us? Stop fretting over the cost of loads. They're a one-time expense, and really represent only a tiny portion of the overall fees we're paying in the funds we buy.

even *after* paying the big fees. Keep in mind, however, that a fund's high expenses are kind of guaranteed. The high return really isn't.

All else being equal, I would choose a fund with lower expenses over a comparable fund that charges a bundle year-in and year-out.

Qualifier 4: Style

The style of a fund helps to achieve the stated investment objectives, and offers you an important selection tool in choosing the right funds for your personal portfolio.

Our style analysis can tell you whether a fund is aggressive or passive, and predict its likely performance in different market environments. Two funds with very similar approaches, which hold similar stocks for similar reasons and sell them at the same time, will undoubtedly have extremely similar performances. Their return pattern will be identical in good times and bad, which means that they'll provide almost no diversification from one another and would therefore be bad complements.

You can begin to see why the selection of each fund must be weighed in the context of your overall portfolio. I will discuss diversification in more detail in Chapter 6. But as you go through my FundMonitor Profiles, watch for the different concepts in style analysis, and the way that channels into a single, overall view of a fund's investment style. The two concepts are well founded in the academic world and are applied by my research team on Canadian mutual funds in an exclusive way for readers of this book.

This first approach is **holdings-based style analysis**. This involves examining the portfolio to determine which style its management employs. In equity funds,

Duff's Tips

Five Core Fund Families

These fund families have a big lineup of good funds, and each family's products are broadly available in Canada through advisors. While some of the funds in these families are better than others, if you build a portfolio around the core holdings of these fund families, you're in good hands:

Altamira
Bissett
Mackenzie
Templeton
Trimark

for example, holdings-based style analysis would do a simple quantitative review on the stocks in the portfolio. In a fund that typically comprised conservative stocks (with very low price-to-earnings (P/E) ratios and very low price-to-book value (P/BV) ratios and slow growth), then holdings-based style analysis would suggest that that fund was a "value fund."

Value and growth represent opposite ends of a continuum of the price in the underlying stocks. Researchers have proven that value and growth styles perform differently enough to allow for legitimate diversification among and between the two approaches. A growth portfolio's holdings would reveal (on average) much higher valuations in terms of P/E ratios and P/BV ratios and so on. Growth stock investing is generally considered a somewhat more aggressive approach than value investing.

But since both value and growth are terms that tend to have positive connotations, the trouble with holdings-based style analysis is that every fund is in the middle, claiming to be at both ends of the value-growth continuum. Everyone wants to be a value investor, but we all want to claim that we own growth companies. Unfortunately, few investors actually have the discipline to be one or the other. That's not bad, but it certainly is frustrating for investors who are trying to diversify among and between hundreds of different mutual fund choices.

This dilemma is one of the key reasons I've embraced a second kind of style analysis. **Returns-based style analysis** is an approach that examines the performance pattern of the fund over the past few years versus other funds and indexes. This approach is not concerned with what the portfolio contains now or in the past. Rather, it simply makes inferences from the return pattern about what is likely in the portfolio or what approach the manager is likely to have been taking. Returns-based style analysis, which I've added to augment our holdings-based style analysis, offers important clues about what style a fund really employs. Technically speaking, it is a co-variance analysis of how a fund has performed versus other funds and indexes — with a very high correlation suggesting a near match in investment approach.

Together, these two forms of style analysis helped me arrive at the overall style of a fund. For details on how to read the style grid in the FundMonitor review legend, read on. Chapter 5 will provide detailed background to our systems.

FundMonitor Profiles:
The Best for 1998

THIS IS REALLY THE MEAT OF THE BOOK.
It's where we profile 68 established funds that have
proven that they are consistently good performers.
Each fund has its own full-page fact sheet.

These funds had to clear some high hurdles to make it on to my list.
While I've offered some of my own personal, subjective comments about
each of the funds, it's a ruthlessly scientific, quantitative system that
actually chooses and analyzes these funds. To reach this level, each
fund had to demonstrate consistent, high average monthly ranks in the
past — compared only against their closest peers. If they failed to make
these rankings, they
were cut. It's that
simple.

To further re-
fine the list for your
needs, read through
the profiles. Each
one will provide a
glimpse of some of
the intimate details
— even the scary

for more
information

www.fundmonitor.com

I'll take just a moment to rave about the Internet, and about my Web site in particular. I'm blown away by the possibilities of interactive communications, and especially by the opportunities that it can provide investors like you.

In addition to this book, I have developed a "living book" on the Internet, which can be personalized for your needs. My new Web site can take you further than the pages of this book, but with all the same principles.

On your first visit to the site, be sure to register. The site offers all of the fund research data tables you see at the back of this book, and even more. But the real bonus is that all of this information can be ranked and sorted, based on your own criteria. It's an amazing service, and I'm indebted to my Web wizards, who told me it was possible and then made it happen.

You will also find an on-line questionnaire, designed to help you identify an optimized asset allocation that's right for you. And if you register yourself for a personalized review, you can have your own personal home page on the FundMonitor site. Your page will greet you with performance monitoring of your real or hypothetical model portfolio. It's available to every investor who signs up for the FundMonitor service (for which there is a fee).

You can make changes on-line. You can find free fund research. You can do anything you like. There is also a live chat room, so you can share your questions and concerns with other readers on-line.

It's informative and it's fun. I look forward to seeing you there!

stuff — on each fund. For example, you'll find out how risky it's really been. Or what style it really employs. (Forget about the manager's claims of being a "value investor"! That's hogwash, if the stocks in the fund are expensive.)

In each essay, you'll find more qualitative information. That's where I'll mention more important issues such as major management changes. If a fund makes the list based on my quantitative, objective analysis, then it stays on the list, even if the management has undergone a change. But I'll let you know about it. You see, most manager changes involve just a small change at the top. Often, another team member takes over. For example, that's what happened recently with the Ivy Funds, where Jerry Javasky has taken over the reins from departed Gerry Coleman, who cut loose and went to C.I. That's a pretty subtle management change. Consequently, I'll do the math to determine which funds have had the best past performance and I'll just give you an overview of what's been happening with the fund.

Each portion of the review page is designed to help you identify critical information fast. Here's an introduction to what it all means.

Up top, you'll see the fund name and a little Canadian flag if it's fully RRSP eligible (🇨🇦). If it's counted only as foreign content for your RRSP, then the flag will look like this 🚫. The team that's specifically responsible for this fund will be shown here along with the date at which they began to manage the fund. If the same people have been responsible for managing this fund since it was launched, then here it will say "since inception." It's important to know who's running the fund and how long they've been there. (So how come this stuff is generally so tough to find?) The management firm that employs the manager is shown here — and it's not always the same as the fund company. Sometimes the fund company has arranged for a sub-advisor: an unrelated firm that they've hired to run the fund. I think subs are slightly better, because if they really stink, it's easier to fire them than it is to fire an entire team within your own company.

Overall performance is a simple representation of the fund's overall historic average rank when compared only against funds within its peer group. The five-star rating is the best available. One star is the worst rating — but remember that only the great funds are profiled here, so nothing here has fewer than three stars. You shouldn't sell your three-star fund to buy one with a four-star rating. The system wasn't meant to be that refined. It's merely meant to portray that some funds have done better than others.

The performance chart simply represents the value of a $10 000 initial investment with all dividends reinvested since inception for the fund or since 1986 — whichever came first. A benchmark for each type of fund is shown that helps investors get an idea of how an unmanaged rival index did in comparison with this fund.

Consistency

My distinctive column graphs show consistency at a glance. This is the first thing I look at in gauging any fund's past performance. Each vertical box represents a single calendar year. If the top quarter of the box is shaded, then the fund did better than a vast majority of its rivals. It placed in the top quartile of its class, meaning that it did better than 75 percent of its peers. Because these boxes are non-overlapping, they don't suffer from the typical distortions you'll find in compound return calculations, where one blockbuster year can skew a whole decade's worth of only mediocre results.

Why Quartile Rankings Change

Historic quartile comparisons with my book this year are a bit different than in prior years. That's because I'm using a much more refined system to do real apples-to-apples comparisons.

It's always been important to my way of measuring mutual funds to be sure to compare only similar funds, to see which do best, and to test for consistency. But now data from PALTrak allows us to group funds in a way that is very specific. A fund that always has lots of big banks, for example, can now be categorized and rated against only similar funds. That way, we find the best of the bank-heavy funds. This more refined system is more fair because even a relatively weak bank-heavy fund would look great lately in comparison to a fund that, as a matter of policy, always has lots of smaller cyclical companies. Truth is, the latter fund would be punished by lumping it with the bank-heavy fund, what with the explosion in bank share prices over the last year or so.

These more refined peer groups neutralize for style and compare only funds with very similar approaches. That way the best funds from each approach will rise to the top — rather than all the funds from one hot approach rising to the top.

Bissett Retirement Fund

Managed by: Michael Quinn, CFA (since inception)

From: Bissett & Associates Investment Management Ltd.

RRSP Eligible: 🍁

Overall performance: ★ ★ ★ ★ ★

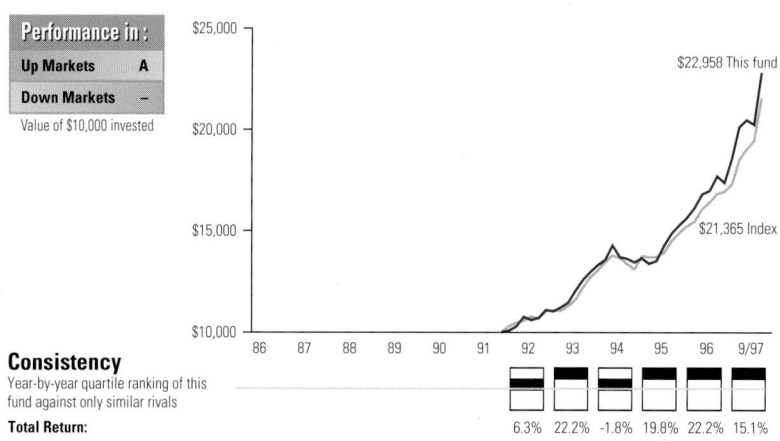

Performance in :	
Up Markets	**A**
Down Markets	**–**

Value of $10,000 invested

$22,958 This fund

$21,365 Index

Consistency
Year-by-year quartile ranking of this
fund against only similar rivals

Total Return: 6.3% 22.2% -1.8% 19.8% 22.2% 15.1%

Risk

% of time fund has lost money over 12-month period	7%
Biggest drop	-8%
Months to recover	14

Efficiency

For every $100	$0.44
which for this class is	Low

Fit (Investment style)

	Value	Blend	Growth
Big			
Medium			
Small			

Opinion

Buy one get many—that's the simple logic behind this special fund. It's less of a bargain than other Bissett funds, because it's merely a collection of them with an extra layer of management expenses—in this case an extra 0.44%. But for investors who are just starting out, or for those wanting a simple one-decision approach, this is a great offering. Quinn actively manages the mix between the various underlying funds in order to profit from changes in interest rates and whatnot.

The Bissett team remains as bullish as they've been for the past few years, primarily because of the positive changes Canada is undergoing, like strong domestic growth, low inflation, and a terrific export sector. With the interest-rate picture still clear, there's little reason to trim the recent 40% or so allocation to fixed income. Still, the fund does have a policy of maxing out its foreign exposure, as do many in its group. In fact, that's what helps my balanced fund benchmark stay so steady (it hasn't had a bear market since 1987).

Balanced

Trimark Income Growth Fund

Managed by: Vito Maida (since 1995) & Patrick Farmer (since 1993)

From: Trimark Investment Management Inc.

RRSP Eligible:

Overall performance: ★ ★ ★ ★ ☆

Performance in :	
Up Markets	**A**
Down Markets	**A**
Value of $10,000 invested	

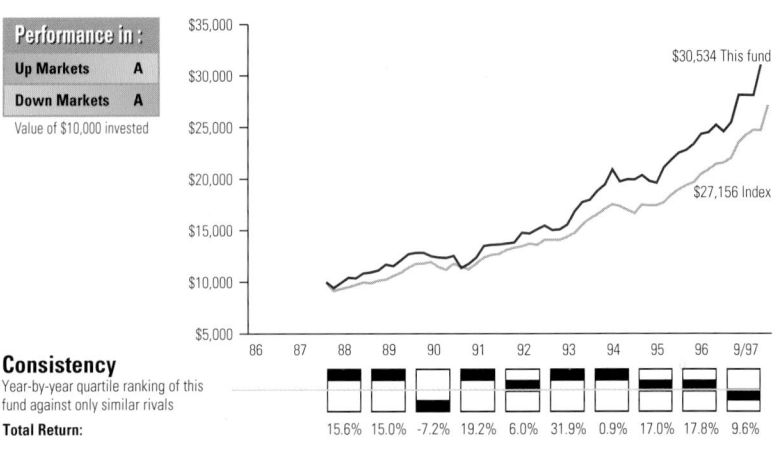

$30,534 This fund

$27,156 Index

Consistency
Year-by-year quartile ranking of this
fund against only similar rivals

Total Return:

15.6%	15.0%	-7.2%	19.2%	6.0%	31.9%	0.9%	17.0%	17.8%	9.6%

Risk

% of time fund has lost money over 12-month period	**9%**
Biggest drop	**-12%**
Months to recover	**15**

Efficiency ◎

For every $100	**$1.60**
which for this class is	**Low**

Fit (Investment style)

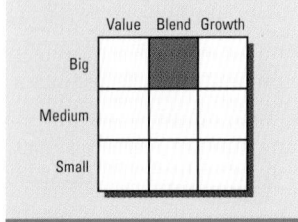

Opinion

Even without manager Wally Kusters, this is a dream fund. He left in 1997, after coming on board just two years earlier. But the mantra at Trimark has always been that the team drives the process and the individuals are less important. Even chairman Bob Krembil would say this about himself; now that the process is refined, even he's replaceable.

Despite the $600 million-plus in its coffers, I'd dare say that this fund's a well-kept secret. That's because this gem is often spurned by investors, who opt instead for its higher-priced clone, the Trimark Select Balanced Fund, which charges 0.6% more every year for the privilege of its rear-end load.

Besides low fees Trimark Income Growth does many things well. First of all, it's conservative. That doesn't sound like much of an attribute in the frothy markets we've had for much of '96 and '97, but it's a valuable trait. Second, the subtle, strategic shifts between asset classes that you'll get in this fund are ideal—both for adding value and for refraining from market timing.

Balanced

Common Sense Asset Builder Fund

Managed by: Jerry Javasky

From: Mackenzie Financial Corporation

RRSP Eligible:

Overall performance: ★ ★ ★ ★ ★

Performance in :	
Up Markets	**A**
Down Markets	–

Value of $10,000 invested

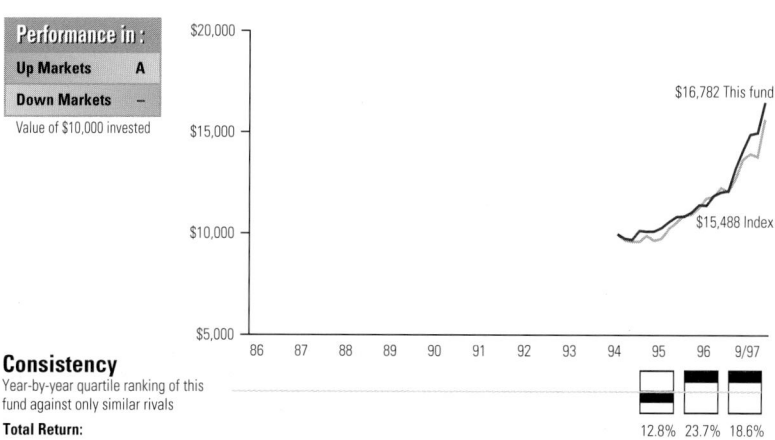

$20,000

$16,782 This fund

$15,000

$15,488 Index

$10,000

$5,000

86 87 88 89 90 91 92 93 94 95 96 9/97

Consistency
Year-by-year quartile ranking of this fund against only similar rivals

Total Return: 12.8% 23.7% 18.6%

Risk

% of time fund has lost money over 12-month period	**0%**
Biggest drop	**-3%**
Months to recover	**5**

Efficiency

For every $100	**$2.26**
which for this class is	**High**

Fit (Investment style)

	Value	Blend	Growth
Big		■	
Medium			
Small			

Opinion

This and others in the family are from Primerica Life Insurance Co., who tapped Mackenzie's Jerry Javasky to run private label funds for them. This one's very similar to Ivy Growth and Income Fund, which is also a good fund.

In this fund you'll find cheap, cheap stocks and government bonds in a mix that can vary widely. By focusing on big cap names, this fund's investors have really made the most of the big cap rally that's dominated recent TSE action. And of course there's the heavy exposure to banks—one of the hottest areas of the market lately. Bear in mind that the other Asset Builder funds are quite similar to this one—offering little diversification from one another. And while this Asset Builder fund is good, it would be ill-suited as a complement to the Ivy fund mentioned above because of the close similarity.

Balanced

Sceptre Balanced Growth Fund

Managed by: Lyle Stein (since 1992)

From: Sceptre Investment Counsel Ltd.

RRSP Eligible:

Overall performance: ★ ★ ★ ✯ ☆

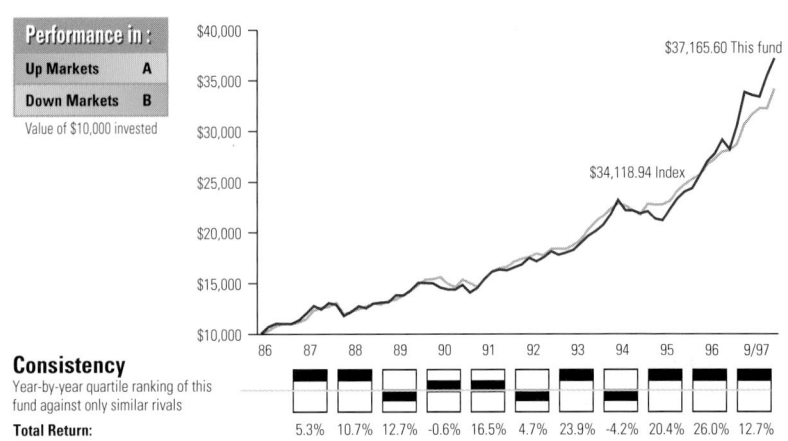

Performance in :	
Up Markets	A
Down Markets	B

Value of $10,000 invested

$37,165.60 This fund

$34,118.94 Index

Consistency
Year-by-year quartile ranking of this
fund against only similar rivals

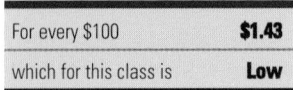

	86	87	88	89	90	91	92	93	94	95	96	9/97
Total Return:	5.3%	10.7%	12.7%	-0.6%	16.5%	4.7%	23.9%	-4.2%	20.4%	26.0%	12.7%

Risk

% of time fund has lost money over 12-month period	**10%**
Biggest drop	**-10%**
Months to recover	**10**

Efficiency

For every $100	**$1.43**
which for this class is	**Low**

Fit (Investment style)

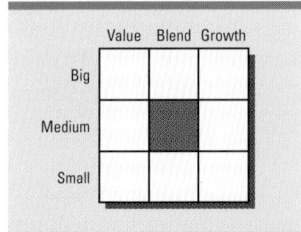

Opinion

Lyle Stein has been busy in his five years or so at the helm of this superb one-decision fund. Of course, with an expense ratio that's about one-third lower than his peer group average, he doesn't have to be as smart as his competition to keep pace with them. But in fact, he is smart. And adroit term selection for bonds and some wins on the stock side have helped him add distance between this fund and his balanced fund rivals.

This is a relatively fixed-mix fund, but Stein is an active manager. He hasn't suffered any bouts of market timing like others who let cash build up to 40%, then pray for a crash. He wouldn't pretend to know when such a thing is coming.

He does, however, know what's coming to Canada: More sustainably good economic performance. And he knows that there will continue to be inefficiently priced companies, so that fundamental equity research will offer rewards. With team members like Allan Jacobs helping to pick stocks, it's easy to add value by finding great companies before the Street does.

Phillips Hager & North Balanced Fund

Managed by: Team (since inception)

From: Phillips Hager & North Investment Management Ltd.

RRSP Eligible:

Overall performance: ★ ★ ★ ✦ ☆

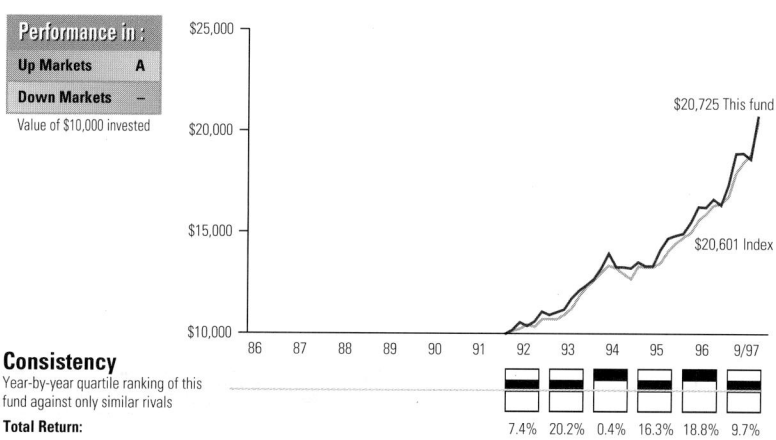

Performance in :	
Up Markets	A
Down Markets	–

Value of $10,000 invested

$25,000

$20,000

$15,000

$10,000

$20,725 This fund

$20,601 Index

86 87 88 89 90 91 92 93 94 95 96 9/97

Consistency
Year-by-year quartile ranking of this fund against only similar rivals

Total Return: 7.4% 20.2% 0.4% 16.3% 18.8% 9.7%

Risk

% of time fund has lost money over 12-month period	2%
Biggest drop	-8%
Months to recover	13

Efficiency

For every $100	$0.91
which for this class is	Low

Fit (Investment style)

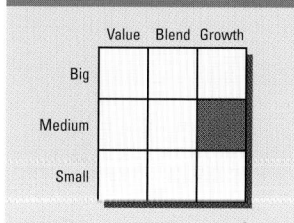

	Value	Blend	Growth
Big			
Medium			
Small			

Opinion

With its low fees, stellar performance, and moderate risk, who wouldn't love this fund?

Your broker, that's who.

Forget the commission thing (this fund doesn't pay one), the problem with PH&N is all about access. Lots and lots of smart financial advisors would love to sell you this fund (even as a loss leader) just to get the rest of your money into load funds. But PH&N isn't on the systems-approved list at most firms. And they have high minimum investments (you'll have to pony up a cool $25 grand). You'll also have to open a special account at PH&N—which means yet another statement every month or quarter.

The firm embodies everything that's good about the mutual fund business. Deep, diligent research; active management that uses both top-down, thematic approaches; and old-fashioned kick-the-tires company research.

Global Strategy Income Plus Fund

Managed by: Tony Massie (since 1992)

From: Global Strategy Financial Inc.

RRSP Eligible:

Overall performance: ★ ★ ★ ⯪ ⯪

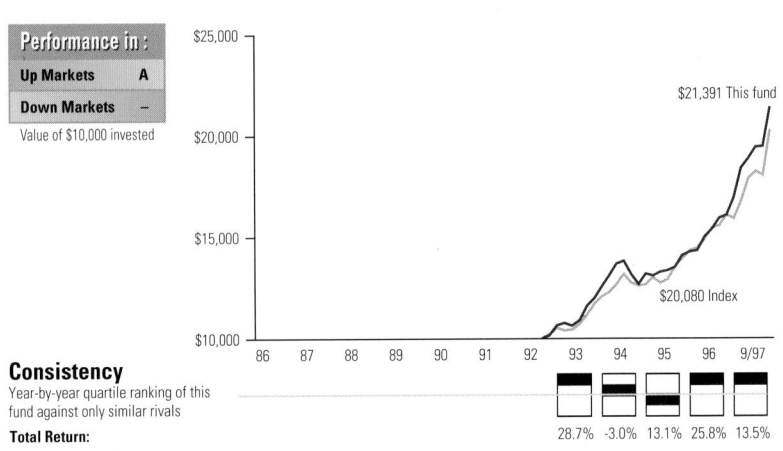

Performance in :	
Up Markets	A
Down Markets	–

Value of $10,000 invested

$25,000

$21,391 This fund

$20,000

$15,000

$20,080 Index

$10,000

86 87 88 89 90 91 92 93 94 95 96 9/97

Consistency
Year-by-year quartile ranking of this
fund against only similar rivals

Total Return: 28.7% -3.0% 13.1% 25.8% 13.5%

Risk

% of time fund has lost money over 12-month period	10%
Biggest drop	-8%
Months to recover	15

Efficiency

For every $100	$2.63
which for this class is	High

Fit (Investment style)

	Value	Blend	Growth
Big	■		
Medium			
Small			

Opinion

I've always been impressed with Tony Massie's ability to understand and follow so many factors. He's both bottom up and top down (meaning that he analyzes macroeconomic trends like the economy and world politics) as well as micro or company-specific factors. In this balanced fund, you won't find much active asset allocation, though there remains a fair bit of uninvested cash. The bonds today are quite short in duration—defensive posturing, to be sure. But the stock market remains rich hunting ground for Massie, who sticks to rock-solid, dividend-paying dirt-cheap companies, and yes, they do still exist—in the utility sector, for example. This conservative fund has done well despite its burdensome expense level of 2.63%.

McLean Budden Balanced Fund

Managed by: Mary Hallward

From: McLean Budden Limited

RRSP Eligible:

Balanced

Overall performance: ★ ★ ★ ✦ ☆

Performance in :	
Up Markets	**A**
Down Markets	**–**
Value of $10,000 invested	

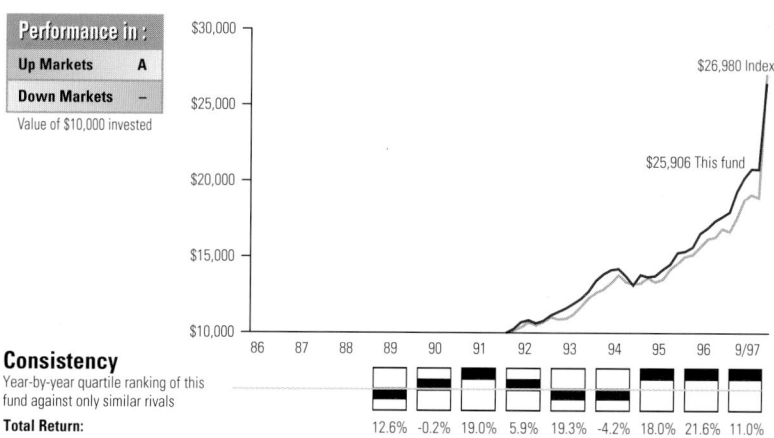

Consistency
Year-by-year quartile ranking of this fund against only similar rivals

Total Return: 12.6% -0.2% 19.0% 5.9% 19.3% -4.2% 18.0% 21.6% 11.0%

Risk

% of time fund has lost money over 12-month period	**14%**
Biggest drop	**-11%**
Months to recover	**15**

Efficiency

For every $100	**$1.75**
which for this class is	**Average**

Fit (Investment style)

	Value	Blend	Growth
Big			
Medium			
Small			

Opinion

Though not well known to retail investors, the McLean Budden team is nonetheless a powerhouse in the pension world—where performance is king. Their conservative style is well-suited to the Canadian market: They charge low fees, employ a bend of disciplines and have patience with their stock holdings.

But don't confuse this fund with McLean Budden Pooled Balanced Fund. The latter is for institutions, even though it shows up alongside the retail fund in the newspaper listings. (If you can afford the six-figure minimum investment, this and other non-bank pooled funds are an excellent bet because of their low, low fees.)

This retail fund charges 1.75% annually, which is a bargain in this country—especially for a fund that's made good money over the years. Credit the success to a relatively fixed mix of big-cap stocks and longer term bonds—a superb combination in a rally that's been especially kind to big stocks

Altamira Growth & Income Fund

Managed by: Cedric Rabin (since inception)

From: Altamira Management Ltd.

RRSP Eligible:

Overall performance: ★ ★ ★ ⅃ ☆

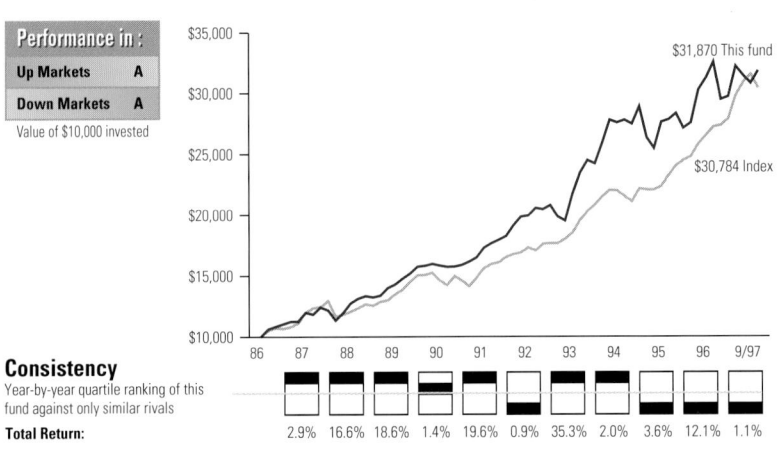

Performance in :	
Up Markets	**A**
Down Markets	**A**

Value of $10,000 invested

$31,870 This fund

$30,784 Index

$35,000
$30,000
$25,000
$20,000
$15,000
$10,000

86 87 88 89 90 91 92 93 94 95 96 9/97

Consistency
Year-by-year quartile ranking of this
fund against only similar rivals

Total Return:

2.9%	16.6%	18.6%	1.4%	19.6%	0.9%	35.3%	2.0%	3.6%	12.1%	1.1%

Risk

% of time fund has lost money over 12-month period	**10%**
Biggest drop	**-13%**
Months to recover	**15**

Efficiency ⊙

For every $100	**$1.40**
which for this class is	**Average**

Fit (Investment style)

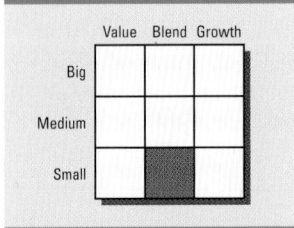

	Value	Blend	Growth
Big			
Medium			
Small			

Opinion

Everyone's dumping on Altamira these days, but most of the criticism is off-base. Yes, returns have been weaker in the past two or three years for this fund and others in the family. But it's not because they changed their style. It's not because they lost great managers. And it's not because they got too big, and thus were forced to become closet indexers.

It's because they simply made two wrong bets: on gold and off banks, to be specific. Both were dead wrong, and since the style at Altamira involves big over- or underweights, the blunder was magnified.

But if you believe at all that talented money managers exist, then you have to resign yourself to believing that Rabin and the others are talented. Their overall performance record has been good, despite the recent weakness. Now, after two dog years, it's clearly the time for patience.

Mutual Premier Diversified Fund

Managed by: Steve Brown & team (since inception)

From: Mutual Asset Management

RRSP Eligible: 🇨🇦

Overall performance: ★ ★ ★ ☆ ☆

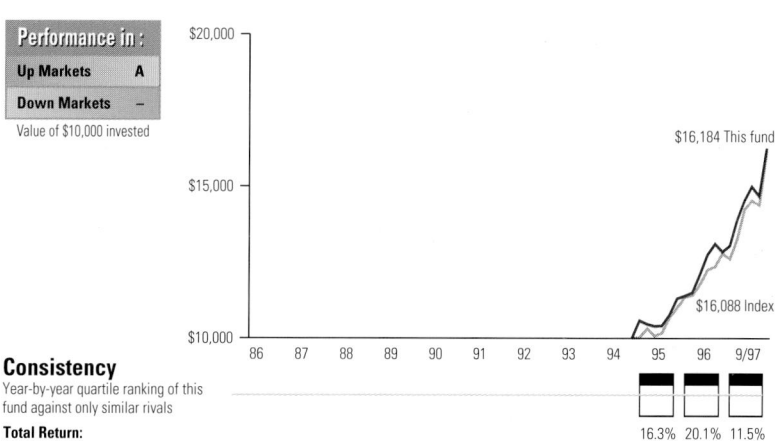

Performance in :	
Up Markets	**A**
Down Markets	**–**

Value of $10,000 invested

$16,184 This fund

$16,088 Index

Consistency
Year-by-year quartile ranking of this
fund against only similar rivals

Total Return: 16.3% 20.1% 11.5%

Risk

% of time fund has lost money over 12-month period	**0%**
Biggest drop	**-5%**
Months to recover	**3**

Efficiency ◉

For every $100	**$2.30**
which for this class is	**High**

Fit (Investment style)

	Value	Blend	Growth
Big			
Medium			
Small			

Opinion

Being able to see the forest through the trees is one of the obvious advantages to being a money manager based outside of Toronto, at least as far as Steve Brown is concerned. His team has seen the Canadian economic big picture very clearly for the past three years on this newer fund. The view has been a good one: government and corporate restructurings have dramatically changed the competitive position of these groups. Now debt reduction and capital spending are taking off— all without any hint of inflation. There's rich hunting in this environment for quality companies that are hitting on all cylinders—and that's what this Waterloo-based team looks for.

In fact, interviewing companies is practically a full time job for the group, whose assets are soaring on the back of good performance numbers. This fund is available no load through mutual agents.

Dynamic Partners Fund

Managed by: Norm Bengough & Jonathan Godman (since inception) & Michael Sprung (since 1995)

From: Godman & Company Investment Counsel

RRSP Eligible:

Overall performance: ★ ★ ★ ↄ ☆

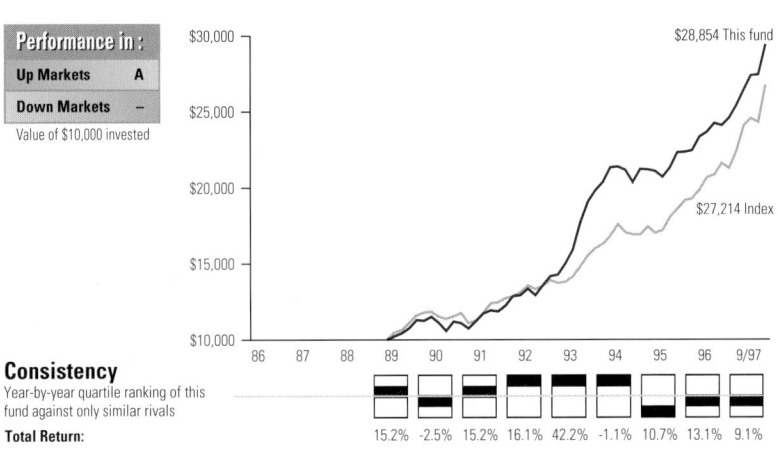

Performance in :	
Up Markets	**A**
Down Markets	**–**

Value of $10,000 invested

$28,854 This fund

$27,214 Index

Consistency
Year-by-year quartile ranking of this fund against only similar rivals

Total Return: 15.2% -2.5% 15.2% 16.1% 42.2% -1.1% 10.7% 13.1% 9.1%

Risk

% of time fund has lost money over 12-month period	**11%**
Biggest drop	**-8%**
Months to recover	**13**

Efficiency

For every $100	**$2.38**
which for this class is	**High**

Fit (Investment style)

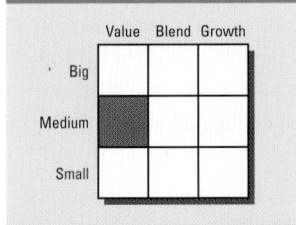

Opinion

You've gotta love it when a smart manager like Norm Bengough is proven wrong on a particular call on the market, because that's when smart people tend to re-double their conviction that things will work out as expected—eventually. That means this fund should have its day—soon.

Bengough's been expecting flat yields and strength in resource stocks for some time. Instead, yields have tumbled and bank shares (of all things!) have zoomed. It just can't last, he'll tell you. We're at a very late stage in the U.S. economic cycle, and worldwide growth is soaring. So Canada's time has indeed come, and should be helped by a cheap loonie.

Partners really is actively managed. The asset-mix shifts in this fund can be big, so the premium pricing of the fund does buy something. But you'd save money by combining a Dynamic stock fund with a Dynamic bond fund in a 60/40 mix.

AGF American Tactical Asset Alloc.

Managed by: Kathy Taylor

From: Barclays Global Investors

RRSP Eligible:

Balanced

Overall performance: ★ ★ ★ ⅟ ☆

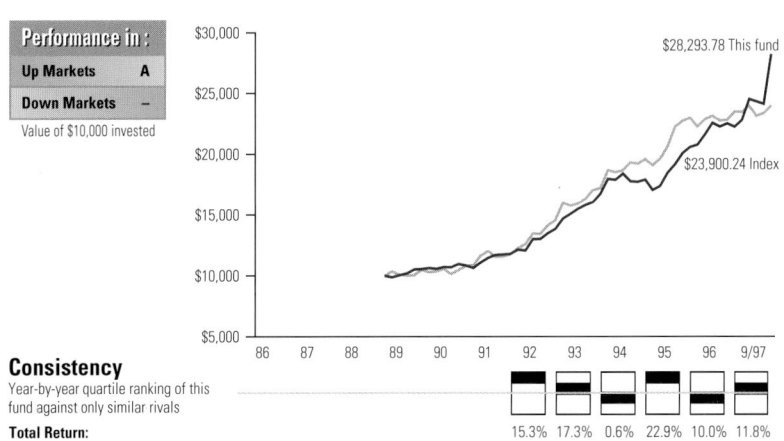

Performance in :	
Up Markets	A
Down Markets	–

Value of $10,000 invested

$30,000

$28,293.78 This fund

$25,000

$20,000

$23,900.24 Index

$15,000

$10,000

$5,000

86 87 88 89 90 91 92 93 94 95 96 9/97

Consistency
Year-by-year quartile ranking of this fund against only similar rivals

Total Return: 15.3% 17.3% 0.6% 22.9% 10.0% 11.8%

Risk

% of time fund has lost money over 12-month period	3%
Biggest drop	-7%
Months to recover	11

Efficiency

For every $100	$2.52
which for this class is	**Average**

Fit (Investment style)

	Value	Blend	Growth
Big			■
Medium			
Small			

Opinion

Since the merger of 20/20 with AGF, the whole fund lineup has been shuffled. Funds with an aggressive tilt have been given the 20/20 moniker, because 20/20 had developed a strong franchise in the area of more aggressive investing. But tame funds like this one were renamed with the AGF label. Despite the new name, the same management team is in place that has always been on the job. It's a powerhouse firm that manages half a trillion bucks using just this strategy on behalf of large institutions.

Why have they won so many big accounts? Because the strategy works. More return, less risk. Active asset mix decisions premised on quant research and contrarian value. But passive investing (indexing) is used to pick stocks. It's a great approach that misfires a little on this fund. First, because the fund charges a hefty 2.52% in fees annually. Second, the big cap stocks that dominate the index have been on an unsustainable tear.

Balanced

Universal World Balanced RRSP

Managed by: Leslie Ferris, Barbara Trebbi, & Michael Landry (since 1994)

From: Mackenzie Investment Management Inc. (Florida)

RRSP Eligible:

Overall performance: ★★★★½

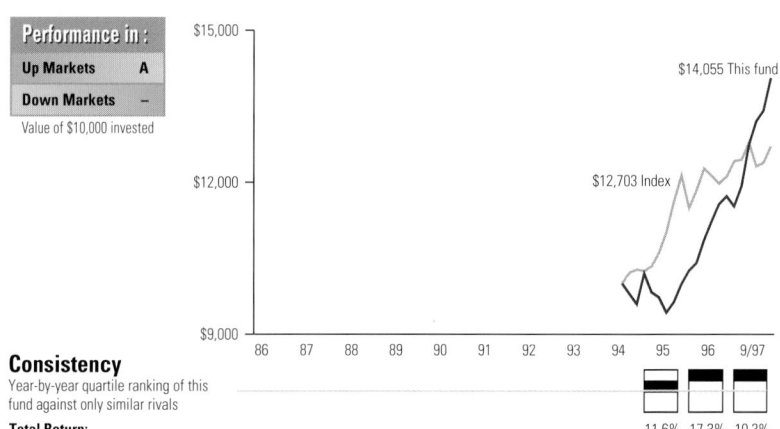

Performance in:	
Up Markets	A
Down Markets	–

Value of $10,000 invested

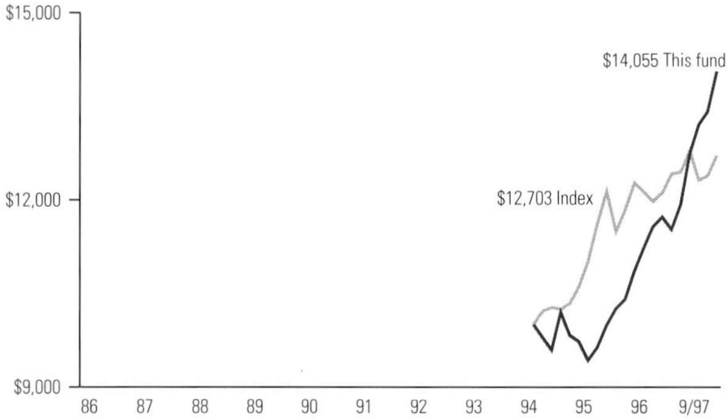
$15,000
$12,000
$9,000
$14,055 This fund
$12,703 Index
86
87
88
89
90
91
92
93
94
95
96
9/97

Consistency

Year-by-year quartile ranking of this fund against only similar rivals

Total Return: 11.6% 17.3% 10.3%

Risk

% of time fund has lost money over 12-month period	10%
Biggest drop	-8%
Months to recover	10

Efficiency

For every $100	$2.43
which for this class is	Average

Fit (Investment style)

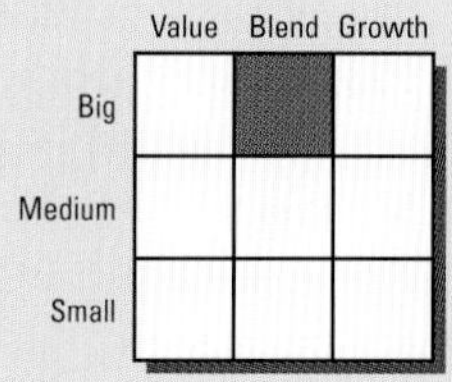
Value
Blend
Growth
Big
Medium
Small

Opinion

Let's say that all of your long-term savings are tied up in your RRSP. This isn't a bad thing. But it does limit your ability to diversify internationally. And that puts a real damper on your ability to limit risk or to make good money. So I'd vigorously encourage investors like you to consider funds like this one. It's fully RRSP-eligible, yet fully foreign. It's a great way to earn non-Canadian returns in an RRSP.

They've done such a good job with this fund, it's tough to figure which moves were best. The currency decisions have been perfect (they've hedged the currencies that subsequently went down, and left unhedged the stronger currencies that went up, like sterling).

The big European stock exposure has been a home run too. As have the mostly European bond holdings.

Phillips Hager & North Bond Fund

Managed by: Team (since inception); Scott Lamont (since 1990)

From: Phillips Hager & North Investment Management Ltd.

RRSP Eligible:

Canadian Bond

Overall performance: ★ ★ ★ ★ ☆

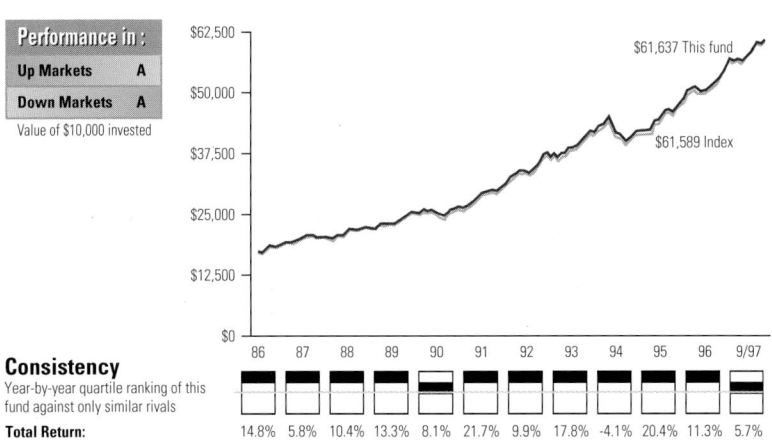

Performance in :	
Up Markets	**A**
Down Markets	**A**

Value of $10,000 invested

$61,637 This fund

$61,589 Index

Consistency
Year-by-year quartile ranking of this fund against only similar rivals

	86	87	88	89	90	91	92	93	94	95	96	9/97
Total Return:	14.8%	5.8%	10.4%	13.3%	8.1%	21.7%	9.9%	17.8%	-4.1%	20.4%	11.3%	5.7%

Risk

% of time fund has lost money over 12-month period	**13%**
Biggest drop	**-17%**
Months to recover	**16**

Efficiency

For every $100	**$0.57**
which for this class is	**Low**

Fit (Investment style)

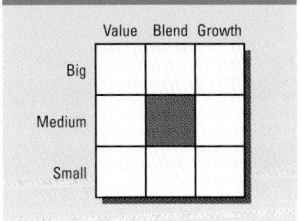

	Value	Blend	Growth
Big			
Medium			
Small			

Opinion

Scott Lamont and others on this respected fixed-income team will be the first to tell you that we're in a vastly different environment for bonds today compared with just a few years ago. Then we had high and falling rates, big coupons and big capital gains. That was when the fund with the longest term won, and expenses didn't matter much. PH&N Bond Fund excelled then too.

But now—with interest rates low and relatively stable—low fees and astute trading will make the difference. At just 0.57% annually (and falling!), this lean fund charges just one-third as much as its average rival.

Low inflation makes for high real rates of return in this environment, and with some good trading, capital gains are still possible, they say. I say this is just about the only bond fund worth owning. Otherwise, just buy a mid-term bond and forget about it.

Green Line Global RRSP Bond Fund

Managed by: Satish Rai (since inception)

From: Toronto Dominion Securities Inc.

RRSP Eligible:

US & Intn'l Bond

Overall performance: ★ ★ ★ ★ ☆

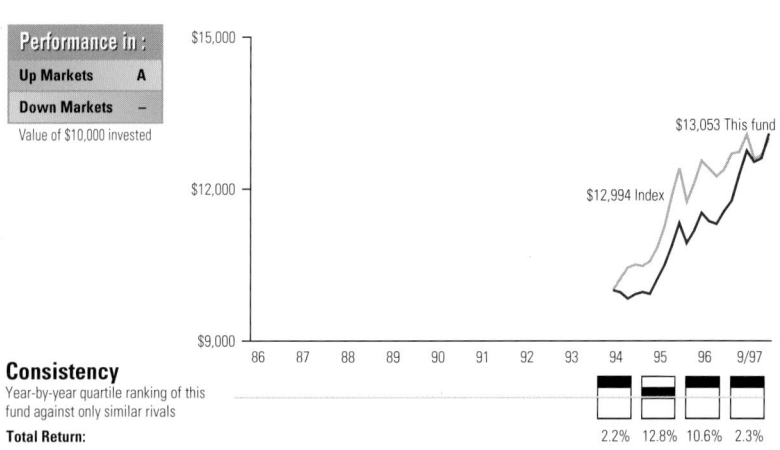

Performance in :	
Up Markets	A
Down Markets	–

Value of $10,000 invested

$13,053 This fund

$12,994 Index

Consistency
Year-by-year quartile ranking of this fund against only similar rivals

Total Return: 2.2% 12.8% 10.6% 2.3%

Risk

% of time fund has lost money over 12-month period	0%
Biggest drop	-4%
Months to recover	4

Efficiency ⊙

For every $100	$2.03
which for this class is	Average

Fit (Investment style)

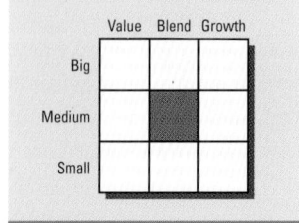

Opinion

Say you're nervous about lofty stock markets, want international diversification, and hope to do better than GICs without a lot of risk. Now suppose that all of your savings are tied up inside your RRSP.

This fund's for you. It's set to do well by profiting from the same course of events today in Europe that set off a Canadian bond rally six years ago. That course of events, simply defined, is the painful restructuring of government and business finances that causes all kinds of dislocations (like unemployment, write-downs, and a falling currency). These events set the stage for a long, sustainable rally in Canadian bond prices when they happened here. Now the same scenario is spreading across Europe.

All of which means that good yields are possible for now, capital gains are likely, and currency protection is vital. This fund can hedge, counts as Canadian content, and beats its peers. What more could you want?

Guardian International Income 'A' Fund

Managed by: Laurence Linklater (since 1993)

From: Kleinwort Guardian Overseas Ltd.

RRSP Eligible:

Overall performance: ★ ★ ☆ ☆ ☆

Performance in :	
Up Markets	**D**
Down Markets	**–**

Value of $10,000 invested

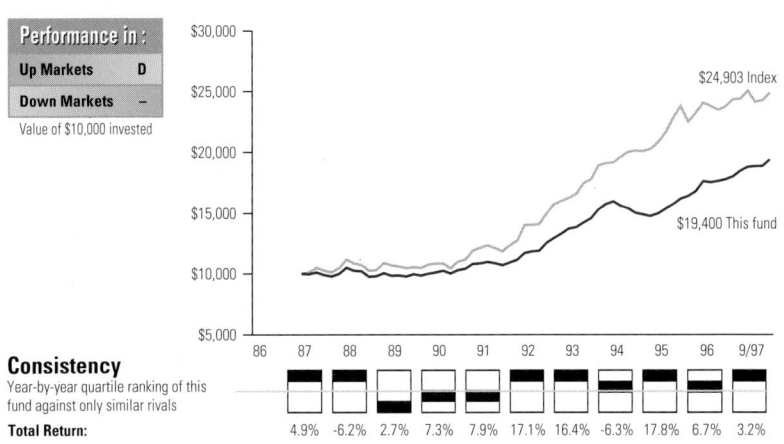

$30,000
$25,000 $24,903 Index
$20,000
$15,000
$10,000 $19,400 This fund
$5,000

86 87 88 89 90 91 92 93 94 95 96 9/97

Consistency
Year-by-year quartile ranking of this
fund against only similar rivals

Total Return:

	4.9%	-6.2%	2.7%	7.3%	7.9%	17.1%	16.4%	-6.3%	17.8%	6.7%	3.2%

Risk

% of time fund has lost money over 12-month period	**15%**
Biggest drop	**-9%**
Months to recover	**32**

Efficiency

For every $100	**$2.10**
which for this class is	**Average**

Fit (Investment style)

	Value	Blend	Growth
Big			
Medium			
Small			

Opinion

Don't be frightened by the use of derivatives in this and other fully RRSP eligible foreign funds. These aren't the same derivatives strategies that buried Orange County. These are very conservative, no-leverage tools that allow the fund to stickhandle its way around the foreign content runes.

The London-based gang responsible for the fund is conservative by nature. (Hey, they're British!) And the record proves their posture: the only negative year they've had was in 1989. You'll get exposure to foreign bond markets like those in Europe (their interest rates are falling, which is good). That way, you can have fixed income without being exposed to the Canadian bond market after an unprecedented 16-year rally. The fund will hedge its currency exposure when warranted and has added to returns in the past through conservative hedging.

Altamira Equity Fund

Managed by: Frank Mersch (since inception)

From: Altamira Management Ltd.

RRSP Eligible:

Overall performance: ★ ★ ★ ★ ★

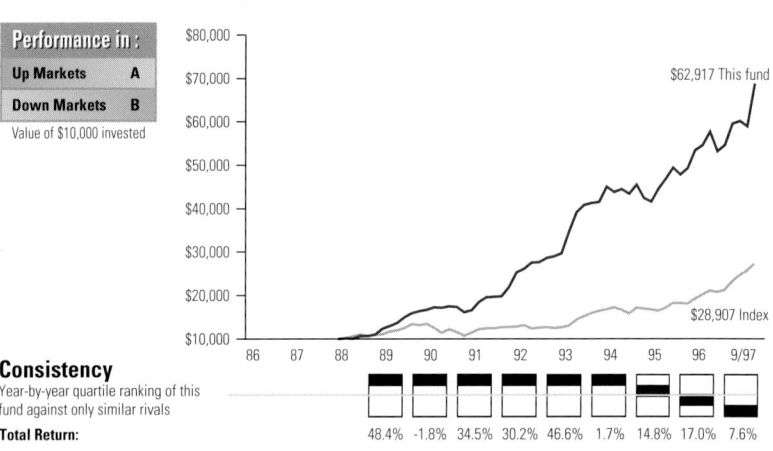

Performance in :	
Up Markets	A
Down Markets	B

Value of $10,000 invested

$62,917 This fund

$28,907 Index

Consistency
Year-by-year quartile ranking of this fund against only similar rivals

Total Return: 48.4% -1.8% 34.5% 30.2% 46.6% 1.7% 14.8% 17.0% 7.6%

Risk

% of time fund has lost money over 12-month period	5%
Biggest drop	-9%
Months to recover	5

Efficiency

For every $100	$2.28
which for this class is	Average

Fit (Investment style)

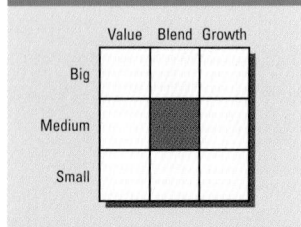

Opinion

What Frank Mersch needed in 1996 was a war, and he got one. But it was the wrong kind.

He was convinced that bank shares, which had already dazzled investors, were finished their show. So he moved on to gold. Bad move. Gold tanked as more and more central bankers and speculators kept selling, producing an artificial and temporary gush of supply. A war or massive crisis would have helped, but instead he got a shareholder battle among different constituencies within his own firm. Their very public fights (in and out of the courtroom) grabbed headlines for some time.

All this has left Altamira's investors wondering what in the heck's going on. And to have the shareholder dispute coincide with weaker-than-most performance has been doubly problematic. But this is still the most enviable track record in Canada, and the team that made it happen is still intact.

Canadian Equity

Industrial Alliance Stock Fund

Managed by: Luc R. Fournier (since inception)

From: Industrial-Alliance Life Insurance Co.

RRSP Eligible:

Overall performance: ★ ★ ★ ★ ★

Canadian Equity

Performance in :	
Up Markets	A
Down Markets	–

Value of $10,000 invested

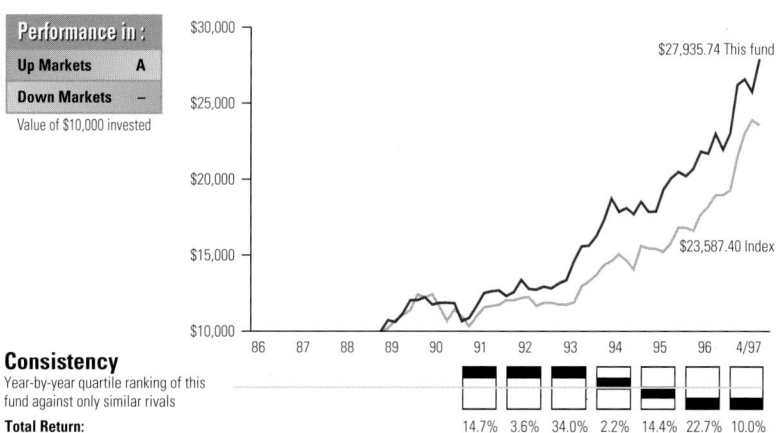

$30,000

$25,000

$20,000

$15,000

$10,000

$27,935.74 This fund

$23,587.40 Index

86 87 88 89 90 91 92 93 94 95 96 4/97

Consistency
Year-by-year quartile ranking of this
fund against only similar rivals

Total Return: 14.7% 3.6% 34.0% 2.2% 14.4% 22.7% 10.0%

Risk

% of time fund has lost money over 12-month period	**15%**
Biggest drop	**-24%**
Months to recover	**22**

Efficiency ◎

For every $100	**$1.61**
which for this class is	**Low**

Fit (Investment style)

	Value	Blend	Growth
Big	■		
Medium			
Small			

Opinion

I know, I know. Seg funds are dull. But this one's done well, and the future looks bright for it. It doesn't charge much in fees and it isn't that risky.

Here's how it works: With a seg fund you get what is, essentially, a mutual fund. But the insurance company that offers it chooses to structure it as an insurance policy. Technically, a seg fund has a little bit of life insurance embedded in it for each investor (if you die, there are certain minimum guarantees). But the thing that makes seg funds attractive is the potential for creditor-proofing, which is very cool for people who might find themselves the target of a lawsuit someday—like professionals or business owners.

So this fund's conservative approach of sticking with big blue chip names (a hot area lately) and its policy of charging just 1.61% in expenses, add up to a good deal for conservative investors.

ABC Fundamental Value Fund

Managed by: Irwin Michael (since inception)

From: I.A. Michael Investment Counsel Ltd.

RRSP Eligible: 🍁

Overall performance: ★ ★ ★ ★ ⯪

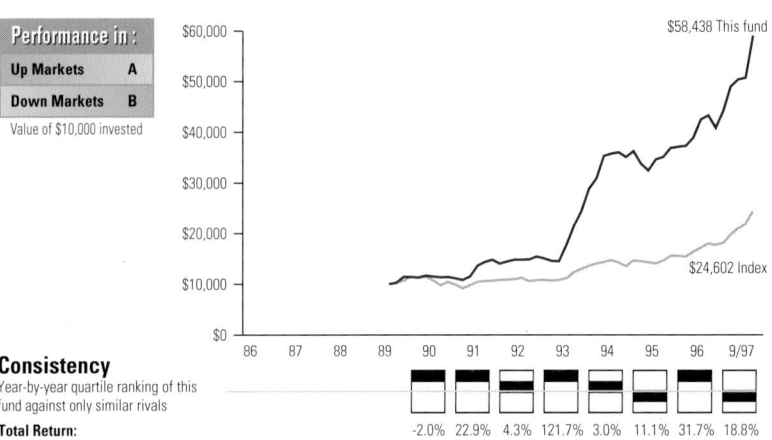

Performance in :	
Up Markets	**A**
Down Markets	**B**

Value of $10,000 invested

$58,438 This fund

$24,602 Index

Consistency
Year-by-year quartile ranking of this fund against only similar rivals

Total Return: -2.0%   22.9%   4.3%   121.7%   3.0%   11.1%   31.7%   18.8%

Risk

% of time fund has lost money over 12-month period	**15%**
Biggest drop	**-11%**
Months to recover	**9**

Efficiency ◎

For every $100	**$2.00**
which for this class is	**Low**

Fit (Investment style)

	Value	Blend	Growth
Big			
Medium			
Small	▨		

Opinion

What doesn't Irwin Michael do well? He's a shareholder activist in takeover battles, a shameless promoter of the concept of buying out-of-favour assets, and an entrepreneur whose entire personal savings sit right alongside yours in his funds. He called the big cap trend beautifully back in my last book and has since done so well that he's back to smaller stocks, whose prices are now relatively low.

Typical of Michael's contrarian approach is Oshawa Group, the grocer. It's dirt cheap (trading miles below break-up value), it makes money, and it pays a good yield. Its crime is that it isn't a bank, so it hasn't doubled. Analysts hate it. But ABC's investors, who have so far done much better than most analysts, know that Irwin Michael's patience is the key to making big money over time.

You'll need $150 000 to get into this fund family and probably much more to diversify by asset class, geography, and investment style.

Clean Environment Equity Fund

Managed by: Ian Ihnatowycz (since inception)

From: Acuity Investment Management

RRSP Eligible:

Overall performance: ★ ★ ★ ⯪ ⯪

Performance in :	
Up Markets	**A**
Down Markets	**D**
Value of $10,000 invested	

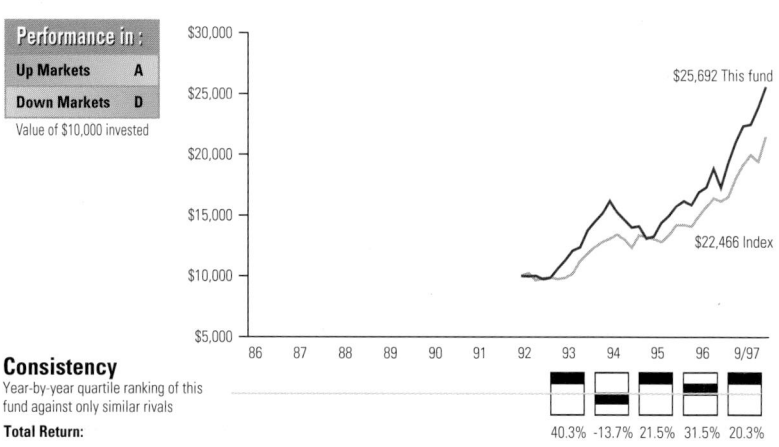

$30,000

$25,000 — $25,692 This fund

$20,000

$15,000

$10,000 — $22,466 Index

$5,000

86 87 88 89 90 91 92 93 94 95 96 9/97

Canadian Equity

Consistency
Year-by-year quartile ranking of this
fund against only similar rivals

Total Return: 40.3% -13.7% 21.5% 31.5% 20.3%

Risk

% of time fund has lost money over 12-month period	**16%**
Biggest drop	**-19%**
Months to recover	**22**

Efficiency

For every $100	**$3.00**
which for this class is	**High**

Fit (Investment style)

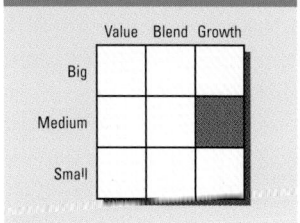

	Value	Blend	Growth
Big			
Medium			▓
Small			

Opinion

It has long been my hypothesis that funds with ethical screens must sacrifice something to find "good" candidates. But both this and Ethical Growth Fund have served their investors—and our world—well. In the case of this Clean Environment fund, credit a growth strategy centered around hot, innovative businesses like YogenFruz and YBM Magnex, for example. The former is a seller of a successful low-fat alternative to ice cream, the latter a maker of high-tech reusable magnets. Both represent forward-thinking management and technology. And both thus epitomize the stock selection process for this fund.

You should own this if you want your investment dollars to speak for you, rewarding "good" companies and, in a small way, punishing the "bad" ones.

Bissett Canadian Equity Fund

Managed by: Fred Pynn & team (since inception)

From: Bissett & Associates Investment Management Ltd.

RRSP Eligible:

Overall performance: ★ ★ ★ ☆ ☆

Performance in :	
Up Markets	**A**
Down Markets	**B**

Value of $10,000 invested

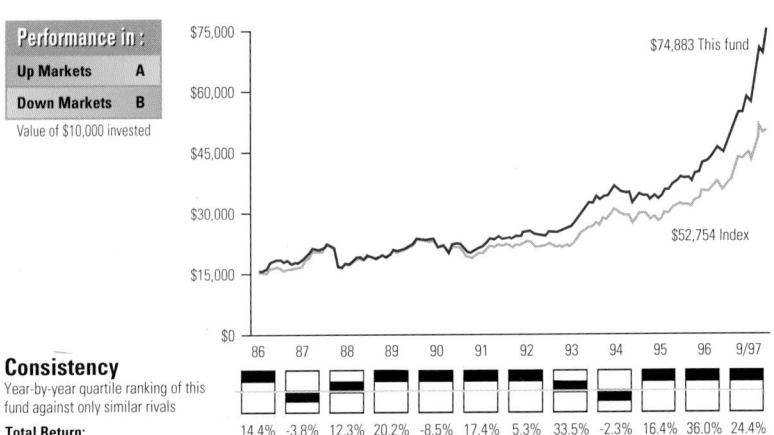

$74,883 This fund

$52,754 Index

Consistency
Year-by-year quartile ranking of this
fund against only similar rivals

	86	87	88	89	90	91	92	93	94	95	96	9/97
Total Return:	14.4%	-3.8%	12.3%	20.2%	-8.5%	17.4%	5.3%	33.5%	-2.3%	16.4%	36.0%	24.4%

Risk

% of time fund has lost money over 12-month period	**17%**
Biggest drop	**-26%**
Months to recover	**23**

Efficiency

For every $100	**$1.35**
which for this class is	**Low**

Fit (Investment style)

	Value	Blend	Growth
Big			
Medium		■	
Small			

Opinion

To be a successful investor long term you've got to get the big picture right. Which just what Fred and the Calgary-based team here at Bissett have done. They don't take a lot of risk. They don't charge a lot of fees. And forget about making big commodity bets—they don't do much of that either.

What they do is achieve consistency by being fully invested in growing companies in Canada and by maximizing their foreign content, a simple trick more investors should do.

Even though valuations are stretched in Canada, according to the firm, opportunities still abound. And the environment for investing is so attractive now, with low inflation and an improving fiscal landscape. Because of that the team has the confidence to invest in good business, to buy more when prices pull back, and to stick around for the long term—which is how long it takes for the benefit of low fees to really manifest themselves.

Guardian Growth Equity Fund 'A'

Managed by: John Priestman (since inception)

From: Guardian Capital Inc.

RRSP Eligible:

Overall performance: ★ ★ ★ ★ ☆

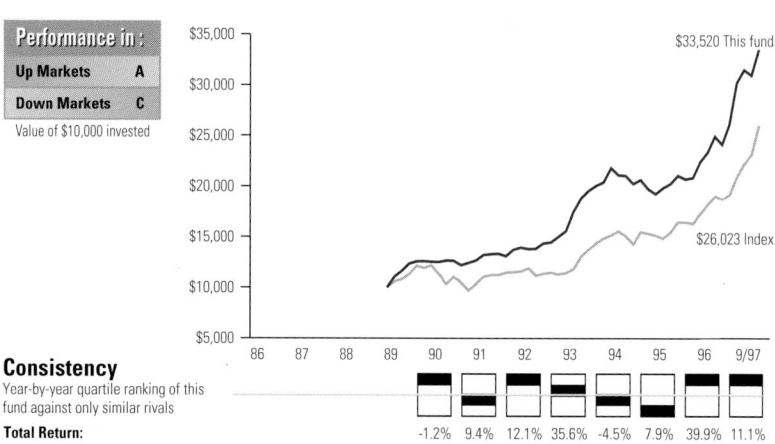

Performance in :	
Up Markets	A
Down Markets	C

Value of $10,000 invested

$33,520 This fund

$26,023 Index

Canadian Equity

Consistency
Year-by-year quartile ranking of this fund against only similar rivals

Total Return: -1.2% 9.4% 12.1% 35.6% -4.5% 7.9% 39.9% 11.1%

Risk

% of time fund has lost money over 12-month period	**17%**
Biggest drop	**-12%**
Months to recover	**23**

Efficiency

For every $100	**$2.24**
which for this class is	**Average**

Fit (Investment style)

	Value	Blend	Growth
Big			
Medium		■	
Small			

Opinion

Guardian uses a fairly simple portfolio-management approach in this and other funds. They do plenty of homework on a slew of companies, pick a fairly tight list, then grill the hell out of management. Most of the time they're looking for bad stuff: risk, worst-case scenarios, etc. By keeping such a strict focus on what could go wrong, a manager like Priestman can avoid leveraged companies or one-product wonders. That diminishes risk for investors.

What's really impressive about this fund, though, is the dough it makes in good markets. With a top-quartile "A" grade in rising markets, this fund really has the oomph you'll need to grow your RRSP through retirement.

Lately there's been more of a shift away from bank and interest-sensitive shares and toward the cyclical and resource companies (except gold). That should work out nicely if the economy keeps chugging along as Priestman expects.

Altafund Investment Corp.

Managed by: Dave Taylor (since 1995)

From: Altamira Management Ltd.

RRSP Eligible:

Overall performance: ★ ★ ★ ★ ☆

Performance in :	
Up Markets	A
Down Markets	C

Value of $10,000 invested

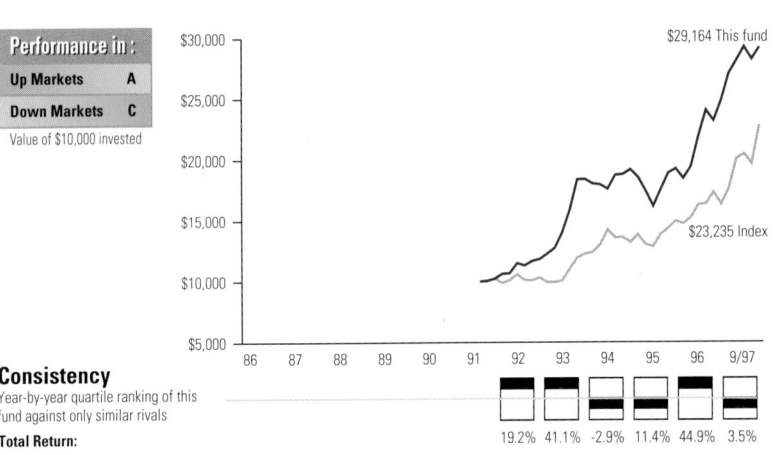

$30,000

$25,000

$20,000

$15,000

$10,000

$5,000

86 87 88 89 90 91 92 93 94 95 96 9/97

$29,164 This fund

$23,235 Index

Consistency

Year-by-year quartile ranking of this fund against only similar rivals

Total Return: 19.2% 41.1% -2.9% 11.4% 44.9% 3.5%

Risk

% of time fund has lost money over 12-month period	**14%**
Biggest drop	**-17%**
Months to recover	**19**

Efficiency

For every $100	**$2.30**
which for this class is	**Average**

Fit (Investment style)

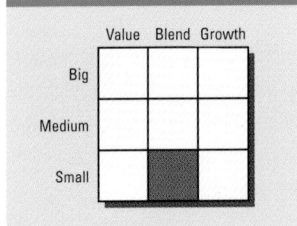

	Value	Blend	Growth
Big			
Medium			
Small		■	

Opinion

This is, and has always been, a more targeted play on resources. At writing, something like 75% of the fund was in the resource group, but interestingly, only a small (underweight) portion of that was in golds—the bait and bane of the Mersch-led equity desk for the past couple of years.

I like this fund, and I own it because it's my sense that this is one of the better ways to play the resource group. Though everyone classifies it as a Canadian equity fund, it's really a unique bird. I like the flexibility the fund has to load up on resources (which are so cyclical anyway) whenever they like.

Going forward, expect the long-heralded recovery in base metals, and of course the oil and gas boom, to translate into real advances for this fully invested fund.

Trimark Canadian Fund

Managed by: Vito Maida (since 1995) & team

From: Trimark Investment Management Inc.

RRSP Eligible:

Overall performance: ★ ★ ★ ★ ☆

Performance in :	
Up Markets	**A**
Down Markets	**A**

Value of $10,000 invested

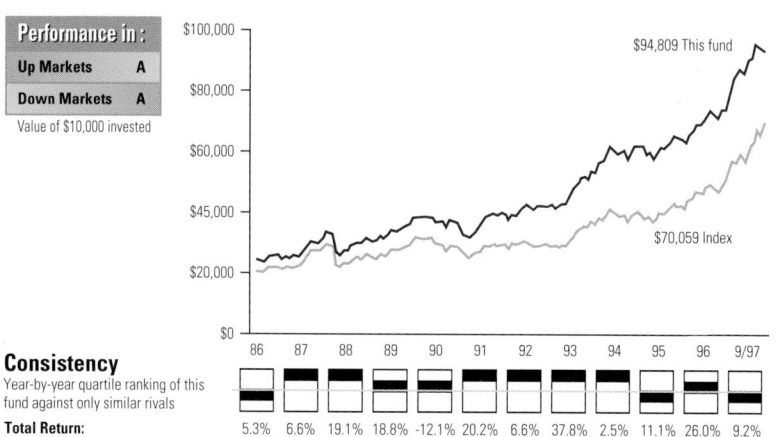

$94,809 This fund

$70,059 Index

Canadian Equity

Consistency
Year-by-year quartile ranking of this
fund against only similar rivals

Total Return:	5.3%	6.6%	19.1%	18.8%	-12.1%	20.2%	6.6%	37.8%	2.5%	11.1%	26.0%	9.2%

Risk

% of time fund has lost money over 12-month period	**11%**
Biggest drop	**-24%**
Months to recover	**17**

Efficiency

For every $100	**$1.52**
which for this class is	**Low**

Fit (Investment style)

	Value	Blend	Growth
Big		■	
Medium			
Small			

Opinion

A year ago I argued with the naysayers who said Trimark was so big that the firm's managers would have trouble trading their positions effectively. At $5 billion in Canadian stocks, I said they'd be fine. After all, their approach is buy and hold—and they buy big-company shares. So trading isn't a big issue.

But they've since almost doubled in assets committed to the relatively small Canadian market. So my resolve is being tested. Yes, at some point, size would become an impediment in the Canadian market. Is Trimark there yet? I'll trust the team to let us know on that score. They're a fiercely competitive bunch. If they thought it would help returns, I'm sure they'd close this puppy.

In fact, Trimark has more resources now (more people) than ever to do all that vaunted bottom-up research. And there's still a low expense ratio for this fund, which bodes very well for the future.

Sprectrum United Canadian Equity

Managed by: Kiki Delaney (since 1992)

From: C.A. Delaney Capital Management Ltd.

RRSP Eligible:

Overall performance: ★ ★ ★ ✦ ✦

Performance in :	
Up Markets	**A**
Down Markets	**A**

Value of $10,000 invested

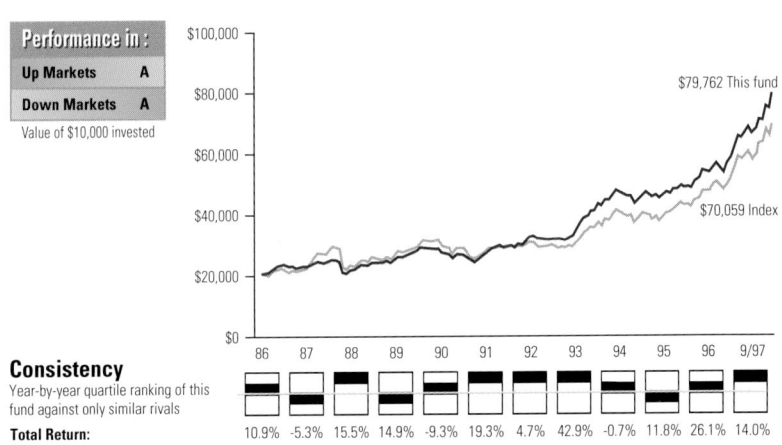

$79,762 This fund

$70,059 Index

Consistency
Year-by-year quartile ranking of this
fund against only similar rivals

Total Return: 10.9% -5.3% 15.5% 14.9% -9.3% 19.3% 4.7% 42.9% -0.7% 11.8% 26.1% 14.0%

Risk

% of time fund has lost money over 12-month period	**20%**
Biggest drop	**-29%**
Months to recover	**20**

Efficiency

For every $100	**$2.35**
which for this class is	**High**

Fit (Investment style)

	Value	Blend	Growth
Big			
Medium		■	
Small			

Opinion

Any marketing department would kill for a track record like this. The fund has done well in good markets. It's done well in bad markets. Its record isn't the result of one huge year. Its record has been, to use a term that's become trite, consistent.

True, manager Kiki Delaney is responsible for only the last five years of the record, which have been great. But look deeper and you'll see real beauty here. The fund hasn't goosed returns by making a killing in some exploration stock, or by being heavily exposed to the hot U.S. market. In fact, it's been very much the wrong environment for Delaney. She's struggling to find great values in a rich market, and the result is a large cash reserve, which naturally reduces risk but also drags down returns in times like these. Something like a fifth of the fund has been in cash lately. You'll want to own this fund before great stock opportunities present themselves.

Green Line Value Fund

Managed by: John Weatherall (since 1993)

From: Toronto Dominion Securities Inc.

RRSP Eligible:

Overall performance: ★ ★ ★ ♩ ☆

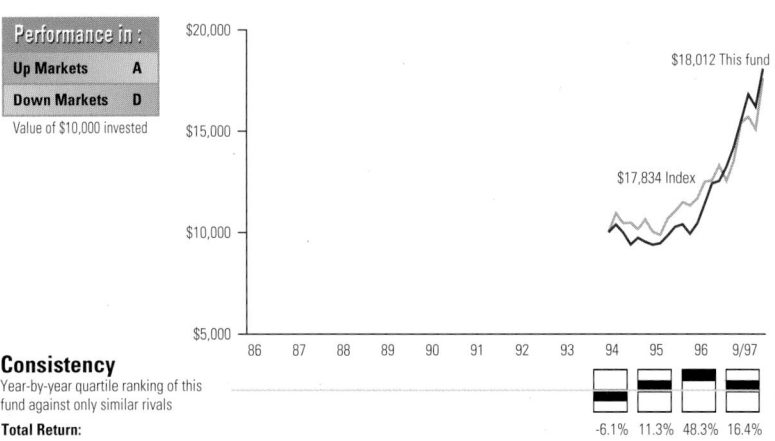

Performance in :	
Up Markets	A
Down Markets	D

Value of $10,000 invested

$18,012 This fund

$17,834 Index

Canadian Equity

Consistency
Year-by-year quartile ranking of this fund against only similar rivals

Total Return: -6.1% 11.3% 48.3% 16.4%

Risk

% of time fund has lost money over 12-month period	**16%**
Biggest drop	**-14%**
Months to recover	**17**

Efficiency

For every $100	**$2.13**
which for this class is	**Average**

Fit (Investment style)

	Value	Blend	Growth
Big			
Medium	■		
Small			

Opinion

Value is just an attractive-sounding word added to the name of many mutual funds. But in this case it means something—it's actually descriptive. Weatherall uses a strict approach to finding cheap stocks and holding them in this strong newer fund. They aren't always big names, but he's certainly profited from the bank rally. He's also been saved by being vastly underweight in the gold and base metals sectors, which have cratered lately.

Since its style is very clear, investors in this fund should diversify into another fund, preferably a terrific small cap growth fund like GBC Canadian Growth or even Guardian Enterprise. There are, after all, cycles when value investing is out of fashion.

Still, with this kind of sizzle in good markets, and expenses that are fair, this is a good fund to buy and hold for the long term.

Ethical Growth Fund

Managed by: Larry Lunn (inception)

From: Connor Clark & Lunn Investment Management Ltd.

RRSP Eligible:

Overall performance: ★ ★ ★ ★ ★

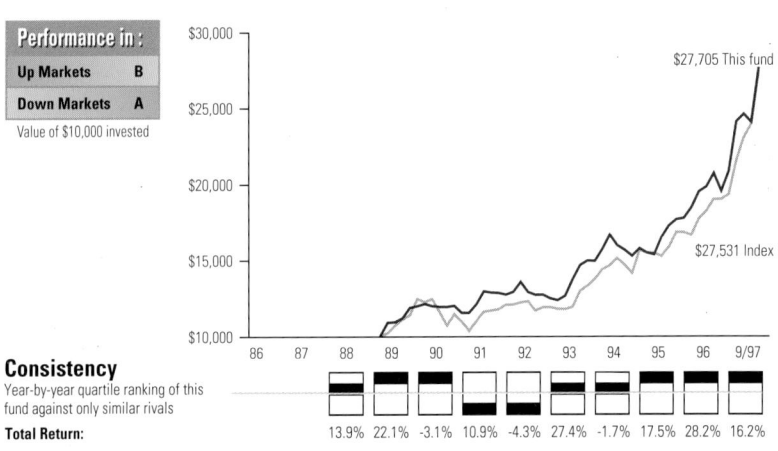

Performance in :	
Up Markets	B
Down Markets	A

Value of $10,000 invested

$30,000

$27,705 This fund

$25,000

$20,000

$15,000

$27,531 Index

$10,000

86 87 88 89 90 91 92 93 94 95 96 9/97

Consistency
Year-by-year quartile ranking of this
fund against only similar rivals

Total Return:

13.9%	22.1%	-3.1%	10.9%	-4.3%	27.4%	-1.7%	17.5%	28.2%	16.2%

Risk

% of time fund has lost money over 12-month period	**18%**
Biggest drop	**-11%**
Months to recover	**15**

Efficiency

For every $100	**$2.14**
which for this class is	**Average**

Fit (Investment style)

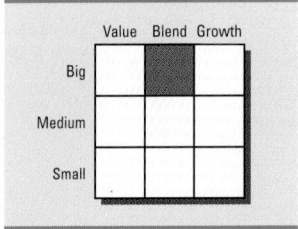

Opinion

If you're big on doing what's right morally, this is a prosperous place to align your values and your wallet. Larry Lunn's risk-averse approach with this fund has long done well for investors. He uses a two-way asset allocation system that permits big cash build-ups when markets look less promising. I wouldn't call that market timing to make extra money; I'd call it protecting capital.

The last couple of years have been well suited to Lunn's approach: big stocks (especially the banks) have moved ahead of everything else, and there's still room for more of the same, according to Lunn, who continues to have little in cash and little outside of Canada.

The rest of the Ethical family also holds some interesting choices for investors, so this family is worth considering when you're standing in line at the credit union.

Empire Elite Equity Fund 5

Managed by: Catharina Van Berkel (since 1993)

From: Empire Life Insurance Company.

RRSP Eligible: 🍁

Overall performance: ★ ★ ★ ★ ★

Canadian Equity

Performance in :	
Up Markets	**B**
Down Markets	**C**

Value of $10,000 invested

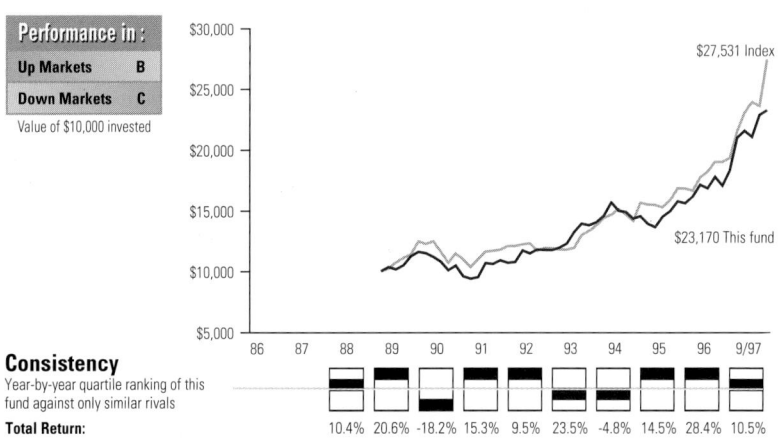

$30,000

$25,000

$20,000

$15,000

$10,000

$5,000

$27,531 Index

$23,170 This fund

86 87 88 89 90 91 92 93 94 95 96 9/97

Consistency
Year-by-year quartile ranking of this
fund against only similar rivals

Total Return: 10.4% 20.6% -18.2% 15.3% 9.5% 23.5% -4.8% 14.5% 28.4% 10.5%

Risk

% of time fund has lost money over 12-month period	**21%**
Biggest drop	**-32%**
Months to recover	**64**

Efficiency

For every $100	**$2.57**
which for this class is	**High**

Fit (Investment style)

	Value	Blend	Growth
Big		■	
Medium			
Small			

Opinion

Despite its heavy overhead (some 2.57% in annual expenses), Van Berkel has managed to do well for the investors in this conservative fund. It is an insurance company seg fund, meaning it's tied to an insurance policy in some remote way. Here's how it works. Seg funds function like mutual funds except that there is an insurance component that will kick in when certain rare circumstances occur. Like, if you buy this fund and the market tanks, they you die, the insurance will kick in to make your account whole again. Or, if you're still under water 10 years after buying the fund, they'll make you whole then too. So the insurance company takes a little bit of risk, for which they are paid (handsomely in this case) out of the management expenses. And you get an investment that's considered an insurance policy if your creditors ask.

The big dividend-paying stocks in this fund and the broad diversification help to temper any market troubles, so it's a good choice for conservative types.

McLean Budden Equity Growth Fund

Managed by: Mary Hallward

From: McLean Budden Limited

RRSP Eligible:

Overall performance: ★ ★ ★ ☆ ☆

Performance in :	
Up Markets	A
Down Markets	C

Value of $10,000 invested

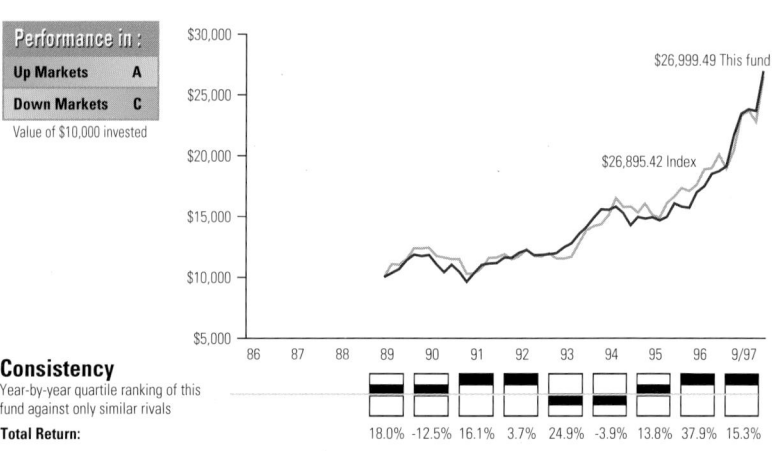

$26,999.49 This fund
$26,895.42 Index

Consistency
Year-by-year quartile ranking of this
fund against only similar rivals

Total Return: 18.0% -12.5% 16.1% 3.7% 24.9% -3.9% 13.8% 37.9% 15.3%

Risk

% of time fund has lost money over 12-month period	**19%**
Biggest drop	**-19%**
Months to recover	**28**

Efficiency ◎

For every $100	**$1.75**
which for this class is	**Average**

Fit (Investment style)

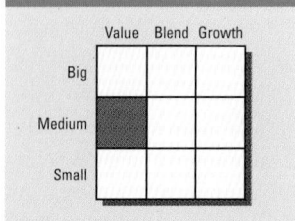

Opinion

Most Canadian equity funds with a track record this good are loaded up with foreign stocks. But this consistent fund has very little beyond our borders. That domestic orientation reflects the management team's conviction that Canada's fundamentals remain very strong. Healthy corporate profits, low interest rates, and improving government finances are all helping to set the stage for an extension of the winning streak in big cap stocks for this team-managed fund.But don't forget the advantage of international diversification in your portfolio. Foreign equities offer not just higher returns over time but also enough diversification to lower your overall risk. That's a one-two punch that makes international investing a must for Canadian investors.

McLean Budden also offers good bond and balanced funds.

Ivy Canadian Fund

Managed by: Jerry Javasky

From: Mackenzie Financial Corporation

RRSP Eligible:

Overall performance: ★ ★ ☆ ☆ ☆

Performance in:	
Up Markets	B
Down Markets	–

Value of $10,000 invested

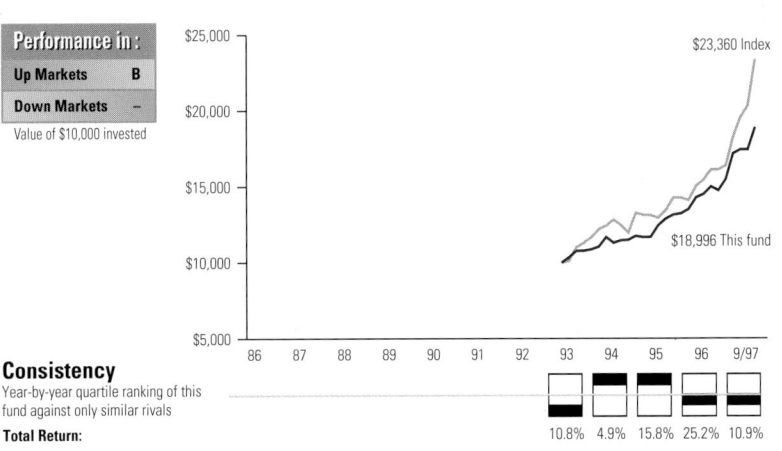

$23,360 Index

$18,996 This fund

Canadian Equity

Consistency
Year-by-year quartile ranking of this
fund against only similar rivals

Total Return: 10.8%   4.9%   15.8%   25.2%   10.9%

Risk

% of time fund has lost money over 12-month period	0%
Biggest drop	-4%
Months to recover	6

Efficiency

For every $100	$2.37
which for this class is	High

Fit (Investment style)

	Value	Blend	Growth
Big			
Medium			
Small			

Opinion

Who could have imagined that this fund, with its perennially huge cash reserves, would ever be able to make much money in a hot bull market? But it has.

For its first couple of years the managers reckoned that stocks were too pricey, so they held 50% or so of the fund in cash. It's still one-third uninvested. Yet with something like half of the stock portion of the fund in bank shares, it has shared in that sector's massive rally. Soon after the bank rally ends, the fund can pounce on cheap stocks.

The loss of Gerry Coleman (who moved to rival C.I. in June) is a blow to investors, but it's tough to argue that Ivy Canadian will be managed any differently in his absence. Jerry Javasky has really been on the case since inception. These guys have always talked about not wanting to dilute their ideas, and so it's interesting to note that the number of stocks in the fund is measurably down already from the 15 names that were held in early 1997.

GBC Canadian Growth Fund

Managed by: Ian Soutar & team (since inception)

From: Pembroke Management Ltd.

RRSP Eligible:

Overall performance: ★ ★ ★ ★ ★

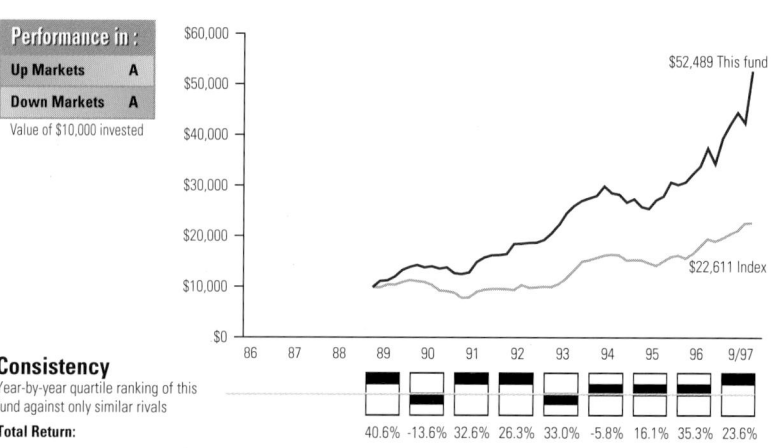

Performance in :	
Up Markets	A
Down Markets	A

Value of $10,000 invested

$52,489 This fund

$22,611 Index

Consistency
Year-by-year quartile ranking of this
fund against only similar rivals

Total Return:

86	87	88	89	90	91	92	93	94	95	96	9/97
			40.6%	-13.6%	32.6%	26.3%	33.0%	-5.8%	16.1%	35.3%	23.6%

Risk

% of time fund has lost money over 12-month period	**20%**
Biggest drop	**-19%**
Months to recover	**14**

Efficiency

For every $100	**$1.85**
which for this class is	**Low**

Fit (Investment style)

	Value	Blend	Growth
Big			
Medium			■
Small			

Opinion

It's easy to make my buy list every year. All you have to do is be like Ian Soutar and the gang here at Pembroke Management: beat your peer group by a mile in three out of every four years. Earn top grades in both rising and falling markets and for that extra measure of safety charge lower fees than the rest of the pack.

How do they manage to accomplish all this? Easy. They do it the old-fashioned way. They work hard to uncover dynamic growth stocks, research them enough that they know more about the company than any Bay Street analyst, diversify into lots of names, and avoid making commodity bets.

Oh yeah, then they put their own money in the fund, right alongside yours.

If these guys spent any money marketing their funds they'd really have a story to tell. Too bad much of Canada's big ad spending is being blown on funds with high fees and poor performance.

Colonia Special Growth Fund

Managed by: Joanne Miller (since inception)

From: Colonia Life Management

RRSP Eligible:

Overall performance: ★ ★ ★ ★ ★

Performance in :	
Up Markets	**A**
Down Markets	**C**
Value of $10,000 invested	

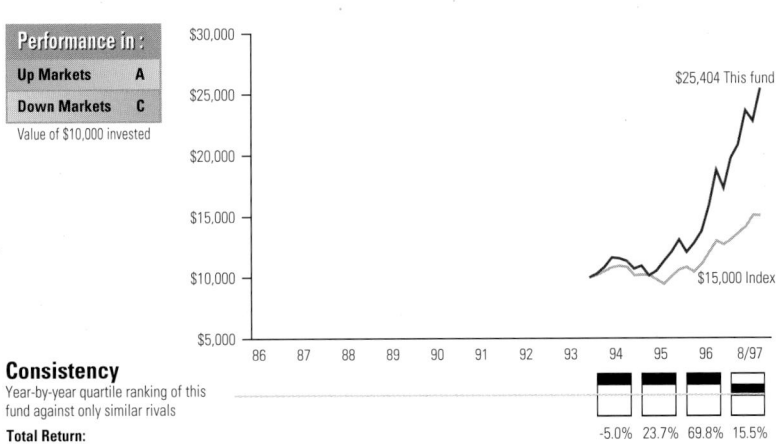

$30,000

$25,404 This fund

$25,000

$20,000

$15,000

$10,000

$15,000 Index

$5,000

86 87 88 89 90 91 92 93 94 95 96 8/97

Consistency
Year-by-year quartile ranking of this
fund against only similar rivals

Total Return: -5.0% 23.7% 69.8% 15.5%

Canadian Small Cap Equity

Risk

% of time fund has lost money over 12-month period	**14%**
Biggest drop	**-13%**
Months to recover	**15**

Efficiency

For every $100	**$2.43**
which for this class is	**Average**

Fit (Investment style)

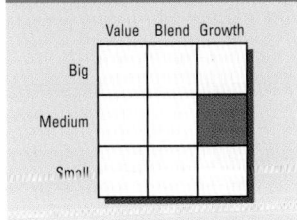

	Value	Blend	Growth
Big			
Medium			
Small			

Opinion

You seldom think of insurance company funds as being dynamic, but this one sure is. In it, Miller owns growth companies that are on the cusp of change; entering new markets, maybe using new technology, or just capitalizing on a new trend.

It's not really as full of small-cap names, though, as one might expect. Fully one-quarter of the fund was recently in cash. And some of the stock holdings are in bigger company shares. But that's just it: Miller is opportunistic. When she sees deals, she'll be ready to pounce. For her, a deal isn't a stock that's cheap. It's a company that's firing on all cylinders and about to hit the gas.

Although it's sad to say, the MER of this fund (2.43%) is very much in line, so this is a candidate with real potential when the small-cap rally eventually comes.

Bissett Small Cap Fund

Managed by: Dave Bissett (since inception)

From: Bissett & Associates Investment Management Ltd.

RRSP Eligible:

Overall performance: ★ ★ ★ ★ ★

Performance in :	
Up Markets	**A**
Down Markets	**D**

Value of $10,000 invested

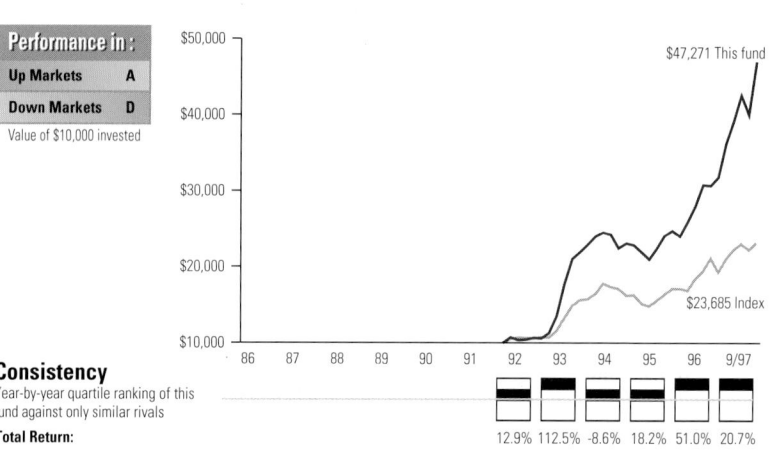

$50,000

$47,271 This fund

$40,000

$30,000

$20,000

$23,685 Index

$10,000

86   87   88   89   90   91   92   93   94   95   96   9/97

Consistency
Year-by-year quartile ranking of this
fund against only similar rivals

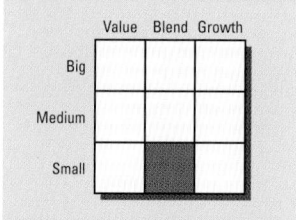

Total Return: 12.9% 112.5% -8.6% 18.2% 51.0% 20.7%

Risk

% of time fund has lost money over 12-month period	**15%**
Biggest drop	**-17%**
Months to recover	**22**

Efficiency

For every $100	**$1.90**
which for this class is	**Low**

Fit (Investment style)

	Value	Blend	Growth
Big			
Medium			
Small			

Opinion

Yet another standout from a superb family, this fund too is overlooked by investors. At less than $100 million, the fund seems to be doing something wrong. Charging too much in expenses maybe?

Nope. It charges just 1.9% annually, which isn't that much for a small cap fund. It's just a simple fund where old-fashioned fundamental analysis counts. Bissett's done well for this fund's investors with what are generally obscure, low P/E stocks in the industrial sector, a huge catch-all that describes any business that makes stuff. There are also some royalty trusts (a group he likes) and a couple of financials that have been strong of late.

While the fund did take almost two years to recover from the small cap meltdown in '94, this one's about as tame as good funds in the small cap world will get. So own it just in combination with other bigger cap funds and foreign funds to wipe out the risk. That way you'll do well in all market environments.

Mawer New Canada Fund

Managed by: Bill MacLachlan

From: Mawer Investment Management

RRSP Eligible:

Overall performance: ★ ★ ★ ★ ★

Performance in :	
Up Markets	**A**
Down Markets	**B**

Value of $10,000 invested

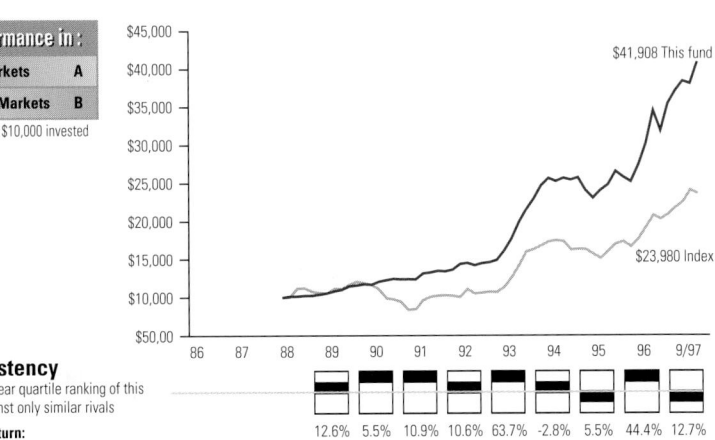

$45,000
$40,000
$35,000
$30,000
$25,000
$20,000
$15,000
$10,000
$50,00

$41,908 This fund

$23,980 Index

86 87 88 89 90 91 92 93 94 95 96 9/97

Consistency
Year-by-year quartile ranking of this fund against only similar rivals

Total Return: 12.6% 5.5% 10.9% 10.6% 63.7% -2.8% 5.5% 44.4% 12.7%

Canadian Small Cap Equity

Risk

% of time fund has lost money over 12-month period	**8%**
Biggest drop	**-11%**
Months to recover	**13**

Efficiency

For every $100	**$1.34**
which for this class is	**Low**

Fit (Investment style)

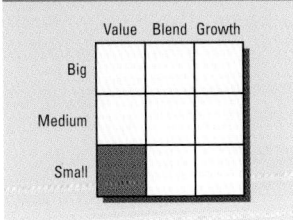

	Value	Blend	Growth
Big			
Medium			
Small			

Opinion

Bill MacLachlan would be the first to tell you not to rush into this fund. At writing, he had real concerns about the level of valuations in the Canadian stock market, and for that matter, the US market. Though he'll cede the point that growth is very impressive and inflation's flat—a super combination for investors—he nonetheless points out that the markets have already priced in this good news. So any change will send stocks reeling.

The gang at Mawer (which is pronounced like lawn "mower") are by no means market timers, though. They use this top-down valuation stuff to suggest how conservative they should be in their stock selection. And here's where the bad news comes in: they feel that smaller companies are more at risk if things go sour.

But this fund's mandate is to invest in smaller companies. So they've stocked it up with cheap holdings—those that couldn't fall far. And they've kept some cash on the sidelines in order to pounce on opportunities when they come. Note that there's a $25,000 minimum to get into this family.

Sceptre Equity Growth Fund

Managed by: Allan Jacobs (since 1993)

From: Sceptre Investment Counsel Ltd.

RRSP Eligible:

Overall performance: ★ ★ ★ ★ ☆

Performance in :	
Up Markets	A
Down Markets	B

Value of $10,000 invested

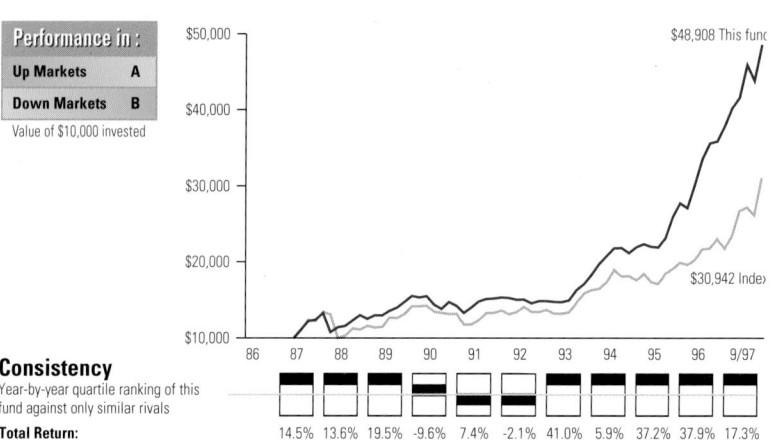

$50,000

$40,000

$30,000

$20,000

$10,000

$48,908 This fund

$30,942 Index

	86	87	88	89	90	91	92	93	94	95	96	9/97

Consistency
Year-by-year quartile ranking of this
fund against only similar rivals

Total Return:

	14.5%	13.6%	19.5%	-9.6%	7.4%	-2.1%	41.0%	5.9%	37.2%	37.9%	17.3%

Risk

% of time fund has lost money over 12-month period	**23%**
Biggest drop	**-19%**
Months to recover	**15**

Efficiency

For every $100	**$1.51**
which for this class is	**Low**

Fit (Investment style)

	Value	Blend	Growth
Big			
Medium			
Small			

Opinion

This fund continues to impress. I've recommended it in every one of my books, starting in 1994. I like it because Jacobs is good at finding value and growth— a combination that's harder to find than most would have you believe. He does it by scouting out-of-the-way names that are off the beaten path of Bay Street analysts. He'll occasionally own IPOs that trade on Alberta, which is not exactly white-shoe territory for a guy who basically makes his living running money for pension plans.

But the upside is enormous, because wins like YBM Magnex (a hi-tech magnet maker) and Hurricane Hydrocarbons (a carbonater of hydro perhaps? no, really, it's a Russian oil producer) offer the chance at a double whammy: rapid profit growth and an expanding valuation multiple for each dollar of earnings.

The fund is cheap, holds up well in tough markets, recovers fast from drops, and offers big long-term gains.

Lotus (MKW) Canadian Equity Fund

Managed by: Greg Bay & team (since 1993)

From: M.K. Wong & Associates Ltd.

RRSP Eligible:

Overall performance: ★ ★ ★ ☆ ☆

Performance in :	
Up Markets	B
Down Markets	C

Value of $10,000 invested

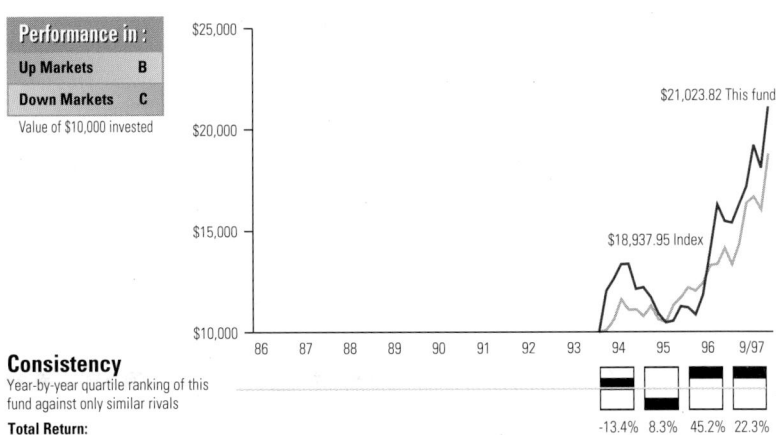

$21,023.82 This fund

$18,937.95 Index

Consistency
Year-by-year quartile ranking of this
fund against only similar rivals

Total Return:

-13.4%	8.3%	45.2%	22.3%

Canadian Small Cap Equity

Risk

% of time fund has lost money over 12-month period	**38%**
Biggest drop	**-22%**
Months to recover	**22**

Efficiency

For every $100	**$2.16**
which for this class is	**Low**

Fit (Investment style)

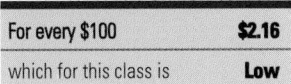

	Value	Blend	Growth
Big			
Medium			
Small			■

Opinion

Small cap stocks are a different beast altogether. Their cycles sometimes seem unrelated to those of the stock market in general—which is exactly why you can benefit from diversifying into these more dynamic growth stories. Such stories are what Bay and the others are all about at M.K. Wong, the firm that produced both Wayne Deans and partner Doug Knight, each a star in his own right today.

There are a few bigger company stocks here, like the stake in Fairfax Financial, the white-hot insurance company. But generally, the fund holds exciting smaller companies on the cusp of change. The strategy can work out very well—as it did in a torrid 1995. Going forward, you can expect leverage to any forthcoming small-cap rally.

Dividend

RoyFund Dividend Fund

Managed by: John Kellett & team

From: Royal Bank Investment Management Inc.

RRSP Eligible:

Overall performance: ★ ★ ★ ✦ ☆

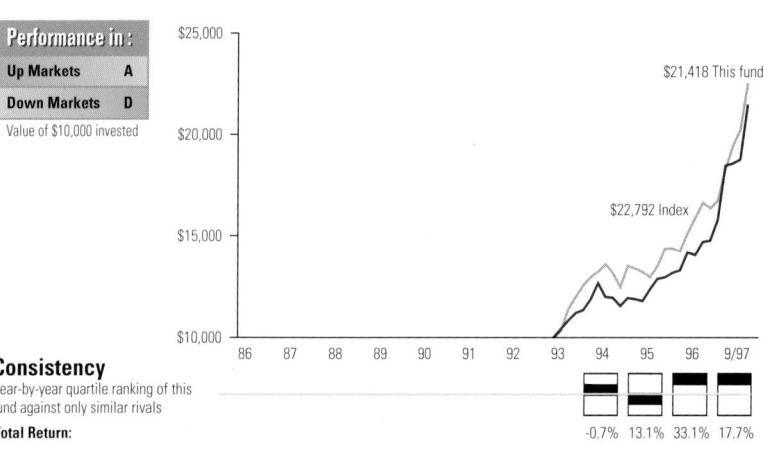

Performance in :	
Up Markets	**A**
Down Markets	**D**

Value of $10,000 invested

$21,418 This fund

$22,792 Index

Consistency
Year-by-year quartile ranking of this fund against only similar rivals

Total Return: -0.7%   13.1%   33.1%   17.7%

Risk

% of time fund has lost money over 12-month period	**7%**
Biggest drop	**-10%**
Months to recover	**15**

Efficiency

For every $100	**$1.84**
which for this class is	**Average**

Fit (Investment style)

	Value	Blend	Growth
Big			
Medium			
Small			

Opinion

These are crazy times for dividend funds. Kellett's made so much money in what is really supposed to be a conservative fund that he struggles with his own analysis of how much more upside is possible. Yet he's convinced that a benign bond market is likely (that means he thinks interest rates aren't headed up). And so financial stocks (like banks) and interest-sensitive stocks (like utilities) continue to dominate the portfolio. He still thinks such shares are reasonably priced, despite their heady advances.

There are more bonds in the fund than in previous years, and with a longer duration, so there's some significant interest-rate risk. Remember that this fund did lose 10% when interest rates rose in 1994, in what was the worst bear market for bonds in 30 years. After the advance we've had for funds like these it's tough to recommend loading up now. Still, this and other good dividend funds should continue to make up a portion of your non-registered portfolio.

AGF Dividend Fund

Managed by: Gord MacDougall (since inception) & Martin Gerber

From: Connor Clark & Lunn Investment Management Ltd.

RRSP Eligible:

Overall performance: ★ ★ ★ ✦ ☆

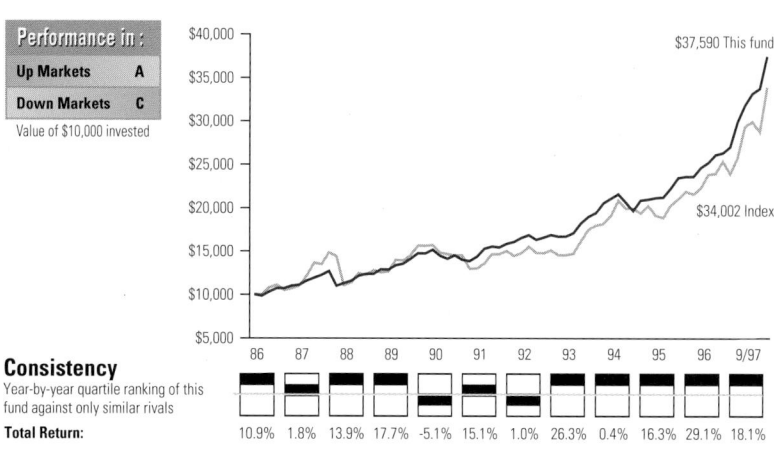

Performance in :	
Up Markets	A
Down Markets	C

Value of $10,000 invested

$37,590 This fund

$34,002 Index

Consistency
Year-by-year quartile ranking of this fund against only similar rivals

Total Return:

86	87	88	89	90	91	92	93	94	95	96	9/97
10.9%	1.8%	13.9%	17.7%	-5.1%	15.1%	1.0%	26.3%	0.4%	16.3%	29.1%	18.1%

Dividend

Risk

% of time fund has lost money over 12-month period	**13%**
Biggest drop	**-14%**
Months to recover	**14**

Efficiency

For every $100	**$1.91**
which for this class is	**Average**

Fit (Investment style)

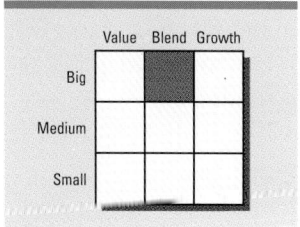

Opinion

It may seem cold and calculated, but it's a hot strategy for income investors in this fund. The Vancouver-based team that's been managing this fund since inception believes in taking the emotion out of investing by applying a consistent quantitative approach all the time. The sterility of this style led them into banks two years ago, when the numbers argued value.

But after a huge run, the team is today moving into names that can provide growth.

Cyclical company shares occasionally play a role in this fund, as does two-way asset allocation between cash and equities. That kind of flexibility has so far added value for investors.

The fund is noticeably light on income trusts, one of the big new areas for funds like these, because Gerber and the others think the retail investors that gobbled them up will choke on the challenges that could lie ahead. If the selling gets overdone, as they think it will, they'll jump in with both feet.

Maxxum Dividend Fund

Managed by: Jackee Pratt (since 1995)

From: London Fund Management Limited

RRSP Eligible:

Overall performance: ★ ★ ★ ⅃ ☆

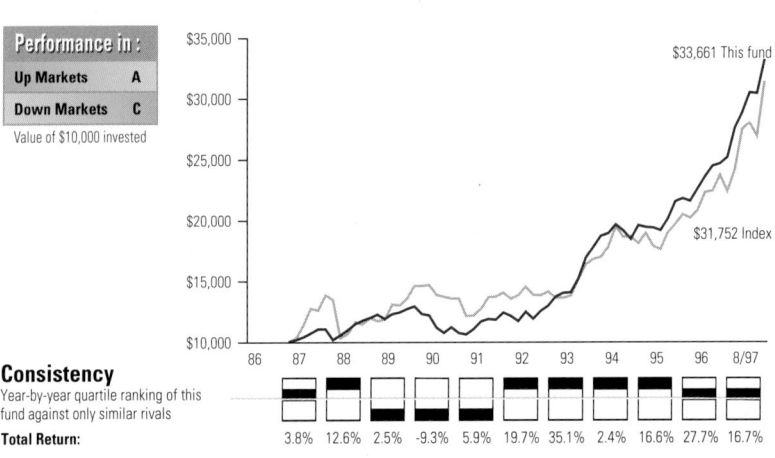

Performance in :	
Up Markets	**A**
Down Markets	**C**

Value of $10,000 invested

$33,661 This fund

$31,752 Index

Consistency
Year-by-year quartile ranking of this
fund against only similar rivals

Total Return:

86	87	88	89	90	91	92	93	94	95	96	8/97
	3.8%	12.6%	2.5%	-9.3%	5.9%	19.7%	35.1%	2.4%	16.6%	27.7%	16.7%

Dividend

Risk

% of time fund has lost money over 12-month period	**13%**
Biggest drop	**-22%**
Months to recover	**35**

Efficiency ◎

For every $100	**$1.75**
which for this class is	**Average**

Fit (Investment style)

	Value	Blend	Growth
Big		■	
Medium			
Small			

Opinion

If you're looking for high, stable income, this isn't the fund for you. This is a conservative common stock fund, despite its dividend category label. But that's not what differentiates it from its peers. After all, most dividend funds are full of common stocks anyway, not the preferreds you'd expect. This fund stands apart because of its excellent record.

Jackee Pratt took over the fund from Veronika Hirsch in late 1995 and has since done a good job in what's been a good environment for the most conservative Canadian blue chip names.

You'll generally find banks, utilities and the pipes in this fund. But there's also more cyclical company shares than most. Names like Inco and Dofasco have added return, as has exposure over the years to the oil patch. It all adds up to a fund with some sizzle in a rising market.

Sceptre International Fund

Managed by: Lennox J.D. McNeely (since inception)

From: Sceptre Investment Counsel Ltd.

RRSP Eligible: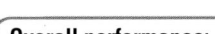

Overall performance: ★ ★ ★ ⯪ ☆

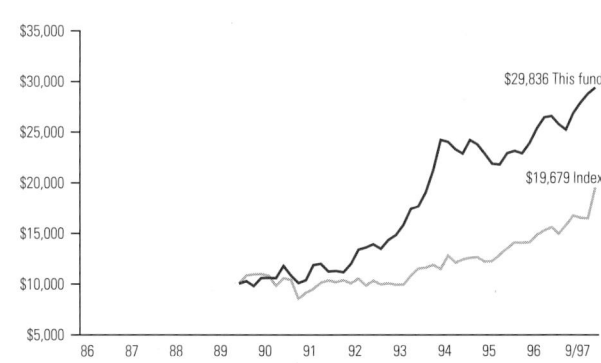

Performance in :	
Up Markets	**A**
Down Markets	**A**

Value of $10,000 invested

$29,836 This fund

$19,679 Index

Consistency
Year-by-year quartile ranking of this
fund against only similar rivals

Total Return:

| 28.1% | -2.0% | 15.6% | 23.6% | 63.6% | -5.6% | 4.6% | 12.3% | 11.2% |

Risk

% of time fund has lost money over 12-month period	**19%**
Biggest drop	**-25%**
Months to recover	**18**

Efficiency

For every $100	**$2.10**
which for this class is	**Low**

Fit (Investment style)

	Value	Blend	Growth
Big	■		
Medium			
Small			

Opinion

Since its inception more than a decade ago, Len McNeely has toiled in relative obscurity next to giants like Templeton Growth Fund. And yet, despite higher expenses, fewer analysts and zero foreign offices, this fund has beaten its nemeses. How? By owning cheap stocks of all sizes. And lots of them—in lots of different countries. And by holding on until the value is realized.

Now could be an especially good time to climb aboard this fund. It endured a butt-kicking in the summer of 1997. The double-digit pullback has dragged down the fund's return numbers over one, three, and five years—making the fund look weak for half a decade. Buy now to enjoy the rebound.

International Equity

Trimark Fund

Managed by: Bob Krembil (since inception), & Richard Jenkins & Angela Eaton

From: Trimark Investment Management Inc.

RRSP Eligible:

Overall performance: ★ ★ ★ ✦ ☆

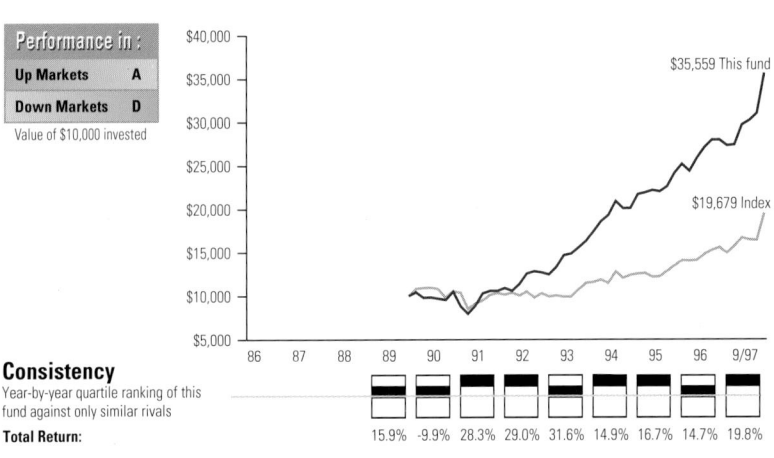

Performance in :	
Up Markets	**A**
Down Markets	**D**

Value of $10,000 invested

$35,559 This fund

$19,679 Index

Consistency
Year-by-year quartile ranking of this fund against only similar rivals

Total Return: 15.9% -9.9% 28.3% 29.0% 31.6% 14.9% 16.7% 14.7% 19.8%

Risk

% of time fund has lost money over 12-month period	**12%**
Biggest drop	**-30%**
Months to recover	**18**

Efficiency ◎

For every $100	**$1.52**
which for this class is	**Low**

Fit (Investment style)

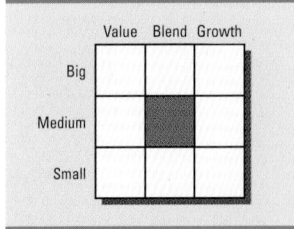

Opinion

Here's an outstanding fund that represents outstanding value for investors. It costs less (in terms of annual expenses) than 90% of its peers and has done better than 95% of its peers.

Credit some (but not all) of that outperformance to a higher-than-most exposure to U.S. stocks, which have led the world in performance ever since this fund opened its doors in 1981.

Even so, picking a few great stocks is what the Trimark team process is all about. By studying competitors, surveying customers, and grilling management they get to know a handful of businesses well. More often than not lately, that's meant that they find great companies then wait and hope for their share price to fall into their buy range. Higher cash levels in this and other Trimark funds have hurt returns lately. Still, I say buy this low-cost front-end load fund now or when stock prices pull back. It should be one of the few to really benefit from a downturn.

International Equity

Green Line Global Select Fund

Managed by: Mandy Elements (since inception)

From: Perpetual Portfolio Management Ltd.

RRSP Eligible:

Overall performance: ★ ★ ★ ✦

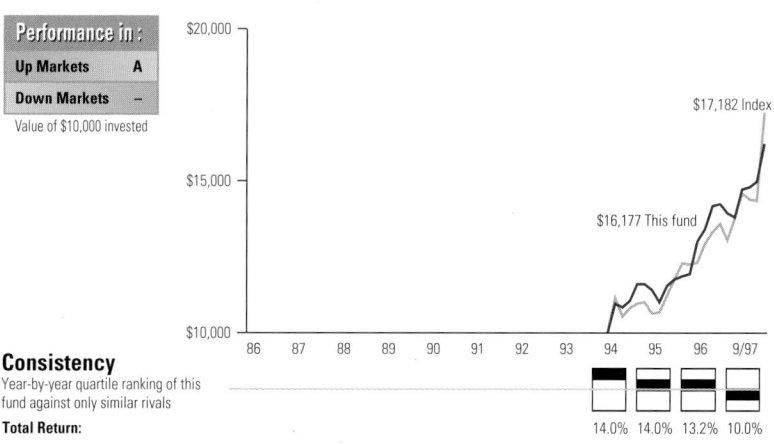

Performance in :	
Up Markets	**A**
Down Markets	**–**

Value of $10,000 invested

$20,000

$17,182 Index

$15,000

$16,177 This fund

$10,000

86 87 88 89 90 91 92 93 94 95 96 9/97

Consistency
Year-by-year quartile ranking of this
fund against only similar rivals

Total Return: 14.0% 14.0% 13.2% 10.0%

Risk

% of time fund has lost money over 12-month period	0%
Biggest drop	-6%
Months to recover	5

Efficiency

For every $100	$2.36
which for this class is	**Average**

Fit (Investment style)

	Value	Blend	Growth
Big			
Medium			
Small			

Opinion

This fund is more diversified than most, with its broad geographic mix (including about one-third in the US), blend of styles (bottom-up and top-down), and even a mix of huge and not-so-huge company shares. All that diversification pays off in stability of returns for investors. But the same factors kill the chance of this fund ever hitting one right out of the park.

That's just fine for the huge team at Perpetual that supports manager Mandy Elements, who is by nature not a gambler. Perpetual needs a big team to do this much research, including macro-economic specialists as well as hands-on, visit-the-company analysts. The award-winning team of 20 managers operates this global business from a converted rectory in the tiny village of Henley-on-Thames in England.

In the UK Perpetual is a famous firm, but in Canada they're unknown. Too bad—their established funds enjoy a great track record

International Equity

MD Growth Fund

Managed by: Templeton Management Team

From: Templeton Global Advisors Ltd.

RRSP Eligible:

Overall performance: ★ ★ ★ ⯰

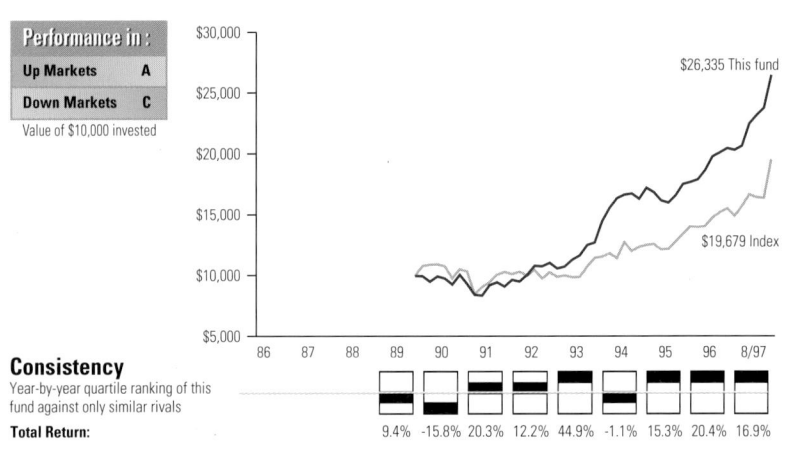

Performance in :	
Up Markets	A
Down Markets	C

Value of $10,000 invested

$26,335 This fund

$19,679 Index

Consistency
Year-by-year quartile ranking of this fund against only similar rivals

	86	87	88	89	90	91	92	93	94	95	96	8/97

Total Return: 9.4% -15.8% 20.3% 12.2% 44.9% -1.1% 15.3% 20.4% 16.9%

International Equity

Risk

% of time fund has lost money over 12-month period	**20%**
Biggest drop	**-28%**
Months to recover	**52**

Efficiency

For every $100	**$1.29**
which for this class is	**Low**

Fit (Investment style)

	Value	Blend	Growth
Big			
Medium			
Small			

Opinion

If you're a doctor and you don't own this fund, you really need to be examined.

It's the Templeton Growth Fund—but physicians and their families get to buy it wholesale. At 1.29% annually, it charges much more than it did just year ago—but still far less than the Templeton offering.

Of course, with this fund you'll get all that famous Templeton management, including broad, broad diversification into 34 countries or so, a true value discipline and a research base that is among the world's largest.

Still, remember that even with low fees and effective diversification, this fund did spend four years recovering from the crash of 1987. That should remind us that even a good fund like this isn't always perfect—but is suitable for long term goals.

Lately the fund's been big on Europe, has had some emerging markets exposure and been famously light on Japan—which was a hot market for a time in 1997.

Saxon World Growth Fund

Managed by: Bob Tattersall

From: Howson Tattersall Investment Counsel Ltd.

RRSP Eligible:

Overall performance: ★ ★ ★ ☆ ☆

Performance in :	
Up Markets	**A**
Down Markets	**D**

Value of $10,000 invested

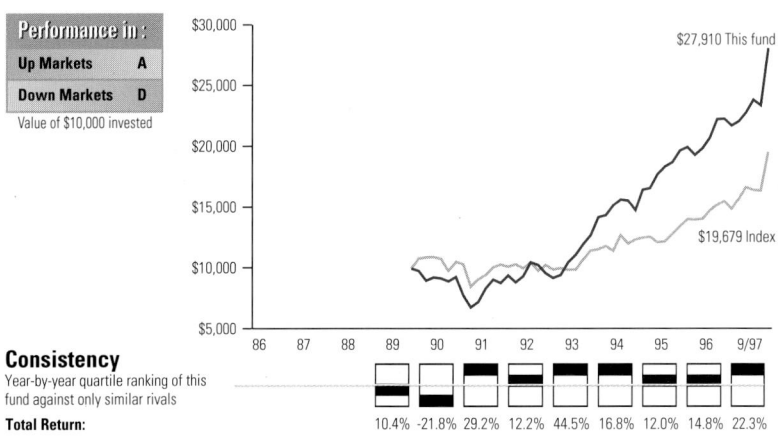

$30,000

$25,000

$20,000

$15,000

$10,000

$5,000

$27,910 This fund

$19,679 Index

86 87 88 89 90 91 92 93 94 95 96 9/97

Consistency
Year-by-year quartile ranking of this
fund against only similar rivals

Total Return: 10.4% -21.8% 29.2% 12.2% 44.5% 16.8% 12.0% 14.8% 22.3%

Risk

% of time fund has lost money over 12-month period	**22%**
Biggest drop	**-32%**
Months to recover	**31**

Efficiency

For every $100	**$1.78**
which for this class is	**Low**

Fit (Investment style)

	Value	Blend	Growth
Big			
Medium			
Small	■		

Opinion

In a rich US equity market, it's nice to see a good manager sticking to his knitting: scouting cheap stocks. Tattersall is a nut for value, a real fundamentalist who does company interviews after screening for statistical cheapness.

So it's not surprising that he's trimming down the US exposure lately (to 50% from 65%), nor is it surprising that he owns no blue chips. They were, after all, the hottest performers in a hot market. What he does own is the occasional country fund, the odd low-tech manufacturer, and even a Japanese holding or two.

Going forward, one would expect that this contrarian, defensive fund would do especially well (in a relative sense) if the market were to come off significantly. Of course, that's just what this manager is hoping for so that he can go shopping.

International Equity

Templeton Growth Fund Ltd.

Managed by: Mark Holowesko (since 1988)

From: Global Advisors

RRSP Eligible:

Overall performance: ★ ★ ★ ☆ ☆

Performance in :	
Up Markets	**A**
Down Markets	**C**
Value of $10,000 invested	

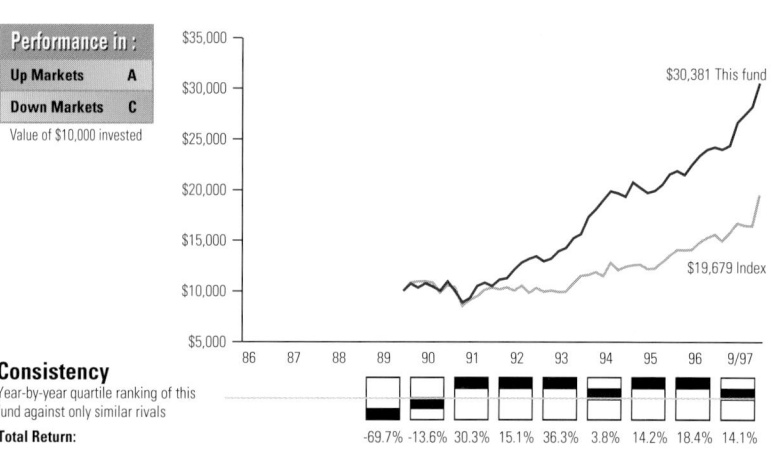

$30,381 This fund

$19,679 Index

Consistency
Year-by-year quartile ranking of this fund against only similar rivals

Total Return: -69.7% -13.6% 30.3% 15.1% 36.3% 3.8% 14.2% 18.4% 14.1%

International Equity

Risk

% of time fund has lost money over 12-month period	**21%**
Biggest drop	**-27%**
Months to recover	**22**

Efficiency

For every $100	**$2.00**
which for this class is	**Low**

Fit (Investment style)

	Value	Blend	Growth
Big	■		
Medium			
Small			

Opinion

When would be a better time to buy this fund? It's got 34 countries, dozens of analysts, 43 great years behind it—and the world's economies are humming along nicely. Valuation disparities among the U.S., Japan, and Europe leave this fund with an easy choice: just buy the cheap stocks. Lately they've been in Europe.

Bypassing Japan's richly valued stocks has helped the fund add distance between itself and the world benchmark index. Having extra weight in Europe's relatively inexpensive stocks has also helped to boost the fund, as has exposure to emerging markets.

Holowesko continues to hold the darlings he's owned for so long, including big-cap telecom stocks, some resources, and cheap (though boring) utility stocks. Don't worry about this fund's largesse—its $7 billion is manageable in such large, liquid stocks.

Trimark Select Growth Fund

Managed by: Bob Krembi (since inception) & team

From: Trimark Investment Management Inc.

RRSP Eligible:

Overall performance: ★ ★ ★ ☆ ☆

Performance in :	
Up Markets	**A**
Down Markets	**C**

Value of $10,000 invested

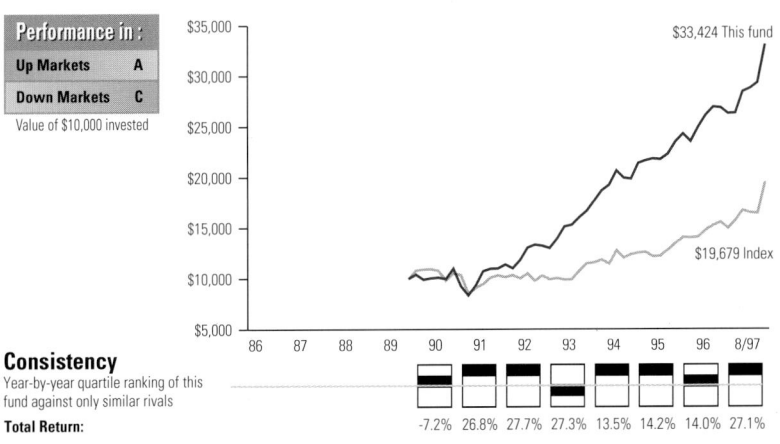

$35,000

$30,000

$25,000

$20,000

$15,000

$10,000

$5,000

$33,424 This fund

$19,679 Index

86 87 88 89 90 91 92 93 94 95 96 8/97

Consistency
Year-by-year quartile ranking of this
fund against only similar rivals

Total Return: -7.2% 26.8% 27.7% 27.3% 13.5% 14.2% 14.0% 27.1%

Risk

% of time fund has lost money over 12-month period	**6%**
Biggest drop	**-24%**
Months to recover	**11**

Efficiency

For every $100	**$2.25**
which for this class is	**Low**

Fit (Investment style)

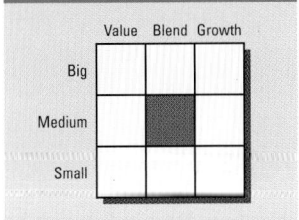

Opinion

There's always a reason for the great performance any star fund enjoys. It would be easy to point to emphasis on the hot U.S. market to explain all of this impressive fund's gains. But in truth, the fund has benefited from more than that. There has been superb stock picking—like the long-held stakes in Caterpillar and FedEx, each of which has grown dramatically in price.

And there have been challenges as well. Consider the heavier expense burden that this fund carries over its front-end load clone, the Trimark Fund (which I recommend over this one, because it is 0.73% cheaper every year to own). Double-digit cash levels haven't helped returns either—at a time when stock markets are roaring.

The premium pricing of the Select funds at Trimark makes them unattractive. You'd be better off to pay the front load for the clone of this fund, and then save a bundle year after year in management expenses.

International Equity

Canada Life US & International S-34

Managed by: Gary Kondrat, Tom Tibbles, and Diane Haslidson

From: Canada Life Investment Management Ltd.

RRSP Eligible::

Overall performance: ★ ★ ★ ☆ ☆

Performance in :	
Up Markets	A
Down Markets	C

Value of $10,000 invested

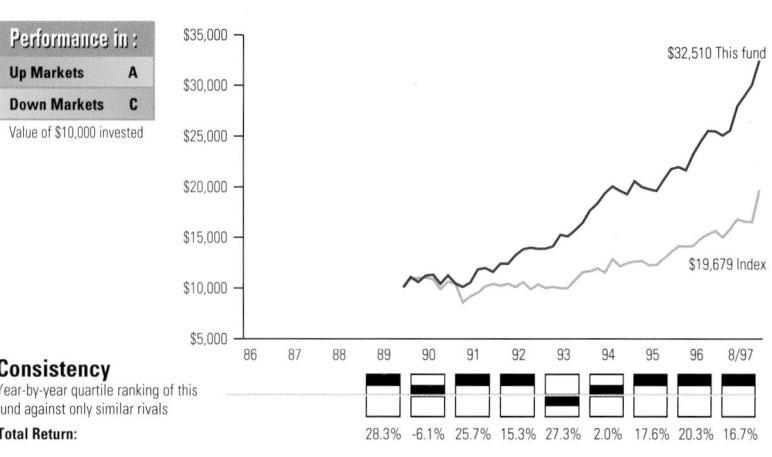

$32,510 This fund

$19,679 Index

Consistency
Year-by-year quartile ranking of this
fund against only similar rivals

Total Return: 28.3% -6.1% 25.7% 15.3% 27.3% 2.0% 17.6% 20.3% 16.7%

Risk

% of time fund has lost money over 12-month period	13%
Biggest drop	-23%
Months to recover	18

Efficiency

For every $100	$2.40
which for this class is	Average

Fit (Investment style)

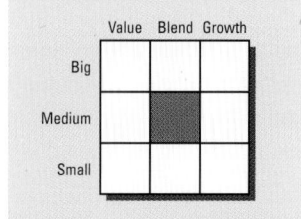

	Value	Blend	Growth
Big			
Medium			
Small			

Opinion

Here are two reasons why this fund makes enough money to appear in my book year after year. First, it has something of a policy constraint to be overweighted to the U.S. market. (The U.S. makes up only about one-third of international equity markets, but this fund's policy is to hold 40%–60% of its assets in the U.S.) The heavy allocation to the U.S. has helped the fund as the U.S. has extended a record 15-year bull market.

Second, Lance Speck and the others continue to add value through stock selection—no small feat in what are highly efficient markets for the big-cap stocks in which they specialized. They employ a relative value approach. Then they buy and hold. And hold.

If only they could convince their marketing department to come up with a better name for the fund than S-34! Helluva name for fund. These insurance marketing departments are just the worst for this arcane terminology.

Nonetheless, this fund has done well since losing star managers Lance Speck and others in 1996.

Fidelity International Portfolio

Managed by: Dick Habermann (since inception)

From: Fidelity Management & Research Co.

RRSP Eligible:

Overall performance: ★ ★ ★ ★ ☆

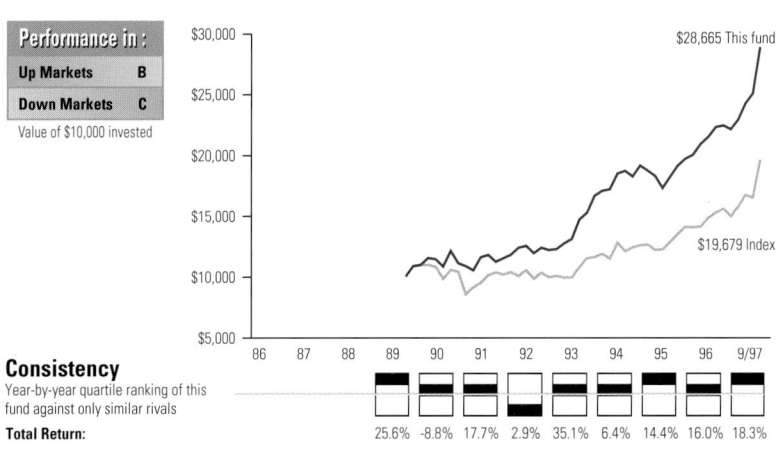

Performance in :	
Up Markets	B
Down Markets	C

Value of $10,000 invested

$30,000

$28,665 This fund

$25,000

$20,000

$15,000

$19,679 Index

$10,000

$5,000

86 87 88 89 90 91 92 93 94 95 96 9/97

Consistency
Year-by-year quartile ranking of this fund against only similar rivals

Total Return: 25.6%   -8.8%   17.7%   2.9%   35.1%   6.4%   14.4%   16.0%   18.3%

Risk

% of time fund has lost money over 12-month period	13%
Biggest drop	-20%
Months to recover	16

Efficiency

For every $100	$2.76
which for this class is	High

Fit (Investment style)

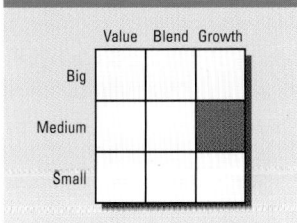

	Value	Blend	Growth
Big			
Medium			■
Small			

Opinion

Cynics would call it overdiversification, but Habermann's got an idea or two about how to manage money. The fund has nearly 500 stock positions, but hasn't lost money in a calendar year and manages to outpace its rivals with consistency. And that's after deducting its heavy expenses.

Get this: as the fund's assets have soared 17-fold in the last five years, its expenses have actually gone up. Still, this is a gem for investors who want broad diversification and don't already own Fidelity's European or Far East funds. After all, they're kind of embedded within this global offering.

And that's exactly why I like it so much. Fidelity's got great regional fund managers and Habermann just taps each to do their work within each region: Yoko Tilley in Japan, Sally Walden in Europe, etc. The formula has worked out well for investors.

International Equity

Cundill Value Fund

Managed by: Peter Cundill (since inception)

From: Peter Cundill & Associates Ltd.

RRSP Eligible:

Overall performance: ★ ★ ★ ★ ★

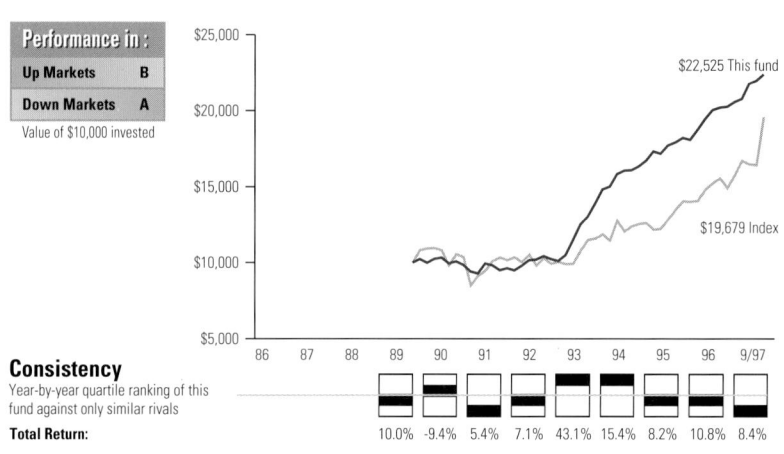

Performance in :	
Up Markets	**B**
Down Markets	**A**

Value of $10,000 invested

$25,000

$22,525 This fund

$20,000

$15,000

$19,679 Index

$10,000

$5,000

86 87 88 89 90 91 92 93 94 95 96 9/97

Consistency
Year-by-year quartile ranking of this
fund against only similar rivals

Total Return: 10.0% -9.4% 5.4% 7.1% 43.1% 15.4% 8.2% 10.8% 8.4%

Risk

% of time fund has lost money over 12-month period	**8%**
Biggest drop	**-16%**
Months to recover	**5**

Efficiency

For every $100	**$2.02**
which for this class is	**Low**

Fit (Investment style)

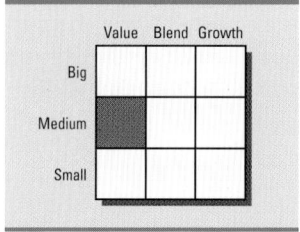

	Value	Blend	Growth
Big			
Medium			
Small			

Opinion

I've long been a fan of this unusual fund. Peter Cundill's conviction that stock markets are simply too high strikes a chord with a few investors. But his approach—and this fund—should strike a chord with you if you've got a lot riding on the current bull market.

He's still positioned quite bearishly, with nearly a third of the fund in cash and the rest in stocks trading at below break-up value. And of course there's the bet against the US market he's been holding on to for some time with futures contracts.

But despite all these hedges the fund has done okay during the last couple of years, which have seen share prices advance to new heights almost daily after a bull market that lasted more than a decade.

Altogether, this fund's aggressively defensive posture may sound like an oxymoron, but it's the Cundill way of making money—a thing he's done since 1974.

Templeton International Stock Fund

Managed by: Don Reed (since inception)

From: Templeton Management Ltd.

RRSP Eligible:

Overall performance: ★ ★ ★ ★

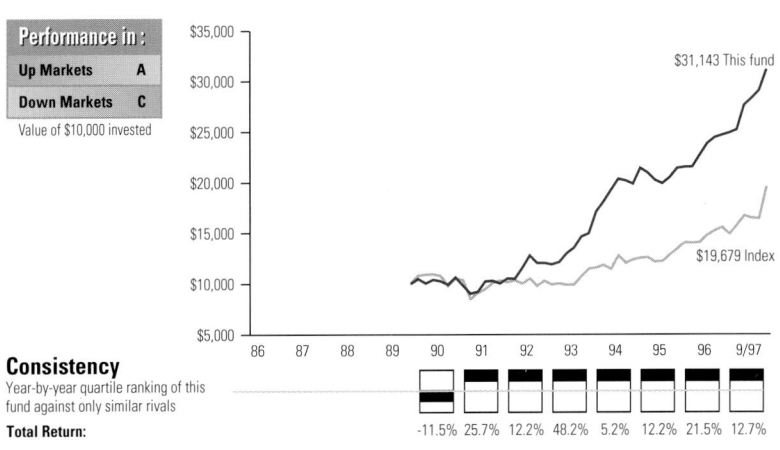

Performance in :	
Up Markets	A
Down Markets	C
Value of $10,000 invested	

$31,143 This fund

$19,679 Index

Consistency
Year-by-year quartile ranking of this fund against only similar rivals

Total Return:

86	87	88	89	90	91	92	93	94	95	96	9/97
				-11.5%	25.7%	12.2%	48.2%	5.2%	12.2%	21.5%	12.7%

Risk

% of time fund has lost money over 12-month period	**13%**
Biggest drop	**-15%**
Months to recover	**18**

Efficiency

For every $100	**$2.51**
which for this class is	**High**

Fit (Investment style)

	Value	Blend	Growth
Big			
Medium			
Small			

Opinion

The outstanding performance of this fund is doubly impressive given its basic constraint: it can't invest in the U.S., and the U.S. has been one of the world's hottest markets.

Credit the strong returns to more than just astute selection on the part of Reed and the gang of five dozen investment professionals scattered around the globe, who speak every other morning at a research call where they tear one another's ideas apart in search of missed opportunities.

Part of the impressive performance is simply attributable to the geographic focus of the fund. Three-quarters of every dollar that's invested in stocks in this fund is invested in Europe—a sizzling market of late. And of course there's almost nothing in Japan, which has been a pig since this fund was launched. Beyond the geographic attribution, there's a strong case for this fund's value discipline—and its ability to make money in any market.

International Equity

Templeton Global Smaller Companies Fund

Managed by: Norm Boersma (since 1997)

From: Templeton Management Ltd.

RRSP Eligible:

Overall performance: ★ ★ ★ ★ ★

Performance in :	
Up Markets	A
Down Markets	D

Value of $10,000 invested

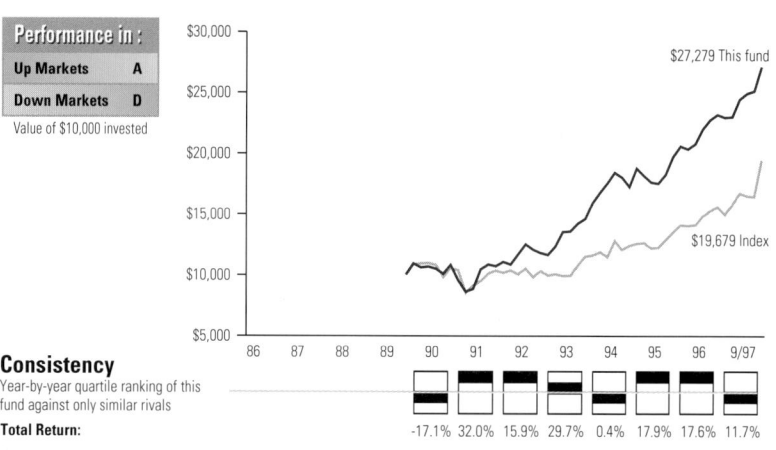

$30,000

$25,000

$20,000

$15,000

$10,000

$5,000

$27,279 This fund

$19,679 Index

86 87 88 89 90 91 92 93 94 95 96 9/97

Consistency
Year-by-year quartile ranking of this fund against only similar rivals

Total Return: -17.1% 32.0% 15.9% 29.7% 0.4% 17.9% 17.6% 11.7%

Risk

% of time fund has lost money over 12-month period	**11%**
Biggest drop	**-22%**
Months to recover	**19**

Efficiency

For every $100	**$2.55**
which for this class is	**Average**

Fit (Investment style)

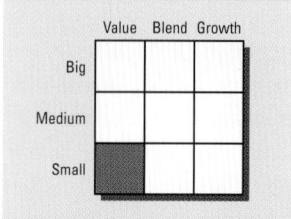

	Value	Blend	Growth
Big			
Medium			
Small			

Opinion

Here's an appealing specialized fund that would nicely complement a position in funds from, say, Trimark, which has lots of bigger companies and lots of exposure to the U.S. market.

By contrast, this fund holds very little in the U.S., where its team of two dozen analysts consider small stocks generally to be of the high-tech, high-price variety. And naturally, there are no big company shares in this portfolio. Which is a good thing. Here's why: 1) small stocks tend to have higher returns; and 2) active management and fundamental research add more value in the area of small stocks because they're less well followed.

The fund has done well by missing Japan (Boersma still thinks prices are too high) and overweighting Europe, where the team continues to think the world's best values lie. As for the U.S., it's anyone's guess what will happen to the market. But they'd be buyers if prices were to plummet.

BPI Global Small Companies Fund

Managed by: Pablo Salas

From: BPI Global Asset Management

RRSP Eligible:

Overall performance: ★ ★ ★ ★ ☆

Performance in :	
Up Markets	B
Down Markets	–

Value of $10,000 invested

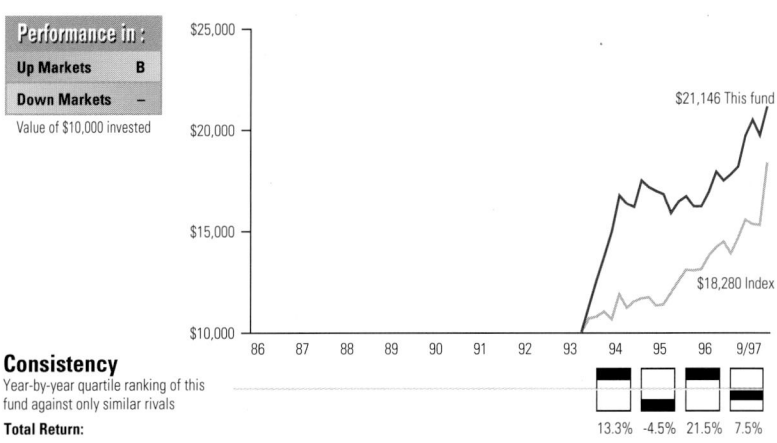

$25,000

$21,146 This fund

$20,000

$15,000

$18,280 Index

$10,000

86 87 88 89 90 91 92 93 94 95 96 9/97

Consistency
Year-by-year quartile ranking of this
fund against only similar rivals

Total Return: 13.3% -4.5% 21.5% 7.5%

Risk

% of time fund has lost money over 12-month period	**21%**
Biggest drop	**-9%**
Months to recover	**19**

Efficiency

For every $100	**$2.83**
which for this class is	**High**

Fit (Investment style)

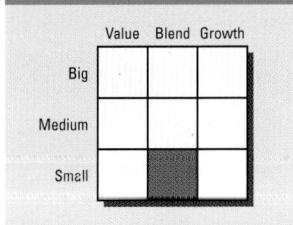

	Value	Blend	Growth
Big			
Medium			
Small		■	

Opinion

If you've seen the brochures, you'll know that Pablo Salas and the rest of the team at Orlando, FL-based BPI Global Advisors look young. But before you pass judgement on their ability to manage money, pepper them with questions about this stock or that industry. These guys are good.

And the time really is right for small caps. The valuation gap between big and small companies is at the lower end of its historical band. The economy is growing nicely and some regions of the world are just beginning to rise from slumber, like Europe. Which happens to be the place where most of this fund's money has been spent.

With rigid screens, management interviews, and clear price targets, this team's active approach to picking stocks covers the world of underfollowed names. Of course, that's where the value should be: in less well known names. But it takes more work to find out about Cochlear Ltd. than it does to find out about Coca-Cola. For that extra work the expenses on this small fund are high at 2.83%.

International Equity

Co-operators U.S. Equity Fund

Managed by: Milton Burns (since inception)

From: Co-Operators Investment Counselling Ltd.

RRSP Eligible

Overall performance: ★ ★ ★ ★ ★

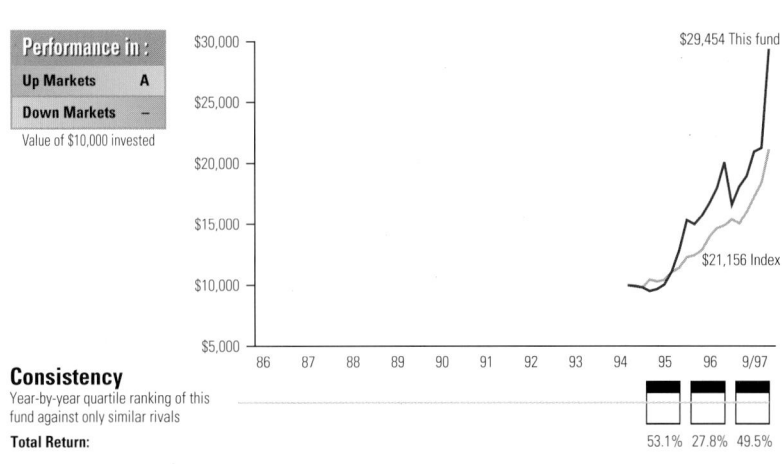

Performance in :	
Up Markets	**A**
Down Markets	**–**

Value of $10,000 invested

$30,000 — $29,454 This fund
$25,000
$20,000
$15,000
$10,000 — $21,156 Index
$5,000

86 87 88 89 90 91 92 93 94 95 96 9/97

Consistency
Year-by-year quartile ranking of this
fund against only similar rivals

Total Return: 53.1% 27.8% 49.5%

Risk

% of time fund has lost money over 12-month period	**0%**
Biggest drop	**-17%**
Months to recover	**7**

Efficiency

For every $100	**$2.07**
which for this class is	**Average**

Fit (Investment style)

	Value	Blend	Growth
Big			
Medium			
Small			

Opinion

Decades of experience and a healthy dose of humble pie keep Milton Burns on top of his peers in this fund that's just barely new enough to make the book. He's on fire, which is what you'd expect from any U.S. fund. But he's done much better than most for his investors—so far at least.

He's not a fighter pilot, and he's not a high-tech whiz kid. And he doesn't work in New York or Toronto. Rather, he works in Waterloo. He attends lots of industry conferences to learn about product developments and to keep abreast of competitive changes.

Mostly, though, he's just a common-sense eclectic value kind of a manager, looking for companies that are going through some kind of dynamic change, like industry consolidation. You'll recognize lots—but not all—of the names in this diversified fund. But remember, average in if you're leery bout lofty stock prices.

C.I. American Fund

Managed by: Bill Priest (since inception)

From: Bea Associates (New York)

RRSP Eligible:

Overall performance: ★ ★ ★ ★ ✦

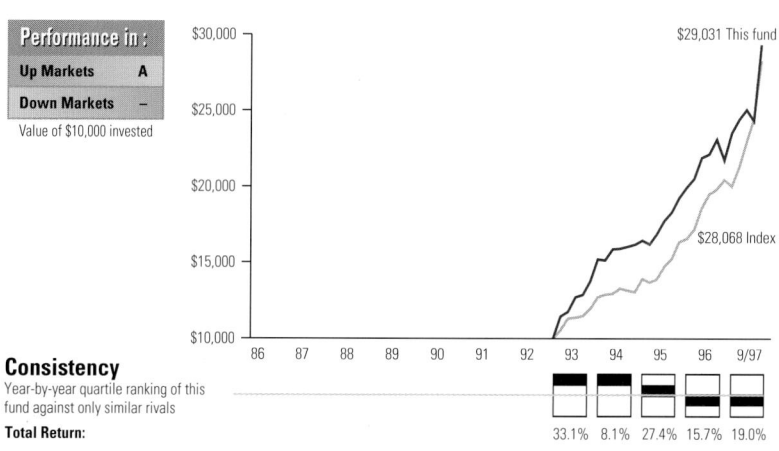

Performance in :	
Up Markets	A
Down Markets	–

Value of $10,000 invested

$29,031 This fund

$28,068 Index

Consistency

Year-by-year quartile ranking of this fund against only similar rivals

Total Return: 33.1% 8.1% 27.4% 15.7% 19.0%

Risk

% of time fund has lost money over 12-month period	0%
Biggest drop	-6%
Months to recover	3

Efficiency

For every $100	$2.46
which for this class is	**Average**

Fit (Investment style)

	Value	Blend	Growth
Big			
Medium			
Small			

Opinion

It's just more of the same from last year's report on this stellar fund. It remains overlooked by investors. It still has only $200 million or so. It still manages to excel despite its heavy 2.46% annual expense burden, and it's still profiting from unit growth in global market leaders like Microsoft, Warner-Lambert, and Heinz.

What lies ahead for Priest and his unitholders? More of the same, he thinks. Sure, stocks have been hot, but the economic environment is superb for corporate—and human—development. Inflation's still dead, so interest rates will stay flat for a while. Freer trade is delivering real productivity gains to all sorts of industries. Increasingly, foreign workers are getting good jobs. And thankfully our own job situation in North America is improving because of a hot domestic economy.

US Equity

Universal U.S. Emerging Growth Fund

Managed by: Jim Broadfoot (since inception)

From: Mackenzie Investment Management Inc. (U.S.)

RRSP Eligible:

Overall performance: ★ ★ ★ ⯨ ⯪

Performance in :	
Up Markets	**A**
Down Markets	**–**

Value of $10,000 invested

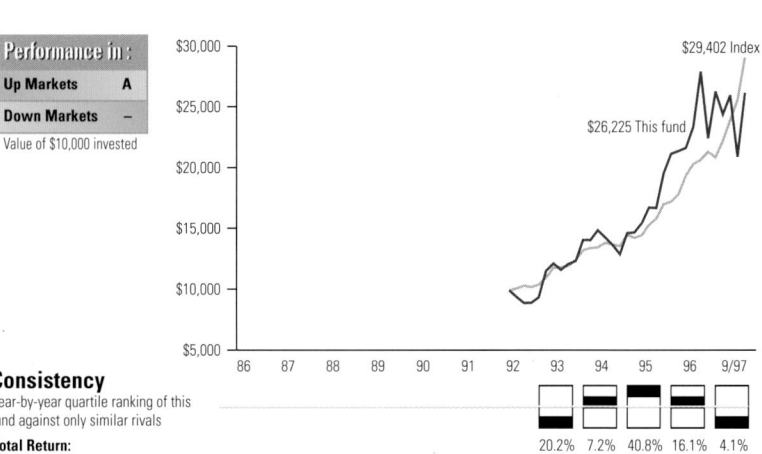

$29,402 Index

$26,225 This fund

Consistency
Year-by-year quartile ranking of this
fund against only similar rivals

Total Return: 20.2% 7.2% 40.8% 16.1% 4.1%

Risk

% of time fund has lost money over 12-month period	**7%**
Biggest drop	**-29%**
Months to recover	**NA**

Efficiency

For every $100	**$2.40**
which for this class is	**Average**

Fit (Investment style)

	Value	Blend	Growth
Big			
Medium			
Small			■

Opinion

Talk about a thumping! The 25% collapse in this fund's share price that ended in the spring of '97 was about as ugly as could have ever been foreseen—especially given the generally favourable market and economic conditions at the time. Who'd a thunk it?

But indeed, the crazy US market had an infatuation with the huge companies that dominate the S&P 500 Index, as index investing became spectacularly popular. With it, the premium to be paid for big, liquid stocks also soared.

Left in the dust were rapid-growth stocks—generally those with a high-tech bent, a couple of which did disappoint the market with poor earnings results. But even at the bottom, Broadfoot's enthusiasm for his smaller, faster-growth stocks was high. He knew that these young companies were maturing quickly; getting FDA approvals, gaining market acceptance and market share, and growing earnings. The rebound has already begun.

US Equity

Fidelity Far East Fund

Managed by: K.C. Lee (since inception)

From: Fidelity International Ltd.

RRSP Eligible:

Overall performance: ★ ★ ★ ★

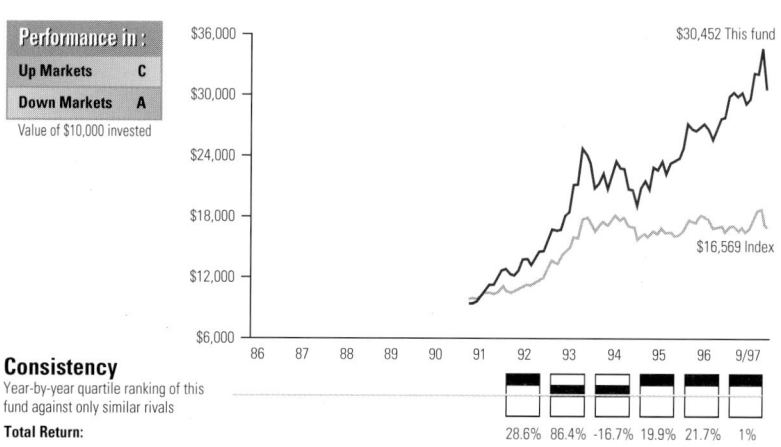

Performance in :	
Up Markets	C
Down Markets	A

Value of $10,000 invested

$36,000
$30,000
$24,000
$18,000
$12,000
$6,000

$30,452 This fund

$16,569 Index

86 87 88 89 90 91 92 93 94 95 96 9/97

Consistency
Year-by-year quartile ranking of this
fund against only similar rivals

Total Return: 28.6% 86.4% -16.7% 19.9% 21.7% 1%

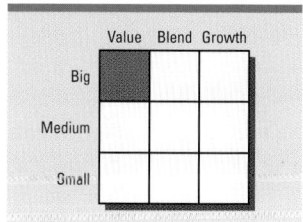

Risk

% of time fund has lost money over 12-month period	11%
Biggest drop	-23%
Months to recover	24

Efficiency

For every $100	$2.83
which for this class is	**Average**

Fit (Investment style)

	Value	Blend	Growth
Big			
Medium			
Small			

Opinion

K.C. Lee's ability to see value in Hong Kong and his courage to bet heavily on the market have made investors in this fund rich, despite a bear market in the region that eroded its peers' unit values. But pulling another rabbit out of the hat will be tough indeed, as Asia grapples with currency turmoil in Thailand and Malaysia that is having sweeping effects on the rest of the region. The greatest risk at writing to the stock markets of the region lies in the interest rate policy of the G7 nations, especially the U.S.

And that looks dicey: U.S. economic growth is strong and, while inflation is still benign, rates are likely to be pushed higher at some point. So just when U.S. and Canadian markets get rained on by higher rates, the Asian markets are also likely to suffer from further currency problems.

Still, Lee makes a powerful argument that now, even under Chinese rule, Hong Kong remains the safest bet. He argues that the Hong Kong dollar can be defended. And once exports pick up again, share prices will recover.

Regional Equity Asia

C.I. Pacific Fund

Managed by: Shaun Chan & Terry Mahoney (since 1996)

From: TCW Asia (Hong Kong)

RRSP Eligible:

Overall performance: ★ ★ ★ ✦ ☆

Performance in :	
Up Markets	**D**
Down Markets	**A**

Value of $10,000 invested

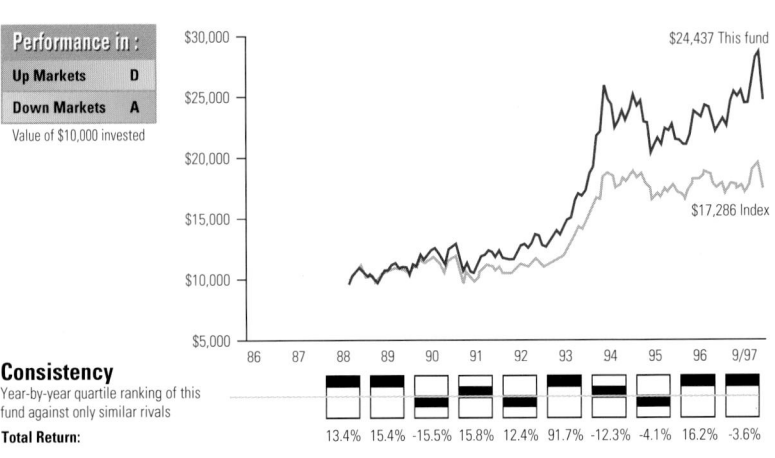

$30,000
$25,000
$20,000
$15,000
$10,000
$5,000

$24,437 This fund

$17,286 Index

86 87 88 89 90 91 92 93 94 95 96 9/97

Consistency
Year-by-year quartile ranking of this
fund against only similar rivals

Total Return: 13.4% 15.4% -15.5% 15.8% 12.4% 91.7% -12.3% -4.1% 16.2% -3.6%

Risk

% of time fund has lost money over 12-month period	**17%**
Biggest drop	**-25%**
Months to recover	**23**

Efficiency

For every $100	**$2.61**
which for this class is	**Average**

Fit (Investment style)

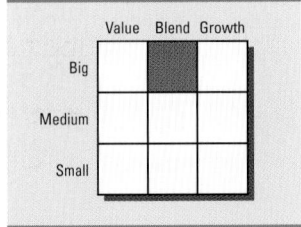

	Value	Blend	Growth
Big		■	
Medium			
Small			

Opinion

Shaun Chan has a paradox of a fund on his hands here. It's suffering through the currency crisis of Southeast Asia and trimming exposure to those markets most affected. But despite the bearishness of these significant events, the fund is fully invested—with half its assets in what was thought to be the more stable Hong Kong market.

So confident is Chan about the liquidity in Hong Kong that he'll spend his free cash there after things settle down. The big names in the Hong Kong market generally benefitted from problems elsewhere in the region because when fund managers move out of Thailand and Malaysia, or wherever, they move into the big liquid markets.

The China question remains: though it's business as usual in Hong Kong now, even after the handover, the Chinese rulers may have their first real test of wills if the Hong Kong dollar gets pushed into the currency turmoil of its southern neighbors. I'd bet that Chan, who's a country allocator, can get it right.

Fidelity European Growth Fund

Managed by: Sally Walden (since inception)

From: Fidelity International Ltd.

RRSP Eligible:

Overall performance: ★ ★ ★ ★ ★

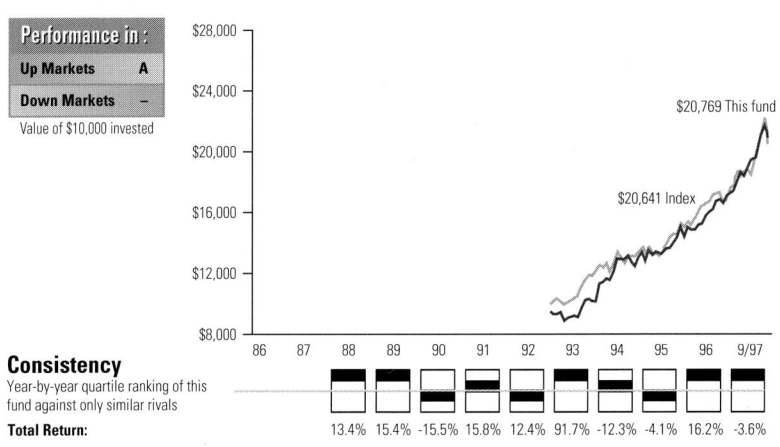

Performance in :	
Up Markets	A
Down Markets	–

Value of $10,000 invested

$28,000

$24,000

$20,000

$16,000

$12,000

$8,000

$20,769 This fund

$20,641 Index

86 87 88 89 90 91 92 93 94 95 96 9/97

Consistency
Year-by-year quartile ranking of this fund against only similar rivals

Total Return: 13.4% 15.4% -15.5% 15.8% 12.4% 91.7% -12.3% -4.1% 16.2% -3.6%

Risk

% of time fund has lost money over 12-month period	0%
Biggest drop	-7%
Months to recover	8

Efficiency

For every $100	$2.80
which for this class is	High

Fit (Investment style)

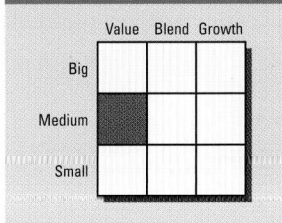

Value Blend Growth

Big

Medium

Small

Opinion

With a mix of both big and smaller companies, and a bottom-up approach to researching them, Sally Walden has hit on the right formula for European investing— just when Europe has been a good place to invest.

Going forward, she's optimistic about the prospects for the region's established markets because of, or in spite of, the economic hardship brought on by the spending restraints necessary to meet the Maastricht requirements. You see, each nation has fiscal hurdles to meet before monetary union can be possible. But high interest rates (to defend each currency) and resulting high unemployment had killed local demand. The inevitable result has been a repeat of the Canadian experience: falling currency values (which have hurt this fund somewhat), improved exports, and lower interest rates to spur the economy. The stock and bond market boom has been welcome, and isn't finished. After all, now employment is growing along with corporate profits.

Regional Equity Europe

Dynamic Europe Fund

Managed by: Joe Evershed (since 1994) & team

From: Goodman & Company Investment Counsel

RRSP Eligible: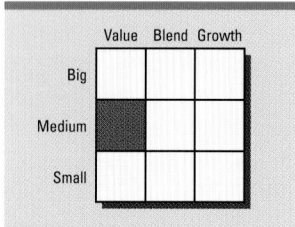

Overall performance: ★ ★ ★ ★ ☆ ☆

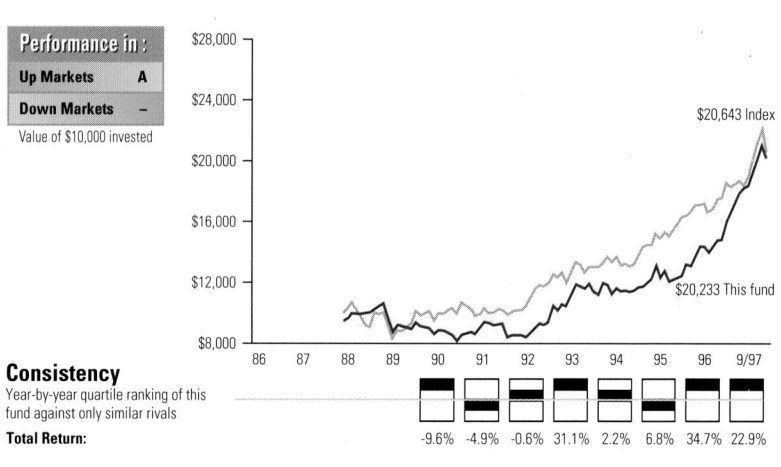

Performance in :	
Up Markets	**A**
Down Markets	**–**

Value of $10,000 invested

$28,000
$24,000
$20,000
$16,000
$12,000
$8,000

$20,643 Index

$20,233 This fund

86 87 88 89 90 91 92 93 94 95 96 9/97

Consistency
Year-by-year quartile ranking of this
fund against only similar rivals

Total Return: -9.6%   -4.9%   -0.6%   31.1%   2.2%   6.8%   34.7%   22.9%

Risk

% of time fund has lost money over 12-month period	33%
Biggest drop	-24%
Months to recover	40

Efficiency

For every $100	$2.64
which for this class is	High

Fit (Investment style)

	Value	Blend	Growth
Big			
Medium			
Small			

Opinion

This fund has stood out in front of its class lately, but had lagged far behind its peers earlier this decade—before Joe Evershed was on the case. Credit strong recent performance to exposure in Eastern Europe, a riskier area that's been hot lately, but still offers bargains.

Bargains, after all, are what Evershed is all about. After restating financials of European companies back to North American standards, his valuation models suggest which companies are attractively priced. He suggests that companies on the continent are some 20% cheaper than those of this side of the pond.

Still, with one-fifth of each actual invested dollar in Eastern Europe, I'm counselling investors that this is a more aggressive fund than most in the group. Mitigating that risk are the diversification benefits and the double-digit cash reserve, which together provide comfort that the fund can still pursue opportunities even if markets rumble before monetary union.

Regional Equity Asia

Spectrum United Emerging Markets

Managed by: Ewen Cameron-Watt (since 1996)

From: Mercury Asset Management

RRSP Eligible:

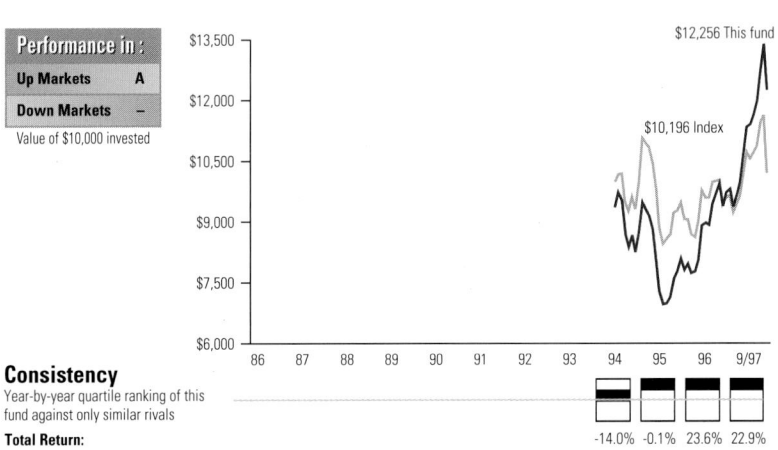

Overall performance: ★ ★ ★ ★ ★

Performance in :	
Up Markets	A
Down Markets	–

Value of $10,000 invested

$13,500 — $12,256 This fund
$12,000
$10,500 — $10,196 Index
$9,000
$7,500
$6,000

86 87 88 89 90 91 92 93 94 95 96 9/97

Consistency
Year-by-year quartile ranking of this
fund against only similar rivals

Total Return: -14.0%   -0.1%   23.6%   22.9%

Risk

% of time fund has lost money over 12-month period	43%
Biggest drop	-28%
Months to recover	28

Efficiency

For every $100	$2.66
which for this class is	**Average**

Fit (Investment style)

	Value	Blend	Growth
Big			
Medium			
Small			

Opinion

Ewen Cameron-Watt called the Asian turmoil right in the first half of 1997. He sold out of Thailand and the Philippines before the currency meltdown. In fact, he's made a number of great moves for investors in this relatively new fund.

It's just old enough to pass my screens for qualification in this book. But what a debut, with top-notch results in the last three years of gut-wrenching change for the liquidity, politics, and valuations of emerging markets.

The fund holds peripheral markets, including some in Eastern Europe and Africa, in addition to standbys like Latin America and the Far East. With its reasonable expenses, broad diversification by country, and good track record, this fund looks promising for the years to come.

Be warned, though, emerging markets will suffer from U.S. interest rate hikes—especially now that defending Asian currencies becomes a major challenge for the industrialized nations. That means that the hedge one might normally get from emerging markets' exposure could be diminished when rates here rise.

Regional Equity—Emerging Markets

Templeton Emerging Markets Fund

Managed by: Mark Mobius (since inception)

From: Templeton Investment Management (Hong Kong) Ltd.

RRSP Eligible:

Overall performance: ★ ★ ★ ☆ ☆

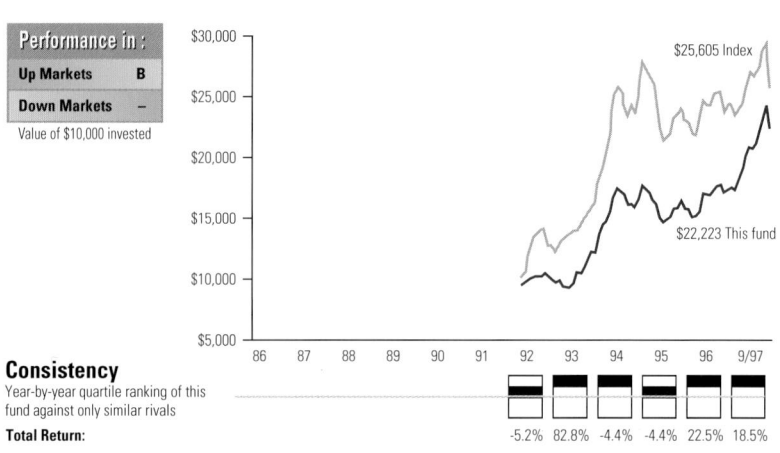

Performance in :	
Up Markets	B
Down Markets	—

Value of $10,000 invested

$25,605 Index

$22,223 This fund

Consistency
Year-by-year quartile ranking of this fund against only similar rivals

Total Return:

-5.2%	82.8%	-4.4%	-4.4%	22.5%	18.5%

Risk

% of time fund has lost money over 12-month period	30%
Biggest drop	-18%
Months to recover	21

Efficiency

For every $100	$3.30
which for this class is	High

Fit (Investment style)

	Value	Blend	Growth
Big			
Medium	■		
Small			

Opinion

Dr. Mobius has earned his reputation for being the father of emerging markets investing the old-fashioned way: he worked his butt off picking dirt cheap stocks with solid fundamentals. And for a time his success was self-fulfilling. When Mobius announced that he was investing in a new market—that the regulatory climate and economic potential were good—that's when scores of others followed, driving up share values in the less-liquid stocks he already owned.

But now this fund and its master have a new challenge: too much success. They manage a whack of dough within the emerging markets group—more than any other player. And while their research continues to be the world's best (thanks to the largest network of buy-side analysts and offices), size could become an impediment at some point.

Maxxum Natural Resource Fund

Managed by: Jackee Pratt (since 1995)

From: London Fund Management Limited

RRSP Eligible:

Overall performance: ★ ★ ★ ★ ★

Performance in :	
Up Markets	A
Down Markets	A

Value of $10,000 invested

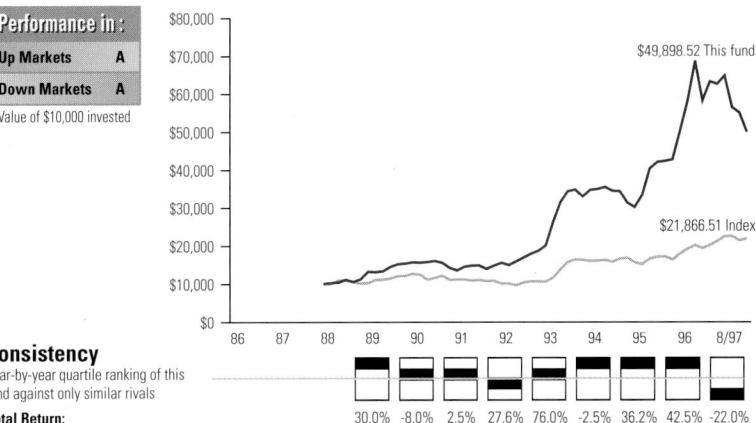

$49,898.52 This fund

$21,866.51 Index

Consistency
Year-by-year quartile ranking of this
fund against only similar rivals

Total Return: 30.0% -8.0% 2.5% 27.6% 76.0% -2.5% 36.2% 42.5% -22.0%

Risk

% of time fund has lost money over 12-month period	25%
Biggest drop	-28%
Months to recover	NA

Efficiency

For every $100	$2.25
which for this class is	Average

Fit (Investment style)

	Value	Blend	Growth
Big			
Medium			
Small			

Opinion

It's a familiar argument, but one that's never out of style: invest a little bit of your money in an aggressive hedge, both for profit and protection. I like broadly diversified resource funds like this one because the experienced manager can have the latitude to play whatever area shows the most promise at any given time.

With newsletters urging investors to dump their resource funds after the recent bloodbath, I'm more inclined than ever to urge you to buy this and other good funds—cheap. Yes, they could fall further. And no, I don't have a crystal ball to let me know when the turn will come. But I know that Pratt is a good manager. And I know that this fund's reasonable expenses auger well for the future, as do the fundamentals of the resource sector.

But don't overdo it. A fund like this could take a long, long time to recover from a big decline.

BPI Canadian Resource Fund Inc.

Managed by: Fred Dalley (since 1994)

From: BPI Mutual Funds

RRSP Eligible:

Overall performance: ★ ★ ★ ★ ★

Performance in :	
Up Markets	B
Down Markets	A

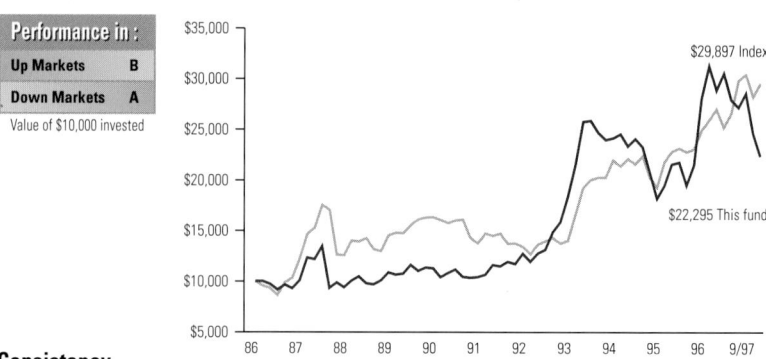

Value of $10,000 invested

$29,897 Index

$22,295 This fund

Consistency
Year-by-year quartile ranking of this
fund against only similar rivals

Total Return: -9.2% 6.2% 2.1% 12.5% -8.8% 13.1% 35.2% 51.5% -13.5% 3.7% 26.3% -17.8%

Risk

% of time fund has lost money over 12-month period	33%
Biggest drop	-36%
Months to recover	22

Efficiency

For every $100	$2.90
which for this class is	High

Fit (Investment style)

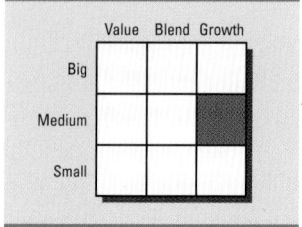

Opinion

Within the general context of a rich bull market, this fund and others like it stand out. Investors must think these guys are stupid to be losing money at a time when even bank shares are doubling.

But that's just it. This is a diversification play, and a good one at that. Dalley's very good at knowing the real poop on little growth resource companies—the kind that can grow their earnings even without advances in the price of their underlying commodity. Trouble is, with a few scandals in the juniors over the last couple of years, nobody's willing to touch even good smaller resource companies.

But they will.

Commodity crunches in gold, gas, and other areas are likely to force price spikes—and once a bull market gets going or becomes apparent in the commodity, investors trip over themselves to get a piece of the dynamic little juniors that offer leveraged exposure to it. With lots of cash lately, the fund is in scavenger mode.

Sector Equity

Altamira Resource Fund

Managed by: David Taylor (since 1995)

From: Altamira Management Ltd.

RRSP Eligible: 🇨🇦

Overall performance: ★ ★ ★ ★ ★

Performance in :	
Up Markets	D
Down Markets	A

Value of $10,000 invested

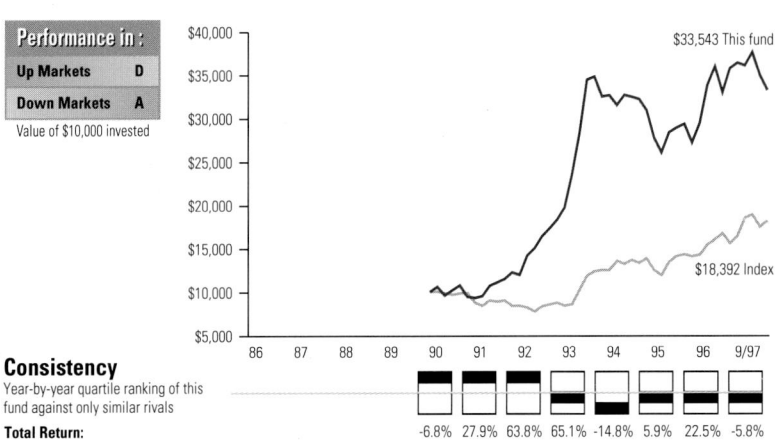

$33,543 This fund

$18,392 Index

Consistency
Year-by-year quartile ranking of this fund against only similar rivals

Total Return: -6.8% 27.9% 63.8% 65.1% -14.8% 5.9% 22.5% -5.8%

Risk

% of time fund has lost money over 12-month period	**28%**
Biggest drop	**-25%**
Months to recover	**31**

Efficiency

For every $100	**$2.28**
which for this class is	**Average**

Fit (Investment style)

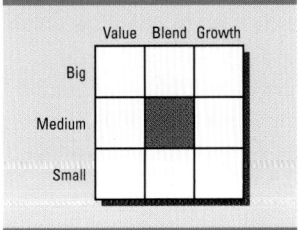

Opinion

Dave Taylor didn't see the gold collapse coming, but he does have something of a road map for how it will end. He argued strongly for some time that other base metals like zinc and copper would come bouncing back, and they did. In those cases he showed that with such low prices, nobody was mining any more of either commodity, nobody was building new smelters, etc. But demand was growing with the world's economic expansion. And so it's likely to be with gold, an area that takes up about a fifth of this diversified resource fund.

This is a very different fund than it was under previous manager Norm Lamarche. It's more concentrated (60-odd names, which is low for this type of fund), it's got more established companies, and it's holding up better in down markets. If you're bullish on gold (like me) this is a sensible, diversified way to play it. Remember, though, to limit this type of fund to no more than 20% and no less than 5% of an aggressive portfolio.

Sector Equity

Green Line Resource Fund

Managed by: Rob Cassels (since 1993) & Jim Steel

From: Toronto Dominion Securities Inc.

RRSP Eligible: 🍁

Overall performance: ★ ★ ★ ☆ ☆

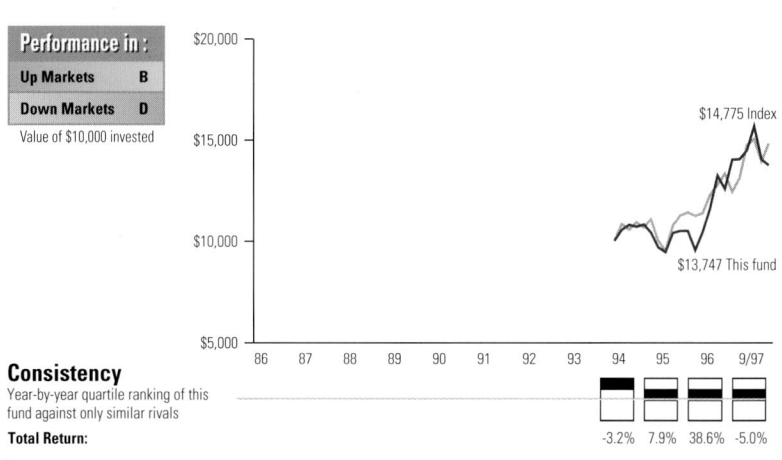

Performance in :	
Up Markets	B
Down Markets	D

Value of $10,000 invested

$14,775 Index

$13,747 This fund

Consistency
Year-by-year quartile ranking of this fund against only similar rivals

Total Return: -3.2% 7.9% 38.6% -5.0%

Risk

% of time fund has lost money over 12-month period	39%
Biggest drop	-17%
Months to recover	20

Efficiency

For every $100	$2.12
which for this class is	Low

Fit (Investment style)

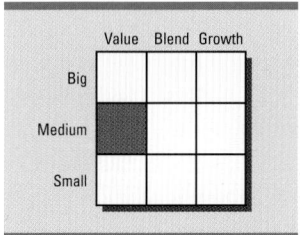

Opinion

Now is a great time to load up on a diversified resource fund like this. Its mandate allows for exposure to golds, trees, mines, or whatever resource areas the team thinks are attractive. That way you'll allow the managers the freedom to move around and buy only those areas that are in the prime of their cycle. Like oil and gas—a big win recently for the fund and an area that continues to dominate its holdings. They also like the tree sector right now.

But that's just it. If you bought a fund that only invested in golds or energy stocks, you'd be constraining your smart manager. A better bet is this unconstrained beauty, with its focus on smallish (but not always small) companies that could be either growth resource or valuation plays.

A word of caution: don't buy a fund like this after it doubles. Most people do, and that's why most people don't do well long term in sector funds.

20/20 Canadian Resources Fund

Managed by: Bob Farquharson (since inception)

From: AGF Funds Inc.

RRSP Eligible:

Overall performance: ★ ★ ★ ★ ★

Performance in :	
Up Markets	**A**
Down Markets	**C**

Value of $10,000 invested

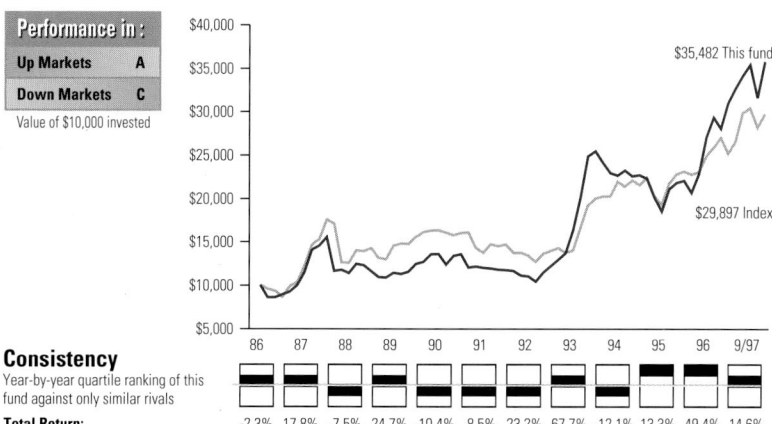

$40,000
$35,000
$30,000
$25,000
$20,000
$15,000
$10,000
$5,000

$35,482 This fund
$29,897 Index

86 87 88 89 90 91 92 93 94 95 96 9/97

Consistency
Year-by-year quartile ranking of this
fund against only similar rivals

Total Return: -2.3% 17.8% -7.5% 24.7% -10.4% -8.5% 23.2% 67.7% -12.1% 13.3% 49.4% 14.6%

Risk

% of time fund has lost money over 12-month period	**50%**
Biggest drop	**-59%**
Months to recover	**147**

Efficiency

For every $100	**$2.88**
which for this class is	**High**

Fit (Investment style)

	Value	Blend	Growth
Big			
Medium			▓
Small			

Opinion

Thirty-year veteran manager Bob Farquharson has seen it all in his days on this fund: supply/demand imbalances, sentiment that contradicts fundamentals—even scandals. So his perspective on today's resource environment in Canada is a valuable one. And he's bullish.

Of course there's the oil and gas story, which is very positive and which dominates the holdings in this fund. There the manager thinks the uptick in activity and the earnings potential of the group look great. Trees and base metals have also done well of late for this broadly diversified fund, and more of the same is expected. The larger names and the focus on gas has helped this fund trounce others like the BPI Canadian Resources Fund over the past few years, after a spectacular run by BPI.

This fund has endured punishing losses in past bear markets. But it does offer tremendous diversification for the other holdings in your portfolio, like bonds and bank shares.

Sector Equity

Royal Precious Metals Fund

Managed by: John Embry

From: Royal Bank Investment Management Inc.

RRSP Eligible:

Overall performance: ★ ★ ★ ★ ★

Performance in :	
Up Markets	B
Down Markets	C

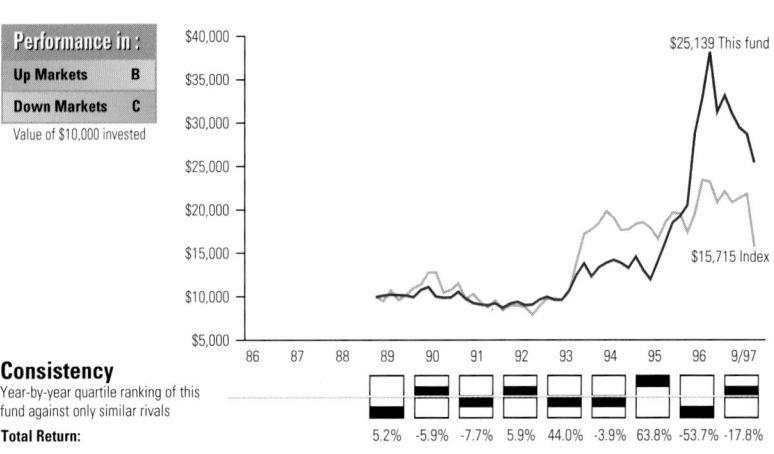

Value of $10,000 invested

$25,139 This fund

$15,715 Index

Consistency
Year-by-year quartile ranking of this fund against only similar rivals

Total Return:

86	87	88	89	90	91	92	93	94	95	96	9/97
			5.2%	-5.9%	-7.7%	5.9%	44.0%	-3.9%	63.8%	-53.7%	-17.8%

Risk

% of time fund has lost money over 12-month period	**43%**
Biggest drop	**-33%**
Months to recover	**NA**

Efficiency

For every $100	**$2.21**
which for this class is	**Average**

Fit (Investment style)

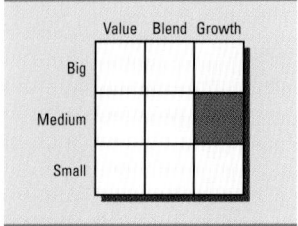

Opinion

There's a simple reason I'm recommending more precious metals funds in this book this year than dividend funds. It's a contrarian thing: dividend funds, and especially bank shares, have exploded in value and now everyone loves them. But gold's in the absolute dumpers.

Embry is a gold hawk. He knows the commodity and the companies. His take on the recent bear market is that fake supply has flooded the market in the form of selling by central banks and short sellers. Shorts will have to repurchase gold to cover their positions. Meanwhile, increasing demand for gold (and silver, which he thinks is an even hotter story) is for real—for industrial uses, for jewellery, or for hoarding (in the event of an inflation scare or currency crisis). People want gold and silver. Especially in the growing economies of Asia, where the perceived value of gold as a store of wealth remains high. Buy this or other gold funds now while they're cheap.

Maxxum Precious Metals Fund

Managed by: Martin Anstee

From: London Fund Management Limited

RRSP Eligible:

Overall performance: ★ ★ ★ ★ ☆

Performance in :	
Up Markets	**A**
Down Markets	**B**

Value of $10,000 invested

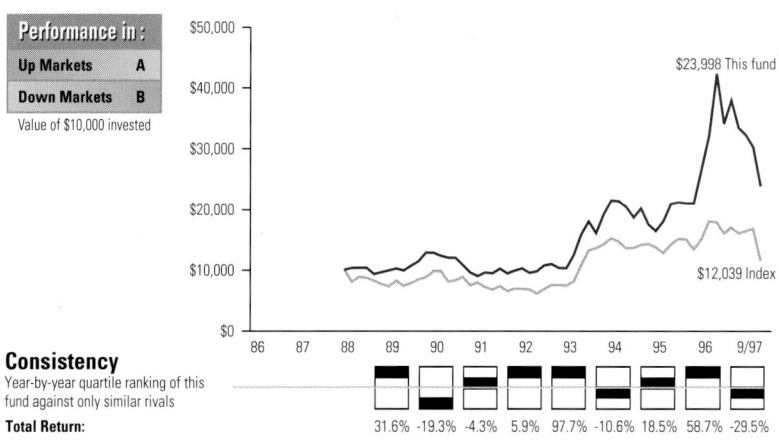

$23,998 This fund

$12,039 Index

$50,000 · $40,000 · $30,000 · $20,000 · $10,000 · $0

86 87 88 89 90 91 92 93 94 95 96 9/97

Consistency
Year-by-year quartile ranking of this fund against only similar rivals

Total Return: 31.6% -19.3% -4.3% 5.9% 97.7% -10.6% 18.5% 58.7% -29.5%

Risk

% of time fund has lost money over 12-month period	**29%**
Biggest drop	**-44%**
Months to recover	**NA**

Efficiency

For every $100	**$2.25**
which for this class is	**Average**

Fit (Investment style)

	Value	Blend	Growth
Big			
Medium			■
Small			

Opinion

Since manager Veronika Hirsch departed in a colourful turn of events, new manager Martin Anstee has been driving this fund through some very difficult times. Even with the terrible bear market for the yellow metal, this fund has underperformed. It lost 40% when gold stocks collapsed in June of '96.

Sector Equity

Dynamic Precious Metals Fund

Managed by: Jonathan Goodman & team

From: Goodman & Company Investment Counsel

RRSP Eligible:

Overall performance: ★ ★ ★ ☆ ☆

Performance in :	
Up Markets	**C**
Down Markets	**A**

Value of $10,000 invested

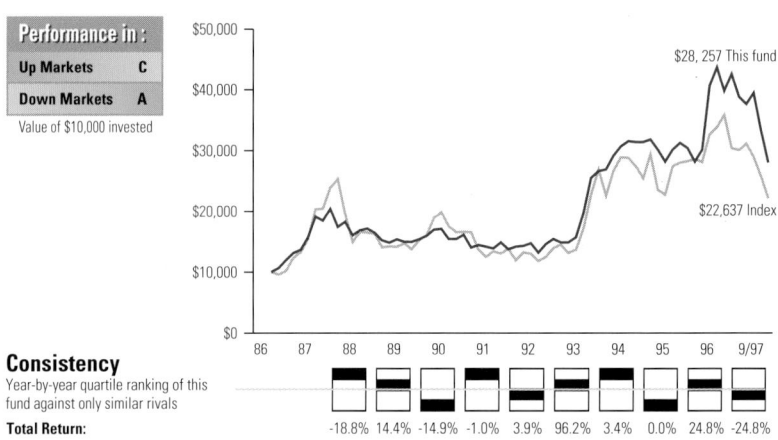

$28, 257 This fund

$22,637 Index

Consistency
Year-by-year quartile ranking of this
fund against only similar rivals

Total Return: -18.8% 14.4% -14.9% -1.0% 3.9% 96.2% 3.4% 0.0% 24.8% -24.8%

Risk

% of time fund has lost money over 12-month period	**43%**
Biggest drop	**-38%**
Months to recover	**69**

Efficiency

For every $100	**$2.49**
which for this class is	**High**

Fit (Investment style)

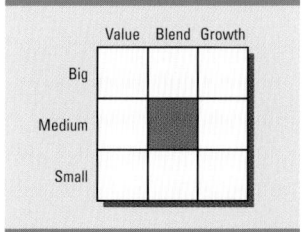

Opinion

Buy this fund now—while investors still hate gold. They loved it at US$430 an ounce, and they hate it at US$320. Go figure.

That the fundamentals are even better than they've been in years (years!) doesn't seem to bother the naysayers. But listen to the persuasive argument from geologist/fund manager Jonathan Goodman. Though his optimistic predictions last year for gold price gains by the year 2000 haven't yet come true, he's nonetheless been right in avoiding overpriced Canadian gold stocks.

The dynamics of gold supply and demand are fascinating and relevant for investors today. You see, Goodman argues convincingly that at such low prices the supply of gold dries up. Many mines cannot economically produce the stuff. Yet demand for it has been quite strong from jewellery buyers and for industrial uses. And don't forget gold's perceived value during currency crises or other dramas.

A stock picker like Goodman can play the rebound nicely.

Asset Allocation and Diversification

TO BEGIN WITH, WE MUST ACKNOWLEDGE that mutual funds can be risky. For this reason, I've devoted space on over 100 pages in this book to describe the losses and loss potential of different funds. The heart-stopping drops in the market this fall were a reminder that investors must learn to manage risk.

What can you do to reduce mutual funds risk? Follow these simple rules:

1. Invest for the long term
2. Develop a balanced portfolio composed of different asset classes
3. Diversify within each asset class

Let's look at each of these.

Invest for the Long Term

You've likely heard this advice before. However, the mathematical support for this truism is powerful.

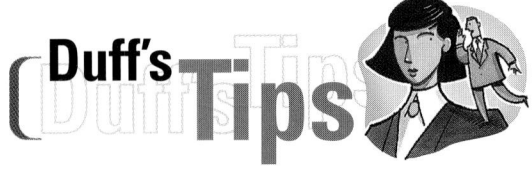

Duff's Tips

Dummy Yields

12% Yield — Buy Now
Better than GICs
Too bad most of that return isn't yield at all.
It's just a return of your money.

Beware of funds with dummy yields. That's what I call the artificially high distribution payout ratios that are policy at some funds. One of the most popular income funds in Canada — the $3-billion Industrial Income Fund — had, at the time of writing, an unsustainably high distribution rate of over 12 percent. The fund company assures me that they work hard to teach advisors not to sell this fund on its high current income. Here are the reasons why.

The underlying portfolio's gross yield is only around six percent, before expenses of almost two percent. That means that this fund actually pays out almost three times what it earns. That's okay in hot markets like the ones we've had recently, but at other times — watch out! Where does the extra dividend money come from? From each investor's own capital, of course.

In recent years, approximately half of this fund's payout has simply been a return of capital. Thus, the fund's investors who take their dividends in cash are on a type of systematic withdrawal plan. These plans are a convenient tool for allowing investors to draw from their capital regularly. Buy why set or maintain a dividend policy that creates a systematic withdrawal plan unless you are trying to convince people that the fund is actually earning high yields?

A true yield of 12 percent really isn't attainable today. You see, mutual fund dividends are very different from common stock dividends. The former are more like a share split and subsequent cashing-in of some shares. Effectively, mutual fund distributions are an administrative event, not an economic one.

If you hear about mutual fund dividends that sound too good to be true, they probably are. Only the net yield on the underlying portfolio is relevant.

We all know that stocks are risky. The shaky October we experienced this year fell on the anniversary of the October 1987 crash, when the market lost about 25 percent of its value — in one day! That's a scary concept to any investor. But the reality of equity investing is that occasionally you are going to be hit with such an event. The past is always a prologue to the future, crashes will recur, and, ultimately, stock prices will continue to grow at a rate faster than other assets such as bonds.

If all of these statements are true, then risk measures from the past will undoubtedly provide some forecasting for the future. Keep in mind, however, that the stock market is a machine driven by crowd psychology. As such, its machinations are often exaggerated — for better or worse. Bull markets generally run too high. Crashes cut too deep. Over time, equity growth rates are fairly steady in the low double digits. But on any given day, anything can happen.

Even though stocks have the potential to lose 25 percent of their value suddenly, the best way to hedge against that occurrence is to extend your holding period.

If stocks can fall 25 percent in a day, how much can they fall in a five-year period? Not much. Strangely, the mathematics works as follows. Over a one-year period, stocks have fairly high variability. There can be terrible years, such as occurred in 1973 and 1974 — in one of the worst bear markets ever. But interestingly, as this chart shows, the longer the time horizon, the more likely that subsequent equity growth will overcome even the scariest losses. Over time, the riskiness of stocks will diminish.

Hold for any five-year period and history tells us that you simply would not have ever lost more than about three percent of your money annually. Hold for 20 years and the same detailed analysis of history in the Canadian market shows that the worst that any investor could have done by holding stock was about plus 15 percent annually.

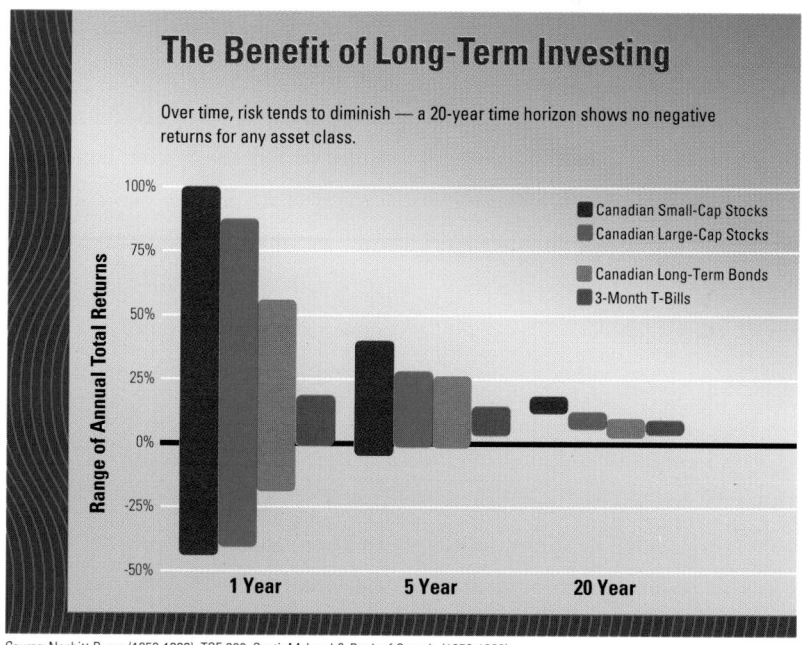

Source: Nesbitt Burns (1959-1996), TSE 300. ScotiaMcLeod & Bank of Canada (1956-1996)

Get a Balanced Portfolio Composed of Different Asset Classes

It's humbling for me to recommend that you diversify broadly. Humbling, that is, because it's an admission that I can't tell you what'll do best in the year ahead.

Zooming in

AIC's Advantage?

Have you seen the figures on this one? AIC's Advantage is Canada's best-performing mutual fund right now.

Heard a little buzz about the fund being badly managed? Couldn't possibly be true, right? Well, let's take a look. I use a technique called "passive benchmarking" to determine whether the manager of any fund adds value through active management of the portfolio.

In the case of the AIC Advantage Fund, I found that investors would have been significantly better off if the managers had taken a five-year vacation. That's right. If you just took the stocks that were held in the portfolio as of June 30, 1992, and stuffed them under your mattress for the last five years, they would have generated a compound annual growth rate of just over 40 percent.

The fund managed to return only 35.9 percent annually. And while that's nothing to shake a stick at, it is shocking to realize that — even in the best-performing fund — active management has dubious benefits. Of course, the fund's return is after fees — which are high in this fund. Still, you have to wonder if investors would rather have paid the managers to take an extended golf vacation, and kept those rich fees for themselves.

Diversification involves owning different kinds of investments, so that at any given time, you'll own some investments that are doing quite well and others that are doing poorly. The idea here is simple: over time, good investments will rise in value. Along the way, the ups and downs can cancel out each other to some degree.

Diversification out of conservative investments (such as bonds, for example) may involve a tough sell for some folks because they believe that bonds are conservative and safe. But stocks sometimes perform well when bonds are having a rough time, and so they can be an ideal match (in some proportion) with bonds, even for conservative investors.

Historically, in fact, as the chart on the following page shows, investors combining stocks with their bond portfolio (in a mix of about half and half) have actually improved returns quite a bit without adding any risk at all. That's the power of diversification by asset class.

You've no doubt heard that asset allocation — your mix between stocks, bonds, cash, and even other types of securities (such as real estate and gold) — is by far the greatest contributor to your return. This means that it doesn't matter whether you own Ford Motor or Apple Computer. What matters is whether you bought any stocks at all. Or cash. Or bonds. And how you balanced your holdings of each asset type.

Since market returns in the future aren't predictable, but risk definitely is, asset allocation approaches that are strategic in nature (which simply means that they are focused on the investor's risk level, not the manager's forecasting abilities) are legitimate ways to structure portfolios that meet a particular investor's need for growth, liquidity, or whatever special circumstances may be necessary.

In Chapter 7, I'll walk you through an example of using strategic asset allocations to structure portfolios to meet the individual needs of the investor. In going through this exercise, we'll show how you can predict fairly accurately the future risk levels and ensure that they are in a range that is tolerable for any individual.

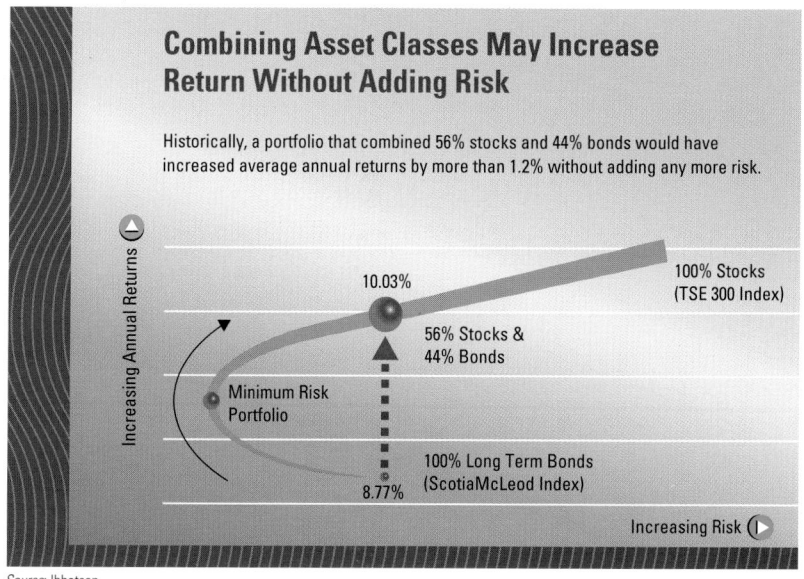

Combining Asset Classes May Increase Return Without Adding Risk

Historically, a portfolio that combined 56% stocks and 44% bonds would have increased average annual returns by more than 1.2% without adding any more risk.

Increasing Annual Returns

10.03%

100% Stocks (TSE 300 Index)

56% Stocks & 44% Bonds

Minimum Risk Portfolio

100% Long Term Bonds (ScotiaMcLeod Index)

8.77%

Increasing Risk

Source: Ibbotson

Diversify Within Each Asset Class

I'll admit it. I have made a big deal about the investment style of each mutual fund shown in my FundMonitor Profiles.

Style is very important. That's because understanding the approach of each fund helps us to choose and pair funds for our own needs. After all, funds of one style will likely perform very well when that style is in vogue. For example, in the 1980s, there was a frenzy of leveraged buyouts, and most acquisitions were targeted at companies with fairly low prices in terms of their book value. These so-called "value" stocks, as they are known, enjoyed a great run at the time, whereas growth stocks faded.

The following chart shows that the difference between growth and value isn't generally predictable but it is sizeable. I can tell you that growth and value funds (and, for that matter, a third unusual stock group called "sector rotation funds") will perform differently in the future. Combining them may reduce your risk without any sacrifices in terms of your return. That's one way to diversify within asset classes.

Diversification by Style

This table shows how two very different styles have performed very differently in the past (these series have a correlation of 0.85). Diversifying by style would have improved your returns in tough years like 1987, 1990 and 1994. Of course, small cap growth funds have done better over time, but with more risk.

	82	83	84	85	86	87	88	89	90	91	92	93	94	95	96
Avg Cdn Large Cap Value	14.9	26.4	1.3	24.1	4.9	-1.4	9.6	22.2	-8.6	9.9	-2.0	23.5	0.5	13.7	24.8
Avg Cdn Small Cap Growth	13.7	32.6	3.9	28.2	25.1	-8.2	10.3	24.0	-13.1	14.7	10.0	53.6	-9.5	18.5	32.4
Difference Amt by which SCG beat LCV	-1.2	6.2	2.6	4.1	20.2	-6.8	0.7	1.8	-4.5	4.8	12.0	30.1	-10.0	4.8	7.6

Let's see if we can diversify in the traditional bond category. Sure, you could only buy Canadian bonds, but history shows us (in a way similar to the growth/value disparity) that global bonds — or for that matter corporate high yield bonds — all move to the beat of different drummers. So, within the bond or fixed income asset class, diversifying into funds of these three distinct asset types (Canadian government, global, and corporate high-yield) can reduce risk by reducing your exposure to the likelihood of one type of bond going down the tubes.

Diversification is inherently conservative. Diversification means never shooting the lights out. Never having a blockbuster year. For that, you have to be "un-diversified." You'd have to be concentrated in one particular "hot" area of whatever market. Diversification's humble nature suggests that none of us try for hot years. Unless you can reliably predict what will be hot next year, diversification is your best strategy.

Diversify Internationally

The argument for international diversification is very powerful. Canada represents a mere three percent of the world's investment opportunities, so investing strictly within Canada means eliminating 97 percent of your options. That would be like walking into a bountifully stocked grocery store, and limiting yourself to one section, of one shelf, of one aisle. You're unlikely to find great bargains with such a narrow approach.

International investing also has merits because often Canada simply isn't the best place to invest. In fact, in the past couple of decades, only occasionally has Canada appeared near the top of the world's best-performing markets list. Trying to determine which markets will have the best performance next year is an impossible task. It's better to recognize that sometimes a diversified portfolio investing in different countries will benefit from the highs and lows experienced

Duff's Tips

The December Tax Whack on Mutual Funds

Over the course of a year, through the buying and selling of their investments, mutual funds accumulate capital gains and distributions, which must be paid out to the investors in the fund.

When do you get paid? It depends on the reporting period of the fund. Sometimes it's quarterly, but more often, any realized capital gains and income distributions are divided up among any current unitholders over the Christmas holidays — when you're not watching. However, if you're holding your fund in a non-registered portfolio, you might want to pay attention.

In a big year — where the markets are very, very strong (as they have been for U.S. stock funds in the past couple of years), large profits will be realized. And here's what happened in the case of those hot U.S. funds. New sales of the U.S. stock funds were quite weak — even in such a hot market — because people seemed afraid of a sudden cold snap. So what we've got is a recipe for high distributions: strong returns and a small number of unitholders to share the tax bill.

This is the reason behind a phenomenon I call the December chill: holding off new purchases until the new year. If you're planning an unregistered investment in a fund where the market has been hot and the assets are stalled, you may want to wait, and let those who have enjoyed the gains foot the bill for the coming distribution. Investors with registered plans needn't worry. The only December chill they'll get is if they forget to wear their woollies.

by each nation's own economic environment. International diversification is not only a great safety blanket, it can be a good strategy for growth. Historically, investors have been able to improve upon returns dramatically without any increase in risk simply by holding one-third of their stock portfolio in Canada and two-thirds internationally.

The European Story

For the same reasons that Canada and the United States experienced a "liquidity-induced" bull market during the 1990s, Europe may be beginning to experience the same thing. Until recently, Europe was (like Canada seven years ago) suffering from a very slow economy, very high unemployment, and unconscionably high interest rates (designed to defend each local currency's value).

Gradually, and thanks to a series of events, European interest rates have begun to fall. The European situation has mirrored Canada's in other ways. New legislation to support corporate restructuring was effective in kicking the Canadian economy out of recession. European corporate restructuring has provided the economic engine there, as well.

Combining International and Canadian Stocks May Increase Return Without Adding Risk

Historically, a portfolio that combined 68% international stocks with 32% Canadian stocks would have increased average annual returns by more than 3% without adding any more risk.

Increasing Annual Returns

14.19%

68% International Stocks & 32% Canadian Stocks

100% International Stocks (MSCI World Index)

Minimum Risk Portfolio

100% Canadian Stocks (TSE 300 Index)

11.00%

Increasing Risk

Source: Ibbotson

Also, while European currencies have been weakening (just like the Canadian dollar has been since 1991), interest rates have been falling and, not surprisingly, company profits and stock prices have been on the move. Today, because of the lag in their economic cycle, Europe looks like an excellent diversification candidate.

Diversify by Management Style

Management styles can vary dramatically — especially in equity fund investing. I have provided a style matrix for each of my FundMonitor picks, which are profiled in Chapter 5.

To achieve extra diversification within a particular category, select funds with different—and therefore complementary—styles.

"Value" and "growth" styles are excellent complements, for example. The chart on page 122 shows the complementary performances of value and growth stocks in an unmanaged index. Managers of the growth and value discipline will perform well at different times.

Building or Rebuilding Your Mutual Fund Portfolio

IN THIS SECTION, I WILL WORK THROUGH A profiling system and look at a case study of the portfolio builder.

The first part of this chapter outlines a new kind of questionnaire that hasn't been used in Canada. I received permission from *Worth* magazine to print it here. This questionnaire is the result of an exclusive study in 1994 with Roper/Starch Worldwide. I believe that the personality profiles that result from this questionnaire offer powerful insights into identifying which kind of portfolio is right for individual investors.

It's a simple exercise. Fill in your best responses to the questionnaire to determine your own "money personality." The results will provide the basis for building your best portfolio solution. You can then determine what kind of investment portfolio would be right for you.

It is important to remember that this is macro stuff. This exercise is not about owning a particular fund. Rather, our goal is simply to determine the right risk level that can drive the best asset mix to meet your objectives. Later, we'll take a look at a case study. Finally, we examine one investor's model portfolio, which we will redesign to match the investor's profile, and to "power up" his growth potential.

The Questionnaire

An exclusive Worth/Roper study.
Republished by permission of *Worth*.

A. I'd rather be safe than sorry in my investment decisions.   0
 • I believe in taking financial risks   1

(1=disagree completely; 7=agree completely)

| 1 | 2 | 3 | 4 | 5 | 6 | 7 |

If you answered 1, then you are a hunter.
If you answered 0, go on to question B.

B. Which do you agree with?
 • When it comes to money, a person has to look out for himself or herself first.   0
 • Even with financial matters, it is important to think of others before yourself.   1

If you answered 0, continue to question C.
If you answered 1, skip to question G.

C. Wealth makes a person more attractive.
 (1=disagree completely; 7=agree completely)

| 1 | 2 | 3 | 4 | 5 | 6 | 7 |

Duff's Tips

Small Investors Aren't as Bad at Choosing Stocks as Most People Think. They're Worse.

In 1997, a U.S. study of 97 000 trades in 1000 randomly selected accounts from one discount brokerage firm demonstrated that people generally sell the stocks they should be buying and buy the turkeys they ought to be selling.

Does time eventually prove them right? Nope. The effect becomes even more pronounced as the time after the trade increases from four months to a year, and then to two years. This startling result, which is measured before commissions, argues strongly that mutual funds — with their professional management and efficient trading — are an excellent alternative for individual investors.

After Two Years	
Stocks sold increased by	2.9%
Stocks bought declined by	0.7%
Difference	3.6%

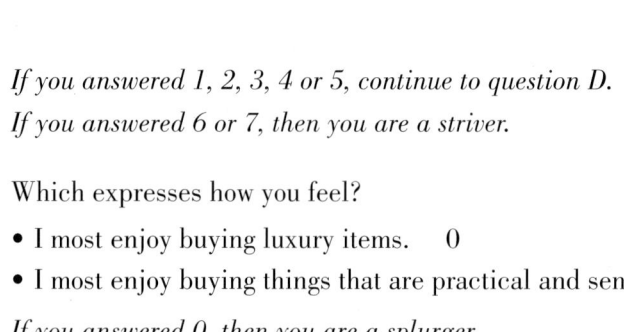

If you answered 1, 2, 3, 4 or 5, continue to question D.
If you answered 6 or 7, then you are a striver.

D. Which expresses how you feel?

- I most enjoy buying luxury items.   0
- I most enjoy buying things that are practical and sensible.   1

If you answered 0, then you are a splurger.
If you answered 1, then skip to question F.

E. With money, I feel that it is more important to plan for the future than to enjoy what I have now.
(1=disagree completely; 7=agree completely)

1   2   3   4   5   6   7

If you answered 1, 2 or 3, then you are a nester. If you answered 4, continue to question F. If you answered 5, 6, or 7, then you are a gatherer.

F. How do you feel about assessing your options when it comes to buying life insurance?

1. Quite competent
2. Somewhat competent
3. Uncertain
4. At a loss

If you answered 1, 2 or 3, then you are a gatherer. If you answered 4, then you are a nester.

G. My top priority is to get ahead financially.
(1=disagree completely; 7=agree completely)

1   2   3   4   5   6   7

If you answered 1 or 2, then you are an idealist. If you answered 3 or 4, then continue to question H. If you answered 5, 6 or 7, then you are a protector.

H. Rate your competence when choosing an investment.

1. Quite competent
2. Somewhat competent

3. Uncertain

4. At a loss

If you answered 1 or 2, then you are a protector. If you answered 3 or 4, then you are an idealist.

For a discussion of what each money personality means, see the sidebar on page 129.

Write your money personality here

_____ .

Money Personality

Whatever your money personality, of course, your current financial situation will also determine the components of your portfolio.

Now take what you've learned about yourself and let's look at our Portfolio Builder chart on page 128.

For example, let's say that you have learned that you are a "hunter." You'll see your money personality profiled, and designated by a colour bar on the risk/return arc.

Below, I have identified a model asset allocation for you. This portfolio is the result of our "optimization analysis." This sophisticated financial engineering looks at historic returns, risk, and the correlation between different kinds of investments to determine which mix would have been best, historically, to achieve the highest return possible from one of the five levels of risk.

If you need investment money within the next 2 to 3 years, or if you are especially bearish, your model portfolio will need to be more conservative (left on the scale).

If you are very bullish, or have many years to invest, you may want to lean to the right of your recommended model, just to customize the asset mix for your personal situation.

The optimization that I've used for this book and that I use in my work is special because it doesn't use traditional risk measures to quantify the pain of risk. My system uses some complex formulae to derive a common sense assessment of a fund's risk of loss — how often, how likely, how severe, how long to recover. This is what dramatically sets apart this strategic asset allocation system from others such as the STAR program from Mackenzie, which uses standard deviation — an old-fashioned idea of risk — as the basis for measuring risk.

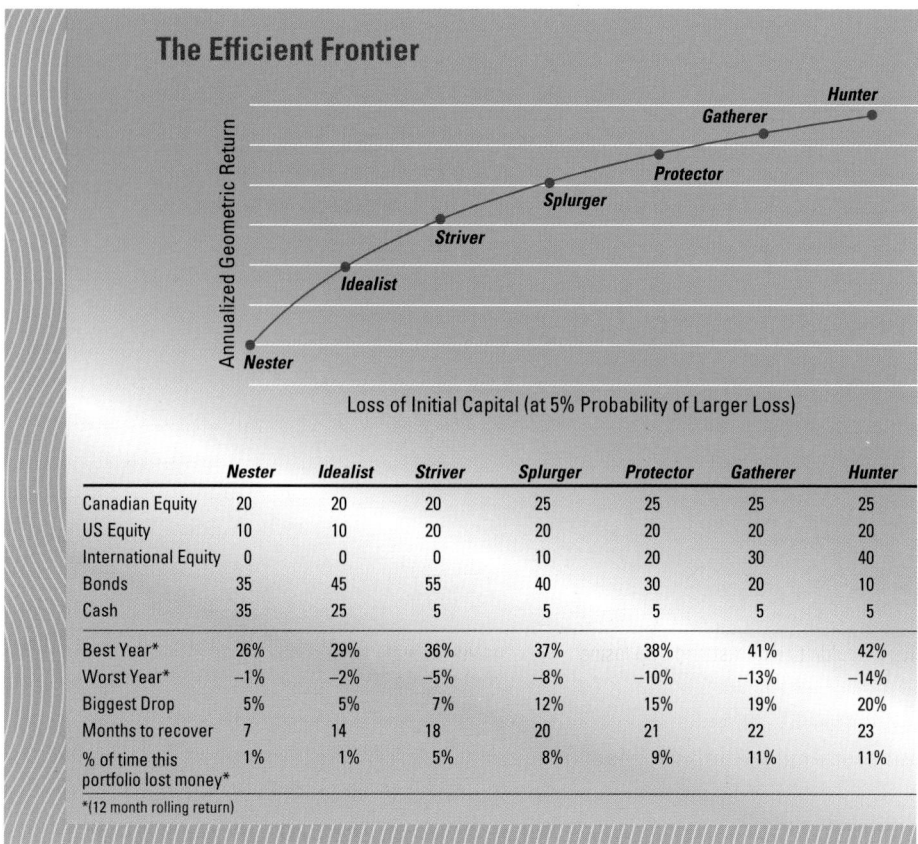

The Efficient Frontier

Annualized Geometric Return (y-axis)

Points along the curve, from bottom-left to top-right: Nester, Idealist, Striver, Splurger, Protector, Gatherer, Hunter

Loss of Initial Capital (at 5% Probability of Larger Loss)

	Nester	Idealist	Striver	Splurger	Protector	Gatherer	Hunter
Canadian Equity	20	20	20	25	25	25	25
US Equity	10	10	20	20	20	20	20
International Equity	0	0	0	10	20	30	40
Bonds	35	45	55	40	30	20	10
Cash	35	25	5	5	5	5	5
Best Year*	26%	29%	36%	37%	38%	41%	42%
Worst Year*	−1%	−2%	−5%	−8%	−10%	−13%	−14%
Biggest Drop	5%	5%	7%	12%	15%	19%	20%
Months to recover	7	14	18	20	21	22	23
% of time this portfolio lost money*	1%	1%	5%	8%	9%	11%	11%

*(12 month rolling return)

Model Portfolios

Forget age minus your shoe size. Today's more sophisticated methods allow for deep, introspective psychological profiling. And that's more than mumbo-jumbo. We've been looking at how values, habits, and goals influence your satisfaction with a given investment portfolio. Since future market returns aren't known (but historic relationships and risk are), we can develop an asset allocation whose risk profile is right for you.

Case Study

Let's walk through a case study of a portfolio, rebuilt for a client I'll call Steve. Steve's responses to the questionnaire revealed that he is a hunter. In terms of business and personal background, Steve runs a family business wholesaling vegetables, and is very confident and well

Zooming in

Profiles of Each Money Personality

Nesters This type of person doesn't care much about managing money. Nesters equate money with comfort, not security. They aren't interested in leaving money for their kids, but rather in living for today. These individuals really don't have much in the way of investments and just want to get by. Nesters do not believe that a person's wealth is equated with his or her worth.

Idealists Idealists are generous, thrifty people who don't much care for money. They wouldn't be devastated by a losing investment — but then again they're not that likely to be involved much in investing. For them money means security, not happiness.

Strivers Strivers are controlled by money and would feel terrible if they lost a nickel. For these individuals, money equals happiness. They believe that luck or connections produce wealth. The striver is not a big saver and generally isn't sophisticated in financial or investment matters.

Splurgers Splurgers buy luxuries. They are also quite risk-averse. These individuals

are hunters but without the financial acumen. They appreciate those who appreciate the best, and aren't very practical.

Protectors Protectors put others first. They are financially savvy and have adequate insurance, or more. They are competent, stable, and think of others first in financial affairs.

Gatherers Gatherers do not have the highest income, but are miserly and wise in many ways. They look out for themselves, are conservative investors, and can afford to recognize and embrace long-term risk in investing. Gatherers are usually comfortable with their ability to choose investments. For them, money equals security.

Hunters Hunters are high-income individuals who are aggressive about making, spending, and investing their money. Sometimes hunters are extravagant, and they generally equate money with happiness, achievement or power. Hunters feel comfortable choosing investments and believe that it takes intelligence and guts to produce wealth.

Duff's Tips

Three Things Some Fund Managers Won't Tell You

1. "I got my clock cleaned by missing the bank rally earlier in the year, so now I'm really swinging for the fences. I need to take some extra risks with the fund if I'm going to make my bonus for the year."

2. "I wish I had never let the marketing department talk me into launching this narrow-mandate sector fund. Sector funds sell, so now I've got a bundle to invest, but I can't sell out of this sector, and I'm bearish."

3. "I hope investors don't flood me with redemptions; I've got some big positions in illiquid stocks that I just couldn't unload in a hurry."

Three Things Your Advisor Won't Tell You

1. *"I make great money but I'm cheaper than you think."*
   Your advisor is your friend. It's natural for investors to haggle over the commissions that they pay, but instead people should be haggling for funds with lower management expenses. That way, investors would save money, year after year.

2. *"I'm really a marketing pro — not a money manager."*
   The mantra for the brokerage business today is "gathering assets." This is a good thing: it keeps advisors focused on dealing with relationships, understanding individual client needs, and providing education and service. All that leaves little time to keep up with all the mountains of research on individual stocks and sectors. Don't expect your financial advisor to see a crash coming. Expect him or her to have understood your psyche and to have structured your account to withstand a crash.

3. *"I'd prefer to liquidate your portfolio up front, and then invest the proceeds."*
   Any advisor stands to make more if you bring in a portfolio of cash than if you bring a portfolio of good mutual funds, good dividend-paying stocks, and quality bonds. Advisors get paid to put you into new stuff, which is often hot stuff and is often unproven. But good financial advisors have your best interests at heart, so be wary when someone advises you to "sell everything."

informed on financial matters. He reads *The Globe and Mail* every day — studying for investment opportunities and following up on matters of general business. He earns good money and is aggressive about how he makes and spends that money. He considers himself to be somewhat extravagant and generally equates money with happiness, achievement, and power.

For Steve, who has about half of his investments within his RRSP, the best portfolio would be one way over to the right of the efficient frontier: the hunter portfolio. Here's the asset mix from page 128: 40% international stock, 20% U.S. stock, 25% Canadian stock, and 15% in bonds and cash.

Steve's long-term horizon, low need for liquidity, and financial savvy suggest that he can withstand tough times in the market. In fact, Steve says he looks forward to a pullback so that he can have the opportunity to go and pick up some more funds. Which is exactly what he did in the mini-meltdown of October 1997.

Although he's not wildly bullish about the market right now, he has faith in the idea that being an owner of companies is far more lucrative than being a loaner to banks and others or just holding fixed income investments. Historically, the hunter's asset mix has had the following risk characteristics (the stats for other money types are shown in the table on page 128):

Best Year: 42%
Worst Year: 14%
Biggest Drop: 20%
Time to recover from that slide: 23 Months
% of the time one-year returns were negative: 11%
(*using data back to 1985)

Remember that we haven't even begun to discuss specific mutual funds yet for Steve — because it doesn't really matter that much. The asset allocation is what really drives his returns. After I suggested the right type of portfolio (the asset allocation) for Steve and showed him the downside risk associated with an aggressive allocation, Steve confirmed that he was comfortable with assuming that much risk. So after getting his buy-in, I drafted the following list of funds for him.

In his RRSP he already owned $50 000 in funds from Mackenzie and Sceptre. Outside his RRSP he owned funds from GT Global, AGF, Trimark, and Templeton. Steve works with a financial advisor.

To achieve the ideal asset allocation targeted above, we needed only to make switches within his current families.

The Basics of Steve's Situation

Here are some of the basic ideas I kept in mind for Steve that apply for most other people.

1. We want to keep his fixed-income stuff inside his RRSP where it will be sheltered from its normally heavy tax burden.

2. We want to maximize the foreign content within the RRSP. If that foreign exposure plus the foreign stuff outside his registered plan

doesn't add up to the target foreign exposure we identified in the personality type, then we'll just have to get more foreign exposure inside his RRSP — beyond the government's 20 percent limit. One way to do that is through the use of fully foreign, fully RRSP-eligible funds that use derivatives. (Canada Trust, Global Strategy, and C.I. all have good choices here.) Steve didn't need to go with derivatives because he had so much savings outside his plan that he could fill up his global shopping basket there.

3. Like many people, Steve had too much in bond funds — which, frankly, are a rip in this interest rate environment (with interest rates so low, a bond fund's expenses gobble up too much of its yield right off the top).

4. Where switches are necessary, I try to first look at the tax bill he might have to pay to sell a position. Second, I try to find a good fund in the same family. Only after failing with that would I make a new sell recommendation for someone. Steve's money was all in good fund families, so the tweaking we had to do was just to improve his asset mix — we had to buy more equity funds.

The Rebuild

Here's the recommended portfolio of the best funds for Steve. The process we are describing here is just a simplified version of what we can do for your portfolio.

	Current Holdings		Changes Needed to Get the Right Asset Mix and Own Great Funds
RRSP Holdings	$40,000	Industrial Income	Switch to Ivy Canadian
	10,000	Sceptre International	Hold
Non-RRSP Holdings	$15,000	Trimark Income Growth	Switch to Trimark Fund
	10,000	AGF Canadian Bond	Switch to AGF Asian Growth
	10,000	GT Global Health Care	Hold
	15,000	Templeton Global Smaller Companies	Hold
Total	$100,000		

Top Ten Picks
for Mutual Fund
Investors

THIS ISN'T A BOOK FOR THE MUTUAL FUND industry; it's a book for investors. And it's about education.

No one cares about your money more than you. That's okay. But it means that — even if you have a planner — it's your responsibility to further educate yourself on money matters.

So I've assembled an honour roll of the ten best investor choices for 1998. I think you'll find that these offer the best education bang for your time and buck:

1. Best Place to Begin

With a book: *The Wealthy Barber*. In my opinion, this is still the best place to begin — or to refresh — your financial education. No book has ever sold as well in Canada, except the Bible.

2. Best Date with Your Spouse

A personal finance course at any local community college, taught by an independent professional. You can also go on this date alone, but bring back everything you learn. You'll both benefit.

3. Best Offering by an Institute of Higher Learning

The Canadian Securities Institute's course on Canadian Investment Management (CIM). Tough, but top rate. Don't confuse this with the Canadian Securities Course (CSC). It's also good, but less relevant for the average investor. Visit the CSI web site at www.csi.ca.

4. Best Virtual Visit to a Mutual Fund Company

The Trimark web site, at www.trimark.com. I know it's been around for a few years, but I still like the downloadable "TimePiece" program. A wealth of information on this site, combined with a very low-key sell. A class act.

5. Best Software Program

PalTrak. You can't beat this program for satisfying breadth and depth of fund information. Of course, you have to really like doing the reading and interpreting. You can check out PalTrak on the web at www.pal.com.

6. Best Kid's Program

The GT Global Henry the Hedgehog program gets my vote this year. My daughter's still a little young, but I think this package looks dynamite. The program includes fun stuff like colouring books, and strolls youngsters through the basics of saving and investing.

7. Best Women's Perspective on Financial Issues

Joanne Thomas Yaccato. I realize that I may not be the best judge of this, but I polled some friends who agree that Ms. Thomas Yaccato does a great job of bringing an "everywoman" perspective to the whole business of financial planning and investing. Mothers especially connect with the writer's many references to her own daughter, Kate. Check your local bookstore, or watch for the writer's regular column in *Chatelaine*.

8. Best Investing Event

The Financial Forum. Absolutely the best, most fun, and most investor-friendly event of its type in Canada. Booths, educational programs, presentations — there's something for everyone here. Watch the speaker schedule so you can come and tune in for your favourite session before or after you browse the floor.

9. Best Daily Read for Mutual Fund Investors

The Globe and Mail. Canada's national newspaper does a great job of covering investment stories in a relevant way. And they now regularly report the calendar year returns for Canadian mutual funds. Watch for the Mutual Fund special sections.

10. Best Financial Friend

Your financial advisor. He or she should be almost as interested in your financial health as you are. If you're not sure you've found your best financial friend yet, you can troll for new connections at financial events and educational seminars. Even after you've found someone you trust, be demanding. Your financial advisor should provide ongoing educational opportunities, timely information about your best mutual fund prospects, and advice on basics like tax reduction.

The Ultimate Fund Tables

THE ULTIMATE FUND TABLES COVER ALL THE funds in Canada with information available at time of printing. Here you'll find information that you won't find anywhere else — the good and the bad.

You'll find one key new feature on this year's Ultimate Fund Tables. Realizing that new investors may be intimidated by a mass of numerical data, I wrote a computer program to translate the statistics into a short, factual sentence. These comments were generated from the following characteristics of each fund:

- age
- past performance
- performance in bull *and* bear markets
- comparison to index.

Obviously, the comments may not tell the whole story, but I hope they serve as useful pointers to potential investors, and complement the statistical figures that are the real meat of the Ultimate Fund Tables.

Overall performance: ★ ★ ★ ★ ★

As with my FundMonitor pages, each commentary begins with a star ranking of the fund's overall performance. This is a good guideline to whether or not the fund is worth further investigation.

Consistency
Year-by-year quartile ranking of this
fund against only similar rivals

Total Return: -9.2% 6.2% 2.1% 12.5% -8.8% 13.1% 35.2% 51.5% -13.5% 3.7% 26.3% -17.8%

The quartile ranking grid shows you how the fund performed against its peers over each calendar year. Look for funds which stay in the top two quartiles most of the time. This measurement strategy is a better indicator than looking at year over year returns, because it is an effective measure in good times as well as bad. If the fund performs in the top two quartiles, its returns may have been low, but it performed better than similar funds.

You'll also find my Management Expense Ratio (MER) stoplight graphic, which offers a guideline to the fund's ongoing expenses. A red light indicates that the fund's MER is in the top one-third of funds of its type. A yellow designates a fund with an MER in the average range, and a green light signifies a fund which is a bargain relative to its peers.

Because I think every investor should have some key information on a fund's darkest hours, I've identified the percentage of times the fund has lost money over any twelve-month period.

I'll also tell you how low the fund has ever gone—its biggest drop. (This isn't information that the fund company is willingly going to share in its marketing materials.) You'll also see how long it took the fund to recover from its worst low; the recovery period is measured from the point at which it began the decline to the point at which it had recovered that original price. Our team at FundMonitor refer to it as the fund's "time under water."

Does a long time "under water" mean that you should reject a fund? Not necessarily. In fact, Canada's best-performing fund over the last decade spent four years of that decade under water as a result of the crash of 1987. Should you be aware of the risk? Absolutely.

Welcome to the Ultimate Fund Tables!

Legend: ★ = overall past performance vs. similar funds (5 ★ max). Boxes show the quartile performance for a fund each calendar year vs. only similar funds (□ is the best score possible). ● = high; ◐ = average; and ● = a fund with low expenses.

Overall Past Performance	Fund Name	Type	88	89	90	91	92	93	94	95	96	Sep-97	Up	Down	% of Time Losing $	Biggest Drop	Date	No. of Mo's to Recover	MER
★	**20/20 Aggressive Global Stock Fund**	FgnEq										□	N/A	N/A	14%	-14%	6/1/96	12	2.88 ●
	This newer international fund has been a dog. High expenses have exacerbated the problem for this actively managed fund.																		
★★★	**20/20 Aggressive Growth Fund**	USEq							□	□	□	□	B	N/A	22%	-15%	6/1/96	13	2.45 ●
	This fund has shown middle-of-the-road performance against similar funds. High expenses haven't been much of a problem for this actively managed fund.																		
★★★	**20/20 Canadian Resources Fund**	CdnEq	□	□	□	□	□	□	□	□	□	□	A	C	50%	-59%	12/1/80	147	2.88 ●
	This well-established fund has shown middle-of-the-road performance against similar funds with top-notch performance in bull markets but disappointing results in bear markets. High expenses haven't been much of a problem for this actively managed fund.																		
★	**20/20 Emerging Markets Value Fund**	FgnEq							□	□	□	□	D	N/A	44%	-30%	9/1/94	N/A	3.80 ●
	This fund has been a dog. High expenses exacerbate the problem for this actively managed fund.																		
	20/20 India Fund	FgnEq								N/A	N/A	□	N/A	N/A	95%	-63%	12/1/94	N/A	3.91 NMG
	There is not too much to say about this new fund.																		
★★★	**20/20 Latin America Fund**	FgnEq							□	□	□	□	A	N/A	31%	-33%	10/1/94	28	3.20 ●
	This fund has had impressive past performance vs. its peers. It is expensive compared to others in its group but worth the extra cost.																		
★★★♪	**20/20 Managed Futures Value Fund**	Spclty									□	□	N/A	N/A	0%	-11%	9/1/96	5	3.94 ◐
	You won't find many like this one! It's done better than most in its class. High expenses haven't hurt the performance for this managed fund.																		
★★★	**20/20 RSP Aggressive Equity**	CdnEq						□	□	□	□	□	B	D	26%	-21%	2/1/94	17	2.45 ●
	A growth fund with a momentum approach, this one bolted out of the gates, but has pulled back lately. A sizzler in frothy markets.																		
★	**20/20 RSP Aggr. Smaller Companies**	CdnEq										□	N/A	N/A	0%	-3%	8/1/97	N/A	2.64 ●
	Here is a fund that's been a dog. This fund's performance has been hindered by its high management expenses.																		
★★★♪	**ABC American Value Fund**	FgnEq									□	□	N/A	N/A	0%	-2%	6/1/96	2	2.00 ●
	This newer fund has done better than most in its class. Lower annual expenses than most bode well for the future of this fund.																		
★★★♪	**ABC Fully-Managed Fund**	Balan				□	□	□	□	□	□	□	A	N/A	10%	-8%	5/1/94	13	2.00 ◐
	Irwin Michael and bonds: a sizzle and steak combo that's just right for the balanced investor. Be sure to add his new American fund too: $150 000 min.																		
★★★★♪	**ABC Fundamental Value Fund**	CdnEq				□	□	□	□	□	□	□	A	B	14%	-11%	10/1/94	9	2.00 ●
	Who couldn't love this one? With more small caps lately, it's set to move. Real bottom-up value investing is what also helps with strong down-market grades.																		
★	**Acadia Balanced Fund**	Balan							□	□	□	□	N/A	N/A	0%	-4%	3/1/97	3	2.27 ●
	Who could love this one? It's been a dog – and at 2.27% annually, it's no bargain either.																		

Legend: ★ = overall past performance vs. similar funds (5 ★ max). Boxes show the quartile performance for a fund each calendar year vs. only similar funds (□ is the best score possible). ● = high; ◐ = average; and ○ = a fund with low expenses.

Consistency		Performance Trend												Risk		% of Time Losing $	Biggest Drop	Date	No. of Mo's to Recover	Efficiency MER
Overall Past Performance	Fund Name	Type	88	89	90	91	92	93	94	95	96	Sep-97	Up	Down					
★★★	**Acadia Bond Fund** Like all the Acadia funds, this charges way too much: 1.97% – for a bond fund! I hate bond funds at 1.50%. Still, it hasn't done badly in the past.	FixInc								□	□	□	N/A	N/A	0%	-2%	7/1/95	1	1.97 ●
★	**Acadia Money Market Fund** This Canadian money market fund has been terrible. High fees exacerbate the problem for this fund.	FixInc					□	□	□	□	□	□	N/A	B	0%	0%		N/A	1.40 ●
★	**Acadia Mortgage Fund** Their mortgage fund has been a dog too. Higher than average expenses exacerbate the problem for this fund.	FixInc					□	□	□	□	□	□	N/A	N/A	0%	0%		2	2.03 ●
★	**ADMAX American Growth Fund** This fund has been a dog. High expenses exacerbate the problem for this American large-cap fund.	USEq					□	□	□	□	□	□	D	N/A	11%	-14%	8/1/95	15	2.88 ●
★	**ADMAX Asset Allocation Fund** This fund has performed as bad as the others from ADMAX. High expenses exacerbate the problem for this tactically managed fund.	Balan					□	□	□	□	□	□	D	N/A	4%	-4%	2/1/94	15	2.61 ●
★★	**ADMAX Canadian Performance Fund** This fund has been set apart from its peers by its weak returns; it's been hit hard in all market conditions. High fees have killed its performance.	CdnEq					□	□	□	□	□	□	D	D	18%	-13%	2/1/94	21	2.67 ●
★	**ADMAX Canadian Select Growth Fund** Here is one that is a dog. This actively managed fund is not worth the extra bucks.	CdnEq			□	□	□	□	□	□	□	□	D	B	35%	-38%	12/1/90	N/A	2.72 ●
★	**ADMAX Cash Performance Fund** This Canadian money market fund has been a dog. Normally I'd say that this actively managed fund has reasonable expenses compared to its peers, but poor overall performance makes that argument weak.	FixInc										□	N/A	N/A	0%	0%		N/A	1.07 ○
★★	**ADMAX Dragon 888 Fund** A China fund. Comparisons here are to Asian funds, which is fair. They left the NAV at $8.88 for a month before opening the fund. 8 is a lucky number to the Chinese. If Hong Kong moves, this could be your lucky number.	FgnEq							□	□	□	□	B	C	67%	-21%	9/1/94	N/A	3.68 ●
★	**ADMAX Europa Performance Fund** This European fund has been a terrible performer. High expenses exacerbate the problem for this actively managed fund.	FgnEq					□	□	□	□	□	□	D	N/A	19%	-8%	8/1/95	12	3.30 ●
★★★┐	**ADMAX Global Health Sciences Fund** This fund has done better than most in its class. The results of having reasonable fees can be seen for this fund of ADMAX's.	SpcIty							□	□	□	□	B	N/A	4%	-15%	6/1/96	12	2.73 ○
★	**ADMAX Global RRSP Index Fund** This newer fund has been keeping the tradition going for ADMAX.	FgnEq										□	N/A	N/A	0%	-2%	3/1/97	2	
★★★★┐	**ADMAX Global Technology Fund** This newer fund is a super fund overall vs. its peers. It is one of the better performing funds offered by ADMAX.	SpcIty										□	N/A	N/A	0%	-6%	2/1/97	2	
★★	**ADMAX International Fund** This fund has been set apart from its peers by its weak returns; it's been hit hard in all market conditions. High expenses exacerbate the problem for this actively managed fund.	FgnEq			□	□	□	□	□	□	□	□	D	D	32%	-23%	8/1/90	32	3.01 ●

Legend: ★ = overall past performance vs. similar funds (5 ★ max). Boxes show the quartile performance for a fund each calendar year vs. only similar funds (□ is the best score possible). ● = high; ◐ = average; and ● = a fund with low expenses.

Overall Past Performance	Fund Name	Type	88	89	90	91	92	93	94	95	96	Sep-97	Up	Down	% of Time Losing $	Biggest Drop	Date	No. of Mo's to Recover	MER
	ADMAX Korea Fund	FgnEq									N/A	N/A	N/A	N/A	57%	-51%	1/1/95	N/A	3.51 ●
★★	**ADMAX Nippon Fund**	FgnEq							□	□	□	□	D	A	42%	-29%	7/1/94	N/A	3.23 ●
★★↗	**ADMAX Tiger Fund**	FgnEq					□	□	□	□	□	□	B	A	37%	-32%	11/1/94	N/A	3.36 ●
★★★	**ADMAX World Income Fund**	FixInc						□	□	□	□	□	B	N/A	0%	-5%	11/1/92	5	2.69 ●
★★★	**AGF American Growth Fund**	USEq	□	□	□	□	□	□	□	□	□	□	B	D	21%	-28%	9/1/87	22	2.79 ●
★★★↗	**AGF American Tactical Asset Alloc.**	Balan					N/A	□	□	□	□	□	A	N/A	3%	-7%	2/1/94	11	2.52 ◐
★★★	**AGF Asian Growth Class**	FgnEq					□	□	□	□	□	□	C	B	21%	-18%	2/1/96	N/A	2.90 ●
★	**AGF Canada Class**	CdnEq										□	N/A	N/A	100%	-10%	3/1/97	4	
★★★	**AGF Canadian Bond Fund**	FixInc	□	□	□	□	□	□	□	□	□	□	A	D	10%	-16%	2/1/94	19	1.88 ●
★★↗	**AGF Canadian Equity Fund**	CdnEq	□	□	□	□	□	□	□	□	□	□	B	B	25%	-31%	7/1/81	18	2.50 ●
★★★	**AGF Canadian Growth Fund**	CdnEq				□	□	□	□	□	□	□	C	C	17%	-11%	1/1/90	14	2.43 ●
★★★	**AGF Canadian Tactical Asset Alloc.**	Balan				□	□	□	□	□	□	□	C	N/A	9%	-11%	2/1/94	21	2.39 ●
★★★↗	**AGF China Focus Fund**	FgnEq							N/A	□	□	□	N/A	N/A	52%	-15%	11/1/94	29	3.49 NMG

ADMAX Korea Fund — Since it's only a one-country fund, this one's suitable only for investors willing to take lots of risk - or those that know something I don't about Korea.

ADMAX Nippon Fund — This fund has been set apart from its peers by its weak returns; it is a great performing fund in bear markets but a disappointment in bull markets. High fees enhance the poor performance.

ADMAX Tiger Fund — This fund has been unimpressive to date. Higher than average expenses exacerbate the problem for this actively managed fund.

ADMAX World Income Fund — ADMAX's global bond fund has shown middle-of-the-road performance against similar funds. This is where the higher fees are worth it.

AGF American Growth Fund — This well-established large-cap fund has shown middle-of-the-road performance against similar funds. It has performed better than most in bull markets but has been hit hard in bear markets. This actively managed fund is expensive but worth it in rising market conditions.

AGF American Tactical Asset Alloc. — This fund has done better than most in its class. Annual fees are reasonable for this reasonably performing actively managed fund.

AGF Asian Growth Class — A better performer than most in down markets, but has shown sub-par results in bullish periods. High expenses haven't been much of a problem for this actively managed fund.

AGF Canada Class — This newer fund has been a dog. Low fees have not helped this fund.

AGF Canadian Bond Fund — Here is an older fund that has shown middle-of-the-road performance against similar funds. It shows top-notch performance in bull markets but has been hit hard in bear markets. This closet indexer is expensive but worth it in rising market conditions.

AGF Canadian Equity Fund — This well-established fund has been unimpressive so far. High expenses exacerbate the problem for this actively managed fund.

AGF Canadian Growth Fund — This fund has shown middle-of-the-road performance against similar funds with disappointing results in all market conditions. High expenses haven't been much of a problem for this fund.

AGF Canadian Tactical Asset Alloc. — This fund has shown middle-of-the-road performance against similar funds. High expenses haven't been much of a problem for this fund.

AGF China Focus Fund — You won't find many like this one! It's done better than most in its class. Lower annual expenses than most bode well for the future of this actively managed fund.

Legend: ★ = overall past performance vs. similar funds (5 ★ max). Boxes show the quartile performance for a fund each calendar year vs. only similar funds (□ is the best score possible). ● = high; ◐ = average; and ○ = a fund with low expenses.

Overall Past Performance	Fund Name	Type	Up	Down	% of Time Losing $	Biggest Drop	Date	No. of Mo's to Recover	MER	Efficiency
★★★⟩	**AGF Dividend Fund**	CdnEq	A	C	13%	-14%	8/1/87	14	1.91	◐
★★★	**AGF European Asset Allocation**	Balan	C	N/A	14%	-8%	5/1/94	14	2.62	●
★★★	**AGF European Growth Fund**	FgnEq	B	N/A	0%	-5%	8/1/95	5	3.01	●
★★★★	**AGF Germany Class 'M'**	FgnEq	N/A	N/A	0%	-7%	8/1/97	N/A	1.60	◐
★	**AGF Germany Fund**	FgnEq	N/A	N/A	0%	-7%	8/1/97	N/A	3.12	●
★★★	**AGF Global Government Bond Fund**	FixInc	C	N/A	14%	-12%	1/1/88	29	1.79	◐
★★★	**AGF Growth & Income Fund**	Balan	B	D	19%	-24%	4/1/81	20	2.50	●
★★★	**AGF Growth Equity Fund**	CdnEq	D	D	27%	-54%	12/1/80	55	2.82	●
★★	**AGF High Income Fund**	CdnEq	D	B	1%	-6%	2/1/94	13	1.92	◐
	AGF Int'l Short Term Income Fund	FixInc	N/A	N/A	32%	-4%	8/1/96	N/A	2.51	NMG
★★★	**AGF International Value Fund**	FgnEq	B	A	7%	-11%	6/1/90	8	2.78	●
★★★⟩	**AGF Japan Class**	FgnEq	B	B	43%	-38%	2/1/90	48	2.97	●
★★★★	**AGF Money Market Account**	FixInc	N/A	N/A	0%	0%	N/A	N/A	1.41	●

AGF Dividend Fund — Managers MacDougall and Gerber have done a great job of steering this fund into the right sectors. This blended style of top-down and bottom-up has led to great performance, while a little below average in down markets.

AGF European Asset Allocation — This fund has shown middle-of-the-road performance against similar funds. High expenses haven't been much of a problem for this actively managed fund.

AGF European Growth Fund — This fund has shown middle-of-the-road performance against similar funds. High expenses haven't been much of a problem for this actively managed fund.

AGF Germany Class 'M' — This fund has off-the-charts performance overall vs. its peers. Reasonable fees represent bargains for this closet indexer.

AGF Germany Fund — This fund has been a dog. High expenses exacerbate the problem for this closet indexer.

AGF Global Government Bond Fund — This well-established fund has shown middle-of-the-road performance against similar funds. Lower annual expenses than most bode well for the future of this actively managed fund.

AGF Growth & Income Fund — This well-established fund has shown middle-of-the-road performance against similar funds. It has performed better than most in bull markets but has been hit hard in bear markets. This actively managed fund is expensive but worth it in rising market conditions.

AGF Growth Equity Fund — This well-established fund has shown middle-of-the-road performance against similar funds. It has been hit hard in all market conditions. High expenses haven't been much of a problem for this actively managed fund.

AGF High Income Fund — This well-established fund has been set apart from its peers by its weak returns. Normally I'd say this fund has reasonable fees, but poor overall performance makes that argument weak.

AGF International Value Fund — Charles Brandes emulates the value style of his mentor Benjamin Graham (for whom he worked early in his career). This fund is a costly one, but it has paid off handsomely so far.

AGF Japan Class — This fund performs better than most of its peers in both up and down markets! For the first half of '97, Nomura managed to squeeze big profits from a sour Japanese market with astute stock picks.

AGF Money Market Account — This well-established fund has impressive past performance characteristics overall vs. its peers. This actively managed fund is expensive but well worth it.

Legend: ★ = overall past performance vs. similar funds (5 ★ max). Boxes show the quartile performance for a fund each calendar year vs. only similar funds (□ is the best score possible). ● = high; ◐ = average; and ◯ = a fund with low expenses.

Overall Past Performance	Fund Name	Type	Up	Down	% of Time Losing $	Biggest Drop	Date	No. of Mo's to Recover	MER
★	AGF RSP Global Bond Fund	FixInc	D	N/A	26%	-9%	2/1/94	17	1.96
★★★	AGF RSP Int'l Equity Allocation	FgnEq	B	N/A	23%	-11%	2/1/94	19	2.44
★★★↗	AGF Special U.S. Class	USEq	A	D	26%	-28%	9/1/87	20	2.81 ●
★★★★	AGF U.S. Dollar Money Market ($US)	FixInc	N/A	N/A	0%	0%	N/A	N/A	0.85 ◯
★	AGF U.S. Income Fund	FixInc	D	N/A	14%	-8%	10/1/93	20	2.50 ●
★★★	AGF U.S. Short-Term High Yield	FixInc	N/A	N/A	4%	-7%	8/1/95	9	2.50 ●
★	AGF World Balanced Fund	Balan	D	N/A	24%	-21%	6/1/90	19	2.35
★	AGF World Equity Fund	FgnEq	N/A	N/A	0%	-5%	8/1/97	N/A	3.03 ●
	AIC Advantage Fund	CdnEq	N/A	N/A	25%	-30%	9/1/87	44	2.45 NMG
★★★★	AIC Advantage Fund II	CdnEq	N/A	N/A	0%	-3%	8/1/97	N/A	2.71 ●
★★★★	AIC Diversified Canada Fund	CdnEq	N/A	N/A	0%	-4%	8/1/97	N/A	2.55 ◐
★	AIC Emerging Markets Fund	FgnEq	N/A	N/A	29%	-25%	10/1/94	N/A	2.78 ◐
★	AIC Money Market Fund	FixInc	N/A	N/A	0%	0%	N/A	N/A	1.00 ◯
★★★↗	AIC Value Fund	FgnEq	A	N/A	7%	-26%	3/1/90	11	2.55 ●

AGF RSP Global Bond Fund — Here is one that is a dog. Normally I'd say that this actively managed fund has reasonable expenses compared to its peers, but poor overall performance makes that argument weak.

AGF RSP Int'l Equity Allocation — This fund has shown middle-of-the-road performance against similar funds. Annual fees are reasonable for this reasonably performing actively managed fund.

AGF Special U.S. Class — You won't find many like this older one! It's done better than most in its class with top-notch performance in bull markets but has been hit hard in bear markets. High expenses haven't been much of a problem for this actively managed fund.

AGF U.S. Dollar Money Market ($US) — This fund has off-the-charts performance overall vs. its peers. No wonder performance has been so good for this actively managed fund, its fees are among the lowest in its group.

AGF U.S. Income Fund — This fund has been a dog. High expenses exacerbate the problem for this actively managed fund.

AGF U.S. Short-Term High Yield — This fund has shown middle-of-the-road performance against similar funds. High expenses haven't been much of a problem for this fund.

AGF World Balanced Fund — Here is one that is a dog. Low fees have not helped this actively managed fund.

AGF World Equity Fund — This fund has been a dog. High expenses exacerbate the problem for this actively managed fund.

AIC Advantage Fund — I didn't compare this sizzler to anything. Really, it's not like the broad Canadian equity funds. It's a theme fund. Remember, too, that this one's closed.

AIC Advantage Fund II — This newer (more costly) clone of AIC Advantage has the same issues: It's very up-market sensitive and holds some illiquid issues.

AIC Diversified Canada Fund — Less focus on fund companies. Long-term buy and hold approach.

AIC Emerging Markets Fund — Tough sector, granted, but this one missed the rally in 1997.

AIC Value Fund — They copy Warren Buffett's successful approach in this fund. So changes to Buffett's holdings could provoke a tax bill for investors here.

Lege nd: ★ = overall past performance vs. similar funds (5 ★ max). Boxes show the quartile performance for a fund each calendar year vs. only similar funds (☐ is the best score possible). ● = high; ◐ = average; and ● = a fund with low expenses.

Overall Past Performance	Fund Name	Type	88	89	90	91	92	93	94	95	96	Sep-97	Up	Down	% of Time Losing $	Biggest Drop	Date	No. of Mo's to Recover	MER
★★	**AIC World Equity Fund**	FgnEq				☐	☐	☐	☐	☐	☐	☐	C	N/A	26%	-10%	2/1/94	27	2.74 ●
	This fund has been set apart from its peers by its weak returns. High expenses exacerbate the problem for this actively managed fund.																		
★★	**All-Canadian CapitalFund**	CdnEq				☐	☐	☐	☐	☐	☐	☐	D	A	12%	-18%	8/1/87	60	2.00 ◐
	This well-established fund has been set apart from its peers by its weak returns, but it's been a top-notch performer in bear markets.																		
★★	**All-Canadian Compound**	CdnEq	☐	☐	☐	☐	☐	☐	☐	☐	☐	☐	D	A	12%	-18%	8/1/87	60	
	I never understood the difference between this one and the others in the family. I haven't bothered to check it out.																		
	All-Canadian ConsumerFund	CdnEq							N/A	N/A	☐	☐	N/A	N/A	2%	-19%	1/1/84	22	1.96 NMG
	We've categorized this as a consumer products fund – so there's nothing to compare it to.																		
★★	**All-Canadian Resources Corporation**	CdnEq	☐	☐	☐	☐	☐	☐	☐	☐	☐	☐	D	B	41%	-52%	8/1/87	79	2.00 ●
	At least it doesn't charge a bundle in fees! That's all I can really say about this underwhelming fund.																		
★★	**Allstar Adrian Day Gold Plus Fund**	Spclty						N/A	☐	☐	☐	☐	N/A	N/A	35%	-35%	12/1/95	N/A	3.34 ●
	High expenses exacerbate the problem for this one.																		
★	**Allstar AIG Asian Fund**	FgnEq										☐	N/A	N/A	0%	-8%	8/1/97	N/A	
	It's new – and it's slow off the block. There's little reason to make this family a part of your holdings.																		
★	**Allstar AIG Canadian Equity Fund**	CdnEq		☐	☐	☐	☐	☐	☐	☐	☐	☐	D	B	30%	-18%	9/1/89	43	3.00 ●
	Wearing a 3% expense anchor tells me there's nothing the current manager could do that could make me think this fund will swim.																		
★ﾉ	**Allstar Money Market Fund**	FixInc				☐	☐	☐	☐	☐	☐	☐	N/A	N/A	16%	-12%	2/1/94	29	2.66 ●
★★★★	**Altafund Investment Corp.**	CdnEq					☐	☐	☐	☐	☐	☐	A	C	14%	-17%	6/1/94	19	2.30 ◐
	It's got the oil and gas. Its got the metals. But it missed the banks. Now people want to split. I think this (mostly resource) fund will come back.																		
★ﾉ	**Altamira Asia Pacific Fund**	FgnEq						☐	☐	☐	☐	☐	C	D	58%	-35%	11/1/94	N/A	2.37 ●
	New manager here. The last guy got Hong Kong and Korea wrong, so he was sent sailing in the South China Sea.																		
★ﾉ	**Altamira Balanced Fund**	Balan			☐	☐	☐	☐	☐	☐	☐	☐	D	C	27%	-26%	8/1/87	66	2.00 ◐
	Not their best offering. Ted Rabin's Growth and Income is a super substitute within the family.																		
★★★ﾉ	**Altamira Bond Fund**	FixInc			☐	☐	☐	☐	☐	☐	☐	☐	A	D	8%	-17%	2/1/94	15	1.29 ◐
	Far lower fees make Altamira Income fund a better buy.																		
	Altamira Capital Growth Fund	CdnEq	N/A	N/A	☐	☐	☐	☐	☐	☐	☐	☐	N/A	N/A	18%	-27%	7/1/87	24	2.00 NMG
	PALTrak says this is a large-cap growth fund, and I'd agree. So there's little else to compare it with.																		

Legend: ★ = overall past performance vs. similar funds (5 ★ max). Boxes show the quartile performance for a fund each calendar year vs. only similar funds (□ is the best score possible). ● = high; ◐ = average; and ● = a fund with low expenses.

Consistency — Overall Past Performance	Fund Name	Type	Risk Up	Risk Down	% of Time Losing $	Biggest Drop	Date	No. of Mo's to Recover	Efficiency MER
★★★	**Altamira Dividend Fund** — A pretty decent fund for taxable investors. But you don't have to buy it – you could just send your money straight to Ottawa.	CdnEq	N/A	N/A	0%	–2%	8/1/97	N/A	1.55
★★★★	**Altamira Equity Fund** — No fund can match this track record. Period. And with the same manager! I'll bet my career that this guy will come back. Hold or buy now.	CdnEq	A	B	5%	–9%	9/1/90	5	2.28
★★★	**Altamira European Equity Fund** — Managed from Europe by the same guy since inception. It's lagged the recent rally but currency dominates the story there.	FgnEq	B	N/A	0%	–7%	9/1/94	8	2.33
★★★	**Altamira Global Bond Fund** — Barry Allan runs this one from Toronto. It's cheaper than its peers – and it's done pretty well. Active currency management is the hook here.	FixInc	B	N/A	20%	–8%	2/1/94	12	1.81
★★★✓	**Altamira Global Discovery Fund** — "Discovery" is a euphemism for "emerging" markets – which some people called "submerging" in the last couple of years. This one's good.	FgnEq	N/A	N/A	18%	–22%	10/1/94	28	2.98
★★	**Altamira Global Diversified Fund** — In a word: underwhelming. Boston-based Wellington Management runs it, and looks for diversification by country, asset and currency.	Balan	D	N/A	29%	–36%	9/1/87	99	2.00
★★★	**Altamira Global Small Co. Fund** — What a compelling asset class. Smaller, faster-growth companies, at the low end of their historical valuation. Run in-house by Altamira.	FgnEq	N/A	N/A	0%	–3%	3/1/97	2	3.02
★★★✓	**Altamira Growth & Income Fund** — This is a cyclical fund. But the same guy runs it – and he hasn't changed his style. Still, with three years in the dumper, waiting can be tough.	Balan	A	A	10%	–13%	10/1/94	15	1.40
★★★✓	**Altamira Income Fund** — Sutherland is one of the very best at managing bonds. When necessary, he'll dabble in US-pay bonds – with or without a hedge.	FixInc	A	D	4%	–15%	2/1/94	15	1.00
★★	**Altamira Japanese Opportunity Fund** — New in-house manager since Jan '97 has turned up the numbers on this single-country fund. And owning Japan really does diversify your other holdings.	FgnEq	N/A	N/A	50%	–23%	10/1/94	N/A	2.36
★★	**Altamira North American Recovery** — Turnarounds, fallen-angels and other special situations make this a different kind of fund – one that can diversify your growth fund holdings.	CdnEq	A	D	24%	–11%	2/1/94	17	2.30
★★	**Altamira Prec. and Strategic Metal** — I always prefer a broader resource play – just to give the manager more room to manoeuvre. But if you want just one sector, look at the risk.	CdnEq	N/A	N/A	27%	–44%	6/1/96	N/A	2.30
★★★	**Altamira Resource Fund** — Dave Taylor's got a good bottom-up approach here. But all of Altamira's funds were mired by the gold thing for a couple of years. I own this one.	CdnEq	D	A	28%	–25%	9/1/93	31	2.28
★★★	**Altamira Science & Technology Fund** — Mostly a US fund, lots of semiconductor and telecom shares. This is a dicey sector, but one with better promise – and value – than the S&P.	Spclty	N/A	N/A	18%	–21%	6/1/96	13	2.31

Legend: ★ = overall past performance vs. similar funds (5 ★ max). Boxes show the quartile performance for a fund each calendar year vs. only similar funds (□ is the best score possible). ● = high; ◐ = average; and ● = a fund with low expenses.

Overall Past Performance	Fund Name	Type	Up	Down	% of Time Losing $	Biggest Drop	Date	No. of Mo's to Recover	MER
★★★	Altamira Select American Fund	USEq	C	N/A	5%	-14%	6/1/96	12	◐ 2.28
★★★	Altamira Short Term Global Income	Spclty	N/A	N/A	11%	-5%	4/1/95	15	1.21 NMG
★★★	Altamira Short Term Gov't Bond Fund	FixInc	N/A	N/A	0%	-1%	7/1/95	1	◐ 1.26
★★★★★	Altamira Spec. High Yield Bond	FixInc	N/A	N/A	0%	-3%	3/1/97	3	● 2.31
★★★	Altamira Special Growth Fund	CdnEq	A	B	24%	-28%	4/1/87	47	◐ 1.80
★★★	Altamira U.S. Larger Company Fund	USEq	B	N/A	3%	-10%	6/1/96	5	◐ 2.30
★★★	AMI Private Capital Equity	CdnEq	A	D	29%	-21%	9/1/89	45	◐ 1.75
★★★	AMI Private Capital Income	FixInc	B	B	9%	-12%	2/1/94	16	◐ 1.25
★★★★★	AMI Private Capital Money Market	FixInc	N/A	N/A	0%	0%	N/A	N/A	● 0.75
★★★	AMI Private Capital Optimix	Balan	C	N/A	12%	-10%	2/1/94	15	● 1.75
★★	APEX Asian Pacific Fund	FgnEq	B	D	40%	-17%	5/1/96	N/A	● 2.76
★	APEX Balanced Allocation Fund	Balan	D	N/A	10%	-10%	2/1/94	16	● 2.96
★	APEX Canadian Stock Fund	CdnEq	N/A	N/A	0%	-4%	8/1/97	N/A	● 2.55
★★	APEX Equity Growth Fund	CdnEq	C	D	15%	-13%	2/1/94	22	● 2.95

Altamira Select American Fund — This smaller-company fund has shown middling performance against similar funds. Abrams targets companies with a capitalization under $3 billion.

Altamira Short Term Global Income — This newer fund can lose money, but represents a good parking lot for those who can accept some risk and need to diversify away from the loonie.

Altamira Short Term Gov't Bond Fund — Great fees and a policy of investing just a little further out the yield curve than the fund above makes this one a touch riskier.

Altamira Spec. High Yield Bond — Great numbers thanks to both high-yield corporates (spreads have tightened) and emerging market debt. Risky but worth it!

Altamira Special Growth Fund — With high P/E stocks, this fund and its group are lagging the bank-loving market we've had lately. But the growth argument remains compelling.

Altamira U.S. Larger Company Fund — Ainsworth played the midcaps for a while and did well. Now he's back to the bigger names. But this is a pricey group today, so be careful!

AMI Private Capital Equity — This fund has shown middle-of-the-road performance against similar funds. It shows top-notch performance in bull markets but has been hit hard in bear markets. Annual fees are reasonable for this reasonably performing fund.

AMI Private Capital Income — This fund has shown middle-of-the-road performance against similar funds along with performing better than most in all market conditions. Annual fees are reasonable for this reasonably performing closet indexer.

AMI Private Capital Money Market — This fund has off-the-charts performance overall vs. its peers. No wonder performance has been so good for this actively managed fund, its fees are among the lowest in its group.

AMI Private Capital Optimix — This fund has shown middle-of-the-road performance against similar funds. Lower annual expenses than most bode well for the future of this fund.

APEX Asian Pacific Fund — This fund has been unimpressive so far; it's performed better than most in bull markets but it's been hit hard in bear markets.

APEX Balanced Allocation Fund — This fund has been a dog. High expenses exacerbate the problem for this actively managed fund.

APEX Canadian Stock Fund — This newer fund isn't yet a dog – but could be in time. High expenses are an obstacle here too.

APEX Equity Growth Fund — This fund has been set apart from its peers by its weak returns, with disappointing results in bull and bear markets. Again, high expenses are an issue.

Legend: ★ = overall past performance vs. similar funds (5 ★ max). Boxes show the quartile performance for a fund each calendar year vs. only similar funds (□ is the best score possible). ● = high; ◐ = average; and ● = a fund with low expenses.

Overall Past Performance	Fund Name	Type	88	89	90	91	92	93	94	95	96	Sep-97	Up	Down	% of Time Losing $	Biggest Drop	Date	No. of Mo's to Recover	MER
★	**APEX Fixed Income Fund**	FixInc							□	□	□	□	D	D	9%	-10%	2/1/94	15	2.27 ●
★★★	**APEX Global Equity Fund**	FgnEq										□	N/A	N/A	0%	-7%	8/1/97	N/A	2.80 ●
★	**APEX Growth & Income Fund**	Balan									□	□	N/A	N/A	0%	-2%	8/1/97	N/A	2.55 ●
★↗	**APEX Money Market Fund**	FixInc								□			N/A	N/A	0%	0%		N/A	1.55 ●
★	**APEX Mortgage Fund**	FixInc									□	□	N/A	N/A	0%	-1%	3/1/97	2	2.00 ●
★★★	**APEX U.S. Equity Fund**	USEq										□	N/A	N/A	0%	-7%	8/1/97	N/A	2.80 ●
★★	**Associate Investors Ltd.**	CdnEq			□	□	□	□	□	□	□	□	D	A	21%	-34%	4/1/81	23	2.09 ◐
★★★↗	**Atlas American Advantage Value**	USEq										□	N/A	N/A	0%	-5%	6/1/96	3	2.60 ●
★★	**Atlas Amer. Large Cap Growth Fund**	USEq	□	□	□	□	□	□	□	□	□	□	D	C	15%	-24%	9/1/87	42	2.67 ●
★	**Atlas American Money Market ($US)**	FixInc										□	N/A	N/A	0%	0%		N/A	1.19 ◐
★	**Atlas American RSP Index Fund**	USEq										□	N/A	N/A	0%	-6%	2/1/97	3	1.61 ◐
★★	**Atlas Canadian Balanced Fund**	Balan	□	□	□	□	□	□	□	□	□	□	D	A	11%	-9%	2/1/94	13	2.26 ●
★★	**Atlas Canadian Bond Fund**	FixInc		□	□	□	□	□	□	□	□	□	C	A	6%	-10%	2/1/94	14	1.97 ●
★↗	**Atlas Cdn. Dividend Growth Fund**	CdnEq										□	N/A	N/A	0%	-2%	8/1/97	N/A	2.50 ●

APEX Fixed Income Fund — Would I be boring you to use the dog reference again? How 'bout the fee problem again too?

APEX Global Equity Fund — Just as weak out of the gate as its mongrel brethren, I'm afraid.

APEX Growth & Income Fund — New and weak. Not cheap either. Big surprise.

APEX Money Market Fund — At a buck and a half, you could predict that this one won't light up the charts. And indeed, it doesn't.

APEX Mortgage Fund — If you're looking for consistency – man, this is it!

APEX U.S. Equity Fund — Not a bad start really. We'll have to wait and see.

Associate Investors Ltd. — Managed by Toronto firm Leon Frazer, this grand-daddy is all big-cap, all value and all-Canadian. Too bad it's underwhelmed investors.

Atlas American Advantage Value — Thank DuPont, Citicorp and McDonnell Douglas for the big wins lately. Thank OpCap Advisors for finding them.

Atlas Amer. Large Cap Growth Fund — A real upturn is under way – as you would expect from any big-cap fund in a big-cap rally. The great returns of the last few years come from a new guy. Watch him.

Atlas American Money Market ($US)

Atlas American RSP Index Fund — I'm in favour of these derivative funds for people whose savings are all tied up in their RRSPs. This one's got low fees.

Atlas Canadian Balanced Fund — Like many Atlas domestic funds, this one's turned way up lately. Jarislowsky, Fraser & Co. run it.

Atlas Canadian Bond Fund — If you like The Bank Credit Analyst, you'd like this fund. The same people are behind it. Of course, the expenses kill it.

Atlas Cdn. Dividend Growth Fund — High fees and a slow start go hand in hand for this Bissett-managed fund.

Legend: ★ = overall past performance vs. similar funds (5 ★ max). Boxes show the quartile performance for a fund each calendar year vs. only similar funds (☐ is the best score possible). ● = high; ● = average; and ● = a fund with low expenses.

(Performance Trend boxes transcribed as quartile numbers: 1 = top quartile … 4 = bottom quartile.)

Consistency			Performance Trend										Risk						Efficiency
Overall Past Performance	Fund Name	Type	88	89	90	91	92	93	94	95	96	Sep-97	Up	Down	% of Time Losing $	Biggest Drop	Date	No. of Mo's to Recover	MER
★★★	**Atlas Canadian Emerging Growth Fund** As Wayne Deans predicted, this fund cooled off in '97. Where it goes next depends on whether you think he was lucky or smart on Bre-X.	CdnEq								1	2	4	N/A	N/A	0%	–10%	3/1/97	N/A	2.50 ●
★★	**Atlas Canadian Emerging Value Fund** Less gold has helped. But the story has been big caps. So this fund won't really move until the page turns to small caps.	CdnEq								3	2	2	N/A	N/A	5%	–11%	8/1/95	6	2.61 ●
★★★★	**Atlas Canadian High Yield Bond Fund** Doug Knight simply has more experience studying more corporate bonds than anyone in Canada. And he doesn't use rating agencies!	FixInc								4	1	1	N/A	N/A	0%	–1%	12/1/94	2	1.88 ●
★★★	**Atlas Canadian Large Cap Growth** Here's a nationally available, low minimum investment, no load way to buy Bissett's excellent management.	CdnEq	2	3	2	3	4	4	1	2	1	1	B	B	28%	–27%	8/1/87	23	2.47 ●
★	**Atlas Canadian Large Cap Value Fund** Managed by RT Capital, this one's moving to cyclical stocks. RT's done well with the fund of late, despite the 2.66 annual clip.	CdnEq								4	4	4	N/A	N/A	0%	–5%	6/1/96	4	2.66 ●
★★★½	**Atlas Canadian Money Market Fund**	FixInc	2	3	2	3	3	3	2	3	3	3	N/A	N/A	0%	0%		N/A	1.10 ●
★★★½	**Atlas Cdn. Small-Cap Growth Fund** With a full 1% more in expenses annually versus the Bissett Small Cap Fund it clones, this poor cousin's never gonna keep pace.	CdnEq										4	N/A	N/A	0%	–6%	3/1/97	2	2.89 ●
★	**Atlas Canadian T-Bill Fund**	FixInc	2	3	3	3	3	4	3	4	3	4	N/A	N/A	0%	0%		N/A	1.30 ●
★★★	**Atlas European Value Fund** The case for Europe right now is very powerful, but few Canadians own it. Pictet run this from the continent, and they're good.	FgnEq							1	2	1	2	B	N/A	0%	–6%	5/1/94	3	2.84 ●
★★	**Atlas Global Value Fund** As you'd expect, this one is light on the rich US market, which isn't helping. But being a contrarian is a lonely job for manager IAI International.	FgnEq				3	3	2	3	3	2	3	D	C	11%	–12%	6/1/90	18	2.73 ●
★★★½	**Atlas Int'l Emerging Mkts. Growth** Three-fifty's a lot of money for expenses. Even for a fund like this. Still, it's roared in a hot market.	FgnEq										4	N/A	N/A	0%	–8%	8/1/97	N/A	3.50 ●
★★★	**Atlas Int'l Large-Cap Growth Fund** The manager's scepticism and plenty of cash are slowing this fund out of the gates. Long term, this bull's very keen.	FgnEq										4	N/A	N/A	0%	–7%	8/1/97	N/A	3.00 ●
★★★★	**Atlas Int'l RSP Index Fund** Low fees, fully Canadian content for RRSPs, and a bullish manager add up to an attractive story for investors here.	FgnEq										4	N/A	N/A	0%	–10%	8/1/97	N/A	2.06 ●
★½	**Atlas Latin American Value Fund** Banker's Trust run this one, and they've been too defensive on Brazil, the Latin star of late.	FgnEq							1	4	2	3	C	N/A	42%	–46%	3/1/94	40	2.94 ●

Legend: ★ = overall past performance vs. similar funds (5 ★ max). Boxes show the quartile performance for a fund each calendar year vs. only similar funds (□ is the best score possible). ● = high; ◐ = average; and ● = a fund with low expenses.

Overall Past Performance	Fund Name	Type	Risk Up	Risk Down	% of Time Losing $	Biggest Drop	Date	No. of Mo's to Recover	MER
★★	**Atlas Pacific Basin Value Fund**	FgnEq	A	D	74%	-26%	9/1/94	N/A	2.88 ●
	With Japan on fire, this one's lagged of late. But a focus on exporters is what'll really work, they say. Currency crises pose real risk.								
★★★	**Atlas World Bond Fund**	FixInc	C	N/A	10%	-7%	2/1/94	14	2.04 ◐
	Salomon Brothers has earned good returns for this fund by actively hedging and the right exposure to Europe. Expenses are reasonable.								
★★	**Azura Balanced Pooled**	Balan	N/A	N/A	0%	-4%	6/1/96	3	2.22 ●
	You'll pay the 2.22% ON TOP of the expenses for the underlying funds. Look out!								
★★★✓	**Azura Balanced RSP Pooled**	Balan	N/A	N/A	0%	-3%	6/1/96	3	2.22 ◐
	Again, the fees are in addition to those of the funds within this fund-of-funds. Very, very expensive.								
★	**Azura Conservative Pooled**	Balan	N/A	N/A	0%	-2%	8/1/97	N/A	2.08 ●
	Double fees are the reason I don't recommend this family.								
★★★	**Azura Growth Pooled**	FgnEq	N/A	N/A	0%	-6%	6/1/96	5	2.28 ●
	Add both layers of fees in this fund and you lose almost 5% of your money annually in expenses.								
★★	**Azura Growth RSP Pooled**	CdnEq	N/A	N/A	0%	-7%	6/1/96	3	2.23 ●
	Again, the fees are in addition to those of the funds within this fund-of-funds. Very, very expensive.								
★	**B.E.S.T. Discoveries Fund**	Labour	N/A	N/A	100%	-2%	8/1/97	N/A	
	This newer fund has been a dog. Low fees have not helped this fund.								
★★	**Batirente – Section Actions**	CdnEq	D	C	32%	-20%	9/1/89	49	1.54 ●
	This fund has been set apart from its peers by its weak returns, but it's been a top-notch performer in bull markets, with disappointing results in bear markets. Low fees have not helped this closet indexer.								
★★★	**Batirente – Section Diversifie**	Balan	B	N/A	14%	-10%	2/1/94	14	1.50 ●
	This fund has shown middle-of-the-road performance against similar funds. Lower annual expenses than most bode well for the future of this fund.								
★★★	**Batirente – Sec. Marche Monetaire**	FixInc	N/A	N/A	0%	0%		1	0.75 ●
	This fund has shown middle-of-the-road performance against similar funds. Lower annual expenses than most bode well for the future of this actively managed fund.								
★★★★★	**Batirente – Section Obligations**	FixInc	A	B	11%	-11%	2/1/94	14	1.50 ◐
	This fund has off-the-charts performance overall vs. its peers with top-notch performance in bull markets as well as performing better than most in bear markets. Reasonable fees represent bargains for this closet indexer.								
★★★	**Beutel Goodman American Equity**	USEq	C	N/A	5%	-10%	3/1/94	12	2.78 ●
	This fund has shown middle-of-the-road performance against similar funds. High expenses haven't been much of a problem for this actively managed fund.								
★★	**Beutel Goodman Balanced Fund**	Balan	C	N/A	4%	-10%	2/1/94	15	2.13 ◐
	This fund has been set apart from its peers by its weak returns. Normally I'd say that this fund has reasonable expenses compared to its peers, but poor overall performance makes that argument weak.								

Performance Trend columns (quartile boxes) shown for years: 88, 89, 90, 91, 92, 93, 94, 95, 96, Sep-97.

Legend: ★ = overall past performance vs. similar funds (5 ★ max). Boxes show the quartile performance for a fund each calendar year vs. only similar funds (□ is the best score possible). ● = high; ◐ = average; and ○ = a fund with low expenses.

Overall Past Performance	Fund Name	Type	Up	Down	% of Time Losing $	Biggest Drop	Date	No. of Mo's to Recover	MER
★★	**Beutel Goodman Canadian Equity**	CdnEq	D	D	20%	-10%	8/1/91	20	2.20
★★★	**Beutel Goodman Income Fund**	FixInc	A	D	13%	-14%	2/1/94	18	0.63
★★★	**Beutel Goodman International Equity**	FgnEq	A	N/A	23%	-14%	3/1/94	25	2.58
★★★★★	**Beutel Goodman Money Market Fund**	FixInc	N/A	N/A	0%	0%	N/A		0.63
★★★★★	**Beutel Goodman Private Balanced**	Balan	A	N/A	4%	-6%	3/1/94	12	1.10
★★★	**Beutel Goodman Private Bond**	FixInc	A	C	18%	-12%	2/1/94	15	0.70
★★★	**Beutel Goodman Small Cap Fund**	CdnEq	N/A	N/A	0%	-11%	8/1/95	4	2.56
★★	**Bissett American Equity Fund**	USEq	D	B	13%	-33%	9/1/87	44	1.50
★★★	**Bissett Bond Fund**	FixInc	A	A	4%	-10%	2/1/94	14	0.75
★★★	**Bissett Canadian Equity Fund**	CdnEq	A	B	17%	-26%	8/1/87	23	1.35
★★★	**Bissett Dividend Income Fund**	CdnEq	B	C	56%	-13%	9/1/89	20	1.50
★★★★	**Bissett Money Market Fund**	FixInc	N/A	N/A	0%	0%	N/A		0.50
★★★★	**Bissett Multinational Growth Fund**	FgnEq	N/A	N/A	0%	-4%	6/1/96	3	1.50

Beutel Goodman Canadian Equity — This fund has been set apart from its peers by its weak returns, but it's been hit hard in all market conditions. Normally I'd say that this fund has reasonable expenses compared to its peers, but poor overall performance makes that argument weak.

Beutel Goodman Income Fund — This fund has done better than most in its class with top-notch performance in bull markets but has been hit hard in bear markets. Lower annual expenses than most bode well for the future of this closet indexer.

Beutel Goodman International Equity — This fund has shown middle-of-the-road performance against similar funds. High expenses haven't been much of a problem for this actively managed fund.

Beutel Goodman Money Market Fund — This fund has off-the-charts performance overall vs. its peers. No wonder performance has been so good for this actively managed fund, its fees are among the lowest in its group.

Beutel Goodman Private Balanced — This fund has off-the-charts performance overall vs. its peers. No wonder performance has been so good for this actively managed fund, its fees are among the lowest in its group.

Beutel Goodman Private Bond — This fund has done better than most in its class with top-notch performance in bull markets but disappointing results in bear markets. Lower annual expenses than most bode well for the future of this closet indexer.

Beutel Goodman Small Cap Fund — You won't find many like this one! It's done better than most in its class. Annual fees are reasonable for this reasonably performing closet indexer.

Bissett American Equity Fund — This well-established fund has been set apart from its peers by its weak returns. Low fees have have not helped this fund.

Bissett Bond Fund — You won't find many like this older one! It's done better than most in its class with top-notch performance in all market conditions. Lower annual expenses than most bode well for the future of this closet indexer.

Bissett Canadian Equity Fund — You won't find many like this older one! It's done better than most in its class with top-notch performance in bull markets as well as performing better than most in bear markets. Lower annual expenses than most bode well for the future of this fund.

Bissett Dividend Income Fund — This fund has shown middle-of-the-road performance against similar funds. Along with performing better than most in bull markets it has been a disappointment in bear markets.

Bissett Money Market Fund — This fund has off-the-charts performance overall vs. its peers. No wonder performance has been so good for this actively managed fund, its fees are among the lowest in its group.

Bissett Multinational Growth Fund — This fund has off-the-charts performance overall vs. its peers. No wonder performance has been so good for this actively managed fund, its fees are among the lowest in its group.

Legend: ★ = overall past performance vs. similar funds (5 ★ max). Boxes show the quartile performance for a fund each calendar year vs. only similar funds (☐ is the best score possible). ● = high; ● = average; and ● = a fund with low expenses.

Consistency			Performance Trend										Risk						Efficiency	
Overall Past Performance	Fund Name	Type	88	89	90	91	92	93	94	95	96	Sep-97	Up	Down	% of Time Losing $	Biggest Drop	Date	No. of Mo's to Recover	MER	
★★★★★	**Bissett Retirement Fund** This fund has off-the-charts performance overall vs. its peers. No wonder performance has been so good for this fund, its fees are among the lowest in its group.	Balan					Q2	Q2	Q2	Q1	Q1	Q1	A	N/A	7%	–8%	2/1/94	14	0.44	●
★★★★★	**Bissett Small Cap Fund** This fund has off-the-charts performance overall vs. its peers with top-notch performance in bull markets but has been hit hard in bear markets. No wonder performance has been so good for this actively managed fund, their fees are among the lowest in its group.	CdnEq					Q2	Q1	Q2	Q2	Q1	Q1	A	D	15%	–17%	2/1/94	22	1.90	●
★★★	**BNP (Canada) Bond Fund** This fund has shown middle-of-the-road performance against similar funds with disappointing results in bull markets and better than average in bear markets. Annual fees are reasonable for this reasonably performing closet indexer.	FixInc					Q3	Q2	Q2	Q2	Q2	Q1	C	B	15%	–12%	2/1/94	16	1.69	●
★	**BNP (Canada) Canadian Money Market** This fund has been a dog. High expenses exacerbate the problem for this actively managed fund.	FixInc					Q3	Q3	Q2	Q3	Q2	Q2	N/A	N/A	0%	0%		N/A	1.26	●
★★	**BNP (Canada) Equity Fund** This fund has been set apart from its peers by its weak returns; it's been hit hard in all market conditions. High expenses exacerbate the problem for this fund.	CdnEq					Q2	Q4	Q3	Q2	Q2	Q1	D	D	10%	–9%	2/1/94	15	2.47	●
★★★	**BPI American Equity Value Fund** This fund has shown middle-of-the-road performance against similar funds with disappointing results in bull markets and better than average in bear markets. High expenses haven't been much of a problem for this actively managed fund.	USEq			Q1	Q3	Q3	Q2	Q2	Q2	Q3	Q3	C	B	5%	–10%	7/1/90	6	2.62	●
★★★	**BPI American Small Companies Fund** This well-established fund has shown middle-of-the-road performance against similar funds. High expenses haven't been much of a problem for this actively managed fund.	USEq				N/A	Q3	Q1	Q1	Q3	Q1	Q1	C	N/A	26%	–41%	8/1/87	63	2.92	●
★★★½	**BPI Asia Pacific Fund** You won't find many new ones like this one! It's done better than most in its class. Annual fees are reasonable for this reasonably performing actively managed fund.	FgnEq										Q4	N/A	N/A	0%	–10%	7/1/97	N/A	2.80	●
★★	**BPI Canadian Balanced Fund** This fund has been set apart from its peers by its weak returns. High expenses exacerbate the problem for this actively managed fund.	Balan		Q2	Q3	Q2	Q1	Q2	Q4	Q3	Q4	Q2	D	N/A	17%	–12%	2/1/94	21	2.47	●
★	**BPI Canadian Bond Fund** This fund has been a dog. Normally I'd say that this fund has reasonable expenses compared to its peers, but poor overall performance makes that argument weak.	FixInc			Q1	Q3	Q4	Q3	Q3	Q4	Q4	Q4	D	C	13%	–13%	2/1/94	20	1.50	●
★★★	**BPI Canadian Equity Value Fund** This fund has shown middle-of-the-road performance against similar funds but has been hit hard in bull markets. With better performance than most in declining markets, high expenses haven't been much of a problem for this actively managed fund.	CdnEq			Q1	Q2	Q1	Q2	Q4	Q1	Q3	Q4	C	B	22%	–15%	2/1/94	21	2.68	●
★★★★★	**BPI Canadian Opportunities RSP Fund** This newer fund has off-the-charts performance overall vs. its peers. This actively managed fund is expensive but well worth it.	CdnEq									Q1	Q4	N/A	N/A	7%	–20%	3/1/97	N/A	2.50	●

Legend: ★ = overall past performance vs. similar funds (5 ★ max). Boxes show the quartile performance for a fund each calendar year vs. only similar funds (□ is the best score possible). ● = high; ◐ = average; and ○ = a fund with low expenses.

Overall Past Performance	Fund Name	Type	Performance Trend (88–Sep-97)	Up	Down	% of Time Losing $	Biggest Drop	Date	No. of Mo's to Recover	MER
★★★	**BPI Canadian Resource Fund Inc.**	CdnEq	□□□□□□□□□□□	B	A	33%	−36%	6/1/81	22	2.90
	Here is an older fund that has shown middle-of-the-road performance against similar funds. As well as performing better than most in bull markets it's been a top-notch performer in bear markets. High expenses haven't been much of a problem for this actively managed fund.									
★★⅃	**BPI Canadian Small Companies Fund**	CdnEq	□□□□□□□□□□□	C	C	29%	−24%	9/1/89	28	2.84
	This fund has been unimpressive so far with disappointing results in all market conditions. High expenses exacerbate the problem for this actively managed fund.									
★★	**BPI Dividend Income Fund**	CdnEq	□□□□□□□□□□□	D	A	10%	−8%	3/1/94	12	1.00
	Lead manager Eric Bushell has done a nice job with this fund since taking over in 1994. The roughly 50% chunk in preferred shares has led to top-notch performance in bear markets. In late 1996, this fund's MER was fixed at 1%.									
★★★★	**BPI Emerging Markets Fund**	FgnEq	□□□□	N/A	N/A	0%	−9%	8/1/97	N/A	2.99
	This newer fund has off-the-charts performance overall vs. its peers. This actively managed fund is expensive but well worth it.									
★★⅃	**BPI Global Balanced RSP Fund**	Balan	□□□□□□□□	C	N/A	8%	−6%	2/1/90	9	2.52
	This fund has been unimpressive so far. Normally I'd say that this actively managed fund has reasonable expenses compared to its peers, but poor overall performance makes that argument weak.									
★★★	**BPI Global Equity Value Fund**	FgnEq	□□□□□□□□□□□	C	A	18%	−29%	9/1/87	32	2.63
	This well-established fund has shown middle-of-the-road performance against similar funds with disappointing results in bull markets and top-notch performance in bear markets. Annual fees are reasonable for this reasonable performing actively managed fund.									
★★★★	**BPI Global Opportunities Fund**	FgnEq	□□	N/A	N/A	0%	−7%	6/1/96	5	2.50
	This fund has off-the-charts performance overall vs. its peers. Reasonable fees represent bargains for this actively managed fund.									
★★★★⅃	**BPI Global RSP Bond Fund**	FixInc	□□	N/A	N/A	0%	−4%	12/1/96	7	1.50
	Who couldn't love this one! It's a super fund overall vs. its peers. No wonder performance has been so good for this actively managed fund, its fees are among the lowest in its group.									
★★★	**BPI Global Small Companies Fund**	FgnEq	□□□□	B	N/A	20%	−9%	9/1/94	19	2.83
	Management of this fund was changed last year to BPI's new global management unit based in Florida. More than half of the fund is invested in Europe, with its US holdings being trimmed in recent months.									
★★	**BPI High Income Fund**	CdnEq	□	N/A	N/A	0%	−1%	3/1/97	2	1.25
	This newer fund has shown middle-of-the-road performance against similar fund. Lower annual expenses than most bode well for the future of this fund.									
★★★★	**BPI T-Bill Fund**	FixInc	□□□□	N/A	N/A	0%	0%	N/A	N/A	0.65
	This well-established fund has off-the-charts performance overall vs. its peers. No wonder performance has been so good for this actively managed fund, its fees are among the lowest in its group.									
★★★	**BPI U.S. Money Market ($US)**	FixInc	□□□□	N/A	N/A	0%	0%	N/A	N/A	0.65
	This newer fund has shown middle-of-the-road performance against similar funds. Lower annual expenses than most bode well for the future of this actively managed fund									
★★★★⅃	**C.I. American Fund**	USEq	□□□	A	N/A	0%	−6%	6/1/96	3	2.46
	Who couldn't love this one! It's a super fund overall vs. its peers. Reasonable fees represent bargains for this actively managed fund.									

Legend: ★ = overall past performance vs. similar funds (5 ★ max). Boxes show the quartile performance for a fund each calendar year vs. only similar funds (☐ is the best score possible). ● = high; ◐ = average; and ○ = a fund with low expenses.

Overall Past Performance	Fund Name	Type	Risk Up	Risk Down	% of Time Losing $	Biggest Drop	Date	No. of Mo's to Recover	MER
★★★	**C.I. American RSP Fund** You won't find many new ones like this one! It's done better than most in its class. Annual fees are reasonable for this reasonably performing actively managed fund.	USEq	N/A	N/A	0%	−5%	8/1/97	N/A	2.46
★★★	**C.I. American Sector Shares** You won't find many like this one! It's done better than most in its class. High expenses haven't been much of a problem for this actively managed fund.	USEq	A	N/A	0%	−6%	6/1/96	3	2.51
★★★	**C.I. Canadian Balanced** This fund has shown middle-of-the-road performance against similar funds. High expenses haven't been much of a problem for this fund.	Balan	B	N/A	2%	−6%	2/1/94	6	2.35
★★★	**C.I. Canadian Bond Fund** This fund has done better than most in its class along with performing better than most in all market conditions. Annual fees are reasonable for this reasonably performing fund.	FixInc	B	B	19%	−9%	2/1/94	14	1.65
★★	**C.I. Canadian Growth Fund** This fund has been set apart from its peers by its weak returns; it's been hit hard in all market conditions. High expenses exacerbate the problem for this fund.	CdnEq	D	D	5%	−8%	10/1/94	7	2.39
★★★★★	**C.I. Canadian Income Fund** This fund has off-the-charts performance overall vs. its peers. Reasonable fees represent bargains for this actively managed fund.	Balan	N/A	N/A	0%	−2%	3/1/97	2	1.90
★	**C.I. Canadian Sector Shares** This fund can be described as having dismal returns. High expenses exacerbate the problem for the fund, especially in declining markets.	CdnEq	D	C	36%	−29%	9/1/89	47	2.44
★★★★★	**C.I. Covington Labour-Sponsored** This fund has off-the-charts performance overall vs. its peers. Reasonable fees represent bargains for this actively managed fund.	Labour	N/A	N/A	0%	−1%	6/1/97	2	4.49
★★★	**C.I. Emerging Markets Fund** This fund has shown middle-of-the-road performance against similar funds. Annual fees are reasonable for this reasonably performing actively managed fund.	FgnEq	C	N/A	32%	−31%	10/1/94	N/A	2.92
★	**C.I. Emerging Markets Sector Shares** Here is one that is a dog. Normally I'd say that this actively managed fund has reasonable expenses compared to its peers, but poor overall performance makes that argument weak.	FgnEq	D	N/A	33%	−31%	10/1/94	N/A	2.97
★★★	**C.I. Global Bond RSP Fund** This fund has shown middle-of-the-road performance against similar funds. Annual fees are reasonable for this reasonably performing fund.	FixInc	A	N/A	21%	−5%	2/1/94	14	2.07
★★	**C.I. Global Equity RSP Fund** This fund has been set apart from its peers by its weak returns. High expenses exacerbate the problem for this actively managed fund.	FgnEq	D	N/A	28%	−14%	2/1/94	23	2.52
★★★★★	**C.I. Global Financial Serv. Sector** This newer fund has off-the-charts performance overall vs. its peers. Reasonable fees represent bargains for this actively managed fund.	FgnEq	N/A	N/A	0%	−5%	8/1/97	N/A	2.47
★★★	**C.I. Global Fund** This well-established fund has shown middle-of-the-road performance against similar funds. Along with performing better than most in bull markets it has been a disappointment in bear markets. Annual fees are reasonable for this reasonably performing actively managed fund.	FgnEq	B	C	25%	−23%	9/1/87	44	2.55

Legend: ★ = overall past performance vs. similar funds (5 ★ max). Boxes show the quartile performance for a fund each calendar year vs. only similar funds (□ is the best score possible). ● = high; ◐ = average; and ○ = a fund with low expenses.

Overall Past Performance	Fund Name	Type	Risk Up	Risk Down	% of Time Losing $	Biggest Drop	Date	No. of Mo's to Recover	MER
★★★★	C.I. Global Health Sciences Sector	Spclty	N/A	N/A	0%	-4%	8/1/97	N/A	2.48 ●
	This newer fund has off-the-charts performance overall vs. its peers. No wonder performance has been so good for this actively managed fund, its fees are among the lowest in its group.								
★★★★	C.I. Global High Yield Fund	FixInc	A	N/A	4%	-13%	10/1/94	11	2.17 ●
	This fund has off-the-charts performance overall vs. its peers. This actively managed fund is expensive but well worth it.								
★★	C.I. Global Resource Sector Shares	FgnEq	N/A	N/A	100%	-13%	2/1/97	5	2.45 ○
	This newer fund has been set apart from its peers by its weak returns. Normally I'd say that this actively managed fund has reasonable expenses compared to its peers, but poor overall performance makes that argument weak.								
★★★	C.I. Global Sector Shares	FgnEq	B	D	17%	-14%	8/1/90	9	2.60 ●
	This fund has shown middle-of-the-road performance against similar funds; it has performed better than most in bull markets but has been hit hard in bear markets. This actively managed fund is expensive but worth it in rising market conditions.								
★★★↗	C.I. Global Tech. Sector Shares	Spclty	N/A	N/A	0%	-11%	2/1/97	4	2.49 ●
	You won't find many new ones like this one! It's done better than most in its class. Lower annual expenses than most bode well for the future of this actively managed fund.								
★★★★↗	C.I. Global Telecom. Sector Shares	Spclty	N/A	N/A	0%	-4%	8/1/97	N/A	2.52 ○
	This newer fund is a super fund overall vs. its peers. Reasonable fees represent bargains for this actively managed fund.								
★★★	C.I. International Balanced Fund	Balan	N/A	N/A	0%	-3%	8/1/97	N/A	2.63 ○
	This fund has impressive past performance characteristics overall vs. its peers. Reasonable fees represent bargains for this actively managed fund.								
★★★↗	C.I. International Balanced RSP	Balan	N/A	N/A	0%	-4%	8/1/97	N/A	2.53 ○
	This fund has done better than most in its class. Annual fees are reasonable for this reasonably performing actively managed fund.								
★★	C.I. Latin American Fund	FgnEq	D	N/A	39%	-40%	2/1/94	40	2.98 ●
	This fund has been set apart from its peers by its weak returns. Normally I'd say that this actively managed fund has reasonable expenses compared to its peers, but poor overall performance makes that argument weak.								
★	C.I. Latin American Sector Shares	FgnEq	N/A	N/A	26%	-39%	10/1/94	32	3.03 ●
	Here is one that is a dog. High expenses exacerbate the problem for this fund.								
★★★★	C.I. Money Market Fund	FixInc	N/A	N/A	0%	0%	N/A	N/A	0.75 ○
	This fund has off-the-charts performance overall vs. its peers. No wonder performance has been so good for this actively managed fund, its fees are among the lowest in its group.								
★★★↗	C.I. Pacific Fund	FgnEq	D	A	17%	-25%	10/1/87	23	2.61 ○
	You won't find many like this one! It's done better than most in its class but has been hit hard in bull markets. A top-notch performer in bear markets makes this reasonably priced actively managed fund well worth it during bearish markets.								
★★	C.I. Pacific Sector Shares	FgnEq	C	A	23%	-22%	1/1/94	40	2.66 ○
	This fund has been set apart from its peers by its weak returns, with disappointing results in a bullish environment. Normally I'd say that this actively managed fund has reasonable expenses compared to its peers, but poor overall performance makes that argument weak.								

Legend: ★= overall past performance vs. similar funds (5 ★ max). Boxes show the quartile performance for a fund each calendar year vs. only similar funds (□ is the best score possible). ● = high; ◐ = average; and ● = a fund with low expenses.

Overall Past Performance	Fund Name	Type	88	89	90	91	92	93	94	95	96	Sep-97	Up	Down	% of Time Losing $	Biggest Drop	Date	No. of Mo's to Recover	MER
★	**C.I. Short-Term Sector Shares**	FixInc	□	□	□	□	□	□	□	□	□	□	N/A	N/A	0%	0%		2	0.05 ●
	This fund has been a dog. Low fees have not helped this actively managed fund.																		
★★★★	**C.I. US Money Market Fund ($US)**	FixInc				□	□	□	□	□	□	□	N/A	N/A	0%	0%		N/A	0.51 ●
	This fund has off-the-charts performance overall vs. its peers. No wonder performance has been so good for this actively managed fund, its fees are among the lowest in its group.																		
★★★	**C.I. World Bond Fund**	FixInc						□	□	□	□	□	A	N/A	18%	−6%	2/1/94	15	2.06 ◐
	This fund has shown middle-of-the-road performance against similar funds. Annual fees are reasonable for this reasonably performing actively managed fund.																		
★★★	**Caldwell Securities Associate Fund**	Balan				□	□	□	□	□	□	□	B	N/A	10%	−10%	3/1/92	13	2.98 ●
	This fund has shown middle-of-the-road performance against similar funds. High expenses haven't been much of a problem for this actively managed fund.																		
★	**Caldwell Securities International**	USEq					□	□	□	□	□	□	D	N/A	11%	−12%	2/1/92	18	3.45 ●
	This fund has been a dog. High expenses exacerbate the problem for this actively managed fund.																		
★★★	**CAMAF(Cdn-Anaest)**	CdnEq	□	□	□	□	□	□	□	□	□	□	B	A	25%	−26%	6/1/81	20	
★	**Cambridge American Growth (Sagit)**	USEq	□	□	□	□	□	□	□	□	□	□	D	N/A	51%	−32%	11/1/93	N/A	2.91 ●
	This fund has been a dog. High expenses exacerbate the problem for this actively managed fund.																		
★	**Cambridge Americas Fund (Sagit)**	FgnEq					□	N/A	□	□	□	□	N/A	N/A	27%	−33%	8/1/87	52	2.88 ●
	This well-established fund has been a dog. High expenses exacerbate the problem for this actively managed fund.																		
★★	**Cambridge Balanced Fund (Sagit)**	Balan	□	□	□	□	□	□	□	□	□	□	D	A	10%	−26%	6/1/96	N/A	2.89 ●
	This well-established fund has been set apart from its peers by its weak returns, but it's been a top-notch performer in bear markets. High fees exacerbate the problem for this actively managed fund, especially in bull markets.																		
★	**Cambridge China Fund (Sagit)**	FgnEq							N/A	N/A	□	□	N/A	N/A	73%	−33%	4/1/95	N/A	2.87 NMG
	Here is one that is a dog. Low fees have not helped this actively managed fund.																		
★	**Cambridge Global Fund (Sagit)**	FgnEq	□	□	□	□	□	□	□	□	□	□	D	D	23%	−58%	10/1/96	N/A	2.91 ●
	This well-established fund can be described as having dismal returns; it's been hit hard in all market conditions. High expenses exacerbate the problem for this actively managed fund.																		
★★	**Cambridge Growth Fund (Sagit)**	CdnEq	□	□	□	□	□	□	□	□	□	□	D	A	22%	−42%	6/1/96	N/A	2.89 ●
	This well-established fund has been set apart from its peers by its weak returns, but it's been a top-notch performer in bear markets. High fees exacerbate the problem for this actively managed fund, especially in bull markets.																		
★	**Cambridge Pacific Fund (Sagit)**	FgnEq	□	□	□	□	□	□	□	□	□	□	D	B	37%	−53%	1/1/94	N/A	2.98 ●
	Here is one that is a dog. This actively managed fund is not worth the extra bucks.																		
★	**Cambridge Precious Metals Fund**	CdnEq										□	N/A	N/A	100%	−61%	10/1/96	N/A	2.81 ●
	This newer fund has been a dog. High expenses exacerbate the problem for this actively managed fund.																		

Legend: ★ = overall past performance vs. similar funds (5 ★ max). Boxes show the quartile performance for a fund each calendar year vs. only similar funds (□ is the best score possible). ● = high; ◐ = average; and ● = a fund with low expenses.

Overall Past Performance	Fund Name	Type	Risk Up	Risk Down	% of Time Losing $	Biggest Drop	Date	No. of Mo's to Recover	MER	Efficiency
★★★	Cambridge Resource Fund (Sagit)	CdnEq	C	B	41%	-57%	6/1/96	N/A	2.92	●
★	Cambridge Special Equity (Sagit)	CdnEq	D	A	51%	-58%	6/1/96	N/A	2.88	●
★↗	Canada Life Asia Pacific S-38	FgnEq	N/A	N/A	88%	-15%	5/1/96	14	2.40	●
★★★	Canada Life Canadian Equity S-9	CdnEq	B	D	22%	-27%	7/1/81	19	2.25	◐
★★★↗	Canada Life European Equity S-37	FgnEq	N/A	N/A	0%	-5%	8/1/97	N/A	2.40	◐
★★	Canada Life Fixed Income S-19	FixInc	C	C	9%	-12%	2/1/94	18	2.00	●
★★★	Canada Life International Bond S-36	FixInc	A	N/A	3%	-4%	1/1/97	7	2.00	◐
★	Canada Life Money Market S-29	FixInc	N/A	N/A	0%	0%		1	1.25	●
★★★	Canada Life U.S. & Int. Equity S-34	FgnEq	A	C	13%	-23%	9/1/87	18	2.40	●
★★★	Canada Trust Everest AmeriGrowth	USEq	B	N/A	5%	-7%	2/1/94	12	1.48	●
★↗	Canada Trust Everest AsiaGrowth	FgnEq	D	D	50%	-23%	2/1/94	N/A	2.46	◐
	Canada Trust Everest Balanced Fund	Balan	N/A	N/A		-3%	8/1/97	N/A	2.13	◐
★★★	Canada Trust Everest Bond Fund	FixInc	B	C	8%	-12%	2/1/94	15	1.36	◐

Performance Trend columns (88 89 90 91 92 93 94 95 96 Sep-97) show quartile boxes for each fund.

Cambridge Resource Fund (Sagit): Here is an older fund that has shown middle-of-the-road performance against similar funds with disappointing results in bull markets and better than average in bear markets. High expenses haven't been much of a problem for this actively managed fund.

Cambridge Special Equity (Sagit): This well-established fund has been a dog, but it's been a top-notch performer in bear markets. High fees exacerbate the problem for this actively managed fund, especially in bull markets.

Canada Life Asia Pacific S-38: This newer fund can be described as having dismal returns. Low fees have not helped this actively managed fund.

Canada Life Canadian Equity S-9: This well-established fund has shown middle-of-the-road performance against similar funds; it has performed better than most in bull markets but has been hit hard in bear markets. Annual fees are reasonable for this reasonably performing fund.

Canada Life European Equity S-37: You won't find many new ones like this one! It's done better than most in its class. Annual fees are reasonable for this reasonably performing actively managed fund.

Canada Life Fixed Income S-19: This well-established fund has been set apart from its peers by its weak returns, with disappointing results in all market conditions. High expenses exacerbate the problem for this closet indexer.

Canada Life International Bond S-36: This fund has shown middle-of-the-road performance against similar funds. Annual fees are reasonable for this reasonably performing actively managed fund.

Canada Life Money Market S-29: This well-established fund has been a dog. High expenses exacerbate the problem for this actively managed fund.

Canada Life U.S. & Int. Equity S-34: Here is an older fund that has shown middle-of-the-road performance against similar funds with top-notch performance in bull markets but disappointing results in bear markets. Annual fees are reasonable for this reasonably performing actively managed fund.

Canada Trust Everest AmeriGrowth: This fund has shown middle-of-the-road performance against similar funds. Lower annual expenses than most bode well for the future of this fund.

Canada Trust Everest AsiaGrowth: This fund can be described as having dismal returns, but it's been hit hard in all market conditions. Normally I'd say that this actively managed fund has reasonable expenses compared to its peers, but poor overall performance makes that argument weak.

Canada Trust Everest Bond Fund: Here is an older fund that has shown middle-of-the-road performance against similar funds; along with performing better than most in bull markets it has been a disappointment in bear markets. Annual fees are reasonable for this reasonably performing closet indexer.

Legend: ★ = overall past performance vs. similar funds (5 ★ max). Boxes show the quartile performance for a fund each calendar year vs. only similar funds (□ is the best score possible). ● = high; ◐ = average; and ○ = a fund with low expenses.

Overall Past Performance	Fund Name	Type	Risk Up	Risk Down	% of Time Losing $	Biggest Drop	Date	No. of Mo's to Recover	MER
★★★◗	**Canada Trust Everest Div. Income** — This fund has done better than most in its class. High expenses haven't been much of a problem for this actively managed fund.	CdnEq	N/A	N/A	0%	−3%	8/1/97	N/A	1.96 ●
★★	**Canada Trust Everest Emerging Mkts.** — This fund has been set apart from its peers by its weak returns. High expenses exacerbate the problem for this closet indexer.	FgnEq	N/A	N/A	6%	−11%	8/1/95	9	3.53 ●
★◗	**Canada Trust Everest EuroGrowth** — This fund can be described as having dismal returns. Low fees have not helped this actively managed fund.	FgnEq	C	N/A	13%	−16%	2/1/94	23	2.30 ◐
★★★★	**Canada Trust Everest Global Growth** — This newer fund has off-the-charts performance overall vs. its peers. This actively managed fund is expensive but well worth it.	Spclty	N/A	N/A	0%	−8%	8/1/97	N/A	2.57 ●
★	**Canada Trust Everest Int'l Bond** — This fund has been a dog. Normally I'd say that this actively managed fund has reasonable expenses compared to its peers, but poor overall performance makes that argument weak.	FixInc	N/A	N/A	14%	−4%	1/1/97	N/A	2.10 ○
★★★	**Canada Trust Everest Int'l Equity** — This fund has shown middle-of-the-road performance against similar funds with disappointing results in bull markets and top-notch performance in bear markets. High expenses haven't been much of a problem for this actively managed fund.	FgnEq	C	A	25%	−16%	9/1/94	19	2.72 ●
★★◗	**Canada Trust Everest Money Market** — This well-established fund has been unimpressive so far. High expenses exacerbate the problem for this actively managed fund.	FixInc	N/A	N/A	0%	0%		N/A	1.09 ●
★★◗	**Canada Trust Everest Mortgage Fund** — This well-established fund has been unimpressive so far with disappointing results in bull markets. High expenses exacerbate the problem for this actively managed fund.	FixInc	C	B	0%	−7%	4/1/81	5	1.60 ●
★★	**Canada Trust Everest North American** — This well-established fund has been set apart from its peers by its weak returns, but it's been a top-notch performer in bear markets. High expenses exacerbate the problem for this actively managed fund, especially in declining markets.	FgnEq	D	C	24%	−31%	12/1/80	25	2.42 ●
★★★★	**Canada Trust Everest Premium Money** — This newer fund has off-the-charts performance overall vs. its peers. No wonder performance has been so good for this actively managed fund, its fees are among the lowest in its group.	FixInc	N/A	N/A	0%	0%		N/A	0.30 ○
★★	**Canada Trust Everest S/T Bond** — This newer fund has been set apart from its peers by its weak returns. Normally I'd say that this actively managed fund has reasonable expenses compared to its peers, but poor overall performance makes that argument weak.	FixInc	N/A	N/A	0%	−1%	12/1/96	5	1.31 ○
★★	**Canada Trust Everest Special Equity** — This well-established fund has been set apart from its peers by its weak returns, performing just slightly better than most in all market conditions. Low fees have not helped this actively managed fund.	CdnEq	B	B	30%	−31%	8/1/87	54	2.18 ◐
★★★	**Canada Trust Everest Stock Fund** — This fund has shown middle-of-the-road performance against similar funds with disappointing results in bull markets and top-notch performance in bear markets. Annual fees are reasonable for this reasonably performing fund.	CdnEq	C	A	15%	−13%	8/1/89	28	1.86 ◐

Legend: ★ = overall past performance vs. similar funds (5 ★ max). Boxes show the quartile performance for a fund each calendar year vs. only similar funds (☐ is the best score possible). ● = high; ◐ = average; and ○ = a fund with low expenses.

Overall Past Performance	Fund Name	Type	88	89	90	91	92	93	94	95	96	Sep-97	Up	Down	% of Time Losing $	Biggest Drop	Date	No. of Mo's to Recover	MER
★★	**Canada Trust Everest U.S. Equity** This fund has been set apart from its peers by its weak returns. Normally I'd say that this actively managed fund has reasonable expenses compared to its peers, but poor overall performance makes that argument weak.	USEq				☐	☐	☐	☐	☐	☐	☐	D	N/A	7%	-10%	9/1/91	4	2.43 ◐
★★	**Canadian Medical Discoveries Fund** This fund has been set apart from its peers by its weak returns. High expenses exacerbate the problem for this actively managed fund.	Labour									☐	☐	N/A	N/A	13%	-5%	3/1/97	N/A	5.00 ●
★↗	**Canadian Protected Fund** This fund can be described as having dismal returns. Normally I'd say that this actively managed fund has reasonable expenses compared to its peers, but poor overall performance makes that argument weak.	Splty							N/A	☐	☐	☐	N/A	N/A	9%	-6%	9/1/93	21	2.40 ◐
★	**Canadian Sci. & Tech. Growth Fund** This newer fund has been a dog. Low fees have not helped this fund.	Labour										☐	N/A	N/A	100%	-1%	3/1/97	4	
★	**Canadian Venture Opportunities Fund** This fund has been a dog. High expenses exacerbate the problem for this actively managed fund.	Labour									☐	☐	N/A	N/A	79%	-40%	3/1/94	N/A	9.11 ●
★	**Capital Alliance Ventures Inc.** This fund has shown middle-of-the-road performance against similar funds. High expenses haven't been much of a problem for this actively managed fund.	Labour									☐	☐	N/A	N/A	6%	-8%	7/1/96	N/A	4.86 ●
★★★★★	**Capstone Cash Management Fund** This fund's off-the-charts performance overall vs. its peers. No wonder performance has been so good for this actively managed fund, its fees are among the lowest in its group.	FixInc	☐	☐	☐	☐	☐	☐	☐	☐	☐	☐	N/A	N/A	0%	0%	N/A	N/A	0.60 ○
★★	**Capstone Int. Investment Trust** This fund has been set apart from its peers by its weak returns, with disappointing results in bull markets. Low fees have not helped this actively managed fund.	FgnEq	☐	☐	☐	☐	☐	☐	☐	☐	☐	☐	C	B	19%	-17%	7/1/90	7	2.14 ◐
★★★	**Capstone Investment Trust** This well-established fund has shown middle-of-the-road performance against similar funds; it has performed better than most in bear markets but has been hit hard in bear markets. Annual fees are reasonable for this reasonably performing actively managed fund.	Balan	☐	☐	☐	☐	☐	☐	☐	☐	☐	☐	B	D	14%	-19%	9/1/87	34	2.14 ◐
★★★	**Cassels Blaikie American Fund ($US)** Here is an older fund that that has shown middle-of-the-road performance against similar funds. Along with performing better than most in bull markets it has been a disappointment in bear markets. Lower annual expenses than most bode well for the future of this fund.	USEq	☐	☐	☐	☐	☐	☐	☐	☐	☐	☐	B	C	23%	-30%	7/1/83	28	1.13 ○
★★★	**Cassels Blaikie Canadian Fund** Here is an older fund that has shown middle-of-the-road performance against similar funds. As well as performing better than most in bull markets it's been a top-notch performer in bear markets. Lower annual expenses than most bode well for the future of this fund.	Balan	☐	☐	☐	☐	☐	☐	☐	☐	☐	☐	B	A	7%	-10%	8/1/87	10	1.04 ○
★★★	**CCPE Diversified Growth Fund R** This well-established fund has shown middle-of-the-road performance against similar funds along with performing better than most in all market conditions. Lower annual expenses than most bode well for the future of this fund.	Balan	☐	☐	☐	☐	☐	☐	☐	☐	☐	☐	B	B	10%	-9%	8/1/87	14	1.35 ○
★★↗	**CCPE Fixed Income Fund** This well-established fund has been unimpressive so far with disappointing results in a bullish environment. Normally I'd say that this fund has reasonable expenses compared to its peers, but poor overall performance makes that argument weak.	FixInc	☐	☐	☐	☐	☐	☐	☐	☐	☐	☐	C	A	7%	-9%	2/1/94	14	1.35 ○

Legend: ★ = overall past performance vs. similar funds (5 ★ max). Boxes show the quartile performance for a fund each calendar year vs. only similar funds (☐ is the best score possible). ● = high; ◐ = average; and ○ = a fund with low expenses.

Consistency			Performance Trend											Risk						Efficiency
Overall Past Performance	Fund Name	Type	88	89	90	91	92	93	94	95	96	Sep-97	Up	Down	% of Time Losing $	Biggest Drop	Date	No. of Mo's to Recover	MER	
★★	**CCPE Global Equity** This fund has been set apart from its peers by its weak returns. Low fees have not helped this actively managed fund.	FgnEq											N/A	N/A	0%	-8%	5/1/96	9	1.75	●
★★★	**CCPE Growth Fund R** This well-established fund has shown middle-of-the-road performance against similar funds along with performing better than most in all market conditions. Lower annual expenses than most bode well for the future of this fund.	CdnEq											B	B	24%	-19%	8/1/87	17	1.35	●
★	**CCPE Money Market Fund** This fund has been a dog. Low fees have not helped this actively managed fund.	FixInc											N/A	N/A	0%	0%		N/A	0.75	●
★★★♪	**CCPE U.S. Equity** This fund has done better than most in its class. Annual fees are reasonable for this reasonably performing actively managed fund.	USEq											N/A	N/A	0%	-6%	6/1/96	3	1.75	◐
★★	**CDA Aggressive Equity (Altamira)** This fund has been set apart from its peers by its weak returns, with disappointing results in bull markets as well as in bear markets. Low fees have not helped this actively managed fund.	CdnEq											C	D	19%	-17%	4/1/94	22	1.00	●
★★★	**CDA Balanced (KBSH)** Here is an older fund that has shown middle-of-the-road performance against similar funds with disappointing results in all market conditions. Lower annual expenses than most bode well for the future of this actively managed fund.	Balan											C	C	17%	-25%	4/1/81	22	0.97	●
★★★	**CDA Bond & Mortgage (Canagex)** Here is an older fund that has shown middle-of-the-road performance against similar funds with disappointing results in bull markets along with being hit hard in bear markets. Annual fees are reasonable for this reasonable performing actively managed fund.	FixInc											C	D	7%	-10%	2/1/94	14	0.91	◐
★	**CDA Canadian Equity (Trimark)** This newer fund has been a dog. Normally I'd say that this fund has reasonable expenses compared to its peers, but poor overall performance makes that argument weak.	CdnEq											N/A	N/A	0%	-3%	3/1/97	2	1.55	●
★★★	**CDA Common Stock (Altamira)** This well-established fund has shown middle-of-the-road performance against similar funds with disappointing results in bull markets and top-notch performance in bear markets. Lower annual expenses than most bode well for the future of this actively managed fund.	CdnEq											C	A	19%	-24%	4/1/81	19	0.96	●
★	**CDA Emerging Markets (KBSH)** Here is one that is a dog. Low fees have not helped this actively managed fund.	FgnEq											N/A	N/A	44%	-21%	6/1/96	N/A	1.45	●
★★★	**CDA European (KBSH)** This fund has shown middle-of-the-road performance against similar funds. Lower annual expenses than most bode well for the future of this actively managed fund.	FgnEq											N/A	N/A	0%	-5%	10/1/95	3	1.45	●
★★★★	**CDA Global (Trimark)** This newer fund has impressive past performance characteristics overall vs. its peers. No wonder performance has been so good for this fund, its fees are among the lowest in its group.	FgnEq											N/A	N/A	0%	-1%	4/1/97	1	1.59	●
★★★♪	**CDA International Equity (KBSH)** You won't find many like this one! It's done better than most in its class. Lower annual expenses than most bode well for the future of this actively managed fund.	FgnEq											N/A	N/A	0%	-10%	8/1/97	N/A	1.45	●

Legend: ★ = overall past performance vs. similar funds; similar funds (5 ★ max). Boxes show the quartile performance for a fund each calendar year vs. only similar funds (☐ is the best score possible). ● = high; ◐ = average; and ○ = a fund with low expenses.

Overall Past Performance	Fund Name	Type	88	89	90	91	92	93	94	95	96	Sep-97	Up	Down	% of Time Losing $	Biggest Drop	Date	No. of Mo's to Recover	MER
★★★	**CDA Money Market (Canagex)**	FixInc			☐	☐	☐	☐	☐	☐	☐	☐	N/A	N/A	0%	0%	0%	1	0.55 ●
★★	**CDA Pacific Basin (KBSH)**	FgnEq							☐	☐	☐	☐	N/A	N/A	22%	-13%	8/1/97	N/A	1.45 ●
★★★★★	**CDA Special Equity (KBSH)**	Spclty									☐	☐	N/A	N/A	0%	-5%	3/1/97	2	1.45 ●
★★★	**CDA U.S. Equity (KBSH)**	USEq									☐	☐	N/A	N/A	0%	-4%	3/1/97	1	1.20 ●
★★★★★	**Centerfire Growth Fund Inc.**	Labour									☐	☐	N/A	N/A	0%	-1%	8/1/97	N/A	1.80 ●
★	**Century DJ Fund**	USEq			☐	☐	☐	☐	☐	☐	☐	☐	D	D	19%	-35%	9/1/87	64	1.80 ●
★★★	**Chou Associates Fund**	FgnEq		☐	☐	☐	☐	☐	☐	☐	☐	☐	B	A	22%	-18%	9/1/89	18	1.96 ◐
★★★	**Chou RRSP Fund**	CdnEq		☐	☐	☐	☐	☐	☐	☐	☐	☐	C	C	20%	-16%	12/1/89	25	2.20 ◐
★★★	**CIBC Balanced Fund**	Balan							☐	☐	☐	☐	C	N/A	13%	-12%	2/1/94	21	2.05 ●
★★★	**CIBC Canadian Bond Fund**	FixInc							☐	☐	☐	☐	B	D	10%	-16%	2/1/94	19	1.50 ●
★	**CIBC Canadian Equity Fund**	CdnEq							☐	☐	☐	☐	D	C	31%	-14%	2/1/94	23	2.05 ◐
★★★	**CIBC Canadian Index Fund**	CdnEq									☐	☐	N/A	N/A	0%	-5%	3/1/97	2	1.00 ●
★	**CIBC Canadian Resource Fund**	CdnEq								☐	☐	☐	N/A	N/A	18%	-11%	6/1/96	7	2.15 ○

CDA Money Market (Canagex): This well-established fund has done better than most in its class. Lower annual expenses than most bode well for the future of this actively managed fund.

CDA Pacific Basin (KBSH): Who couldn't love this one, it's a super fund overall vs. its peers. No wonder performance has been so good for this actively managed fund, its fees are among the lowest in its group.

CDA Special Equity (KBSH): This newer fund has off-the-charts performance overall vs. its peers. No wonder performance has been so good for this closet indexer, its fees are among the lowest in its group.

CDA U.S. Equity (KBSH): This newer fund has shown middle-of-the-road performance against similar funds. Lower annual expenses than most bode well for the future of this closet indexer.

Centerfire Growth Fund Inc.: This newer fund has off-the-charts performance overall vs. its peers. No wonder performance has been so good for this closet indexer, its fees are among the lowest in its group.

Century DJ Fund: This well-established fund has been a dog; it's been hit hard in all market conditions. Low fees have not helped this actively managed fund.

Chou Associates Fund: Here is an older fund that has shown middle-of-the-road performance against similar funds. As well as performing better than most in bull markets it's been a top-notch performer in bear markets. Lower annual expenses than most bode well for the future of this actively managed fund.

Chou RRSP Fund: This well-established fund has shown middle-of-the-road performance against similar funds with disappointing results in all market conditions. Annual fees are reasonable for this reasonably performing actively managed fund.

CIBC Balanced Fund: This fund has shown middle-of-the-road performance against similar funds. Annual fees are reasonable for this reasonably performing closet indexer.

CIBC Canadian Bond Fund: This fund has shown middle-of-the-road performance against similar funds; it has performed better than most in bull markets but has been hit hard in bear markets. Annual fees are reasonable for this reasonably performing closet indexer.

CIBC Canadian Equity Fund: This fund has been a dog. Normally I'd say that this closet indexer has reasonable expenses compared to its peers, but poor overall performance makes that argument weak.

CIBC Canadian Index Fund: This newer fund has impressive past performance characteristics overall vs. its peers. No wonder performance has been so good for this actively managed fund, its fees are among the lowest in its group.

CIBC Canadian Resource Fund: This newer fund has been a dog. Normally I'd say that this actively managed fund has reasonable expenses compared to its peers, but poor overall performance makes that argument weak.

Legend: ★ = overall past performance vs. similar funds (5 ★ max). Boxes show the quartile performance for a fund each calendar year vs. only similar funds (☐ is the best score possible). ● = high; ◐ = average; and ◯ = a fund with low expenses.

Overall Past Performance	Fund Name	Type	Performance Trend (88–Sep-97)	Up	Down	% of Time Losing $	Biggest Drop	Date	No. of Mo's to Recover	MER
★★★	**CIBC Canadian Short-Term Bond**	FixInc		A	D	11%	-8%	2/1/94	14	1.25
★	**CIBC Canadian T-Bill Fund**	FixInc		N/A	N/A	0%	0%	N/A	N/A	0.95
★★	**CIBC Capital Appreciation Fund**	CdnEq		C	D	20%	-19%	2/1/94	27	2.40
★★	**CIBC Dividend Fund**	CdnEq		C	D	19%	-14%	2/1/94	23	1.80
★★	**CIBC Emerging Economies Fund**	FgnEq		N/A	N/A	0%	-13%	2/1/96	11	2.70
★★★★	**CIBC Energy Fund**	CdnEq		N/A	N/A	0%	-10%	2/1/97	5	2.00
★	**CIBC European Equity Fund**	FgnEq		N/A	N/A	0%	-5%	7/1/96	4	2.50
★★★	**CIBC Far East Prosperity Fund**	FgnEq		B	C	50%	-27%	1/1/94	N/A	2.60
★★★	**CIBC Global Bond Fund**	FixInc		N/A	N/A	0%	-4%	8/1/95	3	1.90
★★	**CIBC Global Equity Fund**	FgnEq		D	B	13%	-16%	8/1/90	16	2.40
★★★	**CIBC Global Technology Fund**	SpcIty		N/A	N/A	13%	-17%	6/1/96	7	2.25
★	**CIBC Int'l Index RRSP Fund**	FgnEq		N/A	N/A	0%	-8%	8/1/97	N/A	1.75
★★★★	**CIBC Japanese Equity Fund**	FgnEq		N/A	N/A	36%	-12%	8/1/97	N/A	2.60

CIBC Canadian Short-Term Bond — This fund has shown middle-of-the-road performance against similar funds with top-notch performance in bull markets but has been hit hard in bear markets. Annual fees are reasonable for this reasonably performing closet indexer.

CIBC Canadian T-Bill Fund — This fund has been a dog. Normally I'd say that this actively managed fund has reasonable expenses compared to its peers, but poor overall performance makes that argument weak.

CIBC Capital Appreciation Fund — This fund has been set apart from its peers by its weak returns, with disappointing results in bull markets as well as in bear markets. High expenses exacerbate the problem for this actively managed fund.

CIBC Dividend Fund — This fund has been set apart from its peers by its weak returns, with disappointing results in bull markets as well as in bear markets. Normally I'd say that this actively managed fund has reasonable fees vs. its peers, but its poor overall performance makes that argument weak.

CIBC Emerging Economies Fund — This newer fund has been set apart from its peers by its weak returns. Normally I'd say that this actively managed fund has reasonable expenses compared to its peers, but poor overall performance makes that argument weak.

CIBC Energy Fund — This newer fund has off-the-charts performance overall vs. its peers. No wonder performance has been so good for this actively managed fund, its fees are among the lowest in its group.

CIBC European Equity Fund — This newer fund has been a dog. Normally I'd say that this actively managed fund has reasonable expenses compared to its peers, but poor overall performance makes that argument weak.

CIBC Far East Prosperity Fund — This fund has been unimpressive so far performing just slightly better than most in bull markets, it's been a disappointment in bear markets. Normally I'd say that this actively managed fund has reasonable expenses compared to its peers, but poor overall performance makes that argument weak.

CIBC Global Bond Fund — This fund has shown middle-of-the-road performance against similar funds. Annual fees are reasonable for this reasonably performing actively managed fund.

CIBC Global Equity Fund — This fund has been set apart from its peers by its weak returns, but poor overall performance makes that argument weak. Normally I'd say this fund has reasonable fees, but poor overall performance makes that argument weak.

CIBC Global Technology Fund — You won't find many new ones like this one! It's done better than most in its class. Lower annual expenses than most bode well for the future of this actively managed fund.

CIBC Int'l Index RRSP Fund — This newer fund has been a dog. Low fees have not helped this actively managed fund.

CIBC Japanese Equity Fund — This newer fund has off-the-charts performance overall vs. its peers. Reasonable fees represent bargains for this actively managed fund.

Legend: ★ = overall past performance vs. similar funds (5 ★ max). Boxes show the quartile performance for a fund each calendar year vs. only similar funds (□ is the best score possible). ● = high; ◐ = average; and ○ = a fund with low expenses.

Overall Past Performance	Fund Name	Type	Risk Up	Risk Down	% of Time Losing $	Biggest Drop	Date	No. of Mo's to Recover	MER
★★★	**CIBC Latin American Fund**	FgnEq	N/A	N/A	0%	-7%	8/1/97	N/A	2.50 ●
	This newer fund has shown middle-of-the-road performance against similar funds. Lower annual expenses than most bode well for the future of this actively managed fund.								
★	**CIBC Money Market Fund**	FixInc	N/A	N/A	0%	0%		N/A	0.95 ○
	This fund has been a dog. Normally I'd say that this actively managed fund has reasonable expenses compared to its peers, but poor overall performance makes that argument weak.								
★★★	**CIBC Mortgage Fund**	FixInc	C	B	1%	-6%	3/1/94	11	1.60 ◐
	Here is an older fund that has shown middle-of-the-road performance against similar funds with disappointing results in bull markets and better than average in bear markets. Annual fees are reasonable for this reasonable performing actively managed fund.								
★★★	**CIBC North American Demographics**	FgnEq	N/A	N/A	0%	-4%	8/1/97	N/A	2.50 ●
	This newer fund has shown middle-of-the-road performance against similar funds. High expenses haven't been much of a problem for this actively managed fund.								
★	**CIBC Precious Metals Fund**	CdnEq	N/A	N/A	100%	-41%	9/1/96	N/A	2.00 ●
	This newer fund has been a dog. Low fees have not helped this actively managed fund.								
★★★★	**CIBC Premium T-Bill Fund**	FixInc	N/A	N/A	0%	0%		N/A	0.50 ○
	This fund has impressive past performance characteristics overall vs. its peers. No wonder performance has been so good for this actively managed fund, its fees are among the lowest in its group.								
★★	**CIBC U.S. Dollar Money Market ($US)**	FixInc	N/A	N/A	0%	0%		N/A	0.95 ◐
	This fund has been set apart from its peers by its weak returns. Normally I'd say that this actively managed fund has reasonable expenses compared to its peers, but poor overall performance makes that argument weak.								
★★⅂	**CIBC U.S. Equity Fund**	USEq	C	N/A	0%	-8%	9/1/91	3	2.25 ●
	This fund has been unimpressive so far. Normally I'd say that this actively managed fund has reasonable expenses compared to its peers, but poor overall performance makes that argument weak.								
★★★★★	**CIBC U.S. Index RRSP Fund**	USEq	N/A	N/A	0%	-5%	8/1/97	N/A	1.00 ●
	This newer fund has off-the-charts performance overall vs. its peers. No wonder performance has been so good for this actively managed fund, its fees are among the lowest in its group.								
★★⅂	**CIBC U.S. Opportunities Fund**	USEq	N/A	N/A	38%	-16%	6/1/96	13	2.45 ◐
	This newer fund can be described as having dismal returns. Normally I'd say that this actively managed fund has reasonable expenses compared to its peers, but poor overall performance makes that argument weak.								
★★⅂	**Clarington Canadian Balanced Fund**	Balan	N/A	N/A	0%	-2%	3/1/97	2	2.75 ●
	Check out how unimpressive this new fund has been. High expenses exacerbate the problem for this actively managed fund.								
★★★	**Clarington Canadian Equity Fund**	CdnEq	N/A	N/A	0%	-3%	3/1/97	2	2.75 ●
	This newer fund has shown middle-of-the-road performance against similar funds. High expenses haven't been much of a problem for this actively managed fund.								
★★	**Clarington Canadian Income Fund**	Balan	N/A	N/A	0%	-2%	8/1/97	N/A	1.90 ◐
	This newer fund has been set apart from its peers by its weak returns. Normally I'd say that this closet indexer has reasonable expenses compared to its peers, but poor overall performance makes that argument weak.								

Legend: ★ = overall past performance vs. similar funds (5 ★ max). Boxes show the quartile performance for a fund each calendar year vs. only similar funds (□ is the best score possible). ● = high; ◑ = average; and ○ = a fund with low expenses.

Overall Past Performance	Fund Name	Type	Up	Down	% of Time Losing $	Biggest Drop	Date	No. of Mo's to Recover	MER
★	**Clarington Canadian Small-Cap Fund**	CdnEq	N/A	N/A	0%	0%		N/A	2.75
	This newer fund has been a dog. High expenses exacerbate the problem for this fund.								
★★★★	**Clarington Global Communications**	Spclty	N/A	N/A	0%	-4%	8/1/97	N/A	2.95
	This newer fund has off-the-charts performance overall vs. its peers. This closet indexer is expensive but well worth it.								
★★	**Clarington Global Opportunities**	FgnEq	N/A	N/A	0%	-2%	3/1/97	2	2.95
	This newer fund has been set apart from its peers by its weak returns. High expenses exacerbate the problem for this actively managed fund.								
★★	**Clarington Money Market Fund**	FixInc	N/A	N/A	0%	0%		N/A	0.75
	This newer fund has been set apart from its peers by its weak returns. Low fees have not helped this actively managed fund.								
★★★★	**Clarington U.S. Equity Fund**	USEq	N/A	N/A	0%	-2%	3/1/97	1	2.95
	This newer fund has off-the-charts performance overall vs. its peers. This actively managed fund is expensive but well worth it.								
★	**Clarington U.S. Smaller Co. Growth**	USEq	N/A	N/A	0%	-11%	2/1/97	3	2.95
	This newer fund has been a dog. High expenses exacerbate the problem for this actively managed fund.								
★★★↗	**Clean Environment Balanced Fund**	Balan	B	N/A	15%	-14%	2/1/94	24	3.00
	You won't find many like this one! It's done better than most in its class. High expenses haven't been much of a problem for this actively managed fund.								
★★★↗	**Clean Environment Equity Fund**	CdnEq	A	D	16%	-19%	2/1/94	22	3.00
	This fund has done better than most in its class with top-notch performance in bull markets but has been hit hard in bear markets. High expenses haven't been much of a problem for this actively managed fund.								
★↗	**Clean Environment Income Fund**	FixInc	D	A	0%	-3%	6/1/94	1	2.59
	This fund can be described as having dismal returns, but it's been a top-notch performer in bear markets. High fees exacerbate the problem for this actively managed fund, especially in bull markets.								
★★↗	**Clean Environment Int'l Equity Fund**	FgnEq	D	N/A	21%	-13%	6/1/96	5	3.32
	This fund has been unimpressive so far. High expenses exacerbate the problem for this actively managed fund.								
★★★↗	**Co-operators Balanced Fund**	Balan	A	N/A	7%	-10%	2/1/94	15	2.07
	You won't find many like this one! It's done better than most in its class. Annual fees are reasonable for this reasonably performing fund.								
★★↗	**Co-operators Canadian Equity Fund**	CdnEq	C	D	12%	-8%	6/1/96	4	2.07
	This fund has been unimpressive so far with disappointing results in bull markets as well as in bear markets. Normally I'd say that this fund has reasonable fees vs. its peers, but its poor overall performance makes that argument weak.								
★★★	**Co-operators Fixed Income Fund**	FixInc	A	C	16%	-13%	2/1/94	15	2.07
	This fund has shown middle-of-the-road performance against similar funds with top-notch performance in bull markets but disappointing results in bear markets. High expenses haven't been much of a problem for this closet indexer.								

Legend: ★ = overall past performance vs. similar funds (5 ★ max). Boxes show the quartile performance for a fund each calendar year vs. only similar funds (□ is the best score possible). ● = high; ◐ = average; and ○ = a fund with low expenses.

Overall Past Performance	Fund Name	Type	Up	Down	% of Time Losing $	Biggest Drop	Date	No. of Mo's to Recover	MER
★★★★	**Co-operators U.S. Equity Fund**	USEq	A	N/A	0%	-17%	6/1/96	7	2.07 ◐
	This fund has off-the-charts performance overall vs. its peers. Reasonable fees represent bargains for this actively managed fund.								
★★	**Colonia Bond Fund**	FixInc	D	A	14%	-9%	2/1/94	14	1.74 ◐
	This fund has been set apart from its peers by its weak returns, but it's been a top-notch performer in bear markets. Normally I'd say that this fund has reasonable expenses compared to its peers, but poor overall performance makes that argument weak.								
★⋆	**Colonia Equity Fund**	CdnEq	D	D	24%	-15%	2/1/94	23	2.43 ●
	This fund can be described as having dismal returns; it's been hit hard in all market conditions. High expenses exacerbate the problem for this actively managed fund.								
★★★	**Colonia Money Market Fund**	FixInc	N/A	N/A	0%	-1%	9/1/92	1	1.07 ◐
	This fund has shown middle-of-the-road performance against similar funds. Annual fees are reasonable for this reasonably performing actively managed fund.								
★★	**Colonia Mortgage Fund**	FixInc	C	B	2%	-4%	2/1/94	11	2.01 ●
	This fund has been set apart from its peers by its weak returns, with disappointing results in bull markets. High expenses exacerbate the problem for this actively managed fund.								
★★★★	**Colonia Special Growth Fund**	CdnEq	A	C	14%	-13%	2/1/94	15	2.43 ◐
	This fund has off-the-charts performance overall vs. its peers with top-notch performance in bull markets but disappointing results in bear markets. Reasonable fees represent bargains for this actively managed fund.								
★★⋆	**Colonia Strategic Balanced Fund**	Balan	N/A	N/A	0%	-3%	8/1/97	N/A	0.27 ◐
	This newer fund has been unimpressive so far. Low fees have not helped this actively managed fund.								
★★★⋆	**Common Sense Asset Builder 1**	Balan	A	N/A	0%	-4%	3/1/94	5	2.25 ●
	You won't find many like this one! It's done better than most in its class. High expenses haven't been much of a problem for this actively managed fund.								
★★★⋆	**Common Sense Asset Builder 2**	Balan	A	N/A	0%	-3%	3/1/94	5	2.26 ●
	Who couldn't love this one! It's a super fund overall vs. its peers. This actively managed fund is expensive but well worth it.								
★★★★	**Common Sense Asset Builder 3**	Balan	A	N/A	0%	-3%	3/1/94	5	2.25 ●
	This fund has off-the-charts performance overall vs. its peers. This actively managed fund is expensive but well worth it.								
★★★⋆	**Common Sense Asset Builder 4**	Balan	A	N/A	0%	-2%	3/1/94	5	2.25 ●
	Who couldn't love this one! It's a super fund overall vs. its peers. Reasonable fees represent bargains for this actively managed fund.								
★★★★	**Common Sense Asset Builder 5**	Balan	A	N/A	0%	-3%	3/1/94	5	2.26 ●
	This fund has off-the-charts performance overall vs. its peers. This actively managed fund is expensive but well worth it.								
★★	**Concorde Balanced Fund**	Balan	N/A	N/A	0%	-3%	3/1/97	2	1.95 ◐
	This fund has been set apart from its peers by its weak returns. Normally I'd say that this actively managed fund has reasonable expenses compared to its peers, but poor overall performance makes that argument weak.								

Column group headers: Consistency | Performance Trend (88, 89, 90, 91, 92, 93, 94, 95, 96, Sep-97) | Risk | Efficiency

Legend: ★ = overall past performance for a fund each calendar year vs. similar funds. only similar funds (5 ★ max). Boxes show the quartile performance for a fund each calendar year vs. similar funds (□ is the best score possible). ● = high; ◐ = average; and ○ = a fund with low expenses.

Overall Past Performance	Fund Name	Type	Performance Trend 88–Sep-97	Risk Up	Risk Down	% of Time Losing $	Biggest Drop	Date	No. of Mo's to Recover	MER
★★★	**Concorde Croissance**	CdnEq		B	D	9%	-9%	2/1/94	15	2.18
	This fund has shown middle-of-the-road performance against similar funds; it has performed better than most in bull markets but has been hit hard in bear markets. Annual fees are reasonable for this reasonably performing fund.									
★★★★	**Concorde Dividend Fund**	CdnEq		N/A	N/A	0%	-3%	1/1/95	2	1.90
	This fund has off-the-charts performance overall vs. its peers. Reasonable fees represent bargains for this actively managed fund.									
★	**Concorde Hypotheques**	FixInc		D	C	4%	-7%	2/1/94	13	1.92
	Here is one that is a dog, but it's been a top-notch performer in bear markets. High expenses exacerbate the problem for this actively managed fund, especially in declining markets.									
★	**Concorde International Fund**	FgnEq		N/A	N/A	0%	-8%	6/1/96	11	2.38
	Here is one that is a dog. Normally I'd say that this actively managed fund has reasonable expenses compared to its peers, but poor overall performance makes that argument weak.									
★★	**Concorde Monetaire**	FixInc		N/A	N/A	0%	0%	N/A	N/A	1.17
	This fund has been set apart from its peers by its weak returns. High expenses exacerbate the problem for this actively managed fund.									
★	**Concorde Revenu**	FixInc		D	B	16%	-12%	2/1/94	15	1.96
	This fund can be described as having dismal returns. This closet indexer is not worth the extra bucks.									
★	**Contrarian Strategy Futures L.P.**	Spclty		N/A	N/A	29%	-26%	11/1/95	N/A	1.20
	This fund can be described as having dismal returns. Low fees have not helped this actively managed fund.									
★	**Contrarian Strategy RRSP Futures**	Spclty		N/A	N/A	100%	-21%	3/1/96	N/A	2.50
	This newer fund has been a dog. Normally I'd say that this actively managed fund has reasonable expenses compared to its peers, but poor overall performance makes that argument weak.									
★★★	**Cornerstone Balanced Fund**	Balan		C	D	23%	-32%	6/1/81	22	2.67
	This well-established fund has shown middle-of-the-road performance against similar funds with disappointing results in bull markets along with being hit hard in bear markets. This fund is expensive but worth it in rising market conditions.									
★★★	**Cornerstone Bond Fund**	FixInc		C	A	8%	-12%	4/1/87	9	1.60
	Here is an older fund that has shown middle-of-the-road performance against similar funds with disappointing results in bull markets and top-notch performance in bear markets. Annual fees are reasonable for this reasonable performing closet indexer.									
★★★	**Cornerstone Cdn Growth**	CdnEq		B	C	23%	-25%	9/1/87	52	2.50
	Here is an older fund that has shown middle-of-the-road performance against similar funds. Along with performing better than most in bull markets it has been a disappointment in bear markets. High expenses haven't been much of a problem for this fund.									
★★★	**Cornerstone Global Fund**	FgnEq		C	A	13%	-31%	9/1/87	51	2.75
	Here is an older fund that has shown middle-of-the-road performance against similar funds with disappointing results in bull markets and top-notch performance in bear markets. High expenses haven't been much of a problem for this actively managed fund.									

Legend: ★ = overall past performance vs. similar funds (5 ★ max). Boxes show the quartile performance for a fund each calendar year vs. only similar funds [□ is the best score possible). ● = high; ◐ = average; and ◑ = a fund with low expenses.

Overall Past Performance	Fund Name	Type	Performance Trend 88–Sep-97	Risk Up	Risk Down	% of Time Losing $	Biggest Drop	Date	No. of Mo's to Recover	MER
★	**Cornerstone Gov Money**	FixInc		N/A	N/A	0%	0%		N/A	1.30 ●
	This fund can be described as having dismal returns. High expenses exacerbate the problem for this actively managed fund.									
★★	**Cornerstone U.S. Fund**	USEq		D	B	15%	-32%	9/1/87	52	2.84 ●
	This well-established fund has been set apart from its peers by its weak returns. This fund is not worth the extra bucks.									
	Cote 100 Amerique	FgnEq		N/A	N/A		-2%	8/1/97	N/A	2.00 ◑
★★★	**Cote 100 Amerique REER**	CdnEq		A	D	19%	-20%	2/1/94	22	2.00 ◑
	This fund has done better than most in its class with top-notch performance in bull markets but has been hit hard in bear markets. Annual fees are reasonable for this reasonably performing actively managed fund.									
	Cote 100 EXP	CdnEq		N/A	N/A		-1%	8/1/97	N/A	2.00 ●
★	**Cote 100 REA – Action**	CdnEq		N/A	N/A	13%	-14%	3/1/97	N/A	2.00 ●
	This newer fund has been a dog. Low fees have not helped this actively managed fund.									
★	**Cote 100 U.S.**	USEq		N/A	N/A	0%	-6%	12/1/96	5	2.06 ●
	This newer fund can be described as having dismal returns. Low fees have not helped this closet indexer.									
★★	**Cundill Security Fund**	CdnEq		D	A	30%	-27%	8/1/89	48	2.02 ●
	This well-established fund has been set apart from its peers by its weak returns, but it's been a top-notch performer in bear markets. Its low expenses have not helped this actively managed fund.									
★★★	**Cundill Value Fund**	FgnEq		B	A	8%	-16%	2/1/80	5	2.02 ◐
	Here is an older fund that has shown middle-of-the-road performance against similar funds. As well as performing better than most in bull markets it's been a top-notch performer in bear markets. Lower annual expenses than most bode well for the future of this actively managed fund.									
★★★	**DGC Entertainment Ventures Corp.**	Labour		N/A	N/A	19%	-6%	2/1/96	4	4.80 ●
	This fund has shown middle-of-the-road performance against similar funds. High expenses haven't been much of a problem for this actively managed fund.									
★★	**Dominion Equity Resource Fund Inc.**	CdnEq		C	C	68%	-74%	6/1/81	N/A	2.10 ◐
	This well-established fund has been set apart from its peers by its weak returns, with disappointing results in all market conditions. Low fees have not helped this actively managed fund.									
★★★	**Dynamic Americas Fund**	USEq		B	A	18%	-24%	9/1/87	22	2.48 ●
	Here is an older fund that has shown middle-of-the-road performance against similar funds. As well as performing better than most in bull markets it's been a top-notch performer in bear markets. High expenses haven't been much of a problem for this actively managed fund.									
★★	**Dynamic Canadian Growth Fund**	CdnEq		C	D	27%	-36%	8/1/87	65	2.49 ●
	This well-established fund has been set apart from its peers by its weak returns; it's performed better than most in bull markets but it's been hit hard in bear markets. High expenses exacerbate the problem for this actively managed fund.									

Legend: ★ = overall past performance vs. similar funds (5 ★ max). Boxes show the quartile performance for a fund each calendar year vs. only similar funds (□ is the best score possible). ● = high; ◐ = average; and ○ = a fund with low expenses.

Overall Past Performance	Fund Name	Type	Sep-97	Up	Down	% of Time Losing $	Biggest Drop	Date	No. of Mo's to Recover	MER
★★★★	Dynamic Canadian Real Estate Fund	Spclty	N/A	N/A	N/A	0%	-3%	3/1/97	3	
★★★	Dynamic Dividend Fund	CdnEq		B	B	7%	-7%	2/1/94	15	1.60
★★◐	Dynamic Dividend Growth Fund	CdnEq		C	B	18%	-11%	1/1/90	21	1.83
★★★	Dynamic Europe Fund	FgnEq		A	N/A	33%	-24%	8/1/90	40	2.64
★★★◗	Dynamic Far East Fund	FgnEq		A	B	4%	-15%	7/1/97	N/A	3.57
★★★	Dynamic Fund of Canada	CdnEq		B	B	23%	-33%	4/1/81	23	2.47
★★★	Dynamic Global Bond Fund	FixInc		B	N/A	3%	-14%	2/1/91	10	1.88
★★	Dynamic Global Millennia Fund	Spclty		C	N/A	45%	-24%	2/1/94	25	2.65
★★★	Dynamic Global Partners Fund	Balan		C	N/A	0%	-5%	8/1/94	9	2.60
★★★★	Dynamic Global Precious Metals Fund	Spclty		N/A	N/A	25%	-98%	9/1/96	N/A	2.97
★★★	Dynamic Global Resources Fund	FgnEq		N/A	N/A	5%	-13%	11/1/94	14	2.80
★★★	Dynamic Government Income Fund	FixInc		A	C	24%	-18%	1/1/92	6	0.85
★	Dynamic Income & Growth Fund	FixInc		N/A	N/A	0%	-4%	8/1/97	N/A	

Dynamic Canadian Real Estate Fund — Anne McLean makes a good case for the recovering commercial real estate sector here in Canada. The liquidity problem that plagued real estate funds in the past is bypassed by investing strictly in REITs and stocks of real estate companies.

Dynamic Dividend Fund — This fund is a rarity in a category filled with common stock funds. Lesley Beech's focus on preferred shares still managed to perform above average in all market conditions. More sensitive than most to interest rate movements.

Dynamic Dividend Growth Fund — A heavier emphasis on common shares compared to its more conservative sister fund. Overall performance has been choppy, but better in recent years.

Dynamic Europe Fund — This fund has shown middle-of-the-road performance against similar funds. High expenses haven't been much of a problem for this actively managed fund.

Dynamic Far East Fund — This fund has done better than most in its class with top-notch performance in bull markets as well as performing better than most in bear markets. High expenses haven't been much of a problem for this actively managed fund.

Dynamic Fund of Canada — Here is an older fund that has shown middle-of-the-road performance against similar funds; it performs better than most in all market conditions. High expenses haven't been much of a problem for this actively managed fund.

Dynamic Global Bond Fund — Bond ace Norm Bengough has posted good results with no down years. Performance has suffered since 1996.

Dynamic Global Millennia Fund — This well-established fund has been set apart from its peers by its weak returns. Normally I'd say that this actively managed fund has reasonable expenses compared to its peers, but poor overall performance makes that argument weak.

Dynamic Global Partners Fund — This fund has shown middle-of-the-road performance against similar funds. Annual fees are reasonable for this reasonably performing actively managed fund.

Dynamic Global Precious Metals Fund — This fund holds more than half of its assets in Canada. The fundamentals of gold are very compelling!

Dynamic Global Resources Fund — This fund has shown middle-of-the-road performance against similar funds. High expenses haven't been much of a problem for this actively managed fund.

Dynamic Government Income Fund — This fund has shown middle-of-the-road performance against similar funds with top-notch performance in bull markets but disappointing results in bear markets. Lower annual expenses than most bode well for the future of this closet indexer.

Dynamic Income & Growth Fund — This newer fund has been a dog. Low fees have not helped this fund.

Legend: ★ = overall past performance for a fund each calendar year vs. similar funds (5 ★ max). Boxes show the quartile performance for a fund each calendar year vs. only similar funds (☐ is the best score possible). ● = high; ◐ = average; and ○ = a fund with low expenses.

Overall Past Performance	Fund Name	Type	Risk Up	Risk Down	% of Time Losing $	Biggest Drop	Date	No. of Mo's to Recover	MER
★★★	**Dynamic Income Fund**	FixInc	B	A	2%	−11%	2/1/81	9	1.68
	Lead manager Norm Bengough has put up decent performance and an excellent risk profile. Has never had a losing year since its inception in 1979.								
★★	**Dynamic International Fund**	FgnEq	B	B	27%	−44%	10/1/87	74	2.78
	This well-established fund has been set apart from its peers by its weak returns. This actively managed fund is not worth the extra bucks.								
★	**Dynamic Money Market Fund**	FixInc	N/A	N/A	0%	0%	N/A	N/A	0.79
	This well-established fund has been a dog. Normally I'd say that this actively managed fund has reasonable expenses compared to its peers, but poor overall performance makes that argument weak.								
★★★↗	**Dynamic Partners Fund**	Balan	A	N/A	11%	−8%	1/1/90	13	2.38
	Usually a top-notch performer in hot markets, but not in the last couple of years. A couple of missed market calls have left this actively managed fund trailing in recent years. Expect this one to bounce back.								
★★★	**Dynamic Precious Metals Fund**	CdnEq	C	A	43%	−38%	6/1/96	N/A	2.49
	Goodman tells a compelling story that points to a surge in gold prices by the end of the decade. Goodman knows his stuff; he is one of the only fund managers to completely steer clear of the Bre-X scam.								
★★★↗	**Dynamic Quebec Fund**	CdnEq	N/A	N/A	0%	−3%	3/1/97	2	
	This newer fund has done better than most in its class. Lower annual expenses than most bode well for the future of this fund.								
★★★	**Dynamic Real Estate Equity Fund**	Spclty	N/A	N/A	0%	−3%	7/1/96	1	3.24 NMG
	This mostly US real estate fund holds no direct ownership in properties. Anne McLean buys only quality real estate companies and REITs for this fund, which has so far shown sizzling performance!								
★★	**Dynamic Team Fund**	Balan	C	B	16%	−11%	8/1/87	21	0.86
	Here is an older fund that has shown middle-of-the-road performance against similar funds with disappointing results in bull markets and better than average in bear markets. Lower annual expenses than most bode well for the future of this actively managed fund.								
★★	**Elliott & Page American Growth Fund**	USEq	D	A	17%	−31%	9/1/87	52	1.16
	This well-established fund has been set apart from its peers by its weak returns, but it's been a top-notch performer in bear markets. Its low expenses have not helped this actively managed fund.								
★★★	**Elliott & Page Asian Growth Fund**	FgnEq	N/A	N/A	25%	−15%	8/1/97	N/A	1.36
	This fund has shown middle-of-the-road performance against similar funds. Lower annual expenses than most bode well for the future of this fund.								
★★★	**Elliott & Page Balanced Fund**	Balan	B	N/A	26%	−10%	2/1/94	15	1.99
	This fund has shown middle-of-the-road performance against similar funds. Annual fees are reasonable for this reasonably performing fund.								
★	**Elliott & Page Bond Fund**	FixInc	D	D	10%	−12%	2/1/94	20	1.71
	This fund has been a dog, but it's been hit hard in all market conditions. Normally I'd say that this closet indexer has reasonable expenses compared to its peers, but poor overall performance makes that argument weak.								
★★★	**Elliott & Page Emerging Markets**	FgnEq	N/A	N/A	33%	−24%	9/1/94	33	1.61
	This fund has shown middle-of-the-road performance against similar funds. Lower annual expenses than most bode well for the future of this fund.								

Performance Trend columns: 88, 89, 90, 91, 92, 93, 94, 95, 96, Sep-97 (shown as quartile boxes)

Legend: ★ = overall past performance vs. similar funds (5 ★ max). Boxes show the quartile performance for a fund each calendar year vs. only similar funds (□ is the best score possible). ● = high; ◐ = average; and ○ = a fund with low expenses.

			Performance Trend											Risk						Efficiency
Overall Past Performance	Fund Name	Type	88	89	90	91	92	93	94	95	96	Sep-97	Up	Down	% of Time Losing $	Biggest Drop	Date	No. of Mo's to Recover	MER
★★★	**Elliott & Page Equity Fund**	CdnEq		□	□	□	□	□	□	□	□	□	A	C	15%	-20%	9/1/89	25	1.95 ◐
	This fund has shown middle-of-the-road performance in bull markets but disappointing results in bear markets. Annual fees are reasonable for this reasonably performing fund.																		
★★	**Elliott & Page Global Balanced Fund**	Balan								□	□	□	N/A	N/A	0%	-6%	8/1/95	5	1.96 ●
	This fund has been set apart from its peers by its weak returns. Low fees have not helped this fund.																		
★★	**Elliott & Page Global Bond Fund**	FixInc								□	□	□	N/A	N/A	8%	-6%	7/1/95	5	1.60 ●
	This fund has been set apart from its peers by its weak returns. Low fees have not helped this fund.																		
★★★	**Elliott & Page Global Equity Fund**	FgnEq							□	□	□	□	N/A	N/A	0%	-10%	9/1/94	10	1.51 ●
	This fund has shown middle-of-the-road performance against similar funds. Lower annual expenses than most bode well for the future of this fund.																		
★	**Elliott & Page T-Bill Fund**	FixInc								□	□	□	N/A	N/A	0%	0%	N/A	N/A	1.95 ●
	This fund has been a dog. High expenses exacerbate the problem for this actively managed fund.																		
★★	**Empire Asset Allocation Fund**	Balan									□	□	D	N/A	0%	-2%	3/1/97	2	2.57 ●
	This fund has been set apart from its peers by its weak returns. High expenses exacerbate the problem for this actively managed fund.																		
★★★	**Empire Balanced Fund**	Balan			□	□	□	□	□	□	□	□	B	N/A	11%	-8%	2/1/94	15	2.57 ●
	This fund has shown middle-of-the-road performance against similar funds. High expenses haven't been much of a problem for this fund.																		
★★	**Empire Bond Fund**	FixInc			□	□	□	□	□	□	□	□	C	B	11%	-10%	2/1/94	15	2.18 ●
	This well-established fund has been set apart from its peers by its weak returns, with disappointing results in bull markets. High expenses exacerbate the problem for this closet indexer.																		
★★★	**Empire Elite Equity Fund 5**	CdnEq		□	□	□	□	□	□	□	□	□	B	C	21%	-32%	9/1/87	64	2.57 ●
	Here is an older fund that has shown middle-of-the-road performance against similar funds. Along with performing better than most in bull markets it has been a disappointment in bear markets. High expenses haven't been much of a problem for this fund.																		
★★★★	**Empire Equity Growth Fund 3**	CdnEq		□	□	□	□	□	□	□	□	□	A	C	23%	-24%	6/1/81	18	1.28 ●
	This well-established fund has impressive past performance characteristics overall vs. its peers with top-notch performance in bull markets but disappointing results in bear markets. No wonder performance has been so good for this fund, its fees are among the lowest in its group.																		
★	**Empire Foreign Curr. Cdn Bond Fund**	FixInc								□	□	□	N/A	N/A	33%	-6%	7/1/95	24	2.18 ●
	This fund has been a dog. High expenses exacerbate the problem for this actively managed fund.																		
★★★	**Empire International Fund**	FgnEq							□	□	□	□	C	A	10%	-11%	2/1/94	16	2.57 ○
	This fund has shown middle-of-the-road performance with disappointing results in bull markets and top-notch performance in bear markets. Annual fees are reasonable for this reasonably performing actively managed fund.																		
★	**Empire Money Market Fund**	FixInc				□	□	□	□	□	□	□	N/A	N/A	0%	0%	9/1/92	1	1.54 ●
	This fund has been a dog. High expenses exacerbate the problem for this actively managed fund.																		

Legend: ★ = overall past performance vs. similar funds (5 ★ max). Boxes show the quartile performance for a fund each calendar year vs. only similar funds (☐ is the best score possible). ● = high; ◐ = average; and ● = a fund with low expenses.

THE ULTIMATE FUND TABLES 169

Consistency			Performance Trend										Risk						Efficiency
Overall Past Performance	Fund Name	Type	88	89	90	91	92	93	94	95	96	Sep-97	Up	Down	% of Time Losing $	Biggest Drop	Date	No. of Mo's to Recover	MER
★★★	**Empire Premier Equity Fund 1**	CdnEq	☐	☐	☐	☐	☐	☐	☐	☐	☐	☐	A	B	20%	-27%	5/1/81	19	1.54
	This well-established fund has shown middle-of-the-road performance against similar funds with top-notch performance in bull markets as well as performing better than most in bear markets. Lower annual expenses than most bode well for the future of this fund.																		
★★	**Equitable Life Asset Allocation**	Balan						☐	☐	☐	☐	☐	N/A	N/A	0%	-3%	12/1/96	5	2.25
	This fund has been set apart from its peers by its weak returns. High expenses exacerbate the problem for this actively managed fund.																		
★✦	**Equitable Life Canadian Bond Fund**	FixInc						☐	☐	☐	☐	☐	D	B	18%	-11%	2/1/94	16	2.00
	This fund can be described as having dismal returns. This closet indexer is not worth the extra bucks.																		
★★	**Equitable Life Canadian Stock Fund**	CdnEq						☐	☐	☐	☐	☐	D	D	4%	-7%	2/1/94	6	2.25
	This fund has been set apart from its peers by its weak returns, but it's been hit hard in all market conditions. Normally I'd say that this fund has reasonable expenses compared to its peers, but poor overall performance makes that argument weak.																		
★★★	**Equitable Life International Fund**	FgnEq						☐	☐	☐	☐	☐	N/A	N/A	4%	-11%	11/1/94	12	2.75
	This fund has shown middle-of-the-road performance against similar funds. High expenses haven't been much of a problem for this actively managed fund.																		
★	**Equitable Life Money Market Fund**	FixInc						☐	☐	☐	☐	☐	N/A	N/A	0%	0%		N/A	1.75
	This fund has been a dog. High expenses exacerbate the problem for this actively managed fund.																		
★	**Equitable Life Mortgage Fund**	FixInc						☐	☐	☐	☐	☐	N/A	N/A	0%	-2%	2/1/96	6	2.25
	This fund has been a dog. High expenses exacerbate the problem for this actively managed fund.																		
★★★✦	**Equitable Life Segregated Accum Inc**	FixInc	☐	☐	☐	☐	☐	☐	☐	☐	☐	☐	A	C	5%	-11%	2/1/94	15	0.44
	You won't find many like this older one! It's done better than most in its class with top-notch performance in bull markets but disappointing results in bear markets. Lower annual expenses than most bode well for the future of this closet indexer.																		
★★★	**Equitable Life Seg. Common Stock**	CdnEq	☐	☐	☐	☐	☐	☐	☐	☐	☐	☐	C	B	20%	-25%	8/1/87	69	1.04
	This well-established fund has shown middle-of-the-road performance against similar funds along with performing better than most in all market conditions. Lower annual expenses than most bode well for the future of this fund.																		
★★★	**Ethical Balanced Fund**	Balan						☐	☐	☐	☐	☐	B	N/A	6%	-11%	2/1/94	15	2.06
	This fund has shown middle-of-the-road performance against similar funds. Annual fees are reasonable for this reasonably performing actively managed fund.																		
★★	**Ethical Global Bond Fund**	FixInc						☐	☐	☐	☐	☐	N/A	N/A	0%	-3%	12/1/96	7	2.39
	This fund has been set apart from its peers by its weak returns. High expenses exacerbate the problem for this actively managed fund.																		
★★★	**Ethical Growth Fund**	CdnEq				☐	☐	☐	☐	☐	☐	☐	B	A	18%	-11%	2/1/94	15	2.14
	This well-established fund has shown middle-of-the-road performance against similar funds. As well as performing better than most in bull markets it's been a top-notch performer in bear markets. Annual fees are reasonable for this reasonably performing fund.																		

Legend: ★ = overall past performance vs. similar funds (5 ★ max). Boxes show the quartile performance for a fund each calendar year vs. only similar funds (□ is the best score possible). ● = high; ◐ = average; and ● = a fund with low expenses.

Overall Past Performance	Fund Name	Type	Risk Up	Risk Down	% of Time Losing $	Biggest Drop	Date	No. of Mo's to Recover	MER
★★	**Ethical Income Fund** — This well-established fund has been unimpressive so far with disappointing results in all market conditions. Normally I'd say this fund has reasonable fees, but poor overall performance makes that argument weak.	FixInc	C	C	8%	−13%	2/1/94	15	1.62
★★★	**Ethical Money Market Fund** — This well-established fund has impressive past performance characteristics overall vs. its peers. This actively managed fund is expensive but well worth it.	FixInc	N/A	N/A	0%	0%	N/A	N/A	1.24
★★	**Ethical North American Equity Fund** — This well-established fund has been set apart from its peers by its weak returns, but it's been a top-notch performer in bear markets. High fees exacerbate the problem for this actively managed fund, especially in bull markets.	USEq	D	A	22%	−26%	6/1/81	18	2.49
★★★	**Ethical Pacific Rim Fund** — This fund has done better than most in its class. High expenses haven't been much of a problem for this actively managed fund.	FgnEq	N/A	N/A	0%	−12%	8/1/97	N/A	3.22
★★	**Ethical Special Equity Fund** — This fund can be described as having dismal returns. Normally I'd say that this actively managed fund has reasonable expenses compared to its peers, but poor overall performance makes that argument weak.	CdnEq	N/A	N/A	0%	−6%	6/1/96	4	2.61
★★★	**Ferique American Fund** — You won't find many new ones like this one! It's done better than most in its class. Lower annual expenses than most bode well for the future of this actively managed fund.	USEq	N/A	N/A	0%	−5%	8/1/97	N/A	0.65
★★★	**Ferique Balanced Fund** — This well-established fund has shown middle-of-the-road performance against similar funds with top-notch performance in bull markets with disappointing results in bear markets. Lower annual expenses than most bode well for the future of this actively managed fund.	Balan	A	C	10%	−15%	6/1/81	16	0.44
★★★	**Ferique Bond Fund** — This well-established fund has shown middle-of-the-road performance against similar funds along with performing better than most in all market conditions. Lower annual expenses than most bode well for the future of this fund.	FixInc	B	B	13%	−22%	7/1/79	37	0.60
★★★	**Ferique Equity Fund**	CdnEq	A	B	22%	−41%	6/1/81	22	
★	**Ferique Growth Fund**	CdnEq	N/A	N/A	14%	−8%	6/1/96	5	
★★★	**Ferique International Fund** — This fund has shown middle-of-the-road performance against similar funds. Lower annual expenses than most bode well for the future of this fund.	FgnEq	C	N/A	27%	−9%	9/1/94	16	0.95
★★★★	**Ferique Short Term Income Fund**	FixInc	N/A	N/A	0%	−2%	5/1/79	1	
★	**FESA Enterprise Venture Capital**	Labour	N/A	N/A	53%	−5%	2/1/97	N/A	
★★★	**Fidelity Asset Manager Fund** — This fund has shown middle-of-the-road performance against similar funds. Annual fees are reasonable for this reasonably performing actively managed fund.	Balan	B	N/A	17%	−7%	2/1/94	22	2.69
★★★★	**Fidelity Canadian Asset Allocation** — This fund has off-the-charts performance overall vs. its peers. This actively managed fund is expensive but well worth it.	Balan	N/A	N/A	0%	−4%	6/1/96	2	2.56

Legend: ★ = overall past performance vs. similar funds (5 ★ max). Boxes show the quartile performance for a fund each calendar year vs. only similar funds (□ is the best score possible). ● = high; ◐ = average; and ○ = a fund with low expenses.

Overall Past Performance	Fund Name	Type	Risk Up	Risk Down	% of Time Losing $	Biggest Drop	Date	No. of Mo's to Recover	MER
★★◗	**Fidelity Canadian Bond Fund**	FixInc	C	D	8%	–13%	2/1/94	21	1.34
★★★◗	**Fidelity Canadian Growth Company**	CdnEq	N/A	N/A	0%	–4%	3/1/97	2	2.65
★★★★	**Fidelity Canadian Income Fund**	FixInc	N/A	N/A	0%	–1%	12/1/96	5	1.25
★	**Fidelity Cdn. Short Term Asset Fund**	FixInc	N/A	N/A	0%	0%		N/A	1.25
★★★	**Fidelity Capital Builder Fund**	CdnEq	C	B	21%	–16%	2/1/94	22	2.53
★★★★	**Fidelity Emerging Markets Bond Fund**	FixInc	A	N/A	25%	–21%	10/1/94	14	2.35
★★★★	**Fidelity Emerging Markets Portfolio**	FgnEq	N/A	N/A	6%	–41%	3/1/97	N/A	3.44
★★★◗	**Fidelity European Growth Fund**	FgnEq	A	N/A	0%	–7%	7/1/92	8	2.80
★★★★	**Fidelity Far East Fund**	FgnEq	C	A	11%	–23%	1/1/94	24	2.83
★★★★◗	**Fidelity Growth America Fund**	USEq	A	N/A	3%	–6%	9/1/94	5	2.33
★★★	**Fidelity International Portfolio**	FgnEq	B	C	13%	–20%	8/1/90	16	2.76
★★★	**Fidelity Japanese Growth Fund**	FgnEq	A	C	69%	–35%	7/1/94	N/A	3.13
★★★	**Fidelity Latin American Growth Fund**	FgnEq	C	N/A	41%	–47%	10/1/94	31	3.50

Fidelity Canadian Bond Fund — This fund has been unimpressive so far with disappointing results in bull markets as well as in bear markets. Normally I'd say that this fund has reasonable fees vs. its peers, but its poor overall performance makes that argument weak.

Fidelity Canadian Growth Company — Alan Radlo has done a super job with this fund. This rare fund missed the small-cap meltdown of 1997 by avoiding heavy exposure to golds and resources. Expenses are high but worth it!

Fidelity Canadian Income Fund — This fund has off-the-charts performance overall vs. its peers. Reasonable fees represent bargains for this actively managed fund.

Fidelity Cdn. Short Term Asset Fund — This fund has been a dog. High expenses exacerbate the problem for this actively managed fund.

Fidelity Capital Builder Fund — This fund has shown middle-of-the-road performance against similar funds with disappointing results in bull markets and better than average in bear markets. Annual fees are reasonable for this reasonably performing actively managed fund.

Fidelity Emerging Markets Bond Fund — This fund has off-the-charts performance overall vs. its peers. This actively managed fund is expensive but well worth it.

Fidelity Emerging Markets Portfolio — This fund has off-the-charts performance overall vs. its peers. This closet indexer is expensive but well worth it.

Fidelity European Growth Fund — This fund has done better than most in its class. High expenses haven't been much of a problem for this fund.

Fidelity Far East Fund — K.C. Lee still believes that Hong Kong is the place to be in Asia. Sticking to his convictions is what has led this fund to the top of the charts. This remains an aggressive play on Asian markets with Hong Kong representing well over half of the fund.

Fidelity Growth America Fund — Manager Brad Lewis has navigated this fund past more than half of its competition in each of the last seven years. Expenses for this fund are reasonable, especially in light of Fidelity's massive research staff.

Fidelity International Portfolio — Dick Habermann is the captain of this ship and he makes good use of Fidelity's regional specialists around the world. A rise in the Canadian dollar will cut into the profits of this and all global funds.

Fidelity Japanese Growth Fund — This fund has shown middle-of-the-road performance against similar funds with top-notch performance in bull markets but disappointing results in bear markets. High expenses haven't been much of a problem for this fund.

Fidelity Latin American Growth Fund — This fund has shown middle-of-the-road performance against similar funds. High expenses haven't been much of a problem for this actively managed fund.

Legend: ★ = overall past performance vs. similar funds (5 ★ max). Boxes show the quartile performance for a fund each calendar year vs. only similar funds (□ is the best score possible). ● = high; ◐ = average; and ○ = a fund with low expenses.

Overall Past Performance	Fund Name	Type	Up	Down	% of Time Losing $	Biggest Drop	Date	No. of Mo's to Recover	MER
★★★	**Fidelity North American Income Fund**	FixInc	C	N/A	32%	-15%	2/1/94	N/A	1.75 ●
	This fund has shown middle-of-the-road performance against similar funds. Lower annual expenses than most would bode well for the future of this actively managed fund.								
★ ↗	**Fidelity RSP Global Bond Fund**	FixInc	D	N/A	29%	-11%	2/1/94	15	2.51 ●
	This fund can be described as having dismal returns. High expenses exacerbate the problem for this actively managed fund.								
★★★	**Fidelity Small-Cap America Fund**	USEq	B	N/A	4%	-11%	10/1/95	7	2.66 ●
	This fund has shown middle-of-the-road performance against similar funds. High expenses haven't been much of a problem for this actively managed fund.								
★★★ ↗	**Fidelity True North Fund**	CdnEq	N/A	N/A	0%	-2%	2/1/97	3	2.48 ●
	You won't find many new ones like this one! It's done better than most in its class. High expenses haven't been much of a problem for this actively managed fund.								
★	**Fidelity U.S. Money Market ($US)**	FixInc	N/A	N/A	0%	0%	N/A	N/A	1.25 ●
	This fund has been a dog. High expenses exacerbate the problem for this actively managed fund.								
★	**First American (Guardian Timing)**	FgnEq	D	N/A	30%	-9%	9/1/93	22	2.80 ●
	This fund has been a dog. High expenses exacerbate the problem for this actively managed fund.								
★★	**First Cdn. Asset Allocation**	Balan	D	N/A	17%	-13%	2/1/94	17	2.09 ◐
	This fund has been set apart from its peers by its weak returns. Normally I'd say that this closet indexer has reasonable expenses compared to its peers, but poor overall performance makes that argument weak.								
★★★	**First Canadian Bond Fund**	FixInc	C	C	9%	-12%	2/1/94	15	1.58 ○
	This fund has shown middle-of-the-road performance against similar funds with disappointing results in all market conditions. Annual fees are reasonable for this reasonably performing closet indexer.								
★★★★ ↗	**First Canadian Dividend Income Fund**	CdnEq	N/A	N/A	0%	-4%	8/1/97	N/A	1.66 ○
	This fund is a super fund overall vs. its peers. Reasonable fees represent bargains for this actively managed fund.								
★★★	**First Canadian Emerging Mkts Fund**	FgnEq	N/A	N/A	20%	-26%	12/1/94	29	2.07 ●
	This fund has shown middle-of-the-road performance against similar funds. Lower annual expenses than most would bode well for the future of this actively managed fund.								
★★	**First Canadian Equity Index**	CdnEq	B	D	27%	-21%	9/1/89	43	1.48 ○
	This fund has been set apart from its peers by its weak returns; it's performed better than most in bull markets but it's been hit hard in bear markets. Low fees have not helped this closet indexer.								
★ ↗	**First Canadian European Growth Fund**	FgnEq	N/A	N/A	0%	-5%	8/1/95	6	2.19 ●
	This fund can be described as having dismal returns. Low fees have not helped this actively managed fund.								
★★★★ ↗	**First Canadian Far East Growth Fund**	FgnEq	N/A	N/A	5%	-12%	8/1/97	N/A	2.17 ●
	This fund is a super fund overall vs. its peers. No wonder performance has been so good for this actively managed fund, its fees are among the lowest in its group.								
★★★★	**First Canadian Global Sci. & Tech.**	Spclty	N/A	N/A	0%	-5%	2/1/97	2	2.01 ●
	This newer fund has off-the-charts performance overall vs. its peers. No wonder performance has been so good for this closet indexer, its fees are among the lowest in its group.								

Legend: ★ = overall past performance vs. similar funds (5 ★ max). Boxes show the quartile performance for a fund each calendar year vs. only similar funds (□ is the best score possible). ● = high; ◐ = average; and ● = a fund with low expenses.

Consistency			Performance Trend											Risk						Efficiency
Overall Past Performance	Fund Name	Type	88	89	90	91	92	93	94	95	96	Sep-97	Up	Down	% of Time Losing $	Biggest Drop	Date	No. of Mo's to Recover	MER
★★★	First Cdn. Growth Fund	CdnEq											A	D	19%	-13%	2/1/94	17	2.21
	This fund has shown middle-of-the-road performance against similar funds with top-notch performance in bull markets but has been hit hard in bear markets. Annual fees are reasonable for this reasonably performing fund.																		
★★★	First Cdn. International Bond Fund	FixInc											B	N/A	6%	-5%	1/1/97	N/A	1.97
	This fund has shown middle-of-the-road performance against similar funds. Annual fees are reasonable for this reasonably performing actively managed fund.																		
★★	First Canadian International Growth	FgnEq											D	N/A	21%	-9%	8/1/94	16	2.15
	This fund has been set apart from its peers by its weak returns. Normally I'd say that this fund has reasonable expenses compared to its peers, but poor overall performance makes that argument weak.																		
★★	First Canadian Japanese Growth Fund	FgnEq											N/A	N/A	70%	-27%	11/1/94	N/A	2.06
	This fund has been set apart from its peers by its weak returns. Low fees have not helped this actively managed fund.																		
★★★	First Canadian Latin American Fund	FgnEq											N/A	N/A	0%	-9%	8/1/97	N/A	1.88
	This newer fund has shown middle-of-the-road performance against similar funds. Lower annual expenses than most bode well for the future of this closet indexer.																		
★	First Canadian Money Market	FixInc											N/A	N/A	0%	0%		N/A	1.13
	This fund has been a dog. High expenses exacerbate the problem for this actively managed fund.																		
★★	First Canadian Mortgage Fund	FixInc											D	D	2%	-6%	2/1/94	13	1.47
	This well-established fund has been set apart from its peers by its weak returns; it's been hit hard in all market conditions. Low fees have not helped this actively managed fund.																		
★★	First Canadian N/AFTA Advantage Fund	FgnEq											N/A	N/A	5%	-10%	11/1/94	7	2.00
	This fund has been set apart from its peers by its weak returns. Normally I'd say that this actively managed fund has reasonable expenses compared to its peers, but poor overall performance makes that argument weak.																		
★★★★	First Canadian Precious Metals Fund	CdnEq											N/A	N/A	100%	-33%	3/1/97	N/A	2.07
	This newer fund has off-the-charts performance overall vs. its peers. No wonder performance has been so good for this closet indexer; its fees are among the lowest in its group.																		
★★★	First Cdn. Resource Fund	CdnEq											C	D	35%	-19%	2/1/94	24	2.20
	This fund has shown middle-of-the-road performance against similar funds with disappointing results in bull markets along with being hit hard in bear markets. Annual fees are reasonable for this reasonably performing actively managed fund.																		
★★	First Cdn. Special Growth Fund	CdnEq											B	D	29%	-24%	2/1/94	25	2.17
	This fund has shown middle-of-the-road performance than most but it's been hit hard in bull markets but it's been hit hard in bear markets. Low fees have not helped this fund.																		
★?	First Cdn. T-Bill Fund	FixInc											N/A	N/A	0%	0%		N/A	1.06
	This fund can be described as having dismal returns. Normally I'd say that this actively managed fund has reasonable expenses compared to its peers, but poor overall performance makes that argument weak.																		
★★★★	First Canadian U.S. Equity Index	USEq											N/A	N/A	0%	-6%	8/1/97	N/A	1.16
	This newer fund has off-the-charts performance overall vs. its peers. No wonder performance has been so good for this closet indexer; its fees are among the lowest in its group.																		

Legend: ★ = overall past performance vs. similar funds (5 ★ max). Boxes show the quartile performance for a fund each calendar year vs. only similar funds [ ] is the best score possible). ● = high; ● = average; and ● = a fund with low expenses.

Overall Past Performance	Fund Name	Type	Up	Down	% of Time Losing $	Biggest Drop	Date	No. of Mo's to Recover	MER
★★★	First Cdn. U.S. Growth Fund	USEq	C	N/A	12%	–9%	8/1/95	15	2.21
	This fund has shown middle-of-the-road performance against similar funds. Annual fees are reasonable for this reasonably performing actively managed fund.								
★	First Canadian U.S. Special Growth	USEq	N/A	N/A	0%	–10%	2/1/97	3	1.72
	This newer fund has been a dog. Low fees have not helped this closet indexer.								
★★★★	First Canadian U.S. Value Fund	USEq	N/A	N/A	0%	–2%	3/1/97	1	1.75
	This newer fund has off-the-charts performance overall vs. its peers. Reasonable fees represent bargains for this closet indexer.								
★	First Heritage Fund	CdnEq	D	B	43%	–38%	8/1/87	70	5.16
	This well-established fund has been a dog. This actively managed fund is not worth the extra bucks.								
★★★	Fonds D'Investissement REA	CdnEq	N/A	N/A	0%	0%	N/A	N/A	2.36
★★★	Fonds de Professionnels Balanced	Balan	C	A	7%	–7%	2/1/94	13	0.75
	Here is an older fund that has shown middle-of-the-road performance against similar funds with disappointing results in bull markets and top-notch performance in bear markets. Lower annual expenses than most bode well for the future of this fund.								
★★★	Fonds de Professionnels Bond	FixInc	B	A	4%	–8%	2/1/94	15	0.75
	Here is an older fund that has shown middle-of-the-road performance against similar funds. As well as performing better than most in bull markets it's been a top-notch performer in bear markets. Lower annual expenses than most bode well for the future of this actively managed fund.								
★★♪	Fonds de Professionnels Cdn. Equity	CdnEq	C	C	28%	–17%	9/1/89	42	0.75
	This fund has been unimpressive so far with disappointing results in all market conditions. Low fees have not helped this fund.								
★★♪	Fonds de Professionnels Growth & Inc	Balan	N/A	N/A	0%	–4%	6/1/96	4	0.75
	This fund has been unimpressive so far. Low fees have not helped this actively managed fund.								
★★♪	Fonds de Professionnels Intl Equity	FgnEq	C	N/A	0%	–5%	8/1/97	N/A	0.75
	This fund has been unimpressive so far. Low fees have not helped this actively managed fund.								
★★★★	Fonds de Professionnels Short Term	FixInc	N/A	N/A	12%	0%	N/A	1	0.40
	This fund has off-the-charts performance overall vs. its peers. No wonder performance has been so good for this actively managed fund, its fees are among the lowest in its group.								
★	Fonds de Sold. des Trav. du Quebec	CdnEq	D	B	0%	0%		5	
★★	Fonds Desjardins Actions	CdnEq	C	C	30%	–27%	8/1/87	23	1.94
	This well-established fund has been set apart from its peers by its weak returns, with disappointing results in all market conditions. Normally I'd say this fund has reasonable fees, but poor overall performance makes that argument weak.								
★	Fonds Desjardins Croissance	USEq	D	N/A	13%	–11%	2/1/94	17	1.00
	Here is one that is a dog. Low fees have not helped this actively managed fund.								

Legend: ★ = overall past performance vs. similar funds (5 ★ max). Boxes show the quartile performance for a fund each calendar year vs. only similar funds (□ is the best score possible). ● = high; ◐ = average; and ● = a fund with low expenses.

Overall Past Performance	Fund Name	Type	Performance Trend (88–Sep-97)	Risk Up	Risk Down	% of Time Losing $	Biggest Drop	Date	No. of Mo's to Recover	MER
★★★★	**Fonds Desjardins Divers. Ambitieux**	Balan		N/A	N/A	0%	-4%	8/1/97	N/A	2.17
	This newer fund has off-the-charts performance overall vs. its peers. Reasonable fees represent bargains for this fund.									
★	**Fonds Desjardins Divers. Audacieux**	Balan		N/A	N/A	0%	-3%	8/1/97	N/A	1.97
	Here is one that is a dog. Normally I'd say that this actively managed fund has reasonable expenses compared to its peers, but poor overall performance makes that argument weak.									
★★	**Fonds Desjardins Divers. Modere**	Balan		N/A	N/A	0%	-2%	8/1/97	N/A	1.72
★	**Fonds Desjardins Divers. Secure**	Balan		N/A	N/A	0%	-1%	8/1/97	N/A	1.72
	Here is one that is a dog. Low fees have not helped this actively managed fund.									
★★★	**Fonds Desjardins Dividendes**	CdnEq		A	D	7%	-10%	2/1/94	15	1.94
	This fund has shown middle-of-the-road performance against similar funds with top-notch performance in bull markets but has been hit hard in bear markets. Annual fees are reasonable for this reasonably performing actively managed fund.									
★★	**Fonds Desjardins Environnement**	CdnEq		C	D	14%	-13%	2/1/94	15	2.12
	This fund has been set apart from its peers by its weak returns, with disappointing results in bull markets as well as in bear markets. Normally I'd say that this fund has reasonable fees vs. its peers, but its poor overall performance makes that argument weak.									
★★	**Fonds Desjardins Equilibre**	Balan		C	C	17%	-11%	4/1/87	18	1.94
	This well-established fund has been set apart from its peers by its weak returns, with disappointing results in all market conditions. Normally I'd say this fund has reasonable fees, but poor overall performance makes that argument weak.									
★	**Fonds Desjardins Hypotheques**	FixInc		D	C	1%	-4%	2/1/94	12	1.62
	This well-established fund has been a dog, with disappointing results in bear markets. Normally I'd say that this actively managed fund has reasonable expenses compared to its peers, but poor overall performance makes that argument weak.									
★★★	**Fonds Desjardins International**	FgnEq		A	D	17%	-27%	9/1/87	32	2.37
	Here is an older fund that has shown middle-of-the-road performance against similar funds with top-notch performance in bull markets but has been hit hard in bear markets. Annual fees are reasonable for this reasonable performing actively managed fund.									
★★	**Fonds Desjardins Marche Americain**	USEq		N/A	N/A	0%	-4%	8/1/97	N/A	2.25
	This newer fund has been set apart from its peers by its weak returns. Normally I'd say that this actively managed fund has reasonable expenses compared to its peers, but poor overall performance makes that argument weak.									
★★	**Fonds Desjardins Mondial Equilibre**	Balan		N/A	N/A	0%	-4%	8/1/97	N/A	2.18
	This newer fund can be described as having dismal returns. Low fees have not helped this actively managed fund.									
★	**Fonds Desjardins Monetaire**	FixInc		N/A	N/A	0%	0%	8/1/97	1	1.11
	This fund has been a dog. High expenses exacerbate the problem for this actively managed fund.									

Legend: ★ = overall past performance vs. similar funds (5 ★ max). Boxes show the quartile performance for a fund each calendar year vs. only similar funds (□ is the best score possible). ● = high; ◐ = average; and ● = a fund with low expenses.

Overall Past Performance	Fund Name	Type	Performance Trend 88	89	90	91	92	93	94	95	96	Sep-97	Risk Up	Down	% of Time Losing $	Biggest Drop	Date	No. of Mo's to Recover	MER
★	**Fonds Desjardins Obligations** This well-established fund has been a dog; it has been hit hard in all market conditions. Normally I'd say that this closet indexer has reasonable expenses compared to its peers, but poor overall performance makes that argument weak.	FixInc	□	□	□	□	□	□	□	□	□	□	D	D	9%	-12%	2/1/94	16	1.63
★	**Fonds Ficadre Actions** This well-established fund has been a dog; it has been hit hard in all market conditions. Normally I'd say that this actively managed fund has reasonable expenses compared to its peers, but poor overall performance makes that argument weak.	CdnEq	□	□	□	□	□	□	□	□	□	□	D	D	35%	-46%	4/1/87	114	2.12
★★★	**Fonds Ficadre Equilibre** Here is an older fund that has shown middle-of-the-road performance against similar funds with disappointing results in bull markets along with being hit hard in bear markets. Annual fees are reasonable for this reasonable performing actively managed fund.	Balan	□	□	□	□	□	□	□	□	□	□	C	D	17%	-20%	8/1/87	28	2.13
★	**Fonds Ficadre Hypotheques** This newer fund has been a dog. High expenses exacerbate the problem for this actively managed fund.	FixInc								□	□	□	N/A	N/A	0%	-1%	12/1/96	6	1.66
★★★	**Fonds Ficadre Money Market** This fund has shown middle-of-the-road performance against similar funds. Annual fees are reasonable for this reasonably performing actively managed fund.	FixInc	□	□	□	□	□	□	□	□	□	□	N/A	N/A	0%	0%		N/A	1.07
★	**Fonds Ficadre Obligations** This fund has been a dog; it's been hit hard in all market conditions. Normally I'd say that this fund has reasonable expenses compared to its peers, but poor overall performance makes that argument weak.	FixInc	□	□	□	□	□	□	□	□	□	□	D	D	8%	-11%	2/1/94	15	1.63
★★★↗	**Fonds Optimum Actions** This fund has been unimpressive so far; it's performed better than most in bull markets but it's been hit hard in bear markets. Normally I'd say that this fund has reasonable fees vs. its peers, but its poor overall performance makes that argument weak.	CdnEq	□	□	□	□	□	□	□	□	□	□	B	D	9%	-14%	2/1/94	22	1.62
★★★★	**Fonds Optimum Epargne** This well-established fund has impressive past performance characteristics overall vs. its peers. No wonder performance has been so good for this actively managed fund, its fees are among the lowest in its group.	FixInc	□	□	□	□	□	□	□	□	□	□	N/A	N/A	0%	-1%	1/1/91	2	0.75
★★↗	**Fonds Optimum Equilibre** This well-established fund has been unimpressive so far with disappointing results in bull markets. Low fees have not helped this actively managed fund.	Balan	□	□	□	□	□	□	□	□	□	□	C	B	13%	-10%	2/1/94	14	1.41
★★★	**Fonds Optimum Internationales** This fund has shown middle-of-the-road performance against similar funds. Annual fees are reasonable for this reasonably performing closet indexer.	FgnEq							□	□	□	□	N/A	N/A	13%	-5%	8/1/97	N/A	1.90
★★★↗	**Fonds Optimum Obligations** This well-established fund has done better than most in its class with top-notch performance in bull markets but has been hit hard in bear markets. Annual fees are reasonable for this reasonably performing closet indexer.	FixInc	□	□	□	□	□	□	□	□	□	□	A	D	7%	-12%	2/1/94	14	1.41
★★★	**Franklin U.S. Small-Cap Growth Fund** This newer fund has shown middle-of-the-road performance against similar funds. Lower annual expenses than most bode well for the future of this fund.	USEq									□	□	N/A	N/A	0%	0%		N/A	N/A

Legend: ★ = overall past performance vs. similar funds (5 ★ max). Boxes show the quartile performance for a fund each calendar year vs. only similar funds (□ is the best score possible). ● = high; ◑ = average; and ● = a fund with low expenses.

Consistency			Performance Trend	Risk		Efficiency			
Overall Past Performance	Fund Name	Type	88 89 90 91 92 93 94 95 96 Sep-97	Up	Down	% of Time Losing $	Biggest Drop	Date	No. of Mo's to Recover
★★★	Friedberg Currency Fund	Spclty		N/A	N/A	21%	−31%	12/1/96	N/A
	This fund has shown middle-of-the-road performance against similar funds. Lower annual expenses than most bode well for the future of this actively managed fund.								
★↗	Friedberg Diversified Fund ($US)	Balan		N/A	N/A	0%	−14%	2/1/97	5
	This newer fund can be described as having dismal returns. High expenses exacerbate the problem for this actively managed fund.								
★	Friedberg Double Gold Plus Fund	CdnEq		D	A	63%	−53%	1/1/88	N/A
★★★★	Friedberg Foreign Bond Fund	FixInc		N/A	N/A	0%	−4%	1/1/97	4
	This newer fund has off-the-charts performance overall vs. its peers. No wonder performance has been so good for this actively managed fund, its fees are among the lowest in its group.								
★★★↗	GBC Canadian Bond Fund	FixInc		A	B	6%	−12%	2/1/94	15
	This well-established fund has done better than most in its class with top-notch performance in bull markets as well as performing better than most in bear markets. Lower annual expenses than most bode well for the future of this closet indexer.								
★★★★★	GBC Canadian Growth Fund	CdnEq		A	A	19%	−19%	1/1/90	14
	This fund has off-the-charts performance overall vs. its peers with top-notch performance in all market conditions. No wonder performance has been so good for this actively managed fund, its fees are among the lowest in its group.								
★	GBC International Growth Fund	FgnEq		D	B	40%	−23%	8/1/90	36
	Here is one that is a dog. Normally I'd say this fund has reasonable fees, but poor overall performance makes that argument weak.								
★★★★	GBC Money Market Fund	FixInc		N/A	N/A	0%	0%		N/A
	This fund has impressive past performance characteristics overall vs. its peers. Reasonable fees represent bargains for this actively managed fund.								
★★★	GBC North American Growth Fund Inc.	USEq		D	N/A	27%	−31%	6/1/81	17
	This well-established fund has shown middle-of-the-road performance against similar funds. Lower annual expenses than most bode well for the future of this actively managed fund.								
★★	General Trust of Canada Balanced	Balan		D	A	20%	−11%	1/1/90	13
	This well-established fund has been set apart from its peers by its weak returns, but it's been a top-notch performer in bear markets. Normally I'd say that this actively managed fund has reasonable expenses compared to its peers, but poor overall performance makes that argument weak.								
★★★	General Trust of Canada Bond Fund	FixInc		B	C	11%	−12%	2/1/94	19
	This well-established fund has shown middle-of-the-road performance against similar funds. Along with performing better than most in bull markets it has been a disappointment in bear markets. Annual fees are reasonable for this reasonably performing actively managed fund.								
★★	General Trust of Canada Cdn Equity	CdnEq		D	C	28%	−36%	6/1/81	22
	This well-established fund has been set apart from its peers by its weak returns, with disappointing results in bear markets. Normally I'd say that this actively managed fund has reasonable expenses compared to its peers, but poor overall performance makes that argument weak.								
★★★	General Trust of Canada Growth Fund	CdnEq		C	C	26%	−25%	9/1/89	28
	This fund has shown middle-of-the-road performance against similar funds with disappointing results in all market conditions. Lower annual expenses than most bode well for the future of this actively managed fund.								

Efficiency / MER

Fund Name	MER
Friedberg Currency Fund	5.38 NMG
Friedberg Diversified Fund ($US)	4.30 ●
Friedberg Double Gold Plus Fund	0.93 ◑
Friedberg Foreign Bond Fund	◑
GBC Canadian Bond Fund	1.13 ●
GBC Canadian Growth Fund	1.85 ●
GBC International Growth Fund	1.76 ◑
GBC Money Market Fund	0.75 ◑
GBC North American Growth Fund Inc.	1.83 ●
General Trust of Canada Balanced	2.15 ◑
General Trust of Canada Bond Fund	1.58 ◑
General Trust of Canada Cdn Equity	2.10 ◑
General Trust of Canada Growth Fund	2.13 ●

Legend: ★ = overall past performance vs. similar funds (5 ★ max). Boxes show the quartile performance for a fund each calendar year vs. only similar funds (□ is the best score possible). ● = high; ◐ = average; and ○ = a fund with low expenses.

Overall Past Performance	Fund Name	Type	88	89	90	91	92	93	94	95	96	Sep-97	Up	Down	% of Time Losing $	Biggest Drop	Date	No. of Mo's to Recover	MER	
★★	**General Trust of Canada Intl.**	FgnEq	□	□	□	□	□	□	□	□	□	□	D	B	22%	-17%	7/1/90	17	2.47	●
	This fund has been set apart from its peers by its weak returns. Normally I'd say this fund has reasonable fees, but poor overall performance makes that argument weak.																			
★★★	**General Trust of Canada Money Mkt**	FixInc	□	□	□	□	□	□	□	□	□	□	N/A	N/A	0%	0%			1.09	●
	This well-established fund has shown middle-of-the-road performance against similar funds. High expenses haven't been much of a problem for this actively managed fund.																			
★★★◞	**General Trust of Canada Mortgage**	FixInc		□	□	□	□	□	□	□	□	□	B	A	1%	-5%	8/1/79	9	1.56	○
	You won't find many like this older one! It's done better than most in its class. As well as performing better than most in bull markets it's been a top-notch performer in bear markets. Annual fees are reasonable for this reasonably performing actively managed fund.																			
★★★	**General Trust of Canada U.S. Equity**	USEq	□	□	□	□	□	□	□	□	□	□	B	C	21%	-31%	9/1/87	42	2.15	◐
	This well-established fund has shown middle-of-the-road performance against similar funds. Along with performing better than most in bull markets it has been a disappointment in bear markets. Annual fees are reasonable for this reasonably performing actively managed fund.																			
★★★	**GFM Emerging Markets Country($US)**	FgnEq								□	□	□	N/A	N/A	0%	-7%	10/1/95	3	1.50	●
	This fund has shown middle-of-the-road performance against similar funds. Lower annual expenses than most bode well for the future of this actively managed fund.																			
★	**Global Manager – German Bund Index**	FgnEq								□	□	□	N/A	N/A	45%	-13%	1/1/96	N/A		
★★★★	**Global Manager – German Geared Fund**	FgnEq								□	□	□	N/A	N/A	0%	-21%	8/1/97	N/A		
★	**Global Manager – German Index Fund**	FgnEq								□	□	□	N/A	N/A	0%	-5%	8/1/95	5		
★	**Global Manager – Gold Index Fund**	SpcIty								N/A	□	□	N/A	N/A	91%	-22%	10/1/94	N/A		
★★	**Global Manager – HK Geared Fund**	FgnEq								□	□	□	N/A	N/A	9%	-40%	10/1/94	15		
★★★	**Global Manager – HK Index Fund**	FgnEq								□	□	□	N/A	N/A	0%	-22%	8/1/97	N/A		
★★★	**Global Manager – Japan Geared Fund**	FgnEq								□	□	□	N/A	N/A	45%	-46%	7/1/96	N/A		
★★	**Global Manager – Japan Index Fund**	FgnEq								□	□	□	N/A	N/A	55%	-30%	5/1/96	N/A		
★★★◞	**Global Manager – UK Geared Fund**	FgnEq								□	□	□	N/A	N/A	0%	-10%	11/1/94	4		
★★★◞	**Global Manager – UK Gilt Index Fund**	FgnEq								□	□	□	N/A	N/A	5%	-5%	1/1/96	7		
★★	**Global Manager – UK Index Fund**	FgnEq								□	□	□	N/A	N/A	0%	-5%	11/1/94	4		
★★★★	**Global Manager – US Bond Index Fund**	FixInc								□	□	□	N/A	N/A	36%	-10%	1/1/96	18		
★	**Global Manager – US Dollar Cash**	FixInc								□	□	□	N/A	N/A	0%	-1%	8/1/95	4		

Legend: ★ = overall past performance vs. similar funds (5 ★ max). Boxes show the quartile performance for a fund each calendar year vs. only similar funds (□ is the best score possible). ● = high; ◐ = average; and ○ = a fund with low expenses.

Consistency			Performance Trend											Risk					Efficiency
Overall Past Performance	Fund Name	Type	88	89	90	91	92	93	94	95	96	Sep-97	Up	Down	% of Time Losing $	Biggest Drop	Date	No. of Mo's to Recover	MER
★★★★	**Global Manager – US Geared Fund**	USEq									□	□	N/A	N/A	0%	–13%	6/1/96	3	
★★★⚹	**Global Manager – US Index Fund**	USEq									□	□	N/A	N/A	0%	–6%	6/1/96	3	
★★	**Global Strategy Asia Fund**	FgnEq							□	□	□	□	C	C	44%	–27%	1/1/94	N/A	2.89 ●
	This fund has been set apart from its peers by its weak returns, with disappointing results in all market conditions. High expenses exacerbate the problem for this actively managed fund.																			
★★⚹	**Global Strategy Bond Fund**	FixInc								□	□	□		B	0%	–3%	3/1/94	7	1.50 ●
	This fund has been unimpressive so far with disappointing results in bull markets. High expenses exacerbate the problem for this fund.																			
★★	**Global Strategy Canada Growth Fund**	CdnEq						□		□	□	□	C	D	15%	–13%	2/1/94	23	2.69 ●
	This fund has been set apart from its peers by its weak returns, with disappointing results in bull markets as well as in bear markets. High expenses exacerbate the problem for this actively managed fund.																			
★★★⚹	**Global Strategy Cdn. Opportunities**	CdnEq									□	□	N/A	N/A	0%	–3%	2/1/97	3	2.75 ●
	You won't find many new ones like this one! It's done better than most in its class. High expenses haven't been much of a problem for this fund.																			
★★★⚹	**Global Strategy Cdn Small Cap**	CdnEq								□	□	□	N/A	N/A	0%	–10%	8/1/95	7	2.75 ●
	You won't find many like this one! It's done better than most in its class. High expenses haven't been much of a problem for this actively managed fund.																			
★	**Global Strategy Diversified Asia**	FgnEq								□	□	□	D	D	59%	–25%	11/1/94	N/A	2.69 ◐
	This fund has been a dog, but it's been hit hard in all market conditions. Normally I'd say that this actively managed fund has reasonable expenses compared to its peers, but poor overall performance makes that argument weak.																			
★★	**Global Strategy Diversified Bond**	FixInc					□	□	□	□	□	□	D	N/A	16%	–12%	2/1/94	21	2.24 ●
	This fund has been set apart from its peers by its weak returns. High expenses exacerbate the problem for this actively managed fund.																			
★⚹	**Global Strategy Diversified Europe**	FgnEq						□		□	□	□	C	N/A	19%	–9%	2/1/94	17	2.52 ◐
	This fund can be described as having dismal returns. Normally I'd say that this actively managed fund has reasonable expenses compared to its peers, but poor overall performance makes that argument weak.																			
★★★	**Global Strategy Div Foreign Bond**	FixInc									□	□	N/A	N/A	0%	–4%	1/1/97	5	2.24 ●
	This fund has shown middle-of-the-road performance against similar funds. High expenses haven't been much of a problem for this actively managed fund.																			
★★	**Global Strategy Div. Japan Plus**	FgnEq								□	□	□	D	D	81%	–36%	6/1/94	N/A	2.54 ◐
	This fund has been set apart from its peers by its weak returns, but it's been hit hard in all market conditions. Normally I'd say that this fund has reasonable expenses compared to its peers, but poor overall performance makes that argument weak.																			
★⚹	**Global Strategy Diversified Latin**	FgnEq									□	□	D	N/A	37%	–36%	10/1/94	30	2.95 ◐
	This fund can be described as having dismal returns. Normally I'd say that this actively managed fund has reasonable expenses compared to its peers, but poor overall performance makes that argument weak.																			
★★	**Global Strategy Divers. World Eqt.**	FgnEq									□	□	N/A	N/A	0%	–6%	8/1/97	N/A	2.40 ◐
	This fund has been set apart from its peers by its weak returns. Normally I'd say that this actively managed fund has reasonable expenses compared to its peers, but poor overall performance makes that argument weak.																			

Legend: ★ = overall past performance vs. similar funds (5 ★ max). Boxes show the quartile performance for a fund each calendar year vs. only similar funds (□ is the best score possible). ● = high; ◐ = average; and ○ = a fund with low expenses.

Overall Past Performance	Fund Name	Type	Up	Down	% of Time Losing $	Biggest Drop	Date	No. of Mo's to Recover	Efficiency	MER
★★★	Global Strategy Europe Plus	FgnEq	N/A	N/A	0%	-5%	8/1/95	4	●	2.88
	This fund has shown middle-of-the-road performance against similar funds. High expenses haven't been much of a problem for this actively managed fund.									
★★★	Global Strategy Gold Plus Fund	CdnEq	A	D	21%	-47%	6/1/96	N/A	●	2.89
	This fund has shown middle-of-the-road performance against similar funds with top-notch performance in bull markets but has been hit hard in bear markets. This actively managed fund is expensive but worth it in rising market conditions.									
★★★?	Global Strategy Income Plus Fund	Balan	A	N/A	10%	-8%	2/1/94	15	●	2.63
	You won't find many like this one! It's done better than most in its class. High expenses haven't been a problem for this actively managed fund.									
★	Global Strategy Japan Fund	FgnEq	N/A	N/A	74%	-35%	1/1/95	N/A	●	2.89
	This fund has been a dog. High expenses exacerbate the problem for this actively managed fund.									
★★★	Global Strategy Latin America Fund	FgnEq	B	N/A	33%	-29%	11/1/94	27	◐	2.95
	This fund has shown middle-of-the-road performance against similar funds. Annual fees are reasonable for this reasonably performing actively managed fund.									
★★	Global Strategy Money Market Fund	FixInc	N/A	N/A	0%	0%	N/A	N/A	◐	0.85
	This fund has been set apart from its peers by its weak returns. Normally I'd say that this actively managed fund has reasonable expenses compared to its peers, but poor overall performance makes that argument weak.									
★★★	Global Strategy US Equity	USEq	N/A	N/A	0%	-8%	6/1/96	5	●	2.75
	This fund has shown middle-of-the-road performance against similar funds. High expenses haven't been much of a problem for this actively managed fund.									
★	Global Strategy World Balanced	Balan	N/A	N/A	0%	-3%	8/1/97	N/A	◐	2.41
	Here is one that is a dog. Normally I'd say that this actively managed fund has reasonable expenses compared to its peers, but poor overall performance makes that argument weak.									
★★	Global Strategy World Bond Fund	FixInc	B	N/A	13%	-12%	2/1/94	22	●	2.21
	This fund has shown middle-of-the-road performance against similar funds. High expenses haven't been much of a problem for this actively managed fund.									
★★★★	Global Strategy World Emerging Co.	FgnEq	N/A	N/A	0%	-6%	6/1/96	6	●	2.98
	This fund has off-the-charts performance overall vs. its peers. This actively managed fund is expensive but well worth it.									
★★★	Global Strategy World Equity	FgnEq	N/A	N/A	0%	-5%	6/1/96	5	●	2.87
	This fund has shown middle-of-the-road performance against similar funds. High expenses haven't been much of a problem for this actively managed fund.									
★★	Globelnvest Emerg. Markets Country	FgnEq	N/A	N/A	8%	-7%	3/1/96	10	○	2.72
	This newer fund has been set apart from its peers by its weak returns. Normally I'd say that this actively managed fund has reasonable expenses compared to its peers, but poor overall performance makes that argument weak.									
★★★	Goldfund Ltd. (CSA Mgnt)	SpcIty	N/A	N/A	53%	-58%	10/1/80	75	◐	2.71
	This fund has shown middle-of-the-road performance against similar funds. Annual fees are reasonable for this reasonably performing actively managed fund.									

Performance Trend columns (quartile boxes, years 88, 89, 90, 91, 92, 93, 94, 95, 96, Sep-97) are shown graphically and are not transcribed as text.

Legend: ★ = overall past performance vs. similar funds (5 ★ max). Boxes show the quartile performance for a fund each calendar year vs. only similar funds (□ is the best score possible). ● = high; ● = average; and ● = a fund with low expenses.

Consistency / Overall Past Performance	Fund Name	Type	Risk Up	Risk Down	% of Time Losing $	Biggest Drop	Date	No. of Mo's to Recover	MER
★	**Goldtrust (CSA Mgnt)**	CdnEq	D	B	44%	–58%	10/1/80	71	2.26
★★★	**Green Line Asian Growth Fund**	FgnEq	C	B	32%	–19%	1/1/94	24	2.70
★★★	**Green Line Balanced Growth**	Balan	C	B	17%	–12%	1/1/90	14	2.08
★★	**Green Line Balanced Income Fund**	Balan	D	N/A	14%	–11%	9/1/89	18	2.10
★★★	**Green Line Blue Chip Equity Fund**	CdnEq	C	C	17%	–17%	1/1/90	23	2.27
★★★	**Green Line Canadian Bond Fund**	FixInc	A	D	10%	–13%	2/1/94	15	0.96
★★★	**Green Line Canadian Equity Fund**	CdnEq	B	C	29%	–21%	9/1/89	43	2.11
★★★	**Green Line Canadian Govt. Bond Fund**	FixInc	C	B	16%	–12%	2/1/94	15	0.97
★★	**Green Line Canadian Index Fund**	CdnEq	B	C	29%	–25%	8/1/87	23	1.10
★★★★★	**Green Line Canadian Money Mkt**	FixInc	N/A	N/A	0%	0%		N/A	0.83
★★★	**Green Line Canadian T-Bill Fund**	FixInc	N/A	N/A	4%	0%		N/A	0.83
★★★	**Green Line Dividend Fund**	CdnEq	B	B	15%	–12%	1/1/90	13	2.02
★★★	**Green Line Emerging Markets**	FgnEq	C	N/A	33%	–30%	9/1/94	34	2.69

Fund notes:

- **Goldtrust (CSA Mgnt):** This well-established fund can be described as having dismal returns. Normally I'd say this fund has reasonable fees, but poor overall performance makes that argument weak.
- **Green Line Asian Growth Fund:** This fund has shown middle-of-the-road performance against similar funds with disappointing results in bull markets and better than average in bear markets. Annual fees are reasonable for this reasonably performing actively managed fund.
- **Green Line Balanced Growth:** This fund has been unimpressive so far with disappointing results in bull markets. Normally I'd say this fund has reasonable fees, but poor overall performance makes that argument weak.
- **Green Line Balanced Income Fund:** This fund has been set apart from its peers by its weak returns. Normally I'd say that this fund has reasonable expenses compared to its peers, but poor overall performance makes that argument weak.
- **Green Line Blue Chip Equity Fund:** This fund has been unimpressive so far with disappointing results in all market conditions. Normally I'd say this fund has reasonable fees, but poor overall performance makes that argument weak.
- **Green Line Canadian Bond Fund:** This fund has done better than most in its class with top-notch performance in bull markets but has been hit hard in bear markets. Lower annual expenses than most bode well for the future of this closet indexer.
- **Green Line Canadian Equity Fund:** This fund has shown middle-of-the-road performance against similar funds. Along with performing better than most in bull markets it has been a disappointment in bear markets. Annual fees are reasonable for this reasonable performing fund.
- **Green Line Canadian Govt. Bond Fund:** This fund has been unimpressive so far with disappointing results in bull markets. Low fees have not helped this closet indexer.
- **Green Line Canadian Index Fund:** This well-established fund has shown middle-of-the-road performance against similar funds. Along with performing better than most in bull markets it has been a disappointment in bear markets. Lower annual expenses than most bode well for the future of this fund.
- **Green Line Canadian Money Mkt:** This fund has off-the-charts performance overall vs. its peers. Reasonable fees represent bargains for this actively managed fund.
- **Green Line Canadian T-Bill Fund:** This fund has done better than most in its class. Annual fees are reasonable for this reasonably performing actively managed fund.
- **Green Line Dividend Fund:** This fund has shown middle-of-the-road performance against similar funds; it performs better than most in all market conditions. High expenses haven't been much of a problem for this actively managed fund.
- **Green Line Emerging Markets:** This fund has been unimpressive so far. Normally I'd say that this actively managed fund has reasonable expenses compared to its peers, but poor overall performance makes that argument weak.

Legend: ★ = overall past performance vs. similar funds (5 ★ max). Boxes show the quartile performance for a fund each calendar year vs. only similar funds (1st-quartile box is the best score possible). ● = high; ● = average; and ● = a fund with low expenses.

Consistency			Performance Trend										Risk						Efficiency	
Overall Past Performance	Fund Name	Type	88	89	90	91	92	93	94	95	96	Sep-97	Up	Down	% of Time Losing $	Biggest Drop	Date	No. of Mo's to Recover	MER	
★★★½	**Green Line Energy Fund**	CdnEq								2	1	1	N/A	N/A	5%	–16%	6/1/95	9	2.13	low
	This fund has done better than most in its class. Lower annual expenses than most bode well for the future of this actively managed fund.																			
★★★★★	**Green Line European Growth Fund**	FgnEq								1	1	3	N/A	N/A	0%	–6%	8/1/97	N/A	2.62	high
	This fund has off-the-charts performance overall vs. its peers. This actively managed fund is expensive but well worth it.																			
★★	**Green Line Global Government Bond**	FixInc						1	1	2	3	3	C	N/A	16%	–5%	7/1/95	4	2.10	average
	This fund has been set apart from its peers by its weak returns. Normally I'd say that this actively managed fund has reasonable expenses compared to its peers, but poor overall performance makes that argument weak.																			
★★★★	**Green Line Global RSP Bond Fund**	FixInc							1	2	1	1	A	N/A	0%	–4%	7/1/95	4	2.03	average
	This fund has impressive past performance characteristics overall vs. its peers. Reasonable fees represent bargains for this actively managed fund.																			
★★★½	**Green Line Global Select Fund**	FgnEq							1	2	2	3	A	N/A	0%	–6%	8/1/97	N/A	2.36	average
	This fund has done better than most in its class. Annual fees are reasonable for this reasonably performing actively managed fund.																			
★★	**Green Line Health Sciences Fund**	Spclty										4	N/A	N/A	0%	–6%	3/1/97	2	2.64	average
	This newer fund has been set apart from its peers by its weak returns. Normally I'd say that this actively managed fund has reasonable expenses compared to its peers, but poor overall performance makes that argument weak.																			
★★★	**Green Line International Equity**	FgnEq						2	1	4	3	3	C	N/A	24%	–11%	9/1/94	18	2.35	average
	This fund has shown middle-of-the-road performance against similar funds. Annual fees are reasonable for this reasonably performing actively managed fund.																			
★★★½	**Green Line Japanese Growth Fund**	FgnEq								1	2	2	N/A	N/A	55%	–25%	5/1/96	N/A	2.63	average
	This fund has done better than most in its class. Annual fees are reasonable for this reasonably performing actively managed fund.																			
★	**Green Line Latin Amer. Growth Fund**	FgnEq								2	3	3	N/A	N/A	10%	–38%	12/1/94	29	2.67	low
	This fund has been a dog. Low fees have not helped this actively managed fund.																			
★★	**Green Line Mortgage Fund**	FixInc	1	1	1	2	2	2	3	2	2	3	C	C	1%	–6%	2/1/94	13	1.62	average
	This well-established fund has been set apart from its peers by its weak returns, with disappointing results in all market conditions. Normally I'd say this fund has reasonable fees, but poor overall performance makes that argument weak.																			
★	**Green Line Mortgage-Backed Fund**	FixInc			1	3	4	4	3	4	4	4	D	C	2%	–5%	2/1/94	12	1.56	average
	Here is one that is a dog. Normally I'd say that this actively managed fund has reasonable expenses compared to its peers, but poor overall performance makes that argument weak.																			
★★★½	**Green Line North Amer. Growth 'A'**	FgnEq							2	1	2	4	A	N/A	0%	–8%	6/1/96	3	2.34	average
	This fund has done better than most in its class. Annual fees are reasonable for this reasonably performing actively managed fund.																			
★★★★★	**Green Line Precious Metals Fund**	CdnEq								2	1	2	N/A	N/A	15%	–32%	6/1/96	N/A	2.13	low
	This fund has off-the-charts performance overall vs. its peers. No wonder performance has been so good for this actively managed fund, its fees are among the lowest in its group.																			

Legend: ★ = overall past performance vs. similar funds (5 ★ max). Boxes show the quartile performance for a fund each calendar year vs. only similar funds. □ is the best score possible). ● = high; ◐ = average; and ● = a fund with low expenses.

Fund Name	Type	Overall Past Performance	Up	Down	% of Time Losing $	Biggest Drop	Date	No. of Mo's to Recover	MER
Green Line Real Return Bond Fund	FixInc	★	N/A	N/A	5%	-6%	1/1/96	8	1.61
This fund has been a dog. Normally I'd say that this actively managed fund has reasonable expenses compared to its peers, but poor overall performance makes that argument weak.									
Green Line Resource Fund	CdnEq	★★	B	D	39%	-17%	6/1/94	20	2.12
This fund has shown middle-of-the-road performance against similar funds; it has performed better than most in bull markets but it has been hit hard in bear markets. Lower annual expenses than most bode well for the future of this actively managed fund.									
Green Line Science & Tech. Fund	Spclty	★★★✓	A	N/A	6%	-16%	2/1/97	5	2.59
This fund has done better than most in its class. Annual fees are reasonable for this reasonably performing actively managed fund.									
Green Line Short Term Income Fund	FixInc	★★	C	B	3%	-5%	2/1/94	12	1.14
This fund has been set apart from its peers by its weak returns, with disappointing results in bull markets. Low fees have not helped this actively managed fund.									
Green Line U.S. Blue Chip Equity	USEq	★★	N/A	N/A	0%	-4%	8/1/97	N/A	2.44
This newer fund has been set apart from its peers by its weak returns. Normally I'd say that this actively managed fund has reasonable expenses compared to its peers, but poor overall performance makes that argument weak.									
Green Line U.S. Money Mkt ($US)	FixInc	★✓	N/A	N/A	0%	0%	N/A	N/A	1.27
This fund can be described as having dismal returns. High expenses exacerbate the problem for this actively managed fund.									
Green Line US Index Fund ($US)	USEq	★★★✓	A	B	14%	-29%	9/1/87	22	0.72
This well-established fund has done better than most in its class with top-notch performance in bull markets as well as performing better than most in bear markets. Lower annual expenses than most bode well for the future of this actively managed fund.									
Green Line Value Fund	CdnEq	★★★✓	A	D	15%	-14%	2/1/94	17	2.13
This fund has done better than most in its class with top-notch performance in bull markets but has been hit hard in bear markets. Annual fees are reasonable for this reasonably performing actively managed fund.									
Greystone Managed Global Fund	FgnEq	★★★★	A	N/A	7%	-9%	9/1/94	10	2.46
This fund has impressive past performance characteristics overall vs. its peers. Reasonable fees represent bargains for this actively managed fund.									
Greystone Managed Wealth Fund	Balan	★★	D	N/A	7%	-11%	5/1/94	12	2.50
This fund has been set apart from its peers by its weak returns. High expenses exacerbate the problem for this actively managed fund.									
Growsafe Canadian Balanced Fund	Balan	★	D	N/A	13%	-6%	2/1/94	14	2.30
Here is one that is a dog. High expenses exacerbate the problem for this fund.									
Growsafe Canadian Bond Fund	FixInc	★	D	A	9%	-6%	2/1/94	13	2.10
This fund has been a dog, but it's been a top-notch performer in bear markets. High fees exacerbate the problem for this fund, especially in bull markets.									
Growsafe Canadian Equity Fund	CdnEq	★★	D	D	3%	-6%	2/1/94	13	2.30
This fund has been set apart from its peers by its weak returns; it's been hit hard in all market conditions. Normally I'd say that this fund has reasonable expenses compared to its peers, but poor overall performance makes that argument weak.									

Legend: ★ = overall past performance vs. similar funds (5 ★ max). Boxes show the quartile performance for a fund each calendar year vs. only similar funds (□ is the best score possible). ● = high; ◐ = average; and ◔ = a fund with low expenses.

Overall Past Performance	Fund Name	Type	Performance Trend 88–Sep-97	Risk Up	Down	% of Time Losing $	Biggest Drop	Date	No. of Mo's to Recover	MER
★	**Growsafe Canadian Money Market**	FixInc		N/A	N/A	0%	0%		N/A	0.90
★★★★	**Growsafe European 100 Index Fund**	FgnEq	□ 95 □ 96 □ Sep-97	N/A	N/A	0%	–5%	8/1/97	N/A	1.99
★↗	**Growsafe International Balanced**	Balan	□ 96 □ Sep-97	D	N/A	3%	–5%	8/1/97	N/A	2.60
★★↗	**Growsafe Japanese 225 Index Fund**	FgnEq	□ Sep-97	N/A	N/A	0%	–22%	12/1/96	N/A	1.99
★★★	**Growsafe U.S. 21st Century Index**	USEq	□ Sep-97	N/A	N/A	0%	–11%	2/1/97	N/A	1.99
★★★↗	**Growsafe U.S. 500 Index Fund**	USEq	□ 96	N/A	N/A	0%	–5%	8/1/97	N/A	1.99
★★★↗	**GS American Equity Fund**	USEq	□ Sep-97	N/A	N/A	0%	–5%	6/1/96	2	3.24
★★★★↗	**GS Canadian Balanced Fund**	Balan	□ Sep-97	N/A	N/A	0%	–2%	6/1/96	2	2.80
★★★↗	**GS Canadian Equity Fund**	CdnEq	□ Sep-97	N/A	N/A	0%	–3%	3/1/97	2	2.80
★	**GS International Bond Fund**	FixInc		N/A	N/A	25%	–3%	1/1/97	N/A	2.70
★★	**GS International Equity Fund**	FgnEq		N/A	N/A	0%	–5%	8/1/97	N/A	2.89
★★	**GT Global – Global Theme Class**	FgnEq		N/A	N/A	0%	–12%	2/1/97	4	2.95
★	**GT Global America Growth Class**	USEq	□ 95 □ 96 □ Sep-97	N/A	N/A	24%	–17%	2/1/97	5	2.95
★↗	**GT Global Canada Growth Class**	CdnEq	□ 95 □ 96 □ Sep-97	N/A	N/A	0%	–11%	2/1/97	5	2.57

Growsafe Canadian Money Market — This fund has been a dog. Normally I'd say that this actively managed fund has reasonable expenses compared to its peers, but poor overall performance makes that argument weak.

Growsafe European 100 Index Fund — This newer fund has off-the-charts performance overall vs. its peers. No wonder performance has been so good for this fund, its fees are among the lowest in its group.

Growsafe International Balanced — This fund can be described as having dismal returns. Normally I'd say that this actively managed fund has reasonable expenses compared to its peers, but poor overall performance makes that argument weak.

Growsafe Japanese 225 Index Fund — Check out how unimpressive this new fund has been. Low fees have not helped this fund.

Growsafe U.S. 21st Century Index — This newer fund has impressive past performance characteristics overall vs. its peers. Reasonable fees represent bargains for this fund.

Growsafe U.S. 500 Index Fund — You won't find many new ones like this one! It's done better than most in its class. Annual fees are reasonable for this reasonably performing actively managed fund.

GS American Equity Fund — You won't find many new ones like this one! It's done better than most in its class. High expenses haven't been much of a problem for this actively managed fund.

GS Canadian Balanced Fund — This newer fund has off-the-charts performance overall vs. its peers. This actively managed fund is expensive but well worth it.

GS Canadian Equity Fund — You won't find many new ones like this one! It's done better than most in its class. High expenses haven't been much of a problem for this actively managed fund.

GS International Bond Fund — This newer fund has been a dog. High expenses exacerbate the problem for this actively managed fund.

GS International Equity Fund — This newer fund has shown middle-of-the-road performance against similar funds. High expenses haven't been much of a problem for this actively managed fund.

GT Global – Global Theme Class — This newer fund has been set apart from its peers by its weak returns. High expenses exacerbate the problem for this actively managed fund.

GT Global America Growth Class — This fund has been a dog. High expenses exacerbate the problem for this actively managed fund.

GT Global Canada Growth Class — This fund can be described as having dismal returns. Normally I'd say that this actively managed fund has reasonable expenses compared to its peers, but poor overall performance makes that argument weak.

Legend: ★ = overall past performance vs. similar funds (5 ★ max). Boxes show the quartile performance for a fund each calendar year vs. only similar funds □ is the best score possible). ● = high; ◐ = average; and ● = a fund with low expenses.

Consistency		Performance Trend											Risk						Efficiency
Overall Past Performance	Fund Name	Type	88	89	90	91	92	93	94	95	96	Sep-97	Up	Down	% of Time Losing $	Biggest Drop	Date	No. of Mo's to Recover	MER
★★★★	**GT Global Canada Income Class** This newer fund has off-the-charts performance overall vs. its peers. This fund is expensive but well worth it.	Balan										□	N/A	N/A	0%	-5%	3/1/97	2	2.30 ●
★	**GT Global Canada Money Market** This newer fund has been a dog. Normally I'd say that this actively managed fund has reasonable expenses compared to its peers, but poor overall performance makes that argument weak.	FixInc										□	N/A	N/A	0%	0%	N/A	N/A	0.80 ◐
★★	**GT Global Growth & Income Fund** This fund has been unimpressive so far. High expenses exacerbate the problem for this actively managed fund.	Balan									□	□	N/A	N/A	0%	-4%	8/1/97	N/A	2.95 ●
★★★	**GT Global Health Care Class** This newer fund has shown middle-of-the-road performance against similar funds. High expenses haven't been much of a problem for this fund.	Spclty							□	□	□	□	N/A	N/A	0%	-15%	3/1/97	4	2.88 ●
★	**GT Global Infrastructure Class** This fund has been a dog. High expenses exacerbate the problem for this actively managed fund.	Spclty									□	□	N/A	N/A	0%	-10%	11/1/94	7	2.90 ●
★★★★★	**GT Global Latin America Class** This fund has off-the-charts performance overall vs. its peers. Reasonable fees represent bargains for this actively managed fund.	FgnEq							□	□	□	□	N/A	N/A	10%	-27%	11/1/94	14	2.95 ●
★★	**GT Global Natural Resources Class** This fund has been set apart from its peers by its weak returns. High expenses exacerbate the problem for this actively managed fund.	FgnEq								□	□	□	N/A	N/A	19%	-18%	1/1/97	7	2.95 ●
★★★★★	**GT Global Pacific Growth Class** This fund has off-the-charts performance overall vs. its peers. This actively managed fund is expensive but well worth it.	FgnEq							□	□	□	□	N/A	N/A	5%	-15%	7/1/97	N/A	2.95 ●
★	**GT Global Short-term Income 'A'** This fund has been a dog. High expenses exacerbate the problem for this actively managed fund.	FixInc									□	□	N/A	N/A	0%	-1%	12/1/96	5	1.76 ●
★	**GT Global Short-term Income 'B'** This fund has been a dog. High expenses exacerbate the problem for this actively managed fund.	FixInc									□	□	N/A	N/A	0%	-1%	12/1/96	8	2.25 ●
★★★	**GT Global Telecommunication Class** This fund has shown middle-of-the-road performance against similar funds. High expenses haven't been much of a problem for this actively managed fund.	Spclty							□	□	□	□	N/A	N/A	19%	-23%	6/1/96	13	2.86 ●
★★★	**GT Global World Bond Fund** This fund has shown middle-of-the-road performance against similar funds. High expenses haven't been much of a problem for this actively managed fund.	FixInc							□	□	□	□	N/A	N/A	0%	-2%	6/1/95	3	2.45 ●
★★★	**Guardian American Equity Fund 'A'** This well-established fund has been unimpressive so far with disappointing results in bull markets as well as in bear markets. Normally I'd say that this actively managed fund has reasonable fees vs. its peers, but its poor overall performance makes that argument weak.	USEq	□	□	□	□	□	□	□	□	□	□	C	D	24%	-29%	9/1/87	32	2.37 ◐

Legend: ★ = overall past performance vs. similar funds (5 ★ max). Boxes show the quartile performance for a fund each calendar year vs. only similar funds (☐ is the best score possible). ● = high; ◐ = average; and ○ = a fund with low expenses.

Consistency — Overall Past Performance	Fund Name	Type	Performance Trend (88–Sep-97)	Risk Up	Risk Down	% of Time Losing $	Biggest Drop	Date	No. of Mo's to Recover	Efficiency MER
★	**Guardian American Equity Fund 'B'**	USEq		N/A	N/A	0%	-12%	6/1/96	6	2.97 ●
★★★	**Guardian Asia Pacific Fund 'A'**	FgnEq		N/A	N/A	18%	-14%	8/1/97	N/A	1.84 ◐
★★★	**Guardian Asia Pacific Fund 'B'**	FgnEq		N/A	N/A	67%	-15%	8/1/97	N/A	2.98 ●
★★★	**Guardian Canadian Balanced Fund 'A'**	Balan		C	A	27%	-14%	3/1/81	18	1.90 ○
★	**Guardian Canadian Balanced Fund 'B'**	Balan		N/A	N/A	0%	-2%	8/1/97	N/A	2.67 ●
★★★	**Guardian Canadian Income Fund 'A'**	FixInc		B	A	3%	-5%	2/1/94	12	1.25 ◐
★	**Guardian Canadian Income Fund 'B'**	FixInc		N/A	N/A	0%	-1%	12/1/96	5	1.87 ●
★★★	**Guardian Canadian Money Market 'A'**	FixInc		N/A	N/A	0%	-2%	8/1/79	4	0.85 ○
★	**Guardian Canadian Money Market 'B'**	FixInc		N/A	N/A	0%	0%	N/A	N/A	1.57 ●
★★★★	**Guardian Emerging Markets Fund 'A'**	FgnEq		N/A	N/A	9%	-10%	8/1/95	5	1.51 ◐
★★★	**Guardian Emerging Markets Fund 'B'**	FgnEq		N/A	N/A	0%	-10%	8/1/97	N/A	2.97 ●
★★★	**Guardian Enterprise Fund 'A'**	CdnEq		D	A	21%	-26%	4/1/81	20	2.03 ◐
★★★★★	**Guardian Enterprise Fund 'B'**	CdnEq		N/A	N/A	0%	-8%	6/1/96	3	2.75 ●

Guardian American Equity Fund 'B' — This newer fund has been a dog. High expenses exacerbate the problem for this actively managed fund.

Guardian Asia Pacific Fund 'A' — You won't find many like this one! It's done better than most in its class. Lower annual expenses than most bode well for the future of this actively managed fund.

Guardian Asia Pacific Fund 'B' — This newer fund has shown middle-of-the-road performance against similar funds. High expenses haven't been much of a problem for this actively managed fund.

Guardian Canadian Balanced Fund 'A' — Here is an older fund that has shown middle-of-the-road performance against similar funds with disappointing results in bull markets and top-notch performance in bear markets. Annual fees are reasonable for this reasonable performing fund.

Guardian Canadian Balanced Fund 'B' — This newer fund has been a dog. High expenses exacerbate the problem for this actively managed fund.

Guardian Canadian Income Fund 'A' — This well-established fund has shown middle-of-the-road performance against similar funds. As well as performing better than most in bull markets it's been a top-notch performer in bear markets. Annual fees are reasonable for this reasonably performing actively managed fund.

Guardian Canadian Income Fund 'B' — This newer fund has been a dog. High expenses exacerbate the problem for this actively managed fund.

Guardian Canadian Money Market 'A' — This well-established fund has shown middle-of-the-road performance against similar funds. Annual fees are reasonable for this reasonably performing actively managed fund.

Guardian Canadian Money Market 'B' — This newer fund has been a dog. High expenses exacerbate the problem for this actively managed fund.

Guardian Emerging Markets Fund 'A' — This fund has impressive past performance characteristics overall vs. its peers. No wonder performance has been so good for this actively managed fund, its fees are among the lowest in its group.

Guardian Emerging Markets Fund 'B' — This well-established fund has shown middle-of-the-road performance against similar funds. Annual fees are reasonable for this reasonably performing actively managed fund.

Guardian Enterprise Fund 'A' — This well-established fund has shown middle-of-the-road performance against similar funds but has been hit hard in bull markets. A top-notch performer in bear markets makes this low-priced actively managed fund well worth it.

Guardian Enterprise Fund 'B' — This newer fund has off-the-charts performance overall vs. its peers. This actively managed fund is expensive but well worth it.

Legend: ★ = overall past performance vs. similar funds (5 ★ max). Boxes show the quartile performance for a fund each calendar year vs. only similar funds (☐ is the best score possible). ● = high; ◐ = average; and ○ = a fund with low expenses.

Overall Past Performance	Fund Name	Type	88	89	90	91	92	93	94	95	96	Sep-97	Up	Down	% of Time Losing $	Biggest Drop	Date	No. of Mo's to Recover	MER
★★★✦	**Guardian Foreign Income Fund 'A'** This fund has done better than most in its class. Annual fees are reasonable for this reasonably performing actively managed fund.	FixInc										☐	N/A	N/A	0%	-3%	2/1/96	5	2.05 ○
★★★✦	**Guardian Foreign Income Fund 'B'** You won't find many new ones like this one! It's done better than most in its class. High expenses haven't been much of a problem for this actively managed fund.	FixInc									☐	☐	N/A	N/A	0%	-3%	2/1/96	5	2.95 ●
★★★	**Guardian Global Equity Fund 'A'** Here is an older fund that has shown middle-of-the-road performance against similar funds with disappointing results in all market conditions. Lower annual expenses than most bode well for the future of this actively managed fund.	FgnEq	☐	☐	☐	☐	☐	☐	☐	☐	☐	☐	C	C	25%	-27%	10/1/89	46	1.28 ○
★★★	**Guardian Global Equity Fund 'B'** This newer fund has shown middle-of-the-road performance against similar funds. High expenses haven't been much of a problem for this actively managed fund.	FgnEq									☐	☐	N/A	N/A	0%	-8%	8/1/97	N/A	2.95 ●
★	**Guardian Growth & Income Fund 'A'** This newer fund has been a dog. High expenses exacerbate the problem for this fund.	Balan										☐	N/A	N/A	0%	-3%	3/1/97	2	2.25 ●
★	**Guardian Growth & Income Fund 'B'** This newer fund has been a dog. High expenses exacerbate the problem for this fund.	Balan										☐	N/A	N/A	0%	-3%	3/1/97	2	2.90 ●
★★★★	**Guardian Growth Equity Fund 'A'** This fund has impressive past performance characteristics overall vs. its peers with top-notch performance in bull markets but disappointing results in bear markets. Reasonable fees represent bargains for this actively managed fund.	CdnEq	☐	☐	☐	☐	☐	☐	☐	☐	☐	☐	A	C	16%	-12%	2/1/94	23	2.24 ◐
★★★★★	**Guardian Growth Equity Fund 'B'** This newer fund has off-the-charts performance overall vs. its peers. This actively managed fund is expensive but well worth it.	CdnEq									☐	☐	N/A	N/A	0%	-3%	8/1/97	N/A	2.92 ●
★★	**Guardian International Balanced 'A'** This fund has been set apart from its peers by its weak returns. Low fees have not helped this actively managed fund.	Balan				☐	☐	☐	☐	☐	☐	☐	C	N/A	27%	-10%	2/1/94	21	2.35 ◐
★★★	**Guardian International Balanced 'B'** This newer fund has shown middle-of-the-road performance against similar funds. High expenses haven't been much of a problem for this actively managed fund.	Balan									☐	☐	N/A	N/A	0%	-5%	8/1/97	N/A	2.95 ●
★★	**Guardian International Income 'A'** This well-established fund has been set apart from its peers by its weak returns. Normally I'd say that this actively managed fund has reasonable expenses compared to its peers, but poor overall performance makes that argument weak.	FixInc	☐	☐	☐	☐	☐	☐	☐	☐	☐	☐	D	N/A	15%	-9%	1/1/88	32	2.10 ○
★★★	**Guardian International Income 'B'** This newer fund has shown middle-of-the-road performance against similar funds. High expenses haven't been much of a problem for this actively managed fund.	FixInc									☐	☐	N/A	N/A	0%	-2%	2/1/96	5	2.94 ●
★★★✦	**Guardian Monthly Dividend Fund 'A'** This well-established fund has been unimpressive so far. Low fees have not helped this actively managed fund.	CdnEq							☐	☐	☐	☐	D	B	11%	-6%	3/1/94	13	1.25 ○

Legend: ★ = overall past performance vs. similar funds (5 ★ max). Boxes show the quartile performance for a fund each calendar year vs. only similar funds (□ is the best score possible). ● = high; ◑ = average; and ○ = a fund with low expenses.

Overall Past Performance	Fund Name	Type	Performance Trend (88–Sep-97)	Risk Up	Risk Down	% of Time Losing $	Biggest Drop	Date	No. of Mo's to Recover	MER
★	**Guardian Monthly Dividend Fund 'B'**	CdnEq		N/A	N/A	0%	-3%	12/1/96	5	1.85 ◑
	This newer fund has been a dog. Normally I'd say that this actively managed fund has reasonable expenses compared to its peers, but poor overall performance makes that argument weak.									
★	**Guardian Monthly High Income 'A'**	CdnEq		N/A	N/A	0%	-4%	12/1/96	5	1.46 ●
	This newer fund has been a dog. Low fees have not helped this closet indexer.									
★	**Guardian Monthly High Income 'B'**	CdnEq		N/A	N/A	0%	-4%	12/1/96	5	2.07 ●
	This newer fund has been a dog. High expenses exacerbate the problem for this closet indexer.									
★★★★	**Guardian US Money Market ($US) 'A'**	FixInc		N/A	N/A	0%	0%		1	0.97 ○
	This fund has off-the-charts performance overall vs. its peers. Reasonable fees represent bargains for this actively managed fund.									
★	**Guardian US Money Market ($US) 'B'**	FixInc		N/A	N/A	0%	0%		N/A	1.66 ●
	This newer fund has been a dog. High expenses exacerbate the problem for this actively managed fund.									
★★★	**GWL Advanced Portfolio (G) DSC**	Balan		N/A	N/A	0%	-2%	8/1/97	N/A	2.64 ●
	This newer fund has shown middle-of-the-road performance against similar funds. High expenses haven't been much of a problem for this closet indexer.									
★★◑	**GWL Advanced Portfolio (G) NL**	Balan		N/A	N/A	0%	-2%	8/1/97	N/A	2.88 ●
	This newer fund has been unimpressive so far. High expenses exacerbate the problem for this closet indexer.									
★★★◑	**GWL Aggressive Portfolio (G) DSC**	CdnEq		N/A	N/A	0%	-3%	8/1/97	N/A	2.70 ●
	You won't find many new ones like this one! It's done better than most in its class. High expenses haven't been much of a problem for this closet indexer.									
★★◑	**GWL Aggressive Portfolio (G) NL**	CdnEq		N/A	N/A	0%	-3%	8/1/97	N/A	2.94 ●
	This newer fund has been unimpressive so far. High expenses exacerbate the problem for this closet indexer.									
★	**GWL Balanced Fund (B) DSC**	Balan		N/A	N/A	0%	-3%	3/1/97	2	
★	**GWL Balanced Fund (B) NL**	Balan		N/A	N/A	0%	-3%	3/1/97	2	
★★★	**GWL Balanced Fund (M) DSC**	Balan		N/A	N/A	0%	-3%	2/1/96	3	
★★	**GWL Balanced Fund (M) NL**	Balan		N/A	N/A	0%	-3%	2/1/96	6	
★★★	**GWL Balanced Fund (S) DSC**	Balan		N/A	N/A	0%	-3%	8/1/97	N/A	
★★★	**GWL Balanced Fund (S) NL**	Balan		N/A	N/A	0%	-3%	8/1/97	N/A	
★★★	**GWL Balanced Portfolio (G) DSC**	Balan		N/A	N/A	0%	-3%	8/1/97	N/A	
★★	**GWL Balanced Portfolio (G) NL**	Balan		N/A	N/A	0%	-3%	8/1/97	N/A	

Legend: ★ = overall past performance vs. similar funds (5 ★ max). Boxes show the quartile performance for a fund each calendar year vs. only similar funds (□ is the best score possible). ● = high; ◑ = average; and ● = a fund with low expenses.

Consistency		Performance Trend											Risk						Efficiency
Overall Past Performance	Fund Name	Type	88	89	90	91	92	93	94	95	96	Sep-97	Up	Down	% of Time Losing $	Biggest Drop	Date	No. of Mo's to Recover	MER
★	GWL Bond Fund (B) DSC	FixInc										□	N/A	N/A	0%	-3%	12/1/96	6	
★	GWL Bond Fund (B) NL	FixInc										□	N/A	N/A	0%	-3%	12/1/96	7	
★★★	GWL Bond Fund (M) DSC	FixInc										□	N/A	N/A	0%	-5%	2/1/96	6	
★★★	GWL Bond Fund (M) NL	FixInc										□	N/A	N/A	0%	-5%	2/1/96	6	
★★	GWL Bond Fund (S) DSC	FixInc										□	N/A	N/A	0%	-3%	12/1/96	6	
★	GWL Bond Fund (S) NL	FixInc										□	N/A	N/A	0%	-3%	12/1/96	6	
★	GWL Canadian Bond Fund (G) DSC	FixInc								□	□	□	N/A	N/A	0%	-3%	12/1/96	6	
★★	GWL Canadian Bond Fund (G) NL	FixInc	□	□	□	□	□	□	□	□	□	□	D	C	12%	-12%	2/1/94	16	
★★	GWL Canadian Equity Fund (G) DSC	CdnEq							□			□	N/A	N/A	0%	-10%	9/1/94	9	
★★★	GWL Canadian Equity Fund (G) NL	CdnEq	□	□	□	□	□	□	□	□	□	□	C	A	23%	-26%	8/1/87	50	
★★★	GWL Cdn. Resource Fund (A) DSC	CdnEq											N/A	N/A	17%	-12%	2/1/97	N/A	
★★	GWL Cdn. Resource Fund (A) NL	CdnEq											N/A	N/A	17%	-12%	2/1/97	N/A	
★	GWL Conservative Portfolio (G) DSC	Balan									□	□	N/A	N/A	0%	-2%	12/1/96	5	
★	GWL Conservative Portfolio (G) NL	Balan									□	□	N/A	N/A	0%	-2%	12/1/96	5	
★★	GWL Diversified Fund (G) DSC	Balan								□	□	□	N/A	N/A	0%	-4%	9/1/94	6	
★★	GWL Diversified Fund (G) NL	Balan	□	□	□	□	□	□	□	□	□	□	D	B	12%	-11%	8/1/87	17	
★★★	GWL Equity Fund (M) DSC	CdnEq										□	N/A	N/A	0%	-2%	8/1/97	N/A	
★★	GWL Equity Fund (M) NL	CdnEq										□	N/A	N/A	0%	-3%	8/1/97	N/A	
★★★★	GWL Equity Fund (S) DSC	CdnEq										□	N/A	N/A	0%	-6%	6/1/96	3	
★★★	GWL Equity Fund (S) NL	CdnEq								□	□	□	N/A	N/A	0%	-6%	6/1/96	3	
★★★	GWL Equity Index Fund (G) DSC	CdnEq								□	□	□	N/A	N/A	0%	-8%	10/1/94	7	
★★	GWL Equity Index Fund (G) NL	CdnEq	□	□	□	□	□	□	□	□	□	□	D	D	29%	-26%	8/1/87	23	

Legend: ★ = overall past performance vs. similar funds (5 ★ max). Boxes show the quartile performance for a fund each calendar year vs. only similar funds (□ is the best score possible). ● = high; ◐ = average; and ○ = a fund with low expenses.

Overall Past Performance	Fund Name	Type	Up	Down	% of Time Losing $	Biggest Drop	Date	No. of Mo's to Recover	MER
★★★	GWL Equity/Bond Fund (G) DSC	Balan	N/A	N/A	0%	-6%	9/1/94	8	
★★★	GWL Equity/Bond Fund (G) NL	Balan	C	N/A	14%	-11%	2/1/94	19	
★	GWL Global Inc. Fund (A) DSC	FixInc	N/A	N/A	33%	-4%	2/1/96	9	
★	GWL Global Inc. Fund (A) NL	FixInc	N/A	N/A	33%	-4%	2/1/96	9	
★	GWL Government Bond Fund (G) DSC	FixInc	N/A	N/A	0%	-2%	12/1/96	6	
★★★	GWL Government Bond Fund (G) NL	FixInc	N/A	N/A	0%	-2%	12/1/96	7	
★★	GWL Growth & Income Fund (A) DSC	Balan	N/A	N/A	0%	-7%	6/1/96	5	
★★	GWL Growth & Income Fund (A) NL	Balan	N/A	N/A	0%	-7%	6/1/96	5	
★★★★★	GWL Growth & Income Fund (M) DSC	Balan	N/A	N/A	0%	-2%	8/1/97	N/A	
★★★★	GWL Growth & Income Fund (M) NL	Balan	N/A	N/A	0%	-2%	8/1/97	N/A	
★★★	GWL Growth Equity Fund (A) DSC	CdnEq	N/A	N/A	0%	-8%	6/1/96	3	
★★	GWL Growth Equity Fund (A) NL	CdnEq	N/A	N/A	0%	-8%	6/1/96	3	
★★★★	GWL Income Fund (G) DSC	FixInc	N/A	N/A	0%	-2%	2/1/96	4	
★★★✦	GWL Income Fund (G) NL	FixInc	N/A	N/A	0%	-2%	2/1/96	4	
★★★	GWL International Bond Fund (P) DSC	FixInc	N/A	N/A	5%	-4%	5/1/97	N/A	
★★★	GWL International Bond Fund (P) NL	FixInc	N/A	N/A	5%	-4%	5/1/97	N/A	
★★★✦	GWL Int'l Equity Fund (P) DSC	FgnEq	N/A	N/A	0%	-7%	8/1/97	N/A	
★★★	GWL Int'l Equity Fund (P) NL	FgnEq	N/A	N/A	0%	-7%	8/1/97	N/A	
★	GWL Larger Co. Fund (M) DSC	CdnEq	N/A	N/A	0%	-6%	6/1/96	4	
★	GWL Larger Co. Fund (M) NL	CdnEq	N/A	N/A	0%	-6%	6/1/96	4	
★	GWL Moderate Portfolio (G) DSC	Balan	N/A	N/A	0%	-2%	3/1/97	2	
★	GWL Moderate Portfolio (G) NL	Balan	N/A	N/A	0%	-2%	3/1/97	2	

Legend: ★ = overall past performance vs. similar funds (5 ★ max). Boxes show the quartile performance for a fund each calendar year vs. only similar funds (□ is the best score possible). ● = high; ◐ = average; and ○ = a fund with low expenses.

Consistency		Performance Trend											Risk						Efficiency
Overall Past Performance	Fund Name	Type	88	89	90	91	92	93	94	95	96	Sep-97	Up	Down	% of Time Losing $	Biggest Drop	Date	No. of Mo's to Recover	MER
★	GWL Money Market Fund (G) DSC	FixInc								□	□	□	N/A	N/A	0%	0%		N/A	
★	GWL Money Market Fund (G) NL	FixInc								□	□	□	N/A	N/A	0%	0%		1	
★★★★	GWL Mortgage Fund (G) DSC	FixInc		□	□	□	□	□	□	□	□	□	N/A	N/A	0%	-2%	2/1/96	4	
★★★	GWL Mortgage Fund (G) NL	FixInc	□	□	□	□	□	□	□	□	□	□	C	D	8%	-8%	2/1/94	14	
★★◐	GWL N. A. Equity Fund (B) DSC	FgnEq							□		□	□	N/A	N/A	0%	-5%	3/1/97	2	
★	GWL N. A. Equity Fund (B) NL	FgnEq										□	N/A	N/A	0%	-5%	3/1/97	2	
★★	GWL Smaller Company Fund (M) DSC	CdnEq									□	□	N/A	N/A	0%	-2%	7/1/96	2	
★◐	GWL Smaller Company Fund (M) NL	CdnEq									□	□	N/A	N/A	0%	-2%	7/1/96	2	
★◐	GWL U.S. Equity Fund (G) DSC	USEq								□	□	□	N/A	N/A	0%	-6%	6/1/96	5	
★	GWL U.S. Equity Fund (G) NL	USEq										□	N/A	N/A	0%	-3%	8/1/97	N/A	
★	**Hansberger Asian Fund**	FgnEq				□	□	□	□	□	□	□	D	C	55%	-28%	1/1/94	N/A	2.88 ●
	Here is one that is a dog, but it's been a top-notch performer in bear markets. High expenses exacerbate the problem for this actively managed fund, especially in declining markets.																		
★	**Hansberger Asian Sector Shares**	FgnEq							□	□	□	□	N/A	N/A	57%	-22%	9/1/94	N/A	2.93 ●
	Here is one that is a dog. High expenses exacerbate the problem for this fund.																		
★	**Hansberger Developing Markets Fund**	FgnEq										□	N/A	N/A	0%	-7%	8/1/97	N/A	3.00 ●
	This newer fund has been a dog. High expenses exacerbate the problem for this actively managed fund.																		
★	**Hansberger Developing Mkts Sector**	FgnEq										□	N/A	N/A	0%	-6%	8/1/97	N/A	2.95 ◐
	This newer fund has been a dog. Normally I'd say that this actively managed fund has reasonable expenses compared to its peers, but poor overall performance makes that argument weak.																		
★	**Hansberger European Fund**	FgnEq					□	□	□	□	□	□	D	N/A	28%	-16%	6/1/92	14	2.56 ◐
	Here is one that is a dog. Normally I'd say that this fund has reasonable expenses compared to its peers, but poor overall performance makes that argument weak.																		
★	**Hansberger European Sector Shares**	FgnEq								□	□	□	D	N/A	19%	-10%	8/1/95	9	2.61 ●
	Here is one that is a dog. High expenses exacerbate the problem for this fund.																		
★★	**Hansberger Global Small-Cap Fund**	FgnEq									□	□	N/A	N/A	0%	-5%	7/1/96	5	2.90 ●
	This newer fund has been set apart from its peers by its weak returns. High expenses exacerbate the problem for this actively managed fund.																		

Legend: ★ = overall past performance vs. similar funds (5 ★ max). Boxes show the quartile performance for a fund each calendar year vs. only similar funds (□ is the best score possible). ● = high; ◐ = average; and ○ = a fund with low expenses.

Consistency (Overall Past Performance)	Fund Name	Type	Performance Trend (88–Sep-97)	Risk Up	Risk Down	% of Time Losing $	Biggest Drop	Date	No. of Mo's to Recover	Efficiency MER
★★	**Hansberger Global Small-Cap Sector**	FgnEq		N/A	N/A	0%	-2%	10/1/96	1	2.95 ●
	This newer fund has been set apart from its peers by its weak returns. High expenses exacerbate the problem for this actively managed fund.									
★★★	**Hansberger International Fund**	FgnEq		N/A	N/A	0%	-5%	8/1/97	N/A	2.60 ●
	This newer fund has shown middle-of-the-road performance against similar funds. High expenses haven't been much of a problem for this actively managed fund.									
★★★	**Hansberger Int'l Sector Shares**	FgnEq		N/A	N/A	0%	-5%	8/1/97	N/A	2.65 ●
	This newer fund has shown middle-of-the-road performance against similar funds. High expenses haven't been much of a problem for this actively managed fund.									
★★★★	**Hansberger Value Fund**	FgnEq		N/A	N/A	0%	-3%	8/1/97	N/A	2.53 ◐
	This newer fund has off-the-charts performance overall vs. its peers. Reasonable fees represent bargains for this actively managed fund.									
★★★◐	**Hansberger Value Sector Shares**	FgnEq		N/A	N/A	0%	-3%	8/1/97	N/A	2.58 ◐
	You won't find many new ones like this one! It's done better than most in its class. Annual fees are reasonable for this reasonably performing actively managed fund.									
★★★★★	**Hongkong Bank Americas Fund**	FgnEq		N/A	N/A	0%	-5%	8/1/97	N/A	2.34 ◐
	This fund has off-the-charts performance overall vs. its peers. No wonder performance has been so good for this actively managed fund. Its fees are among the lowest in its group.									
★★★	**Hongkong Bank Asian Growth Fund**	FgnEq		B	B	35%	-18%	9/1/94	16	2.29 ◐
	This fund has shown middle-of-the-road performance against similar funds along with performing better than most in all market conditions. Lower annual expenses than most bode well for the future of this actively managed fund.									
★★★	**Hongkong Bank Balanced Fund**	Balan		B	N/A	9%	-10%	2/1/94	21	1.92 ○
	This fund has shown middle-of-the-road performance against similar funds. Annual fees are reasonable for this reasonably performing fund.									
★★★◐	**Hongkong Bank Canadian Bond Fund**	FixInc		N/A	N/A	0%	-2%	2/1/96	5	1.24 ○
	You won't find many like this one! It's done better than most in its class. Lower annual expenses than most bode well for the future of this actively managed fund.									
★★★★	**Hongkong Bank Dividend Income Fund**	CdnEq		N/A	N/A	0%	-2%	3/1/97	2	1.96 ●
	This fund has impressive past performance characteristics overall vs. its peers. This actively managed fund is expensive but well worth it.									
★◐	**Hongkong Bank Emerging Markets Fund**	FgnEq		N/A	N/A	16%	-23%	12/1/94	N/A	2.72 ◐
	This fund can be described as having dismal returns. Normally I'd say that this actively managed fund has reasonable expenses compared to its peers, but poor overall performance makes that argument weak.									
★★★	**Hongkong Bank Equity Fund**	CdnEq		B	C	35%	-18%	9/1/89	41	1.96 ◐
	This fund has shown middle-of-the-road performance against similar funds. Along with performing better than most in bull markets it has been a disappointment in bear markets. Annual fees are reasonable for this reasonable performing fund.									
★★★	**Hongkong Bank European Growth Fund**	FgnEq		N/A	N/A	0%	-6%	8/1/95	4	2.31 ◐
	This fund has shown middle-of-the-road performance against similar funds. Annual fees are reasonable for this reasonably performing actively managed fund.									

Legend: ★ = overall past performance vs. similar funds (5 ★ max). Boxes show the quartile performance for a fund each calendar year vs. only similar funds (□ is the best score possible). ● = high; ◐ = average; and ○ = a fund with low expenses.

Overall Past Performance	Fund Name	Type	Risk Up	Risk Down	% of Time Losing $	Biggest Drop	Date	No. of Mo's to Recover	MER
★★	**Hongkong Bank Global Bond Fund**	FixInc	N/A	N/A	11%	-4%	8/1/95	3	2.07
	This fund has been set apart from its peers by its weak returns. Normally I'd say that this actively managed fund has reasonable expenses compared to its peers, but poor overall performance makes that argument weak.								
★	**Hongkong Bank Money Market Fund**	FixInc	N/A	N/A	0%	0%		N/A	0.92
	This fund has been a dog. Normally I'd say that this actively managed fund has reasonable expenses compared to its peers, but poor overall performance makes that argument weak.								
★★★★	**Hongkong Bank Mortgage Fund**	FixInc	A	A	0%	-2%	3/1/94	5	1.47
	This fund has off-the-charts performance overall vs. its peers with top-notch performance in all market conditions. No wonder performance has been so good for this actively managed fund. Its fees are among the lowest in its group.								
★★⌐	**Hongkong Bank Small Cap Growth Fund**	CdnEq	N/A	N/A	0%	-9%	6/1/96	3	2.31
	This fund has been unimpressive so far. Normally I'd say that this actively managed fund has reasonable expenses compared to its peers, but poor overall performance makes that argument weak.								
★	**Horizons 1 Multi-Asset Fund Inc.**	Balan	D	N/A	13%	-11%	4/1/97	N/A	3.60
	This fund has been a dog. High expenses exacerbate the problem for this actively managed fund.								
★★⌐	**HRL Balanced Fund**	Balan	C	B	16%	-11%	2/1/94	21	1.75
	This well-established fund has been unimpressive so far with disappointing results in bull markets. Normally I'd say this fund has reasonable fees, but poor overall performance makes that argument weak.								
★★	**HRL Bond Fund**	FixInc	C	C	16%	-17%	9/1/86	33	1.50
	This well-established fund has been set apart from its peers by its weak returns, with disappointing results in all market conditions. Normally I'd say this fund has reasonable fees, but poor overall performance makes that argument weak.								
★★	**HRL Canadian Fund**	CdnEq	D	C	37%	-20%	2/1/94	31	1.75
	This well-established fund has been set apart from its peers by its weak returns, with disappointing results in bear markets. Normally I'd say that this actively managed fund has reasonable expenses compared to its peers, but poor overall performance makes that argument weak.								
★★★★★	**HRL Instant $$ Fund**	FixInc	N/A	N/A	0%	0%		N/A	0.50
	This fund has off-the-charts performance overall vs. its peers. No wonder performance has been so good for this actively managed fund, its fees are among the lowest in its group.								
★★	**HRL Overseas Growth Fund**	FgnEq	C	N/A	26%	-12%	9/1/94	17	1.75
	This fund has been set apart from its peers by its weak returns. Low fees have not helped this fund.								
★★★	**Hyperion Asian Fund**	FgnEq	A	A	28%	-30%	1/1/94	N/A	3.25
	This fund has shown middle-of-the-road performance against similar funds with top-notch performance in all market conditions. High expenses haven't been much of a problem for this actively managed fund.								
★★★★★	**Hyperion Cdn. Equity Growth**	CdnEq	N/A	N/A	0%	-5%	3/1/97	2	2.62
	This newer fund has off-the-charts performance overall vs. its peers. This fund is expensive but well worth it.								
★★★	**Hyperion European Fund**	FgnEq	B	N/A	7%	-19%	8/1/90	21	3.00
	This fund has shown middle-of-the-road performance against similar funds. High expenses haven't been much of a problem for this fund.								

Legend: ★ = overall past performance vs. similar funds (5 ★ max). Boxes show the quartile performance for a fund each calendar year vs. only similar funds [□ is the best score possible). ● = high; ◐ = average; and ● = a fund with low expenses.

Overall Past Performance	Fund Name	Type	Risk Up	Risk Down	% of Time Losing $	Biggest Drop	Date	No. of Mo's to Recover	MER
★★★ⱼ	**Hyperion Global Health Care Fund** — You won't find many new ones like this one! It's done better than most in its class. High expenses haven't been much of a problem for this closet indexer.	SpcIty	N/A	N/A	0%	-6%	3/1/97	2	3.30 ●
★★★	**Hyperion Global Science & Tech.** — This well-established fund has shown middle-of-the-road performance against similar funds. Lower annual expenses than most bode well for the future of this fund.	SpcIty	D	N/A	16%	-34%	9/1/87	23	2.25 ◐
★★★ⱼ	**Hyperion High Yield Bond Fund** — You won't find many like this one! It's done better than most in its class with top-notch performance in bull markets but has been hit hard in bear markets. High expenses haven't been much of a problem for this closet indexer.	FixInc	A	D	13%	-16%	2/1/94	19	2.10 ●
★★★	**Hyperion Small-Cap Canadian Equity** — This fund has shown middle-of-the-road performance against similar funds with top-notch performance in bull markets but has been hit hard in bear markets. Annual fees are reasonable for this reasonably performing actively managed fund.	CdnEq	A	D	17%	-20%	2/1/94	24	2.50 ◐
★★★ⱼ	**Hyperion Value Line U.S. Equity** — You won't find many like this one! It's done better than most in its class. High expenses haven't been much of a problem for this actively managed fund.	USEq	A	N/A	8%	-12%	3/1/94	11	3.00 ●
★★★ⱼ	**ICM Balanced Fund** — You won't find many like this one! It's done better than most in its class with top-notch performance in bull markets but has been hit hard in bear markets. Lower annual expenses than most bode well for the future of this fund.	Balan	A	D	15%	-18%	9/1/87	19	0.30 ◐
★★★	**ICM Bond Fund** — This fund has shown middle-of-the-road performance against similar funds along with performing better than most in all market conditions. Lower annual expenses than most bode well for the future of this closet indexer.	FixInc	B	B	11%	-10%	2/1/94	14	0.14 ●
★★★	**ICM Equity Fund** — This well-established fund has shown middle-of-the-road performance against similar funds with performing better than most in all market conditions. Lower annual expenses than most bode well for the future of this fund.	CdnEq	B	B	18%	-31%	6/1/87	68	0.12 ●
★★★	**ICM International Equity Fund** — This fund has shown middle-of-the-road performance against similar funds. Lower annual expenses than most bode well for the future of this fund.	FgnEq	B	N/A	2%	-6%	8/1/97	N/A	0.35 ●
★★★★★	**ICM Short Term Investment Fund** — This fund has off-the-charts performance overall vs. its peers. No wonder performance has been so good for this actively managed fund. Its fees are among the lowest in its group.	FixInc	N/A	N/A	0%	0%		N/A	0.12 ●
★★★	**IG Beutel Goodman Cdn. Balanced** — This newer fund has shown middle-of-the-road performance against similar funds. High expenses haven't been much of a problem for this actively managed fund.	Balan	N/A	N/A	0%	-3%	3/1/97	2	2.99 ●
★★★ⱼ	**IG Beutel Goodman Cdn. Equity Fund** — You won't find many new ones like this one! It's done better than most in its class. High expenses haven't been much of a problem for this actively managed fund.	CdnEq	N/A	N/A	0%	-4%	3/1/97	2	3.17 ●
★★★★	**IG Beutel Goodman Cdn. Small-Cap** — This newer fund has off-the-charts performance overall vs. its peers. This actively managed fund is expensive but well worth it.	CdnEq	N/A	N/A	0%	-3%	3/1/97	2	2.86 ●

Performance Trend columns shown as quartile boxes for calendar years: 88, 89, 90, 91, 92, 93, 94, 95, 96, Sep-97.

Lege d: ★ = overall past performance vs. similar funds (5 ★ max). Boxes show the quartile performance for a fund each calendar year vs. only similar funds □ is the best score possible. ● = high; ◐ = average; and ● = a fund with low expenses.

Consistency (Overall Past Performance)	Fund Name	Type	Performance Trend (88–Sep-97)	Risk Up	Risk Down	% of Time Losing $	Biggest Drop	Date	No. of Mo's to Recover	MER (Efficiency)
★★	**IG Sceptre Canadian Balanced Fund**	Balan		N/A	N/A	0%	-3%	8/1/97	N/A	2.95 ●
	This newer fund has been set apart from its peers by its weak returns. High expenses exacerbate the problem for this actively managed fund.									
★	**IG Sceptre Canadian Bond Fund**	FixInc		N/A	N/A	0%	-3%	12/1/96	5	2.64 ●
	This newer fund has been a dog. High expenses exacerbate the problem for this actively managed fund.									
★★★✓	**IG Sceptre Canadian Equity Fund**	CdnEq		N/A	N/A	0%	-5%	8/1/97	N/A	2.83 ●
	You won't find many new ones like this one! It's done better than most in its class. High expenses haven't been much of a problem for this actively managed fund.									
★★★	**Imperial Growth Canadian Equity**	CdnEq		B	B	16%	-27%	7/1/81	18	1.96 ◐
	This well-established fund has shown middle-of-the-road performance against similar funds along with performing better than most in all market conditions. Annual fees are reasonable for this reasonably performing fund.									
★★	**Imperial Growth Diversified Fund**	Balan		D	N/A	8%	-8%	2/1/94	13	2.00 ◐
	This fund has been set apart from its peers by its weak returns. Normally I'd say that this fund has reasonable expenses compared to its peers, but poor overall performance makes that argument weak.									
★	**Imperial Growth Money Market Fund**	FixInc		N/A	N/A	0%	0%		1	1.50 ●
	This fund has been a dog. High expenses exacerbate the problem for this actively managed fund.									
★★★	**Imperial Growth North American Eqt.**	FgnEq		B	B	29%	-29%	7/1/81	19	1.60 ●
	Here is an older fund that has shown middle-of-the-road performance against similar funds along with performing better than most in all market conditions. Lower annual expenses than most bode well for the future of this actively managed fund.									
★★★	**Industrial Alliance Bond Fund**	FixInc		B	B	6%	-11%	2/1/94	15	1.61 ◐
	This well-established fund has shown middle-of-the-road performance against similar funds along with performing better than most in all market conditions. Annual fees are reasonable for this reasonably performing closet indexer.									
★★★	**Industrial Alliance Bond Fund – 2**	FixInc		N/A	N/A	0%	-1%	3/1/97	1	1.61 ◐
	This newer fund has shown middle-of-the-road performance against similar funds. Annual fees are reasonable for this reasonably performing fund.									
★★★	**Industrial Alliance Diversified**	Balan		B	C	8%	-10%	4/1/87	18	1.61 ◐
	Here is an older fund that has shown middle-of-the-road performance against similar funds. Along with performing better than most in bull markets it has been a disappointment in bear markets. Annual fees are reasonable for this reasonably performing closet indexer.									
★	**Industrial Alliance Diversified – 2**	Balan		N/A	N/A	100%	-7%	3/1/97	4	1.61 ◐
	This newer fund has been a dog. Normally I'd say that this fund has reasonable expenses compared to its peers, but poor overall performance makes that argument weak.									
★	**Industrial Alliance Ecoflex Fund A**	CdnEq		D	N/A	2%	-10%	2/1/94	13	2.14 ◐
	Here is one that is a dog. Normally I'd say that this fund has reasonable expenses compared to its peers, but poor overall performance makes that argument weak.									
★	**Industrial Alliance Ecoflex Fund B**	FixInc		D	C	23%	-12%	2/1/94	15	1.55 ◐
	This fund has been a dog. Normally I'd say that this closet indexer has reasonable expenses compared to its peers, but poor overall performance makes that argument weak.									

Legend: ★ = overall past performance vs. similar funds (5 ★ max). Boxes show the quartile performance for a fund each calendar year vs. only similar funds (□ is the best score possible). ● = high; ● = average; and ● = a fund with low expenses.

Consistency			Performance Trend										Risk						Efficiency
Overall Past Performance	Fund Name	Type	88	89	90	91	92	93	94	95	96	Sep-97	Up	Down	% of Time Losing $	Biggest Drop	Date	No. of Mo's to Recover	MER
★★★⟩	**Industrial Alliance Ecoflex Fund D**	Balan											C	N/A	7%	−10%	2/1/94	13	2.14
	This fund has been unimpressive so far. Normally I'd say that this closet indexer has reasonable expenses compared to its peers, but poor overall performance makes that argument weak.																		
★⟩	**Industrial Alliance Ecoflex Fund E**	FgnEq											N/A	N/A	0%	−8%	8/1/97	N/A	2.14
	This newer fund can be described as having dismal returns. Low fees have not helped this fund.																		
★	**Industrial Alliance Ecoflex Fund G**	FixInc											N/A	N/A	0%	−1%	5/1/97	N/A	1.55
	This newer fund has been a dog. Low fees have not helped this fund.																		
★	**Industrial Alliance Ecoflex Fund H**	FixInc											D	B	5%	−5%	3/1/94	11	1.55
	This fund has been a dog. Low fees have not helped this actively managed fund.																		
★★★⟩	**Industrial Alliance Ecoflex Fund I**	FgnEq											N/A	N/A	0%	−3%	8/1/97	N/A	2.14
	You won't find many new ones like this one! It's done better than most in its class. Annual fees are reasonable for this reasonably performing actively managed fund.																		
★	**Industrial Alliance Ecoflex Fund M**	FixInc											N/A	N/A	0%	−1%	11/1/92	1	1.02
	This fund has been a dog. Normally I'd say that this actively managed fund has reasonable expenses compared to its peers, but poor overall performance makes that argument weak.																		
★	**Industrial Alliance Ecoflex Fund S**	USEq											N/A	N/A	0%	−6%	2/1/97	2	2.14
	This newer fund has been a dog. Normally I'd say that this fund has reasonable expenses compared to its peers, but poor overall performance makes that argument weak.																		
★★★	**Industrial Alliance Emerging Market**	FgnEq											N/A	N/A	0%	−8%	8/1/97	N/A	1.61
	This newer fund has shown middle-of-the-road performance against similar funds. Lower annual expenses than most bode well for the future of this fund.																		
★	**Industrial Alliance Global Bond Fund**	FixInc											N/A	N/A	0%	−1%	5/1/97	N/A	1.61
	This newer fund has been a dog. Low fees have not helped this fund.																		
★★★★	**Industrial Alliance Int'l Fund**	FgnEq											N/A	N/A	0%	−3%	8/1/97	N/A	1.61
	This newer fund has off-the-charts performance overall vs. its peers. No wonder performance has been so good for this actively managed fund. Its fees are among the lowest in its group.																		
★	**Industrial Alliance Money Mkt. Fund**	FixInc											N/A	N/A	0%	−1%	11/1/92	1	1.61
	This fund has been a dog. High expenses exacerbate the problem for this actively managed fund.																		
★★★⟩	**Industrial Alliance Mortgage Fund**	FixInc											A	B	1%	−4%	3/1/94	11	1.61
	You won't find many like this older one! It's done better than most in its class with top-notch performance in bull markets as well as performing better than most in bear markets. Annual fees are reasonable for this reasonable performing actively managed fund.																		
★★★★	**Industrial Alliance Stock Fund**	CdnEq		N/A									A	N/A	15%	−24%	9/1/87	22	1.61
	This well-established fund has off-the-charts performance overall vs. its peers. No wonder performance has been so good for this fund. Its fees are among the lowest in its group.																		

Legend: ★ = overall past performance vs. similar funds (5 ★ max). Boxes show the quartile performance for a fund each calendar year vs. only similar funds (□ is the best score possible). ● = high; ◐ = average; and ○ = a fund with low expenses.

Overall Past Performance	Fund Name	Type	Risk Up	Risk Down	% of Time Losing $	Biggest Drop	Date	No. of Mo's to Recover	MER
★	Industrial Alliance Stock Fund – 2	CdnEq	N/A	N/A	0%	-4%	3/1/97	2	1.61
★★	Industrial Alliance US Stock Fund	USEq	N/A	N/A	0%	-6%	2/1/97	2	1.61
★★★	Industrial American Fund	USEq	C	C	14%	-29%	9/1/87	22	2.38
★★★	Industrial Balanced Fund	Balan	B	N/A	9%	-10%	2/1/94	15	2.37
★★★	Industrial Bond Fund	FixInc	A	D	12%	-16%	2/1/94	19	1.98
★★★★★	Industrial Cash Management	FixInc	N/A	N/A	0%	0%	N/A	N/A	0.50
★★★	Industrial Dividend Growth Fund Ltd.	CdnEq	A	B	27%	-33%	9/1/89	45	2.39
★★	Industrial Equity Fund Ltd.	CdnEq	B	D	38%	-37%	8/1/87	67	2.41
★★★	Industrial Future Fund	CdnEq	C	C	26%	-21%	9/1/89	42	2.38
★★★	Industrial Growth Fund	CdnEq	C	A	24%	-24%	8/1/87	17	2.38
★★↗	Industrial Horizon Fund	CdnEq	D	B	22%	-17%	9/1/89	43	2.38
★★★	Industrial Income Fund	Balan	B	B	19%	-20%	7/1/79	37	1.87
★★★↗	Industrial Mortgage Securities	FixInc	B	D	9%	-12%	1/1/90	13	1.86

Performance Trend columns (88, 89, 90, 91, 92, 93, 94, 95, 96, Sep-97) show quartile boxes for each fund.

Industrial Alliance Stock Fund – 2: This newer fund has been a dog. Normally I'd say that this fund has reasonable expenses compared to its peers, but poor overall performance makes that argument weak.

Industrial Alliance US Stock Fund: This newer fund has been set apart from its peers by its weak returns. Low fees have not helped this fund.

Industrial American Fund: This well-established fund has shown middle-of-the-road performance against similar funds with disappointing results in all market conditions. Annual fees are reasonable for this reasonably performing actively managed fund.

Industrial Balanced Fund: This fund has shown middle-of-the-road performance against similar funds. High expenses haven't been much of a problem for this fund.

Industrial Bond Fund: This fund has shown middle-of-the-road performance against similar funds with top-notch performance in bull markets but has been hit hard in bear markets. This closet indexer is expensive but worth it in rising market conditions.

Industrial Cash Management: This well-established fund has off-the-charts performance overall vs. its peers. No wonder performance has been so good for this actively managed fund, its fees are among the lowest in its group.

Industrial Dividend Growth Fund Ltd.: Here is an older fund that has shown middle-of-the-road performance against similar funds with top-notch performance in bull markets as well as performing better than most in bear markets. High expenses haven't been much of a problem for this actively managed fund.

Industrial Equity Fund Ltd.: This well-established fund has been set apart from its peers by its weak returns; it's performed better than most in bull markets but it's been hit hard in bear markets. High expenses exacerbate the problem for this fund.

Industrial Future Fund: This fund has shown middle-of-the-road performance against similar funds with disappointing results in all market conditions. High expenses haven't been much of a problem for this actively managed fund.

Industrial Growth Fund: Here is an older fund that has shown middle-of-the-road performance against similar funds with disappointing results in bull markets and top-notch performance in bear markets. High expenses haven't been much of a problem for this actively managed fund.

Industrial Horizon Fund: This well-established fund has been unimpressive so far. This fund is not worth the extra bucks.

Industrial Income Fund: Beware of this fund's fixed quarterly payout. Over the last couple of years, about 60% of this fund's distributions were actually a return of capital. It has a substantial holding in bonds.

Industrial Mortgage Securities: You won't find many like this older one! It's done better than most in its class; it has performed better than most in bull markets but has been hit hard in bear markets. High expenses haven't been much of a problem for this actively managed fund.

Legend: ★ = overall past performance vs. similar funds (5 ★ max). Boxes show the quartile performance for a fund each calendar year vs. only similar funds (□ is the best score possible). ● = high; ◐ = average; and ● = a fund with low expenses.

Consistency			Performance Trend	Risk						Efficiency
Overall Past Performance	Fund Name	Type	88 89 90 91 92 93 94 95 96 Sep-97	Up	Down	% of Time Losing $	Biggest Drop	Date	No. of Mo's to Recover	MER
★★★	**Industrial Pension Fund**	Balan		C	D	32%	-34%	9/1/89	50	2.44 ●
	Here is an older fund that has shown middle-of-the-road performance against similar funds with disappointing results in bull markets along with being hit hard in bear markets. This actively managed fund is expensive but worth it in rising market conditions.									
★	**Industrial Short-Term Fund**	FixInc		N/A	N/A	0%	0%	N/A	N/A	1.23 ●
	This fund has been a dog. High expenses exacerbate the problem for this actively managed fund.									
★★★★	**Infinity Canadian Fund**	Balan		N/A	N/A	0%	-4%	8/1/97	N/A	2.95 ●
	This newer fund has off-the-charts performance overall vs. its peers. This fund is expensive but well worth it.									
★★	**Infinity Income Fund**	CdnEq		D	A	7%	-5%	3/1/94	12	2.24 ●
	This well-established fund has been set apart from its peers by its weak returns, but it's been a top-notch performer in bear markets. High fees exacerbate the problem for this fund, especially in bull markets.									
★★★♪	**Infinity International Fund**	Balan		N/A	N/A	0%	-8%	8/1/97	N/A	2.95 ●
	You won't find many new ones like this one! It's done better than most in its class. High expenses haven't been much of a problem for this fund.									
★★★★★	**Infinity T-Bill Fund**	FixInc		N/A	N/A	0%	0%	N/A	N/A	1.00 ◐
	This newer fund has off-the-charts performance overall vs. its peers. Reasonable fees represent bargains for this actively managed fund.									
★★	**Infinity Wealth Management Fund**	FgnEq		D	D	22%	-33%	12/1/80	26	2.95 ●
	This well-established fund has been set apart from its peers by its weak returns; it's been hit hard in all market conditions. High expenses exacerbate the problem for this fund.									
★	**InvesNat Blue Chip Amer Equity ($US)**	USEq		D	N/A	27%	-11%	2/1/94	21	2.33 ◐
	Here is one that is a dog. Normally I'd say that this actively managed fund has reasonable expenses compared to its peers, but poor overall performance makes that argument weak.									
★♪	**InvesNat Canadian Bond Fund**	FixInc		D	B	19%	-9%	2/1/94	15	1.46 ◐
	This fund can be described as having dismal returns. Normally I'd say this fund has reasonable fees, but poor overall performance makes that argument weak.									
★★	**InvesNat Canadian Equity Fund**	CdnEq		C	C	14%	-11%	2/1/94	15	2.12 ◐
	This fund has shown middle-of-the-road performance against similar funds with disappointing results in all market conditions. Annual fees are reasonable for this reasonably performing fund.									
★★★★	**InvesNat Corporate Cash Mgmt Fund**	FixInc		N/A	N/A	0%	0%	N/A	N/A	0.52 ●
	This fund has off-the-charts performance overall vs. its peers. No wonder performance has been so good for this actively managed fund, its fees are among the lowest in its group.									
★	**InvesNat Dividend Fund**	CdnEq		D	D	6%	-4%	2/1/94	13	1.70 ◐
	This fund has been a dog, but it's been hit hard in all market conditions. Normally I'd say that this actively managed fund has reasonable expenses compared to its peers, but poor overall performance makes that argument weak.									
★★♪	**InvesNat European Equity Fund**	FgnEq		C	N/A	4%	-14%	9/1/92	11	2.31 ◐
	This fund has been unimpressive so far. Normally I'd say that this fund has reasonable expenses compared to its peers, but poor overall performance makes that argument weak.									

Legend: ★ = overall past performance vs. similar funds (5 ★ max). Boxes show the quartile performance for a fund each calendar year vs. only similar funds (□ is the best score possible). ● = high; ◐ = average; and ● = a fund with low expenses.

Overall Past Performance (Consistency)	Fund Name	Type	Risk Up	Risk Down	% of Time Losing $	Biggest Drop	Date	No. of Mo's to Recover	MER (Efficiency)
★★★♪	**InvesNat Far East Equity Fund** — You won't find many like this one! It's done better than most in its class. Lower annual expenses than most bode well for the future of this actively managed fund.	FgnEq	N/A	N/A	9%	-15%	1/1/97	N/A	2.45 ●
★★♪	**InvesNat International RSP Bond** — This fund has been unimpressive so far. Normally I'd say that this actively managed fund has reasonable expenses compared to its peers, but poor overall performance makes that argument weak.	FixInc	N/A	N/A	6%	-5%	1/1/97	6	2.12 ◐
★★	**InvesNat Japanese Equity Fund** — This fund has been set apart from its peers by its weak returns. Normally I'd say that this actively managed fund has reasonable expenses compared to its peers, but overall performance makes that argument weak.	FgnEq	N/A	N/A	74%	-34%	9/1/94	N/A	2.43 ◐
★★★	**InvesNat Money Market Fund** — This fund has shown middle-of-the-road performance against similar funds. Annual fees are reasonable for this reasonably performing actively managed fund.	FixInc	N/A	N/A	0%	0%	N/A	N/A	1.05 ◐
★★★♪	**InvesNat Mortgage Fund** — This fund has done better than most in its class. As well as performing better than most in bull markets it's been a top-notch performer in bear markets. Lower annual expenses than most bode well for the future of this actively managed fund.	FixInc	B	A	0%	-4%	3/1/94	8	1.55 ●
★♪	**InvesNat Retirement Balanced Fund** — This fund can be described as having dismal returns. Normally I'd say that this fund has reasonable expenses compared to its peers, but poor overall performance makes that argument weak.	Balan	D	N/A	16%	-9%	1/1/90	12	2.14 ◐
★★★	**InvesNat Short Term Government Bond** — This fund has shown middle-of-the-road performance against similar funds; it has performed better than most in bull markets but has been hit hard in bear markets. Annual fees are reasonable for this reasonably performing actively managed fund.	FixInc	B	D	4%	-5%	2/1/94	13	1.35 ◐
★★★★	**InvesNat Treasury Bill Plus Fund** — This fund has off-the-charts performance overall vs. its peers. Reasonable fees represent bargains for this actively managed fund.	FixInc	N/A	N/A	0%	0%	N/A	N/A	0.77 ◐
★	**InvesNat U.S. Money Market ($US)** — This fund has been a dog. Normally I'd say that this actively managed fund has reasonable expenses compared to its peers, but poor overall performance makes that argument weak.	FixInc	N/A	N/A	0%	0%	N/A	N/A	1.11 ◐
★★★	**Investors Asset Allocation Fund** — This fund has shown middle-of-the-road performance against similar funds. High expenses haven't been much of a problem for this fund.	Balan	B	N/A	7%	-9%	2/1/94	17	2.73 ●
★★★	**Investors Canadian Equity Fund** — This well-established fund has shown middle-of-the-road performance against similar funds; it performs better than most in all market conditions. High expenses haven't been much of a problem for this fund.	CdnEq	B	B	16%	-23%	8/1/87	23	2.46 ●
★★	**Investors Cdn. Natural Resource** — This newer fund has been set apart from its peers by its weak returns. High expenses exacerbate the problem for this actively managed fund.	CdnEq	N/A	N/A	0%	-6%	3/1/97	3	2.85 ●
★★★★	**Investors Canadian Small-Cap Fund** — This newer fund has off-the-charts performance overall vs. its peers. This actively managed fund is expensive but well worth it.	CdnEq	N/A	N/A	0%	-3%	3/1/97	2	2.79 ●

Legend: ★ = overall past performance vs. similar funds (5 ★ max). Boxes show the quartile performance for a fund each calendar year vs. only similar funds (□ is the best score possible). ● = high; ● = average; and ● = a fund with low expenses.

Consistency		Performance Trend											Risk						Efficiency
Overall Past Performance	Fund Name	Type	88	89	90	91	92	93	94	95	96	Sep-97	Up	Down	% of Time Losing $	Biggest Drop	Date	No. of Mo's to Recover	MER
★★★	**Investors Corporate Bond Fund**	FixInc											B	A	0%	−2%	2/1/96	4	1.89 ●
★★★	**Investors Dividend Fund**	CdnEq											B	A	12%	−18%	4/1/81	18	2.34 ●
★★⟩	**Investors European Growth Fund**	FgnEq											C	N/A	7%	−10%	3/1/91	9	2.45 ●
★★	**Investors Global Bond Fund**	FixInc											D	N/A	18%	−5%	8/1/95	4	2.18 ●
★★★	**Investors Global Fund**	FgnEq											C	B	16%	−23%	9/1/87	34	2.46 ●
★★⟩	**Investors Government Bond Fund**	FixInc											C	C	12%	−13%	8/1/79	27	1.90 ●
★★★	**Investors Growth Plus Portfolio**	Balan											A	N/A	8%	−9%	1/1/90	13	0.17 ●
★★★	**Investors Growth Portfolio Fund**	FgnEq											B	N/A	11%	−17%	1/1/90	18	0.18 ●
★★	**Investors Income Plus Portfolio**	Balan											D	N/A	8%	−8%	2/1/94	15	0.15 ●
★★	**Investors Income Portfolio Fund**	FixInc											D	A	10%	−9%	2/1/94	14	0.16 ●
★★⟩	**Investors Japanese Growth Fund**	FgnEq											C	B	43%	−36%	10/1/89	45	2.46 ●
★★★★	**Investors Latin American Growth**	FgnEq											N/A	N/A	0%	−8%	8/1/97	N/A	3.00 ●

Investors Corporate Bond Fund — This fund has shown middle-of-the-road performance against similar funds. As well as performing better than most in bull markets it's been a top-notch performer in bear markets. High expenses haven't been much of a problem for this fund.

Investors Dividend Fund — Here is an older fund that has shown middle-of-the-road performance against similar funds. As well as performing better than most in bull markets it's been a top-notch performer in bear markets. High expenses haven't been much of a problem for this actively managed fund.

Investors European Growth Fund — This fund has been unimpressive so far. Normally I'd say that this closet indexer has reasonable expenses compared to its peers, but poor overall performance makes that argument weak.

Investors Global Bond Fund — This fund has been set apart from its peers by its weak returns. High expenses exacerbate the problem for this actively managed fund.

Investors Global Fund — This well-established fund has shown middle-of-the-road performance against similar funds with disappointing results in bull markets and better than average in bear markets. Annual fees are reasonable for this reasonable performing fund.

Investors Government Bond Fund — This well-established fund has been unimpressive so far with disappointing results in all market conditions. High expenses exacerbate the problem for this closet indexer.

Investors Growth Plus Portfolio — This fund has shown middle-of-the-road performance against similar funds. Lower annual expenses than most bode well for the future of this actively managed fund.

Investors Growth Portfolio Fund — This fund has shown middle-of-the-road performance against similar funds; it has performed better than most in bull markets but it has been hit hard in bear markets. Lower annual expenses than most bode well for the future of this fund.

Investors Income Plus Portfolio — This fund has been set apart from its peers by its weak returns. Low fees have not helped this fund.

Investors Income Portfolio Fund — This fund has been set apart from its peers by its weak returns, but it's been a top-notch performer in bear markets. This low-priced closet indexer is well worth it.

Investors Japanese Growth Fund — This well-established fund has been unimpressive so far with disappointing results in bull markets. Normally I'd say this fund has reasonable fees, but poor overall performance makes that argument weak.

Investors Latin American Growth — This newer fund has off-the-charts performance overall vs. its peers. This actively managed fund is expensive but well worth it.

Legend: ★ = overall past performance vs. similar funds (5 ★ max). Boxes show the quartile performance for a fund each calendar year vs. only similar funds (☐ is the best score possible). ● = high; ◐ = average; and ○ = a fund with low expenses.

Overall Past Performance	Fund Name	Type	88	89	90	91	92	93	94	95	96	Sep-97	Up	Down	% of Time Losing $	Biggest Drop	Date	No. of Mo's to Recover	MER
★★	**Investors Money Market Fund**	FixInc	☐	☐	☐	☐	☐	☐	☐	☐	☐	☐	N/A	N/A	0%	0%	N/A	N/A	1.07 ◐
	This well-established fund has been set apart from its peers by its weak returns. Normally I'd say that this actively managed fund has reasonable expenses compared to its peers, but poor overall performance makes that argument weak.																		
★★★☂	**Investors Mortgage Fund**	FixInc	☐	☐	☐	☐	☐	☐	☐	☐	☐	☐	B	D	4%	-7%	2/1/94	13	1.89 ●
	You won't find many like this older one! It's done better than most in its class. It has performed better than most in bull markets but has been hit hard in bear markets. High expenses haven't been much of a problem for this actively managed fund.																		
★★★	**Investors Mutual of Canada**	Balan	☐	☐	☐	☐	☐	☐	☐	☐	☐	☐	B	D	18%	-22%	12/1/80	23	2.34 ●
	Here is an older fund that has shown middle-of-the-road performance against similar funds; it has performed better than most in bull markets but has been hit hard in bear markets. This fund is expensive but worth it in rising market conditions.																		
★★★	**Investors North American Growth**	FgnEq	☐	☐	☐	☐	☐	☐	☐	☐	☐	☐	C	D	17%	-26%	12/1/80	24	2.38 ◐
	Here is an older fund that has shown middle-of-the-road performance against similar funds with disappointing results in bull markets along with being hit hard in bear markets. Annual fees are reasonable for this reasonable performing actively managed fund.																		
★★☂	**Investors N.A. High-Yield Bond**	FixInc										☐	N/A	N/A	0%	-2%	3/1/97	2	2.21 ●
	Check out how unimpressive this new fund has been. High expenses exacerbate the problem for this actively managed fund.																		
★★★	**Investors Pacific International**	FgnEq				☐	☐	☐	☐	☐	☐	☐	B	A	16%	-16%	8/1/97	N/A	2.56 ◐
	This fund has shown middle-of-the-road performance against similar funds. As well as performing better than most in bull markets it's been a top-notch performer in bear markets. Annual fees are reasonable for this reasonable performing actively managed fund.																		
★★★★	**Investors Real Property Fund**	SpcIty				N/A	N/A	☐	☐	☐	☐	☐	N/A	N/A	14%	-4%	10/1/92	34	2.39 ◐
	This fund has off-the-charts performance overall vs. its peers. Reasonable fees represent bargains for this actively managed fund.																		
★★★	**Investors Retirement Gth. Portfolio**	CdnEq	☐	☐	☐	☐	☐	☐	☐	☐	☐	☐	C	C	13%	-14%	9/1/89	20	0.18 ●
	This fund has shown middle-of-the-road performance against similar funds with disappointing results in all market conditions. Lower annual expenses than most bode well for the future of this fund.																		
★★★	**Investors Retirement Mutual Fund**	CdnEq	☐	☐	☐	☐	☐	☐	☐	☐	☐	☐	B	A	21%	-28%	6/1/81	20	2.40 ●
	Here is an older fund that has shown middle-of-the-road performance against similar funds. As well as performing better than most in bull markets it's been a top-notch performer in bear markets. High expenses haven't been much of a problem for this closet indexer.																		
★★	**Investors Retirement Plus Portfolio**	Balan	☐	☐	☐	☐	☐	☐	☐	☐	☐	☐	D	N/A	8%	-7%	1/1/90	13	0.17 ●
	This fund-of-funds has been set apart from its peers by its weak returns. The low fees shown are on top of each fund's fees.																		
★★★	**Investors Special Fund**	FgnEq	☐	☐	☐	☐	☐	☐	☐	☐	☐	☐	B	C	21%	-33%	6/1/81	19	2.39 ◐
	This well-established fund has shown middle-of-the-road performance against similar funds. Along with performing better than most in bull markets it has been a disappointment in bear markets. Annual fees are reasonable for this reasonably performing actively managed fund.																		

Legend: ★ = overall past performance vs. similar funds (5 ★ max). Boxes show the quartile performance for a fund each calendar year vs. only similar funds (□ is the best score possible). ● = high; ◐ = average; and ● = a fund with low expenses.

Overall Past Performance	Fund Name	Type	Risk Up	Risk Down	% of Time Losing $	Biggest Drop	Date	No. of Mo's to Recover	MER
★★★	Investors Summa Fund	CdnEq	B	C	24%	-24%	9/1/89	27	2.43
★★★	Investors U.S. Growth Fund	USEq	B	A	18%	-29%	10/1/87	39	2.35
★★★↗	Investors U.S. Opportunities Fund	USEq	N/A	N/A	0%	-3%	3/1/97	2	2.61
★★★	Investors World Growth Portfolio	FgnEq	B	N/A	5%	-7%	8/1/97	N/A	0.18
★★	Ivy Canadian Fund	CdnEq	B	N/A	0%	-4%	2/1/94	6	2.37
★★	Ivy Enterprise Fund	CdnEq	D	A	81%	-32%	9/1/89	49	2.43
★★★	Ivy Foreign Equity Fund	FgnEq	B	N/A	0%	-4%	7/1/96	2	2.40
★★★	Ivy Growth & Income Fund	Balan	B	N/A	11%	-5%	2/1/94	12	2.13
★★★↗	Ivy Mortgage Fund	FixInc	A	C	3%	-6%	2/1/94	13	1.90
★★	Jones Heward American Fund	USEq	C	D	19%	-31%	9/1/87	22	2.50
★★	Jones Heward Bond Fund	FixInc	C	D	8%	-13%	2/1/94	19	1.75
★★	Jones Heward Canadian Balanced Fund	Balan	C	C	20%	-14%	9/1/87	21	2.40
★★★	Jones Heward Fund Ltd.	CdnEq	A	B	27%	-37%	5/1/81	23	2.50

Investors Summa Fund — This well-established fund has shown middle-of-the-road performance against similar funds with top-notch performance in bull markets but disappointing results in bear markets. High expenses haven't been much of a problem for this actively managed fund.

Investors U.S. Growth Fund — This well-established fund has shown middle-of-the-road performance against similar funds. As well as performing better than most in bull markets it's been a top-notch performer in bear markets. Annual fees are reasonable for this reasonably performing actively managed fund.

Investors U.S. Opportunities Fund — You won't find many new ones like this one! It's done better than most in its class. High expenses haven't been much of a problem for this actively managed fund.

Investors World Growth Portfolio — This fund has shown middle-of-the-road performance against similar funds. Lower annual expenses than most bode well for the future of this fund.

Ivy Canadian Fund — A changing of the guard at Ivy Canadian leaves Jerry Javasky at the helm of this conservative fund. With more than 30% in cash, Javasky will be opportunistic when markets eventually sour.

Ivy Enterprise Fund — This well-established fund has been a dog. Normally I'd say this fund has reasonable fees, but poor overall performance makes that argument weak.

Ivy Foreign Equity Fund — This fund has shown middle-of-the-road performance against similar funds. Annual fees are reasonable for this reasonably performing actively managed fund.

Ivy Growth & Income Fund — This fund has shown middle-of-the-road performance against similar funds. Annual fees are reasonable for this reasonably performing actively managed fund.

Ivy Mortgage Fund — You won't find many like this one! It's done better than most in its class with top-notch performance in bull markets but disappointing results in bear markets. High expenses haven't been much of a problem for this actively managed fund.

Jones Heward American Fund — This well-established fund has been set apart from its peers by its weak returns, with disappointing results in bull markets as well as in bear markets. High expenses exacerbate the problem for this actively managed fund.

Jones Heward Bond Fund — This fund has been set apart from its peers by its weak returns, with disappointing results in bull markets as well as in bear markets. High expenses exacerbate the problem for this closet indexer.

Jones Heward Canadian Balanced Fund — This well-established fund has been set apart from its peers by its weak returns, with disappointing results in all market conditions. High expenses exacerbate the problem for this fund.

Jones Heward Fund Ltd. — Here is an older fund that has shown middle-of-the-road performance against similar funds with top-notch performance in bull markets as well as performing better than most in bear markets. High expenses haven't been much of a problem for this actively managed fund.

Legend: ★ = overall past performance vs. similar funds. Boxes show the quartile performance for a fund each calendar year vs. only similar funds (5 ★ max). □ is the best score possible). ● = high; ◐ = average; and ● = a fund with low expenses.

Consistency			Performance Trend										Risk						Efficiency
Overall Past Performance	Fund Name	Type	88	89	90	91	92	93	94	95	96	Sep-97	Up	Down	% of Time Losing $	Biggest Drop	Date	No. of Mo's to Recover	MER
★★★	**Jones Heward Money Market Fund**	FixInc											N/A	N/A	0%	0%		N/A	1.00
	This fund has shown middle-of-the-road performance against similar funds. Annual fees are reasonable for this reasonably performing actively managed fund.																		
★★	**Laurentian American Equity Fund Ltd**	USEq											D	B	18%	-25%	9/1/87	20	2.65
	This well-established fund has been set apart from its peers by its weak returns. This actively managed fund is not worth the extra bucks.																		
★★↑	**Laurentian Asia Pacific Fund**	FgnEq											N/A	N/A	37%	-13%	5/1/96	N/A	2.65
	This fund has been unimpressive so far. Normally I'd say that this actively managed fund has reasonable expenses compared to its peers, but overall performance makes that argument weak.																		
★	**Laurentian Canadian Balanced Fund**	Balan											D	N/A	12%	-9%	2/1/94	15	2.65
	This fund has been a dog. High expenses exacerbate the problem for this closet indexer.																		
★★	**Laurentian Canadian Equity Fund Ltd**	CdnEq											D	D	25%	-28%	6/1/81	19	2.65
	This well-established fund has been set apart from its peers by its weak returns; it's been hit hard in all market conditions. High expenses exacerbate the problem for this closet indexer.																		
★★	**Laurentian Commonwealth Fund Ltd.**	FgnEq											C	B	12%	-18%	9/1/87	16	2.65
	This well-established fund has been set apart from its peers by its weak returns, with disappointing results in bull markets. Normally I'd say this fund has reasonable fees, but poor overall performance makes that argument weak.																		
★★★	**Laurentian Dividend Fund Ltd.**	CdnEq											B	A	14%	-16%	4/1/81	18	2.65
	Here is an older fund that has shown middle-of-the-road performance against similar funds. As well as performing better than most in bull markets it's been a top-notch performer in bear markets. High expenses haven't been much of a problem for this actively managed fund.																		
★★★	**Laurentian Emerging Markets Fund**	FgnEq											N/A	N/A	5%	-12%	8/1/97	N/A	2.95
	This fund has shown middle-of-the-road performance against similar funds. Annual fees are reasonable for this reasonably performing actively managed fund.																		
★★	**Laurentian Europe Fund**	FgnEq											N/A	N/A	0%	-5%	8/1/95	4	2.65
	This fund has been set apart from its peers by its weak returns. High expenses exacerbate the problem for this actively managed fund.																		
★★	**Laurentian Global Balanced Fund**	Balan											C	N/A	9%	-11%	8/1/90	16	2.65
	This fund has been set apart from its peers by its weak returns. Normally I'd say that this actively managed fund has reasonable expenses compared to its peers, but overall performance makes that argument weak.																		
★★	**Laurentian Government Bond Fund**	FixInc											D	C	5%	-5%	2/1/94	12	2.15
	This fund has been set apart from its peers by its weak returns, but it's been a top-notch performer in bear markets. High expenses exacerbate the problem for this closet indexer, especially in declining markets.																		
★★↑	**Laurentian Income Fund**	FixInc											C	A	12%	-16%	7/1/79	33	2.15
	This well-established fund has been unimpressive so far with disappointing results in a bullish environment. High expenses exacerbate the problem for this closet indexer.																		
★★	**Laurentian International Fund Ltd**	FgnEq											D	B	17%	-25%	9/1/87	22	2.65
	This well-established fund has been set apart from its peers by its weak returns. This fund is not worth the extra bucks.																		

Legend: ★ = overall past performance vs. similar funds (5 ★ max). Boxes show the quartile performance for a fund each calendar year vs. only similar funds (□ is the best score possible). ● = high; ◐ = average; and ● = a fund with low expenses.

Overall Past Performance	Fund Name	Type	Up	Down	% of Time Losing $	Biggest Drop	Date	No. of Mo's to Recover	MER
★★♪	**Laurentian Money Market Fund** This well-established fund has been unimpressive so far. High expenses exacerbate the problem for this actively managed fund.	FixInc	N/A	N/A	0%	0%	—	N/A	1.15
★★	**Laurentian Special Equity Fund** This fund has been set apart from its peers by its weak returns, with disappointing results in bull markets. High expenses exacerbate the problem for this actively managed fund.	CdnEq	C	B	15%	-13%	2/1/94	16	2.65
★★★♪	**Leith Wheeler Balanced Fund** This fund has done better than most in its class with top-notch performance in all market conditions. Lower annual expenses than most bode well for the future of this fund.	Balan	A	A	11%	-10%	2/1/94	15	1.16
★★★	**Leith Wheeler Canadian Equity Fund** This fund has shown middle-of-the-road performance against similar funds. Along with performing better than most in bull markets it has been a disappointment in bear markets. Lower annual expenses than most bode well for the future of this actively managed fund.	CdnEq	B	C	0%	-5%	6/1/94	1	1.40
★★★♪	**Leith Wheeler Fixed Income Fund** You won't find many like this one! It's done better than most in its class with top-notch performance in bull markets but disappointing results in bear markets. Lower annual expenses than most bode well for the future of this fund.	FixInc	A	C	0%	-2%	6/1/94	2	0.80
★★★★★	**Leith Wheeler Money Market Fund** This fund has off-the-charts performance overall vs. its peers. No wonder performance has been so good for this actively managed fund, its fees are among the lowest in its group.	FixInc	N/A	N/A	0%	0%	—	N/A	0.60
★★★	**Leith Wheeler U.S. Equity Fund** This fund has shown middle-of-the-road performance against similar funds. Lower annual expenses than most bode well for the future of this actively managed fund.	USEq	C	N/A	4%	-73%	6/1/97	N/A	1.36
★★★	**London Life Bond** This well-established fund has shown middle-of-the-road performance against similar funds; it has performed better than most in bull markets but has been hit hard in bear markets. This closet indexer is expensive but worth it in rising market conditions.	FixInc	B	D	11%	-13%	2/1/94	15	2.00
★★★	**London Life Canadian Equity** Here is an older fund that has shown middle-of-the-road performance against similar funds with top-notch performance in all market conditions. Annual fees are reasonable for this reasonably performing fund.	CdnEq	A	A	21%	-25%	9/1/89	42	2.00
★★★	**London Life Diversified** This fund has shown middle-of-the-road performance against similar funds. Annual fees are reasonable for this reasonably performing actively managed fund.	Balan	B	N/A	15%	-10%	9/1/89	18	2.00
★	**London Life International Equity** This newer fund has been a dog. High expenses exacerbate the problem for this actively managed fund.	FgnEq	N/A	N/A	29%	-10%	8/1/95	5	2.50
★★★♪	**London Life Money Market** This fund has done better than most in its class. High expenses haven't been much of a problem for this actively managed fund.	FixInc	N/A	N/A	0%	0%	—	2	1.30
★★★	**London Life Mortgage** This well-established fund has shown middle-of-the-road performance against similar funds. Along with performing better than most in bull markets it has been a disappointment in bear markets. High expenses haven't been much of a problem for this actively managed fund.	FixInc	B	C	6%	-14%	7/1/80	21	2.00

Legend: ★ = overall past performance vs. similar funds (5 ★ max). Boxes show the quartile performance for a fund each calendar year vs. only similar funds (□ is the best score possible). ● = high; ◑ = average; and ◐ = a fund with low expenses.

Consistency			Performance Trend											Risk						Efficiency
Overall Past Performance	Fund Name	Type	88	89	90	91	92	93	94	95	96	Sep-97		Up	Down	% of Time Losing $	Biggest Drop	Date	No. of Mo's to Recover	MER
★★★	**Lotus (MKW) Balanced Fund**	Balan												C	C	20%	–18%	8/1/87	23	2.14
	Here is an older fund that has shown middle-of-the-road performance against similar funds with disappointing results in all market conditions. Annual fees are reasonable for this reasonably performing fund.																			
★★★	**Lotus (MKW) Bond Fund**	FixInc												A	A	0%	–7%	3/1/94	11	0.98
	This fund has impressive past performance characteristics overall vs. its peers with top-notch performance in all market conditions. No wonder performance has been so good for this closet indexer, their fees are among the lowest in its group.																			
★★★↗	**Lotus (MKW) Canadian Equity Fund**	CdnEq												B	C	38%	–22%	4/1/94	22	2.16
	You won't find many like this one! It's done better than most in its class. Along with performing better than most in bull markets it has been a disappointment in bear markets. Lower annual expenses than most bode well for the future of this actively managed fund.																			
★★★★	**Lotus (MKW) Income Fund**	FixInc												N/A	N/A	0%	0%	N/A	N/A	0.80
	This fund has off-the-charts performance overall vs. its peers. Reasonable fees represent bargains for this actively managed fund.																			
★★★	**Lutheran Life Balanced Fund**	Balan												N/A	N/A	0%	–3%	3/1/97	2	
★	**Lutheran Life Canadian Bond Fund**	FixInc												N/A	N/A	0%	–2%	2/1/96	6	
★★★	**Lutheran Life Canadian Equity Fund**	CdnEq												N/A	N/A	0%	–5%	3/1/97	2	
★★	**Lutheran Life Int'l Bond Fund**	FixInc												N/A	N/A	5%	–4%	1/1/97	N/A	
★★★★↗	**Lutheran Life Int'l Equity Fund**	FgnEq												N/A	N/A	0%	–6%	8/1/97	N/A	
★	**Lutheran Life Money Market Fund**	FixInc												N/A	N/A	0%	0%	N/A	N/A	
★★↗	**Mackenzie Sentinel Canada Equity**	CdnEq												C	B	39%	–29%	7/1/87	70	1.98
	This well-established fund has been unimpressive so far with disappointing results in bull markets. Normally I'd say this fund has reasonable fees, but poor overall performance makes that argument weak.																			
★	**Mackenzie Sentinel Global Fund**	FgnEq												D	D	42%	–33%	10/1/87	75	0.51
	This well-established fund has been a dog; it's been hit hard in all market conditions. Low fees have not helped this fund.																			
★★	**Mandate National Mortgage Corp.**	FixInc												C	A	0%	0%	N/A	N/A	
★★★★	**Manulife Cabot Blue Chip Fund**	CdnEq												A	N/A	0%	–6%	10/1/94	6	2.50
	This fund has off-the-charts performance overall vs. its peers. This fund is expensive but well worth it.																			
★★★↗	**Manulife Cabot Canadian Equity Fund**	CdnEq												A	N/A	0%	–8%	10/1/94	7	2.50
	This fund is a super fund overall vs. its peers. This fund is expensive but well worth it.																			

Legend: ★ = overall past performance vs. similar funds (5 ★ max). Boxes show the quartile performance for a fund each calendar year vs. only similar funds (▀ is the best score possible). ● = high; ◌ = average; and ◍ = a fund with low expenses.

Consistency			Performance Trend										Risk						Efficiency
Overall Past Performance	Fund Name	Type	88	89	90	91	92	93	94	95	96	Sep-97	Up	Down	% of Time Losing $	Biggest Drop	Date	No. of Mo's to Recover	MER
★★½	**Manulife Cabot Canadian Growth Fund**	CdnEq								3	2	2	C	D	24%	–21%	4/1/94	22	2.50 ◌
	This fund has been unimpressive so far with disappointing results in bull markets as well as in bear markets. Normally I'd say that this actively managed fund has reasonable fees vs. its peers, but its poor overall performance makes that argument weak.																		
★	**Manulife Cabot Diversified Bond**	FixInc								4	4	4	D	B	3%	–8%	3/1/94	14	2.00 ●
	Here is one that is a dog. This actively managed fund is not worth the extra bucks.																		
★★½	**Manulife Cabot Emerging Growth Fund**	CdnEq								3	2	3	B	C	24%	–18%	4/1/94	21	2.50 ●
	This fund has been unimpressive so far. Performing just slightly better than most in bull markets, it's been a disappointment in bear markets. High expenses exacerbate the problem for this actively managed fund.																		
★★★	**Manulife Cabot Global Equity Fund**	FgnEq								2	3	3	B	N/A	3%	–6%	8/1/97	N/A	2.50 ◌
	This fund has shown middle-of-the-road performance against similar funds. Annual fees are reasonable for this reasonably performing fund.																		
★★	**Manulife Cabot Money Market Fund**	FixInc								2	4	4	N/A	N/A	0%	0%		N/A	1.25 ●
	This fund has been set apart from its peers by its weak returns. High expenses exacerbate the problem for this actively managed fund.																		
★★★	**Manulife Vistafund 1 Amer. Stock**	USEq								1	2	2	N/A	N/A	0%	–10%	6/1/96	5	1.63 ◍
	This fund has shown middle-of-the-road performance against similar funds. Lower annual expenses than most bode well for the future of this actively managed fund.																		
★★★	**Manulife Vistafund 1 Bond Fund**	FixInc	1	2	2	3	1	2	4	3	4	2	B	D	5%	–15%	2/1/94	20	1.63 ◌
	This well-established fund has shown middle-of-the-road performance against similar funds. It has performed better than most in bull markets but has been hit hard in bear markets. Annual fees are reasonable for this reasonably performing closet indexer.																		
★★★	**Manulife Vistafund 1 Cap. Gains Gth**	CdnEq	2	1	3	2	1	2	3	2	3	3	B	B	20%	–28%	8/1/87	23	1.63 ◌
	Here is an older fund that has shown middle-of-the-road performance against similar funds along with performing better than most in all market conditions. Annual fees are reasonable for this reasonably performing actively managed fund.																		
★★★	**Manulife Vistafund 1 Diversified**	Balan	2	1	4	3	2	2	2	2	4	3	C	C	18%	–14%	8/1/87	17	1.63 ◍
	Here is an older fund that has shown middle-of-the-road performance against similar funds with disappointing results in all market conditions. Lower annual expenses than most bode well for the future of this fund.																		
★★★	**Manulife Vistafund 1 Equity Fund**	CdnEq	2	2	3	2	2	3	1	2	3	3	D	A	22%	–26%	8/1/87	23	1.63 ◌
	Here is an older fund that has shown middle-of-the-road performance against similar funds but has been hit hard in bull markets. A top-notch performer in bear markets makes this reasonably priced fund well worth it during bearish markets.																		
★★	**Manulife Vistafund 1 Global Bond**	FixInc								4	1	4	N/A	N/A	6%	–8%	1/1/97	N/A	1.63 ◍
	This fund has been set apart from its peers by its weak returns. Low fees have not helped this actively managed fund.																		
★★★	**Manulife Vistafund 1 Global Equity**	FgnEq								2	3	4	N/A	N/A	0%	–8%	8/1/97	N/A	1.63 ◍
	This fund has shown middle-of-the-road performance against similar funds. Lower annual expenses than most bode well for the future of this actively managed fund.																		

Legend: ★ = overall past performance vs. similar funds (5 ★ max). Boxes show the quartile performance for a fund each calendar year vs. only similar funds (□ is the best score possible). ● = high; ◐ = average; and ○ = a fund with low expenses.

Consistency			Performance Trend											Risk					Efficiency
Overall Past Performance	Fund Name	Type	88	89	90	91	92	93	94	95	96	Sep-97	Up	Down	% of Time Losing $	Biggest Drop	Date	No. of Mo's to Recover	MER
★★★	**Manulife Vistafund 1 Short Term Sec**	FixInc											N/A	N/A	0%	−1%	9/1/92	1	1.63 ●
	This well-established fund has shown middle-of-the-road performance against similar funds. High expenses haven't been much of a problem for this actively managed fund.																		
★★	**Manulife Vistafund 2 Amer. Stock**	USEq											N/A	N/A	0%	−10%	6/1/96	5	2.38 ●
	This fund has been set apart from its peers by its weak returns. High expenses exacerbate the problem for this actively managed fund.																		
★★★	**Manulife Vistafund 2 Bond Fund**	FixInc											C	D	5%	−15%	2/1/94	21	2.38 ●
	This well-established fund has been set apart from its peers by its weak returns, with disappointing results in bull markets as well as in bear markets. High expenses exacerbate the problem for this closet indexer.																		
★★	**Manulife Vistafund 2 Cap. Gains Gth**	CdnEq											D	B	21%	−28%	8/1/87	24	2.38 ●
	This well-established fund has been set apart from its peers by its weak returns. This actively managed fund is not worth the extra bucks.																		
★	**Manulife Vistafund 2 Diversified**	Balan											D	C	19%	−14%	8/1/87	20	2.38 ●
	This well-established fund has been a dog, but it's been a top-notch performer in bear markets. High expenses exacerbate the problem for this fund, especially in declining markets.																		
★★	**Manulife Vistafund 2 Equity Fund**	CdnEq											D	A	24%	−26%	8/1/87	23	2.38 ●
	This well-established fund has been set apart from its peers by its weak returns, but it's been a top-notch performer in bear markets. High fees exacerbate the problem for this fund, especially in bull markets.																		
★	**Manulife Vistafund 2 Global Bond**	FixInc											N/A	N/A	6%	−9%	1/1/97	N/A	2.38 ●
	This fund has been a dog. High expenses exacerbate the problem for this actively managed fund.																		
★★	**Manulife Vistafund 2 Global Equity**	FgnEq											N/A	N/A	0%	−8%	8/1/97	N/A	2.38 ○
	This fund has been set apart from its peers by its weak returns. Normally I'd say that this actively managed fund has reasonable expenses compared to its peers, but overall performance makes that argument weak.																		
★	**Manulife Vistafund 2 Short Term Sec**	FixInc											N/A	N/A	0%	−1%	9/1/92	1	2.38 ●
	This well-established fund has been a dog. High expenses exacerbate the problem for this actively managed fund.																		
★★★	**Marathon Equity Fund**	CdnEq											B	A	29%	−43%	4/1/87	59	2.49 ○
	This well-established fund has shown middle-of-the-road performance against similar funds. As well as performing better than most in bull markets it's been a top-notch performer in bear markets. Annual fees are reasonable for this reasonably performing actively managed fund.																		
★	**Marathon Resource Fund**	CdnEq											N/A	N/A	100%	−10%	3/1/97	N/A	2.47 ●
	This newer fund has been a dog. High expenses exacerbate the problem for this fund.																		
★★★	**Margin of Safety Fund (Hillery Inv)**	USEq											B	C	8%	−19%	10/1/89	15	1.87 ○
	This fund has shown middle-of-the-road performance against similar funds. Along with performing better than most in bull markets it has been a disappointment in bear markets. Annual fees are reasonable for this reasonable performing actively managed fund.																		
★	**Maritime Life Aggr. Equity – 'B'**	CdnEq											N/A	N/A	0%	−6%	2/1/97	4	2.30 ○
	This newer fund can be described as having dismal returns. Normally I'd say that this fund has reasonable expenses compared to its peers, but poor overall performance makes that argument weak.																		

Legend: ★ = overall past performance vs. similar funds (5 ★ max). Boxes show the quartile performance for a fund each calendar year vs. only similar funds (□ is the best score possible). ● = high; ◐ = average; and ● = a fund with low expenses.

Consistency			Performance Trend	Risk						Efficiency
Overall Past Performance	Fund Name	Type	88 89 90 91 92 93 94 95 96 Sep-97	Up	Down	% of Time Losing $	Biggest Drop	Date	No. of Mo's to Recover	MER
★★	**Maritime Life Aggr. Equity –'A & C'** This newer fund has been set apart from its peers by its weak returns. Normally I'd say that this actively managed fund has reasonable expenses compared to its peers, but poor overall performance makes that argument weak.	CdnEq	□ (Sep-97)	N/A	N/A	0%	-6%	2/1/97	4	2.30
★★	**Maritime Life Amer Gth & Inc 'A&C'** This fund has been set apart from its peers by its weak returns. Normally I'd say that this actively managed fund has reasonable expenses compared to its peers, but poor overall performance makes that argument weak.	USEq	□ (96, Sep-97)	C	N/A	0%	-6%	9/1/94	4	2.30
★★★♪	**Maritime Life Amer. Gth. & Inc – 'B'** This newer fund has done better than most in its class. Annual fees are reasonable for this reasonably performing fund.	USEq	□ (Sep-97)	N/A	N/A	0%	-5%	8/1/97	N/A	2.30
★	**Maritime Life Balanced – 'B'** This newer fund has been a dog. High expenses exacerbate the problem for this fund.	Balan	□	N/A	N/A	0%	-3%	8/1/97	N/A	2.30
★★	**Maritime Life Bond – 'B'** This newer fund has been set apart from its peers by its weak returns. High expenses exacerbate the problem for this fund.	FixInc	□	N/A	N/A	0%	-2%	12/1/96	5	1.90
★★★♪	**Maritime Life Cdn. Equity –'A & C'** This fund has done better than most in its class. High expenses haven't been much of a problem for this closet indexer.	CdnEq	□ (94, Sep-97)	N/A	N/A	0%	-7%	2/1/97	4	2.30
★	**Maritime Life Cdn. Equity – 'B'** This newer fund has been a dog. High expenses exacerbate the problem for this fund.	CdnEq	□ (Sep-97)	N/A	N/A	0%	-7%	2/1/97	4	2.30
★	**Maritime Life Discovery –'A & C'** This newer fund has been a dog. High expenses exacerbate the problem for this actively managed fund.	USEq	□ (Sep-97)	N/A	N/A	0%	-15%	2/1/97	4	2.30
★	**Maritime Life Discovery – 'B'** This newer fund has been a dog. High expenses exacerbate the problem for this fund.	USEq	□	N/A	N/A	0%	-15%	2/1/97	4	2.30
★★★♪	**Maritime Life Dividend Inc. – 'B'** You won't find many new ones like this one! It's done better than most in its class. High expenses haven't been much of a problem for this fund.	CdnEq	□ (Sep-97)	N/A	N/A	0%	-3%	8/1/97	N/A	2.05
★	**Maritime Life Dividend Inc.–'A & C'** This newer fund has been a dog. High expenses exacerbate the problem for this actively managed fund.	CdnEq	□ (95, 96, Sep-97)	N/A	N/A	0%	-3%	8/1/97	N/A	2.05
★★★♪	**Maritime Life Eurasia – 'A & C'** This newer fund has been unimpressive so far. Normally I'd say that this actively managed fund has reasonable expenses compared to its peers, but poor overall performance makes that argument weak.	FgnEq	□	N/A	N/A	0%	-9%	8/1/97	N/A	2.30
★★	**Maritime Life Eurasia – 'B'** This newer fund has been set apart from its peers by its weak returns. Normally I'd say that this fund has reasonable expenses compared to its peers, but poor overall performance makes that argument weak.	FgnEq	□	N/A	N/A	0%	-9%	8/1/97	N/A	2.30
★★★♪	**Maritime Life Global Equity – 'B'** Check out how unimpressive this new fund has been. Normally I'd say that this fund has reasonable expenses compared to its peers, but poor overall performance makes that argument weak.	FgnEq	□	N/A	N/A	0%	-7%	8/1/97	N/A	2.55

Legend: ★ = overall past performance vs. similar funds (5 ★ max). Boxes show the quartile performance for a fund each calendar year vs. only similar funds (□ is the best score possible). ● = high; ◐ = average; and ○ = a fund with low expenses.

Consistency Overall Past Performance	Fund Name	Type	Performance Trend (88–Sep-97)	Risk Up	Risk Down	% of Time Losing $	Biggest Drop	Date	No. of Mo's to Recover	Efficiency MER
★	**Maritime Life Global Equity – 'A & C'**	FgnEq		N/A	N/A	0%	-7%	8/1/97	N/A	2.55
	Here is one that is a dog. Normally I'd say that this actively managed fund has reasonable expenses compared to its peers, but poor overall performance makes that argument weak.									
★★★	**Maritime Life Growth – 'B'**	CdnEq		N/A	N/A	0%	-5%	3/1/97	2	2.30
	This newer fund has done better than most in its class. Annual fees are reasonable for this reasonably performing fund.									
★	**Maritime Life Money Market – 'B'**	FixInc		N/A	N/A	0%	0%	N/A	N/A	1.50 ●
	This newer fund has been a dog. High expenses exacerbate the problem for this actively managed fund.									
★★★	**Maritime Life Pacific Basin – 'A&C'**	FgnEq		A	C	46%	-15%	9/1/94	32	2.55
	This fund has shown middle-of-the-road performance against similar funds. Annual fees are reasonable for this reasonably performing actively managed fund.									
★	**Maritime Life Pacific Basin – 'B'**	FgnEq		N/A	N/A	0%	-14%	8/1/97	N/A	2.55
	This newer fund has been a dog. Normally I'd say that this fund has reasonable expenses compared to its peers, but poor overall performance makes that argument weak.									
★★★★	**Maritime Life S&P 500 – 'A & C'**	USEq		N/A	N/A	0%	-6%	8/1/97	N/A	2.05
	This fund has off-the-charts performance overall vs. its peers. Reasonable fees represent bargains for this actively managed fund.									
★★★	**Maritime Life S&P 500 – 'B'**	USEq		N/A	N/A	0%	-6%	8/1/97	N/A	2.05
	This newer fund has shown middle-of-the-road performance against similar funds. Annual fees are reasonable for this reasonably performing fund.									
★★★	**Mawer Cdn. Balanced RSP Fund**	Balan		B	N/A	9%	-9%	2/1/94	15	0.89
	This fund has shown middle-of-the-road performance against similar funds. Lower annual expenses than most bode well for the future of this fund.									
★★★	**Mawer Canadian Bond Fund**	FixInc		B	B	16%	-12%	2/1/94	15	0.89
	This fund has shown middle-of-the-road performance along with performing better than most in all market conditions. Lower annual expenses than most bode well for the future of this closet indexer.									
★★★	**Mawer Cdn. Diversified Investment**	Balan		B	N/A	9%	-9%	2/1/94	15	0.98
	This fund has shown middle-of-the-road performance against similar funds. Lower annual expenses than most bode well for the future of this fund.									
★★	**Mawer Canadian Equity Fund**	CdnEq		D	N/A	18%	-11%	2/1/94	16	1.07
	This fund has been set apart from its peers by its weak returns. Low fees have not helped this fund.									
★★★★	**Mawer Canadian Income Fund**	FixInc		A	A	18%	-10%	2/1/94	15	0.88
	This fund has impressive past performance characteristics overall vs. its peers with top-notch performance in all market conditions. No wonder performance has been so good for this fund. Its fees are among the lowest in its group.									
★★★	**Mawer Canadian Money Market Fund**	FixInc		N/A	N/A	0%	0%	N/A	N/A	0.57
	This fund has shown middle-of-the-road performance against similar funds. Lower annual expenses than most bode well for the future of this actively managed fund.									
★	**Mawer High Yield Bond Fund**	FixInc		N/A	N/A	0%	-2%	3/1/97	4	1.16
	This newer fund has been a dog. Low fees have not helped this fund.									

Legend: ★= overall past performance vs. similar funds (5 ★ max). Boxes show the quartile performance for a fund each calendar year vs. only similar funds (▢ is the best score possible). ● = high; ◐ = average; and ◔ = a fund with low expenses.

Overall Past Performance	Fund Name	Type	88	89	90	91	92	93	94	95	96	Sep-97	Up	Down	% of Time Losing $	Biggest Drop	Date	No. of Mo's to Recover	MER
★★★★	**Mawer New Canada Fund**	CdnEq		▢	▢	▢	▢	▢	▢	▢	▢	▢	A	B	8%	-11%	5/1/94	13	1.34
★★★	**Mawer U.S. Equity Fund**	USEq						▢	▢	▢	▢	▢	B	N/A	0%	-5%	6/1/96	3	1.18
★★★⯪	**Mawer World Investment Fund**	FgnEq				▢	▢	▢	▢	▢	▢	▢	A	A	6%	-11%	9/1/94	10	1.29
★★★★★	**Maxxum American Equity Fund**	USEq									▢	▢	N/A	N/A	0%	-10%	6/1/96	3	2.50
★★★	**Maxxum Canadian Balanced Fund**	Balan				▢	▢	▢	▢	▢	▢	▢	A	N/A	19%	-14%	2/1/94	19	2.15
★★★	**Maxxum Canadian Equity Growth Fund**	CdnEq	▢	▢	▢	▢	▢	▢	▢	▢	▢	▢	A	B	26%	-37%	12/1/80	28	2.15
★★★⯪	**Maxxum Dividend Fund**	CdnEq	▢	▢	▢	▢	▢	▢	▢	▢	▢	▢	A	C	13%	-22%	8/1/89	35	1.75
★★★	**Maxxum Global Equity Fund**	FgnEq									▢	▢	N/A	N/A	0%	-6%	6/1/96	6	2.50
★★★	**Maxxum Income Fund**	FixInc	▢	▢	▢	▢	▢	▢	▢	▢	▢	▢	B	D	8%	-14%	2/1/94	16	1.75
★★★★★	**Maxxum Money Market Fund**	FixInc		▢	▢	▢	▢	▢	▢	▢	▢	▢	N/A	N/A	0%	0%	N/A	N/A	0.85
★★★★★	**Maxxum Natural Resource Fund**	CdnEq							▢	▢	▢	▢	A	A	25%	-28%	6/1/96	N/A	2.25
★★★⯪	**Maxxum Precious Metals Fund**	CdnEq	▢	▢	▢	▢	▢	▢	▢	▢	▢	▢	A	B	29%	-44%	6/1/96	N/A	2.25

Mawer New Canada Fund — This fund has off-the-charts performance overall vs. its peers with top-notch performance in bull markets as well as performing better than most in bear markets. No wonder performance has been so good for this actively managed fund, its fees are among the lowest in its group.

Mawer U.S. Equity Fund — This fund has shown middle-of-the-road performance against similar funds. Lower annual expenses against similar funds.

Mawer World Investment Fund — You won't find many like this one! It's done better than most in its class with top-notch performance in all market conditions. Lower annual expenses than most bode well for the future of this actively managed fund.

Maxxum American Equity Fund — This fund has off-the-charts performance overall vs. its peers. This actively managed fund is expensive but well worth it.

Maxxum Canadian Balanced Fund — This fund has shown middle-of-the-road performance against similar funds. Annual fees are reasonable for this reasonably performing fund.

Maxxum Canadian Equity Growth Fund — This well-established fund has shown middle-of-the-road performance against similar funds with top-notch performance in bull markets as well as performing better than most in bear markets. Annual fees are reasonable for this reasonably performing actively managed fund.

Maxxum Dividend Fund — This well-established fund has done better than most in its class with top-notch performance in bull markets but disappointing results in bear markets. Annual fees are reasonable for this reasonably performing actively managed fund.

Maxxum Global Equity Fund — This fund has shown middle-of-the-road performance against similar funds. Annual fees are reasonable for this reasonably performing actively managed fund.

Maxxum Income Fund — This well-established fund has shown middle-of-the-road performance against similar funds; it has performed better than most in bull markets but has been hit hard in bear markets. This closet indexer is expensive but worth it in rising market conditions.

Maxxum Money Market Fund — This well-established fund has off-the-charts performance overall vs. its peers. Reasonable fees represent bargains for this actively managed fund.

Maxxum Natural Resource Fund — This fund has off-the-charts performance overall vs. its peers with top-notch performance in all market conditions. Reasonable fees represent bargains for this actively managed fund.

Maxxum Precious Metals Fund — You won't find many like this one! It's done better than most in its class with top-notch performance in bull markets as well as performing better than most in bear markets. Annual fees are reasonable for this reasonable performing actively managed fund.

Legend: ★= overall past performance vs. similar funds (5 ★ max). Boxes show the quartile performance for a fund each calendar year vs. only similar funds (□ is the best score possible). ● = high; ◐ = average; and ◑ = a fund with low expenses.

Consistency (Overall Past Performance)	Fund Name	Type	88	89	90	91	92	93	94	95	96	Sep-97	Up	Down	% of Time Losing $	Biggest Drop	Date	No. of Mo's to Recover	MER
★★	**McDonald Asia Plus**	FgnEq									□	□	N/A	N/A	14%	-8%	2/1/96	10	3.46 ●
	This newer fund has been set apart from its peers by its weak returns. High expenses exacerbate the problem for this actively managed fund.																		
★★	**McDonald Canada Plus**	Balan								□	□	□	D	N/A	23%	-12%	1/1/94	23	2.41 ●
	This fund has been set apart from its peers by its weak returns. High expenses exacerbate the problem for this actively managed fund.																		
★	**McDonald Emerging Economies**	FgnEq									□	□	N/A	N/A	0%	-7%	6/1/96	7	3.42 ●
	This newer fund has been a dog. High expenses exacerbate the problem for this actively managed fund.																		
★	**McDonald Enhanced Bond**	FixInc									□	□	N/A	N/A	0%	-2%	12/1/96	7	2.22 ●
	This newer fund has been a dog. High expenses exacerbate the problem for this actively managed fund.																		
★	**McDonald Euro Plus**	FgnEq									□	□	N/A	N/A	0%	-5%	8/1/97	N/A	2.48 ◐
	This newer fund has been a dog. Normally I'd say that this actively managed fund has reasonable expenses compared to its peers, but poor overall performance makes that argument weak.																		
★	**McDonald New America**	USEq									□	□	N/A	N/A	0%	-8%	3/1/97	2	2.03 ●
	This newer fund has been a dog. Low fees have not helped this actively managed fund.																		
★★	**McDonald New Japan**	FgnEq									□	□	N/A	N/A	86%	-23%	5/1/96	N/A	2.67 ●
	This newer fund has been set apart from its peers by its weak returns. High expenses exacerbate the problem for this actively managed fund.																		
★★★	**McLean Budden American Growth Fund**	USEq			□	□	□	□	□	□	□	□	B	A	1%	-9%	8/1/90	5	1.75 ◐
	This fund has done better than most in its class. As well as performing better than most in bull markets it's been a top-notch performer in bear markets. Lower annual expenses than most bode well for the future of this fund.																		
★★★	**McLean Budden Balanced Fund**	Balan					□	□	□	□	□	□	A	N/A	14%	-11%	2/1/94	15	1.75 ◐
	You won't find many like this one! It's done better than most in its class. Annual fees are reasonable for this reasonably performing fund.																		
★★★	**McLean Budden Equity Growth Fund**	CdnEq		□	□	□	□	□	□	□	□	□	A	C	19%	-19%	8/1/89	28	1.75 ◐
	This fund has shown middle-of-the-road performance against similar funds with top-notch performance in bull markets but disappointing results in bear markets. Annual fees are reasonable for this reasonably performing fund.																		
★★★	**McLean Budden Fixed Income Fund**	FixInc							□	□	□	□	A	C	10%	-13%	2/1/94	15	1.00 ●
	This fund has impressive past performance characteristics overall vs. its peers with top-notch performance in bull markets but disappointing results in bear markets. No wonder performance has been so good for this closet indexer, its fees are among the lowest in its group.																		
★★★	**McLean Budden Global Equity Fund**	FgnEq									□	□	N/A	N/A	0%	-6%	8/1/97	15	N/A
	This newer fund has shown middle-of-the-road performance against similar funds. Lower annual expenses than most bode well for the future of this fund.																		
★★★★	**McLean Budden Int'l Fixed Income**	FixInc									□	□	N/A	N/A	0%	-2%	12/1/96	4	
	This newer fund has off-the-charts performance overall vs. its peers. No wonder performance has been so good for this fund, its fees are among the lowest in its group.																		

Legend: ★ = overall past performance vs. similar funds (5 ★ max). Boxes show the quartile performance for a fund each calendar year vs. only similar funds (□ is the best score possible). ● = high; ● = average; and ● = a fund with low expenses.

Consistency (Overall Past Performance)	Fund Name	Type	Performance Trend (88–Sep-97)	Risk Up	Risk Down	% of Time Losing $	Biggest Drop	Date	No. of Mo's to Recover	MER	Efficiency
★★★↗	**McLean Budden Money Market Fund** — This fund has done better than most in its class. Lower annual expenses than most bode well for the future of this actively managed fund.	FixInc		N/A	N/A	0%	0%	N/A	N/A	0.75	●
★★★	**McLean Budden Pooled American Eqt.** — This well-established fund has impressive past performance characteristics overall vs. its peers with top-notch performance in bull markets but disappointing results in bear markets. No wonder performance has been so good for this fund, its fees are among the lowest in its group.	USEq		A	C	10%	-32%	9/1/87	28	0.00	●
★★★↗	**McLean Budden Pooled Balanced Fund** — This well-established fund is a super fund overall vs. its peers with top-notch performance in bull markets but has been hit hard in bear markets. No wonder performance has been so good for this fund, its fees are among the lowest in its group.	Balan		A	D	12%	-16%	8/1/87	17	0.00	●
★★★↗	**McLean Budden Pooled Canadian Eqt.** — This well-established fund has done better than most in its class with top-notch performance in bull markets but has been hit hard in bear markets. Lower annual expenses than most bode well for the future of this fund.	CdnEq		A	D	23%	-25%	8/1/87	21	0.00	●
★★★★	**McLean Budden Pooled Fixed Income** — This well-established fund has off-the-charts performance overall vs. its peers with top-notch performance in bull markets as well as performing better than most in bear markets. No wonder performance has been so good for this closet indexer, its fees are among the lowest in its group.	FixInc		A	B	5%	-16%	2/1/81	14	0.00	●
★★↗	**McLean Budden Pooled Offshore Eqt.** — This fund has been unimpressive so far with disappointing results in all market conditions. Low fees have not helped this actively managed fund.	FgnEq		C	C	29%	-21%	8/1/90	32		
★★★★★	**McLean Budden Registered Balanced**	Balan		A	N/A	8%	-10%	2/1/94	15	1.30	●
★★★↗	**MD Balanced Fund** — This fund has done better than most in its class. Lower annual expenses than most bode well for the future of this fund.	Balan		A	N/A	9%	-9%	2/1/94	15	1.30	●
★★★	**MD Bond and Mortgage Fund** — This newer fund has shown middle-of-the-road performance against similar funds. Lower annual expenses than most bode well for the future of this actively managed fund.	FixInc		N/A	N/A	0%	-1%	12/1/96	6	1.06	●
★★★★	**MD Bond Fund** — This fund has impressive past performance characteristics overall vs. its peers with top-notch performance in bull markets as well as performing better than most in bear markets. No wonder performance has been so good for this fund, their fees are among the lowest in its group.	FixInc		A	B	8%	-12%	2/1/94	15	1.02	●
★★	**MD Dividend Fund** — This fund has been set apart from its peers by its weak returns; it's been hit hard in all market conditions. Low fees have not helped this actively managed fund.	CdnEq		D	D	7%	-8%	2/1/94	14	1.30	●
★★★★	**MD Emerging Markets Fund** — This fund has impressive past performance characteristics overall vs. its peers. No wonder performance has been so good for this actively managed fund, its fees are among the lowest in its group.	FgnEq		N/A	N/A	20%	-11%	8/1/97	N/A	2.46	●
★★★	**MD Equity Fund** — This well-established fund has shown middle-of-the-road performance against similar funds with disappointing results in bull markets and top-notch performance in bear markets. Lower annual expenses than most bode well for the future of this actively managed fund.	CdnEq		B	A	23%	-19%	8/1/87	16	1.28	●

Legend: ★ = overall past performance vs. similar funds (5 ★ max). Boxes show the quartile performance for a fund each calendar year vs. only similar funds (top-quartile box is the best score possible). ● = high; ● = average; and ● = a fund with low expenses.

Consistency			Performance Trend										Risk						Efficiency
Overall Past Performance	Fund Name	Type	88	89	90	91	92	93	94	95	96	Sep-97	Up	Down	% of Time Losing $	Biggest Drop	Date	No. of Mo's to Recover	MER
★	**MD Global Bond Fund** Here is one that is a dog. Low fees have not helped this actively managed fund.	FixInc								2	3	4	N/A	N/A	20%	–5%	6/1/95	6	1.11 (low)
★★★½	**MD Growth Fund** You won't find many like this older one! It's done better than most in its class with top-notch performance in bull markets but disappointing results in bear markets. Lower annual expenses than most bode well for the future of this actively managed fund.	FgnEq	2	3	4	2	2	1	3	1	1	1	A	C	20%	–28%	9/1/87	52	1.29 (low)
★★★	**MD Money Fund** This well-established fund has shown middle-of-the-road performance against similar funds. Lower annual expenses than most bode well for the future of this actively managed fund.	FixInc	3	4	3	2	3	1	1	1	4	1	N/A	N/A	5%	–8%	7/1/96	N/A	0.54 (low)
★★★	**MD Select Fund** This fund has shown middle-of-the-road performance against similar funds; it has performed better than most in bull markets but it has been hit hard in bear markets. Lower annual expenses than most bode well for the future of this actively managed fund.	CdnEq							3	3	1	1	B	D	24%	–10%	2/1/94	22	1.31 (low)
★★★½	**MD U.S. Equity Fund** You won't find many like this one! It's done better than most in its class. Lower annual expenses than most bode well for the future of this actively managed fund.	USEq						1	3	1	2	1	A	N/A	2%	–8%	3/1/96	8	1.31 (low)
★	**Merrill Lynch Canadian Equity Fund** This newer fund has been a dog. High expenses exacerbate the problem for this actively managed fund.	CdnEq										2	N/A	N/A	0%	–7%	6/1/96	4	2.88 (high)
★★★	**Merrill Lynch Capital Asset Fund** This newer fund has shown middle-of-the-road performance against similar funds. High expenses haven't been much of a problem for this actively managed fund.	Balan										1	N/A	N/A	0%	–3%	2/1/96	7	3.05 (high)
★★★	**Merrill Lynch Emerging Markets Fund** This newer fund has shown middle-of-the-road performance against similar funds. High expenses haven't been much of a problem for this actively managed fund.	FgnEq										3	N/A	N/A	0%	–11%	8/1/97	N/A	3.21 (high)
★★★	**Merrill Lynch World Allocation Fund** This newer fund has shown middle-of-the-road performance against similar funds. High expenses haven't been much of a problem for this actively managed fund.	Balan										1	N/A	N/A	0%	–6%	8/1/97	N/A	2.97 (high)
★★★	**Merrill Lynch World Bond Fund** This newer fund has shown middle-of-the-road performance against similar funds. High expenses haven't been much of a problem for this actively managed fund.	FixInc										2	N/A	N/A	20%	–5%	12/1/96	N/A	2.28 (high)
★★★★★	**Metlife MVP Asian-Pacific RSP Eq.** This newer fund has off-the-charts performance overall vs. its peers. This fund is expensive but well worth it.	FgnEq										4	N/A	N/A	0%	–11%	8/1/97	N/A	2.90 (high)
½	**Metlife MVP Balanced Fund** This well-established fund can be described as having dismal returns. Normally I'd say this fund has reasonable fees, but poor overall performance makes that argument weak.	Balan	3	2	3	4	3	4	4	4	3	2	D	B	19%	–14%	8/1/87	21	2.22 (average)
★	**Metlife MVP Bond Fund** This well-established fund has been set apart from its peers by its weak returns, with disappointing results in all market conditions. High expenses exacerbate the problem for this fund.	FixInc	4	4	2	4	3	4	3	4	4	4	C	C	8%	–12%	2/1/94	18	2.22 (high)

Legend: ★ = overall past performance vs. similar funds (5 ★ max). Boxes show the quartile performance for a fund each calendar year vs. only similar funds (□ is the best score possible). ● = high; ◐ = average; and ○ = a fund with low expenses.

Overall Past Performance	Fund Name	Type	Performance Trend (88–Sep-97)	Risk Up	Risk Down	% of Time Losing $	Biggest Drop	Date	No. of Mo's to Recover	MER
★	**Metlife MVP Equity Fund**	CdnEq		D	C	36%	-29%	8/1/87	70	2.23 ◐
	This well-established fund has been a dog, with disappointing results in bear markets. Normally I'd say that this closet indexer has reasonable expenses compared to its peers, but poor overall performance makes that argument weak.									
★★↗	**Metlife MVP Global Equity Fund**	FgnEq		N/A	N/A	0%	-6%	8/1/97	N/A	2.90 ●
	This newer fund can be described as having dismal returns. High expenses exacerbate the problem for this fund.									
★★★	**Metlife MVP Growth Fund**	CdnEq		B	C	17%	-14%	5/1/94	14	2.23 ◐
	This fund has shown middle-of-the-road performance against similar funds. Along with performing better than most in bull markets it has been a disappointment in bear markets. Annual fees are reasonable for this reasonable performing actively managed fund.									
★	**Metlife MVP Money Market Fund**	FixInc		N/A	N/A	0%	0%		3	1.72 ●
	This fund has been a dog. High expenses exacerbate the problem for this actively managed fund.									
★★★↗	**Metlife MVP U.S. Equity Fund**	USEq		A	N/A	15%	-8%	3/1/94	12	2.23 ◐
	You won't find many like this one! It's done better than most in its class. Annual fees are reasonable for this reasonably performing fund.									
★	**Middlefield Global Technology Fund**	Spclty		N/A	N/A	100%	-30%	10/1/96	N/A	2.75 ●
	This newer fund has been a dog. High expenses exacerbate the problem for this actively managed fund.									
★★	**Middlefield Growth Fund**	CdnEq		D	D	26%	-25%	9/1/93	36	2.78 ●
	This fund has been set apart from its peers by its weak returns; it's been hit hard in all market conditions. High expenses exacerbate the problem for this actively managed fund.									
★	**Middlefield Money Market Fund**	FixInc		N/A	N/A	0%	0%		N/A	0.54 ○
	This newer fund has been a dog. Low fees have not helped this actively managed fund.									
★	**Millennia III American Equity 1**	USEq		N/A	N/A	0%	-6%	6/1/96	5	2.77 ●
	This newer fund has been a dog. High expenses exacerbate the problem for this actively managed fund.									
★	**Millennia III American Equity 2**	USEq		N/A	N/A	0%	-6%	6/1/96	5	2.95 ●
	This newer fund has been a dog. High expenses exacerbate the problem for this actively managed fund.									
★	**Millennia III Canadian Balanced 1**	Balan		N/A	N/A	0%	-3%	8/1/97	N/A	2.71 ●
	This newer fund has been a dog. High expenses exacerbate the problem for this actively managed fund.									
★	**Millennia III Canadian Balanced 2**	Balan		N/A	N/A	0%	-3%	8/1/97	N/A	2.89 ●
	This newer fund has been a dog. High expenses exacerbate the problem for this actively managed fund.									
★	**Millennia III Canadian Equity 1**	CdnEq		N/A	N/A	0%	-5%	6/1/96	3	2.72 ●
	This newer fund has been a dog. High expenses exacerbate the problem for this actively managed fund.									

Legend: ★ = overall past performance for a fund each calendar year vs. only similar funds (5 ★ max). Boxes show the quartile performance vs. similar funds (□ is the best score possible). ● = high; ◑ = average; and ● = a fund with low expenses.

Overall Past Performance	Fund Name	Type	Performance Trend 88 89 90 91 92 93 94 95 96 Sep-97	Risk Up	Risk Down	% of Time Losing $	Biggest Drop	Date	No. of Mo's to Recover	MER
★	**Millennia III Canadian Equity 2** This newer fund has been a dog. High expenses exacerbate the problem for this actively managed fund.	CdnEq	□ □ □ □ □	N/A	N/A	0%	-5%	6/1/96	3	2.90 ●
★	**Millennia III Income Fund 1** This newer fund has been a dog. High expenses exacerbate the problem for this actively managed fund.	FixInc	□ □ □	N/A	N/A	0%	-2%	2/1/96	5	2.19 ●
★	**Millennia III Income Fund 2** This newer fund has been a dog. High expenses exacerbate the problem for this actively managed fund.	FixInc	□ □ □	N/A	N/A	0%	-2%	2/1/96	5	2.37 ●
★	**Millennia III Int'l Equity 1** This newer fund has been a dog. High expenses exacerbate the problem for this actively managed fund.	FgnEq	□ □ □	N/A	N/A	20%	-7%	8/1/97	N/A	2.90 ●
★	**Millennia III Int'l Equity 2** This newer fund has been a dog. High expenses exacerbate the problem for this actively managed fund.	FgnEq	□ □	N/A	N/A	20%	-7%	8/1/97	N/A	3.08 ●
★	**Millennia III Money Market Fund 1** This newer fund has been a dog. High expenses exacerbate the problem for this actively managed fund.	FixInc	□ □	N/A	N/A	0%	0%		N/A	1.38 ●
★	**Millennia III Money Market Fund 2** This newer fund has been a dog. High expenses exacerbate the problem for this actively managed fund.	FixInc	□ □	N/A	N/A	0%	0%		N/A	1.56 ●
★★★	**Millennium Diversified Fund** This fund has shown middle-of-the-road performance against similar funds. High expenses haven't been much of a problem for this fund.	Balan	C	N/A	19%	-12%	2/1/94	19	2.50 ●
★★★★	**Millennium Income Fund** This newer fund has off-the-charts performance overall vs. its peers. This fund is expensive but well worth it.	CdnEq	□	N/A	N/A	0%	-3%	3/1/97	1	2.50 ●
★★★★↑	**Millennium Next Generation Fund** Who couldn't love this one! It's a super fund overall vs. its peers with top-notch performance in bull markets but has been hit hard in bear markets. Reasonable fees in bull markets represent real bargains for this actively managed fund.	CdnEq	□ □	A	D	16%	-10%	2/1/94	15	2.50 ◑
★	**Monarch Canadian Fund** This newer fund has been a dog. High expenses exacerbate the problem for this fund.	CdnEq	□	N/A	N/A	100%	-6%	2/1/97	4	2.41 ●
★	**Monarch Canadian Sector Shares** This newer fund has been a dog. High expenses exacerbate the problem for this fund.	CdnEq		N/A	N/A	100%	-7%	2/1/97	4	2.46 ●
★★	**Monarch Dividend Fund** This newer fund has been set apart from its peers by its weak returns. Normally I'd say that this fund has reasonable expenses compared to its peers, but poor overall performance makes that argument weak.	CdnEq	□	N/A	N/A	0%	-2%	3/1/97	2	1.91 ◑
★★★	**Multiple Opportunities Fund** This well-established fund has shown middle-of-the-road performance against similar funds. Along with performing better than most in bull markets it has been a disappointment in bear markets. Annual fees are reasonable for this reasonably performing actively managed fund.	CdnEq	□ □ □ □ □	B	C	37%	-62%	10/1/87	72	2.74 ◑

Legend: ★ = overall past performance vs. similar funds (5 ★ max). Boxes show the quartile performance for a fund each calendar year vs. only similar funds (□ is the best score possible). ● = high; ◑ = average; and ● = a fund with low expenses.

Overall Past Performance	Fund Name	Type	Performance Trend 88–Sep-97	Risk Up	Risk Down	% of Time Losing $	Biggest Drop	Date	No. of Mo's to Recover	MER
★	Mutual Bond Fund	FixInc	(quartile boxes)	D	A	13%	-12%	2/1/94	18	1.87
★★⅟	Mutual Diversifund 40	Balan	(quartile boxes)	C	C	16%	-12%	9/1/89	18	1.77
★★⅟	Mutual Equifund	CdnEq	(quartile boxes)	B	C	30%	-27%	9/1/89	49	1.79
★	Mutual Money Market	FixInc	(quartile boxes)	N/A	N/A	0%	0%	N/A	N/A	1.03
★★★	Mutual Premier American Fund	USEq	(quartile boxes)	C	N/A	8%	-8%	6/1/96	4	2.34
★★	Mutual Premier Blue Chip Fund	CdnEq	(quartile boxes)	C	N/A	9%	-9%	2/1/94	15	2.29
★	Mutual Premier Bond Fund	FixInc	(quartile boxes)	D	B	20%	-12%	2/1/94	16	1.90
★★★⅟	Mutual Premier Diversified Fund	Balan	(quartile boxes)	A	N/A	0%	-5%	6/1/96	3	2.30
★	Mutual Premier Emerging Markets	FgnEq	(quartile boxes)	N/A	N/A	0%	-12%	8/1/97	N/A	3.76
★★	Mutual Premier Growth Fund	CdnEq	(quartile boxes)	C	B	9%	-11%	2/1/94	14	2.28
★★★	Mutual Premier International Fund	FgnEq	(quartile boxes)	B	N/A	13%	-8%	9/1/94	10	2.38
★★★	Mutual Premier Mortgage Fund	FixInc	(quartile boxes)	C	B	3%	-6%	3/1/94	11	1.58
★★★★	NAL-Balanced Growth Fund	Balan	(quartile boxes)	N/A	N/A	0%	-3%	8/1/97	N/A	2.00

Mutual Bond Fund — This fund has been a dog, but it's been a top-notch performer in bear markets. High fees exacerbate the problem for this closet indexer, especially in bull markets.

Mutual Diversifund 40 — This well-established fund has been unimpressive so far with disappointing results in all market conditions. Normally I'd say this fund has reasonable fees, but poor overall performance makes that argument weak.

Mutual Equifund — This well-established fund has been unimpressive so far. Performing just slightly better than most in bull markets, it's been a disappointment in bear markets. Normally I'd say that this closet indexer has reasonable expenses compared to its peers, but poor overall performance makes that argument weak.

Mutual Money Market — This well-established fund has been a dog. Normally I'd say that this actively managed fund has reasonable expenses compared to its peers, but poor overall performance makes that argument weak.

Mutual Premier American Fund — This fund has shown middle-of-the-road performance against similar funds. Annual fees are reasonable for this reasonably performing fund.

Mutual Premier Blue Chip Fund — This fund has been set apart from its peers by its weak returns. Normally I'd say that this closet indexer has reasonable expenses compared to its peers, but poor overall performance makes that argument weak.

Mutual Premier Bond Fund — Here is one that is a dog. This closet indexer is not worth the extra bucks.

Mutual Premier Diversified Fund — This fund has done better than most in its class. High expenses haven't been much of a problem for this fund.

Mutual Premier Emerging Markets — This newer fund has been a dog. High expenses exacerbate the problem for this actively managed fund.

Mutual Premier Growth Fund — This fund has shown middle-of-the-road performance against similar funds with disappointing results in bull markets and better than average in bear markets. Annual fees are reasonable for this reasonably performing actively managed fund.

Mutual Premier International Fund — This fund has shown middle-of-the-road performance against similar funds. Annual fees are reasonable for this reasonably performing actively managed fund.

Mutual Premier Mortgage Fund — This fund has shown middle-of-the-road performance against similar funds with disappointing results in bull markets and better than average in bear markets. Annual fees are reasonable for this reasonably performing actively managed fund.

NAL-Balanced Growth Fund — This fund has off-the-charts performance overall vs. its peers. Reasonable fees represent bargains for this actively managed fund.

Legend: ★ = overall past performance vs. similar funds (5 ★ max). Boxes show the quartile performance for a fund each calendar year vs. only similar funds (□ is the best score possible). ● = high; ◐ = average; and ● = a fund with low expenses.

Overall Past Performance	Fund Name	Type	88	89	90	91	92	93	94	95	96	Sep-97	Up	Down	% of Time Losing $	Biggest Drop	Date	No. of Mo's to Recover	MER
★★★	**NAL-Canadian Bond Fund**	FixInc											C	B	8%	−11%	2/1/94	15	1.75 ●
★★★	**NAL-Canadian Diversified Fund**	Balan											B	C	16%	−10%	8/1/87	14	1.75 ◐
★★★	**NAL-Canadian Equity Fund**	CdnEq											C	B	26%	−22%	9/1/87	22	1.75 ◐
★	**NAL-Canadian Money Market Fund**	FixInc											N/A	N/A	0%	0%		N/A	1.25 ●
★★★↘	**NAL-Equity Growth Fund**	CdnEq											N/A	N/A	0%	−4%	8/1/97	N/A	2.00 ◐
★★	**NAL-Global Equity Fund**	FgnEq											C	N/A	16%	−11%	3/1/92	13	2.50 ◐
★★★	**NAL-U.S. Equity Fund**	USEq											B	N/A	0%	−9%	9/1/94	5	2.25 ◐
★★★	**National Life Balanced Fund**	Balan											B	N/A	10%	−11%	2/1/94	16	2.00 ◐
★★★	**National Life Equities Fund**	CdnEq											C	A	24%	−31%	7/1/81	20	2.00 ◐
★★★	**National Life Fixed Income Fund**	FixInc											B	C	7%	−13%	2/1/94	15	2.00 ●
★★★↘	**National Life Global Equities Fund**	FgnEq											A	B	10%	−19%	8/1/90	17	2.40 ◐
✶	**National Life Money Market Fund**	FixInc											N/A	N/A	0%	0%		N/A	1.60 ●

NAL-Canadian Bond Fund — Here is an older fund that has shown middle-of-the-road performance against similar funds with disappointing results in bull markets and better than average in bear markets. High expenses haven't been much of a problem for this closet indexer.

NAL-Canadian Diversified Fund — This well-established fund has shown middle-of-the-road performance against similar funds. Along with performing better than most in bull markets it has been a disappointment in bear markets. Annual fees are reasonable for this reasonably performing fund.

NAL-Canadian Equity Fund — This well-established fund has shown middle-of-the-road performance against similar funds with disappointing results in bull markets and better than average in bear markets. Annual fees are reasonable for this reasonable performing fund.

NAL-Canadian Money Market Fund — This fund has been a dog. High expenses exacerbate the problem for this actively managed fund.

NAL-Equity Growth Fund — This fund has done better than most in its class. Annual fees are reasonable for this reasonably performing actively managed fund.

NAL-Global Equity Fund — This fund has been set apart from its peers by its weak returns. Normally I'd say that this actively managed fund has reasonable expenses compared to its peers, but poor overall performance makes that argument weak.

NAL-U.S. Equity Fund — This fund has shown middle-of-the-road performance against similar funds. Annual fees are reasonable for this reasonably performing actively managed fund.

National Life Balanced Fund — This fund has shown middle-of-the-road performance against similar funds. Annual fees are reasonable for this reasonably performing closet indexer.

National Life Equities Fund — Here is an older fund that has shown middle-of-the-road performance against similar funds with disappointing results in bull markets and top-notch performance in bear markets. Annual fees are reasonable for this reasonable performing fund.

National Life Fixed Income Fund — Here is an older fund that has shown middle-of-the-road performance against similar funds. Along with performing better than most in bull markets it has been a disappointment in bear markets. High expenses haven't been much of a problem for this closet indexer.

National Life Global Equities Fund — You won't find many like this one! It's done better than most in its class with top-notch performance in bull markets as well as performing better than most in bear markets. Annual fees are reasonable for this reasonable performing actively managed fund.

National Life Money Market Fund — This fund has been a dog. High expenses exacerbate the problem for this actively managed fund.

Legend: ★ = overall past performance vs. similar funds (5 ★ max). Boxes show the quartile performance for a fund each calendar year vs. only similar funds (□ is the best score possible). ● = high; ◐ = average; and ● = a fund with low expenses.

Overall Past Performance	Fund Name	Type	Risk Up	Risk Down	% of Time Losing $	Biggest Drop	Date	No. of Mo's to Recover	MER
★★	**National Trust American Equity Fund** This fund has been set apart from its peers by its weak returns. High expenses exacerbate the problem for this actively managed fund.	USEq	C	N/A	13%	−9%	2/1/94	16	2.59 ●
★★★	**National Trust Balanced Fund** This fund has shown middle-of-the-road performance against similar funds. Annual fees are reasonable for this reasonably performing fund.	Balan	B	N/A	10%	−11%	2/1/94	15	1.81 ◐
★★★	**National Trust Canadian Bond Fund** Here is an older fund that has shown middle-of-the-road performance against similar funds. Along with performing better than most in bull markets it has been a disappointment in bear markets. Annual fees are reasonable for this reasonably performing closet indexer.	FixInc	B	C	15%	−14%	7/1/80	16	1.34 ◐
★★★	**National Trust Canadian Equity Fund** Here is an older fund that has shown middle-of-the-road performance against similar funds with disappointing results in bull markets and top-notch performance in bear markets. Annual fees are reasonable for this reasonable performing fund.	CdnEq	C	A	23%	−29%	8/1/87	47	1.60 ◐
★★★★★	**National Trust Canadian Index Fund** This newer fund has off-the-charts performance overall vs. its peers. No wonder performance has been so good for this fund, its fees are among the lowest in its group.	CdnEq	N/A	N/A	0%	−5%	3/1/97	2	N/A ◐
★★★	**National Trust Dividend Fund** This fund has shown middle-of-the-road performance against similar funds; it has performed better than most in bull markets but has been hit hard in bear markets. Annual fees are reasonable for this reasonably performing actively managed fund.	CdnEq	B	D	14%	−9%	2/1/94	22	1.84 ◐
★	**National Trust Emerging Markets** Here is one that is a dog. High expenses exacerbate the problem for this fund.	FgnEq	N/A	N/A	29%	−37%	9/1/94	N/A	3.08 ●
★	**National Trust Int'l Equity Fund** Here is one that is a dog. High expenses exacerbate the problem for this fund.	FgnEq	N/A	N/A	23%	−12%	9/1/94	15	2.79 ●
★★★	**National Trust Int'l RSP Bond Fund** This fund has done better than most in its class. High expenses haven't been much of a problem for this fund.	FixInc	N/A	N/A	0%	−3%	5/1/97	N/A	2.15 ●
★	**National Trust Money Market Fund** This fund can be described as having dismal returns. High expenses exacerbate the problem for this actively managed fund.	FixInc	N/A	N/A	0%	0%	N/A	N/A	1.16 ●
★★★	**National Trust Mortgage Fund** This fund has shown middle-of-the-road performance against similar funds. Along with performing better than most in bull markets it has been a disappointment in bear markets. Lower annual expenses than most should bode well for the future of this actively managed fund.	FixInc	B	C	7%	−6%	3/1/94	11	1.52 ◐
★★	**National Trust Special Equity Fund** This fund has been set apart from its peers by its weak returns, with disappointing results in bull markets as well as in bear markets. Normally I'd say that this actively managed fund has reasonable fees vs. its peers, but its poor overall performance makes that argument weak.	CdnEq	C	D	30%	−23%	2/1/94	26	2.50 ◐

Performance Trend columns (quartile boxes shown for years): 88, 89, 90, 91, 92, 93, 94, 95, 96, Sep-97.

Legend: ★ = overall past performance vs. similar funds (5 ★ max). Boxes show the quartile performance for a fund each calendar year vs. only similar funds. [□] is the best score possible). ● = high; ◐ = average; and ◔ = a fund with low expenses.

Consistency	Fund Name	Performance Trend											Risk						Efficiency
Overall Past Performance		Type	88	89	90	91	92	93	94	95	96	Sep-97	Up	Down	% of Time Losing $	Biggest Drop	Date	No. of Mo's to Recover	MER
★★★★	**National Trust U.S. Index Fund** This newer fund has off-the-charts performance overall vs. its peers. No wonder performance has been so good for this fund, its fees are among the lowest in its group.	USEq											N/A	N/A	0%	-5%	8/1/97	N/A	
★★★	**Navigator American Growth Fund** This newer fund has been set apart from its peers by its weak returns. Low fees have not helped this fund.	USEq											N/A	N/A	31%	-14%	7/1/95	6	
★★	**Navigator American Value Inv.** This fund has been set apart from its peers by its weak returns. High expenses exacerbate the problem for this actively managed fund.	USEq											N/A	N/A	0%	-7%	8/1/97	N/A	2.95 ●
★★★★↗	**Navigator Asia Pacific Fund** Who couldn't love this one! It's a super fund overall vs. its peers. No wonder performance has been so good for this actively managed fund, its fees are among the lowest in its group.	FgnEq											N/A	N/A	7%	-13%	8/1/95	8	2.39 ◐
★★★★	**Navigator Canadian Income Fund** This fund has off-the-charts performance overall vs. its peers. This actively managed fund is expensive but well worth it.	FixInc											A	N/A	0%	-1%	3/1/97	1	3.15 ●
★★★↗	**Navigator Value Inv. Retirement** You won't find many like this one! It's done better than most in its class with top-notch performance in bull markets but disappointing results in bear markets. High expenses haven't been much of a problem for this actively managed fund.	CdnEq											A	C	11%	-16%	4/1/94	12	2.88 ●
★★★	**NN Asset Allocation Fund** Here is an older fund that had slightly disappointing results in all market conditions. The fees aren't too bad.	Balan											C	C	17%	-11%	9/1/87	16	2.25 ◔
★★★	**NN Can-Am Fund** This fund has shown middle-of-the-road performance against similar funds. Annual fees are reasonable for this reasonably performing actively managed fund.	USEq											A	N/A	9%	-7%	2/1/94	12	2.25 ◔
★★	**NN Can-Asian Fund** This fund has been set apart from its peers by its weak returns. Low fees have not helped this actively managed fund.	FgnEq											D	B	40%	-23%	2/1/94	23	2.25 ●
★↗	**NN Can-Daq 100 Fund** This newer fund can be described as having dismal returns. Normally I'd say that this fund has reasonable expenses compared to its peers, but poor overall performance makes that argument weak.	USEq											N/A	N/A	0%	-13%	2/1/97	3	2.25 ●
★	**NN Can-Emerge Fund** This newer fund has been a dog. Low fees have not helped this actively managed fund.	FgnEq											N/A	N/A	0%	-10%	8/1/97	N/A	2.25 ●
★★★↗	**NN Can-Euro Fund** You won't find many new ones like this one! It's done better than most in its class. Lower annual expenses than most bode well for the future of this actively managed fund.	FgnEq											N/A	N/A	0%	-8%	8/1/97	N/A	2.25 ◐
★★	**NN Can-Global Bond Fund** This newer fund has shown middle-of-the-road performance against similar funds. Annual fees are reasonable for this reasonably performing actively managed fund.	FixInc											N/A	N/A	0%	-4%	12/1/96	7	2.00 ◔

Legend: ★ = overall past performance vs. similar funds (5 ★ max). Boxes show the quartile performance for a fund each calendar year vs. only similar funds (☐ is the best score possible). ● = high; ◐ = average; and ● = a fund with low expenses.

Consistency			Performance Trend											Risk						Efficiency	
Overall Past Performance	Fund Name	Type	88	89	90	91	92	93	94	95	96	Sep-97	Up	Down	% of Time Losing $	Biggest Drop	Date	No. of Mo's to Recover		MER
★	**NN Elite Fund** Balan											☐	☐	N/A	N/A	0%	-4%	9/1/95	6	●	2.75
	This fund has been a dog. High expenses exacerbate the problem for this actively managed fund.																				
★★★★	**NN Money Market Fund** FixInc							☐	☐	☐	☐	☐	N/A	N/A	0%	0%		N/A	◐	0.75
	This fund has off-the-charts performance overall vs. its peers. Reasonable fees represent bargains for this actively managed fund.																				
★	**NN T-Bill Fund** FixInc				☐	☐	☐	☐	☐	☐	☐	☐	N/A	N/A	0%	0%		N/A	●	1.25
	This well-established fund has been a dog. High expenses exacerbate the problem for this actively managed fund.																				
★★	**North-West Life Ecoflex 'A'** CdnEq											☐	N/A	N/A	0%	-5%	3/1/97	2	◐	2.14
	This newer fund has been set apart from its peers by its weak returns. Normally I'd say that this fund has reasonable expenses compared to its peers, but poor overall performance makes that argument weak.																				
★	**North-West Life Ecoflex 'B'** FixInc											☐	N/A	N/A	0%	-1%	3/1/97	2	◐	1.55
	This newer fund has been a dog. Normally I'd say that this fund has reasonable expenses compared to its peers, but poor overall performance makes that argument weak.																				
★	**North-West Life Ecoflex 'D'** Balan											☐	N/A	N/A	0%	-3%	3/1/97	2	◐	2.14
	This newer fund has been a dog out of the gate, but let's wait and see how it does in time.																				
★	**North-West Life Ecoflex 'E'** FgnEq											☐	N/A	N/A	0%	-8%	8/1/97	N/A	●	2.14
	This newer fund has been a dog. Normally I'd say that this fund has reasonable expenses compared to its peers, but poor overall performance makes that argument weak.																				
★	**North-West Life Ecoflex 'G'** FixInc											☐	N/A	N/A	0%	-1%	5/1/97	N/A	●	1.55
	This newer fund has been a dog. Low fees have not helped this fund.																				
★	**North-West Life Ecoflex 'H'** FixInc											☐	N/A	N/A	0%	0%	3/1/97	2	●	1.55
	This newer fund has been a dog. Low fees have not helped this fund.																				
★	**North-West Life Ecoflex 'I'** FgnEq											☐	N/A	N/A	0%	-3%	8/1/97	N/A	●	2.14
	This newer fund has been a dog. Normally I'd say that this fund has reasonable expenses compared to its peers, but poor overall performance makes that argument weak.																				
★	**North-West Life Ecoflex 'M'** FixInc											☐	N/A	N/A	0%	0%		N/A	◐	1.02
	This newer fund has been a dog. Normally I'd say that this actively managed fund has reasonable expenses compared to its peers, but poor overall performance makes that argument weak.																				
★	**North-West Life Ecoflex 'S'** USEq											☐	N/A	N/A	0%	-6%	2/1/97	2	●	2.14
	This newer fund has been a dog. Normally I'd say that this fund has reasonable expenses compared to its peers, but poor overall performance makes that argument weak.																				
★	**O'Donnell American Sector Growth** USEq										☐	☐	N/A	N/A	57%	-9%	6/1/96	11	●	2.90
	This newer fund has been a dog. High expenses exacerbate the problem for this actively managed fund.																				
★	**O'Donnell Balanced Fund** Balan											☐	N/A	N/A	0%	-2%	3/1/97	3	●	2.40
	This newer fund has been a dog. High expenses exacerbate the problem for this fund.																				

Legend: ★ = overall past performance vs. similar funds (5 ★ max). Boxes show the quartile performance for a fund each calendar year vs. only similar funds (□ is the best score possible). ● = high; ◐ = average; and ● = a fund with low expenses.

Overall Past Performance	Fund Name	Type	Risk Up	Risk Down	% of Time Losing $	Biggest Drop	Date	No. of Mo's to Recover	MER
★★	O'Donnell Canadian Emerging Growth	CdnEq	N/A	N/A	0%	-7%	3/1/97	N/A	2.75
★★★	O'Donnell Growth Fund	CdnEq	N/A	N/A	0%	-8%	3/1/97	4	2.75
★★★★★	O'Donnell High Income Fund	FixInc	N/A	N/A	0%	-1%	3/1/97	1	2.00
★	O'Donnell Money Market Fund	FixInc	N/A	N/A	0%	0%		N/A	1.10
★	O'Donnell Short Term Fund	FixInc	N/A	N/A	0%	0%		N/A	1.35
★	O'Donnell U.S. Mid-Cap Fund	USEq	N/A	N/A	0%	-6%	6/1/96	8	2.90
★	O'Donnell World Equity Fund	FgnEq	N/A	N/A	0%	0%	2/1/97	3	2.75
★★★★	O'Donnell World Prec. Metals Fund	SpcIty	N/A	N/A	100%	-17%	6/1/97	N/A	2.90
★★★	OHA Balanced Fund	Balan	C	N/A	17%	-8%	2/1/94	14	0.90
★★★	OHA Bond Fund	FixInc	B	C	17%	-13%	2/1/94	15	0.90
★?	OHA Canadian Equity Fund	CdnEq	B	D	26%	-21%	9/1/93	31	0.90
★★	OHA Foreign Equity Fund	FgnEq	C	N/A	0%	-9%	6/1/96	4	1.70
★★★★	OHA Short Term Fund	FixInc	N/A	N/A	0%	0%		N/A	0.70

O'Donnell Canadian Emerging Growth: This newer fund has been set apart from its peers by its weak returns. High expenses exacerbate the problem for this actively managed fund.

O'Donnell Growth Fund: This newer fund has shown middle-of-the-road performance against similar funds. High expenses haven't been much of a problem for this actively managed fund.

O'Donnell High Income Fund: This newer fund has shown off-the-charts performance overall vs. its peers. This actively managed fund is expensive but well worth it.

O'Donnell Money Market Fund: This newer fund has been a dog. High expenses exacerbate the problem for this actively managed fund.

O'Donnell Short Term Fund: This newer fund has been a dog. High expenses exacerbate the problem for this actively managed fund.

O'Donnell U.S. Mid-Cap Fund: This newer fund has been a dog. High expenses exacerbate the problem for this actively managed fund.

O'Donnell World Equity Fund: This newer fund has been a dog. High expenses exacerbate the problem for this fund.

O'Donnell World Prec. Metals Fund: This newer fund has off-the-charts performance overall vs. its peers. Reasonable fees represent bargains for this fund.

OHA Balanced Fund: This fund has shown middle-of-the-road performance against similar funds. Lower annual expenses than most bode well for the future of this actively managed fund.

OHA Bond Fund: This fund has shown middle-of-the-road performance against similar funds. Along with performing better than most in bull markets it has been a disappointment in bear markets. Lower annual expenses than most bode well for the future of this fund.

OHA Canadian Equity Fund: This fund has been unimpressive so far with disappointing results in bull markets as well as in bear markets. Low fees have not helped this actively managed fund.

OHA Foreign Equity Fund: This fund has shown middle-of-the-road performance against similar funds. Lower annual expenses than most bode well for the future of this actively managed fund.

OHA Short Term Fund: This fund has off-the-charts performance overall vs. its peers. No wonder performance has been so good for this actively managed fund, its fees are among the lowest in its group.

Legend: ★ = overall past performance vs. similar funds (5 ★ max). Boxes show the quartile performance for a fund each calendar year vs. only similar funds (□ is the best score possible). ● = high; ◐ = average; and ● = a fund with low expenses.

Overall Past Performance	Fund Name	Type	Up	Down	% of Time Losing $	Biggest Drop	Date	No. of Mo's to Recover	MER
★★★	**Ontario Teachers Group Balanced** — Here is an older fund that has shown middle-of-the-road performance against similar funds. As well as performing better than most in bull markets it's been a top-notch performer in bear markets. Lower annual expenses than most bode well for the future of this fund.	Balan	B	A	10%	-10%	8/1/87	14	1.00
★★★	**Ontario Teachers Group Diversified** — Here is an older fund that has shown middle-of-the-road performance against similar funds with disappointing results in bull markets and top-notch performance in bear markets. Lower annual expenses than most bode well for the future of this fund.	CdnEq	C	A	26%	-27%	4/1/81	20	1.00
★★★★	**Ontario Teachers Group Fixed Value** — This well-established fund has impressive past performance characteristics overall vs. its peers. No wonder performance has been so good for this actively managed fund, its fees are among the lowest in its group.	FixInc	N/A	N/A	0%	0%	N/A	N/A	0.50
★★	**Ontario Teachers Group Global** — This fund has been set apart from its peers by its weak returns. Low fees have not helped this actively managed fund.	FgnEq	D	N/A	6%	-7%	2/1/94	15	1.00
★★	**Ontario Teachers Group Growth** — This well-established fund has been set apart from its peers by its weak returns, but it's been a top-notch performer in bear markets. Its low expenses have not helped this actively managed fund.	CdnEq	D	A	32%	-29%	7/1/81	17	1.00
★★	**Ontario Teachers Group Mortgage Inc** — This well-established fund has been set apart from its peers by its weak returns, but it's been a top-notch performer in bear markets. Its low expenses have not helped this actively managed fund.	FixInc	D	A	6%	-20%	12/1/86	30	0.75
★★★	**Optima Strategy Canadian Equity** — Here is an older fund that has shown middle-of-the-road performance against similar funds. As well as performing better than most in bull markets it's been a top-notch performer in bear markets. Lower annual expenses than most bode well for the future of this actively managed fund.	CdnEq	B	A	19%	-26%	8/1/87	23	0.41
★	**Optima Strategy Cdn Fixed Income** — This well-established fund can be described as having dismal returns. Low fees have not helped this closet indexer.	FixInc	D	B	10%	-12%	2/1/90	10	0.40
★★★	**Optima Strategy Global Fixed Income** — This fund has shown middle-of-the-road performance against similar funds. Lower annual expenses than most bode well for the future of this actively managed fund.	FixInc	B	N/A	4%	-5%	7/1/95	4	0.48
★★★	**Optima Strategy Int'l Equity** — You won't find many like this one! It's done better than most in its class. Lower annual expenses than most bode well for the future of this actively managed fund.	FgnEq	A	N/A	0%	-8%	11/1/94	6	0.47
★★	**Optima Strategy Short Term Income** — This fund has been unimpressive so far but it's been a top-notch performer in bear markets. This low-priced closet indexer is well worth it.	FixInc	D	A	2%	-4%	2/1/94	12	0.28
★★★★	**Optima Strategy U.S. Equity** — This fund is a super fund overall vs. its peers. No wonder performance has been so good for this fund, its fees are among the lowest in its group.	USEq	A	N/A	0%	-7%	9/1/94	6	0.42
★★★★	**Orbit North American Equity Fund** — This newer fund is a super fund overall vs. its peers. This actively managed fund is expensive but well worth it.	FgnEq	N/A	N/A	0%	-3%	7/1/96	2	2.50

Legend: ★ = overall past performance vs. similar funds (5 ★ max). Boxes show the quartile performance for a fund each calendar year vs. only similar funds (☐ is the best score possible). ● = high; ◐ = average; and ● = a fund with low expenses.

Overall Past Performance	Fund Name	Type	88	89	90	91	92	93	94	95	96	Sep-97	Up	Down	% of Time Losing $	Biggest Drop	Date	No. of Mo's to Recover	MER
★★⟋	**Orbit World Fund** This fund can be described as having dismal returns, but it's been a top-notch performer in bear markets. Normally I'd say that this actively managed fund has reasonable expenses compared to its peers, but poor overall performance makes that argument weak	FgnEq							☐	☐	☐	☐	D	A	20%	-14%	11/1/94	29	2.50
★★★	**Pacific Special Equity Fund** This fund has shown middle-of-the-road performance against similar funds; it has performed better than most in bull markets but has been hit hard in bear markets. This actively managed fund is expensive but worth it in rising market conditions.	CdnEq								☐	☐	☐	B	D	23%	-23%	6/1/96	N/A	2.80
★	**Pacific Total Return Fund** This newer fund has been a dog. High expenses exacerbate the problem for this fund.	CdnEq									☐	☐	N/A	N/A	100%	-15%	3/1/97	N/A	2.90
★★★⟋	**Phillips Hager & North Balanced** This fund has done better than most in its class. Lower annual expenses than most bode well for the future of this fund.	Balan				☐	☐	☐	☐	☐	☐	☐	A	N/A	2%	-8%	2/1/94	13	0.91
★★★★	**Phillips Hager & North Bal Pens Tr** This fund has off-the-charts performance overall vs. its peers. No wonder performance has been so good for this fund, its fees are among the lowest in its group.	Balan					☐	☐	☐	☐	☐	☐	A	N/A	6%	-8%	2/1/94	13	0.00
★★★	**Phillips Hager & North Bond Fund** This well-established fund has impressive past performance characteristics overall vs. its peers with top-notch performance in all market conditions. No wonder performance has been so good for this fund, its fees are among the lowest in its group	FixInc								☐	☐	☐	A	A	13%	-17%	7/1/80	16	0.57
★★★	**Phillips Hager & North Cdn. Equity** This well-established fund has shown middle-of-the-road performance against similar funds with top-notch performance in bull markets as well as performing better than most in bear markets. Lower annual expenses than most bode well for the future of this closet indexer.	CdnEq			☐	☐	☐	☐	☐	☐	☐	☐	A	B	24%	-42%	6/1/81	23	1.09
★★★	**PH & N Canadian Equity Plus Fund** Here is an older fund that has shown middle-of-the-road performance against similar funds with top-notch performance in all market conditions. Lower annual expenses than most bode well for the future of this fund.	CdnEq			☐	☐	☐	☐	☐	☐	☐	☐	A	A	21%	-40%	6/1/81	22	1.18
★★★★★	**PH & N Canadian Money Market** This well-established fund has off-the-charts performance overall vs. its peers. No wonder performance has been so good for this actively managed fund, its fees are among the lowest in its group.	FixInc				☐	☐	☐	☐	☐	☐	☐	N/A	N/A	0%	0%		N/A	0.48
★★★⟋	**Phillips Hager & North Div. Income** This well-established fund has done better than most in its class with top-notch performance in all market conditions. Lower annual expenses than most bode well for the future of this actively managed fund.	CdnEq			☐	☐	☐	☐	☐	☐	☐	☐	C	A	12%	-16%	5/1/81	17	1.21
★★	**PH & N International Equity Fund** This fund has been set apart from its peers by its weak returns. Low fees have not helped this fund.	FgnEq							☐	☐	☐	☐	C	N/A	7%	-7%	9/1/94	8	1.49
★★★	**PH & N North American Equity Fund** This fund has shown middle-of-the-road performance against similar funds. Lower annual expenses than most bode well for the future of this actively managed fund.	FgnEq							☐	☐	☐	☐	C	N/A	26%	-23%	2/1/94	23	1.18

Legend: ★ = overall past performance vs. similar funds (5 ★ max). Boxes show the quartile performance for a fund each calendar year vs. only similar funds (☐ is the best score possible). ● = high; ◐ = average; and ● = a fund with low expenses.

Overall Past Performance	Fund Name	Type	Up	Down	% of Time Losing $	Biggest Drop	Date	No. of Mo's to Recover	MER
★★★?	PH & N Short Term Bond & Mortgage	FixInc	A	C	3%	-6%	2/1/94	12	0.64
★★★★	PH & N $US Money Market	FixInc	N/A	N/A	0%	0%		N/A	0.52
★★★?	Phillips Hager & North U.S. Equity	USEq	A	D	16%	-32%	9/1/87	22	1.10
★★★★	Phillips Hager & North Vintage	CdnEq	A	A	15%	-29%	8/1/87	23	1.76
★?	Protected American Fund	Balan	D	A	21%	-8%	4/1/96	N/A	2.30
★★	Pursuit Canadian Bond Fund	FixInc	D	A	6%	-6%	2/1/94	15	0.80
★★?	Pursuit Canadian Equity Fund	CdnEq	C	A	24%	-32%	6/1/87	71	1.50
★★	Pursuit Global Bond Fund	FixInc	N/A	N/A	0%	-4%	12/1/96	6	1.25
★★★?	Pursuit Global Equity Fund	FgnEq	N/A	N/A	0%	-4%	8/1/97	N/A	1.75
★	Pursuit Growth Fund	USEq	D	A	21%	-18%	9/1/87	22	1.75
★★★★	Pursuit Money Market Fund	FixInc	N/A	N/A	0%	-1%	6/1/88	1	0.50
★★	Quebec Growth Fund	CdnEq	C	C	36%	-74%	5/1/87	108	1.89
★★?	Resolute Growth Fund	CdnEq	D	B	32%	-18%	7/1/96	N/A	2.00

PH & N Short Term Bond & Mortgage: This fund has done better than most in its class with top-notch performance in bull markets but disappointing results in bear markets. Lower annual expenses than most bode well for the future of this closet indexer.

PH & N $US Money Market: This fund has off-the-charts performance overall vs. its peers. No wonder performance has been so good for this actively managed fund, its fees are among the lowest in its group.

Phillips Hager & North U.S. Equity: This well-established fund has done better than most in its class with top-notch performance in bull markets but has been hit hard in bear markets. Lower annual expenses than most bode well for the future of this actively managed fund.

Phillips Hager & North Vintage: Wow! Here is an established fund that has off-the-charts performance overall vs. its peers with top-notch performance in all market conditions. No wonder performance has been so good for this actively managed fund, their fees are among the lowest in its group.

Protected American Fund: This well-established fund can be described as having dismal returns, but it's been a top-notch performer in bear markets. High fees exacerbate the problem for this actively managed fund, especially in bull markets.

Pursuit Canadian Bond Fund: This fund has been set apart from its peers by its weak returns, but it's been a top-notch performer in bear markets. This low-priced actively managed fund is well worth it.

Pursuit Canadian Equity Fund: This well-established fund has been unimpressive so far with disappointing results in a bullish environment. Low fees have not helped this actively managed fund.

Pursuit Global Bond Fund: This newer fund has shown middle-of-the-road performance against similar funds. Lower annual expenses than most bode well for the future of this actively managed fund.

Pursuit Global Equity Fund: This newer fund is a super fund overall vs. its peers. No wonder performance has been so good for this actively managed fund, its fees are among the lowest in its group.

Pursuit Growth Fund: This well-established fund has been a dog, but it's been a top-notch performer in bear markets. Its low expenses have not helped this actively managed fund.

Pursuit Money Market Fund: This fund has off-the-charts performance overall vs. its peers. No wonder performance has been so good for this actively managed fund, its fees are among the lowest in its group.

Quebec Growth Fund: This well-established fund has been set apart from its peers by its weak returns. Performing just slightly better than most in bull markets, it's been a disappointment in bear markets. Low fees have not helped this actively managed fund.

Resolute Growth Fund: This fund has been unimpressive so far. Low fees have not helped this actively managed fund.

Legend: ★ = overall past performance vs. similar funds (5 ★ max). Boxes show the quartile performance for a fund each calendar year vs. only similar funds. □ is the best score possible). ● = high; ◐ = average; and ● = a fund with low expenses.

Overall Past Performance	Fund Name	Type	Performance Trend 88–Sep-97	Risk Up	Risk Down	% of Time Losing $	Biggest Drop	Date	No. of Mo's to Recover	MER
★★	**Retrocom Growth Fund Inc.**	Labour		N/A	N/A	33%	-1%	9/1/95	11	4.61
	This fund has been unimpressive so far. Normally I'd say that this actively managed fund has reasonable expenses compared to its peers, but poor overall performance makes that argument weak.									
★★	**Royal Asian Growth Fund**	FgnEq		D	C	51%	-25%	1/1/94	N/A	2.84
	This fund has been set apart from its peers by its weak returns, but it's been a top-notch performer in bear markets. High expenses exacerbate the problem for this actively managed fund, especially in declining markets.									
★★★	**Royal Balanced Fund**	Balan		C	N/A	10%	-8%	2/1/94	15	2.31
	This fund has shown middle-of-the-road performance against similar funds. High expenses haven't been much of a problem for this fund.									
★	**Royal Canadian Growth Fund**	CdnEq		C	C	21%	-17%	2/1/94	22	2.30
	This fund can be described as having dismal returns with disappointing results in all market conditions. Normally I'd say this fund has reasonable fees, but poor overall performance makes that argument weak.									
★	**Royal Canadian Small Cap**	CdnEq		D	D	24%	-19%	2/1/94	23	2.27
	This fund has been a dog, but it's been hit hard in all market conditions. Normally I'd say that this fund has reasonable expenses compared to its peers, but poor overall performance makes that argument weak.									
★★★	**Royal Energy Fund**	CdnEq		A	C	44%	-48%	7/1/81	72	2.32
	Here is an older fund that has shown middle-of-the-road performance against similar funds with top-notch performance in bull markets but disappointing results in bear markets. Annual fees are reasonable for this reasonable performing actively managed fund.									
★★★	**Royal European Growth Fund**	FgnEq		D	N/A	25%	-30%	9/1/87	71	2.66
	This fund has shown middle-of-the-road performance against similar funds. High expenses haven't been much of a problem for this actively managed fund.									
★★	**Royal International Equity Fund**	FgnEq		B	N/A	9%	-8%	9/1/94	10	2.49
	This fund has shown middle-of-the-road performance against similar funds. High expenses haven't been much of a problem for this actively managed fund.									
★★	**Royal Japanese Stock Fund**	FgnEq		C	D	51%	-48%	5/1/88	73	2.95
	This well-established fund has been set apart from its peers by its weak returns, with disappointing results in bull markets as well as in bear markets. High expenses exacerbate the problem for this fund.									
★	**Royal Latin American Fund**	FgnEq		N/A	N/A	0%	-4%	8/1/95	5	3.00
	This newer fund has been a dog. High expenses exacerbate the problem for this actively managed fund.									
★	**Royal Lepage Commercial Real Estate**	Spclty		N/A	N/A	38%	-6%	6/1/93	15	3.40
	This fund has been a dog. High expenses exacerbate the problem for this actively managed fund.									
★★	**Royal Life Balanced Fund**	Balan		C	N/A	9%	-11%	2/1/94	15	2.34
	This fund has been unimpressive so far. High expenses exacerbate the problem for this closet indexer.									
★★★	**Royal Life Canadian Growth Fund**	CdnEq		N/A	N/A	0%	-8%	6/1/96	5	2.35
	This fund has shown middle-of-the-road performance against similar funds. Lower annual expenses than most bode well for the future of this actively managed fund.									

Legend: ★ = overall past performance vs. similar funds (5 ★ max). Boxes show the quartile performance for a fund each calendar year vs. only similar funds (☐ is the best score possible), ● = high; ◐ = average; and ○ = a fund with low expenses.

Consistency		Performance Trend											Risk						Efficiency
Overall Past Performance	Fund Name	Type	88	89	90	91	92	93	94	95	96	Sep-97	Up	Down	% of Time Losing $	Biggest Drop	Date	No. of Mo's to Recover	MER
★★★	**Royal Life Equity Fund** This fund has shown middle-of-the-road performance against similar funds. Along with performing better than most in bull markets it has been a disappointment in bear markets. High expenses haven't been much of a problem for this fund.	CdnEq											B	C	9%	-15%	2/1/90	13	2.37 ●
★★★	**Royal Life Income Fund** This fund has shown middle-of-the-road performance against similar funds with disappointing results in bull markets along with being hit hard in bear markets. This closet indexer is expensive but worth it in rising market conditions.	FixInc											C	D	11%	-12%	2/1/94	16	1.88 ●
★★	**Royal Life Int'l Equity Fund** This fund has been set apart from its peers by its weak returns. High expenses exacerbate the problem for this actively managed fund.	FgnEq											N/A	N/A	5%	-6%	8/1/97	N/A	2.60 ●
★★★★★	**Royal Life Money Market Fund** This fund has off-the-charts performance overall vs. its peers. Reasonable fees represent bargains for this actively managed fund.	FixInc											N/A	N/A	0%	0%	N/A	N/A	1.00 ○
★★★	**Royal Life Science & Technology** This newer fund has shown middle-of-the-road performance against similar funds. High expenses haven't been much of a problem for this actively managed fund.	Spclty											N/A	N/A	0%	-15%	6/1/96	7	2.81 ●
★★★★★	**Royal Life U.S. Equity Fund** This newer fund has off-the-charts performance overall vs. its peers. No wonder performance has been so good for this actively managed fund, its fees are among the lowest in its group.	USEq											N/A	N/A	0%	-8%	6/1/96	3	2.21 ◐
★★★↗	**Royal Precious Metals Fund** This fund has done better than most in its class. Along with performing better than most in bull markets it has been a disappointment in bear markets. Annual fees are reasonable for this reasonably performing actively managed fund.	CdnEq											B	C	43%	-36%	6/1/96	N/A	2.21 ◐
★★★★★	**Royal Premium Money Market Fund** This newer fund has off-the-charts performance overall vs. its peers. No wonder performance has been so good for this actively managed fund, its fees are among the lowest in its group.	FixInc											N/A	N/A	0%	0%	N/A	N/A	0.35 ●
★★★	**Royal Trust Advantage Balanced Fund** This well-established fund has shown middle-of-the-road performance against similar funds. Along with performing better than most in bull markets it has been a disappointment in bear markets. Annual fees are reasonable for this reasonably performing actively managed fund.	Balan											B	C	14%	-11%	8/1/87	17	1.78 ◐
★★★	**Royal Trust Advantage Growth Fund** This well-established fund has shown middle-of-the-road performance against similar funds with disappointing results in bull markets along with being hit hard in bear markets. Annual fees are reasonable for this reasonable performing fund.	Balan											C	D	17%	-17%	9/1/87	20	1.92 ◐
★★↗	**Royal Trust Advantage Income Fund** This well-established fund has been unimpressive so far with disappointing results in bull markets. Low fees have not helped this fund.	Balan											C	B	3%	-7%	2/1/94	15	1.65 ●
★★↗	**Royal Trust American Stock Fund** This well-established fund has been unimpressive so far with disappointing results in bull markets. Normally I'd say this fund has reasonable fees, but poor overall performance makes that argument weak.	USEq											C	B	23%	-27%	9/1/87	24	2.18 ◐
★★★	**Royal Trust Bond Fund** This well-established fund has shown middle-of-the-road performance against similar funds along with performing better than most in all market conditions. Annual fees are reasonable for this reasonably performing closet indexer.	FixInc											B	B	10%	-12%	2/1/94	15	1.39 ◐

Legend: ★ overall past performance vs. similar funds (5 ★ max). Boxes show the quartile performance for a fund each calendar year vs. only similar funds (□ is the best score possible). ● = high; ◐ = average; and ◑ = a fund with low expenses.

Consistency Overall Past Performance	Fund Name	Type	Risk Up	Risk Down	% of Time Losing $	Biggest Drop	Date	No. of Mo's to Recover	Efficiency MER
★	Royal Trust Canadian Money Market	FixInc	N/A	N/A	0%	0%	—	N/A	1.00 ●
★★	Royal Trust Canadian Stock Fund	CdnEq	C	A	23%	−35%	12/1/80	26	1.95 ●
★	Royal Trust Canadian T-Bill Fund	FixInc	N/A	N/A	0%	0%	—	N/A	0.93 ●
★★	Royal Trust Growth and Income Fund	CdnEq	C	C	18%	−10%	1/1/90	14	1.77 ●
★★★	Royal Trust International Bond Fund	FixInc	A	N/A	9%	−4%	10/1/92	4	1.87 ●
★★★	Royal Trust Mortgage Fund	FixInc	B	D	3%	−5%	2/1/94	13	1.73 ●
★	Royal Trust U.S. Money Market ($US)	FixInc	N/A	N/A	0%	0%	—	N/A	1.12 ●
★★★	RoyFund Bond Fund	FixInc	C	A	4%	−10%	2/1/94	15	1.56 ●
★★★	RoyFund Canadian Equity Fund	CdnEq	A	A	25%	−41%	6/1/81	22	2.10 ●
★	RoyFund Canadian Money Market Fund	FixInc	N/A	N/A	0%	0%	—	N/A	1.00 ●
★★★	RoyFund Canadian T-Bill Fund	FixInc	N/A	N/A	0%	0%	—	N/A	0.93 ●
★★★	RoyFund Dividend Fund	CdnEq	A	D	7%	−10%	2/1/94	15	1.84 ●

Performance Trend columns: 88 89 90 91 92 93 94 95 96 Sep-97

Royal Trust Canadian Money Market — This fund has been a dog. Normally I'd say that this actively managed fund has reasonable expenses compared to its peers, but poor overall performance makes that argument weak.

Royal Trust Canadian Stock Fund — This well-established fund has been set apart from its peers by its weak returns, with disappointing results in a bullish environment. Normally I'd say that this closet indexer has reasonable expenses compared to its peers, but poor overall performance makes that argument weak.

Royal Trust Canadian T-Bill Fund — This fund has been a dog. Normally I'd say that this actively managed fund has reasonable expenses compared to its peers, but poor overall performance makes that argument weak.

Royal Trust Growth and Income Fund — This well-established fund has been set apart from its peers by its weak returns, with disappointing results in all market conditions. Normally I'd say this fund has reasonable fees, but poor overall performance makes that argument weak.

Royal Trust International Bond Fund — This fund has done better than most in its class. Annual fees are reasonable for this reasonably performing actively managed fund.

Royal Trust Mortgage Fund — You won't find many like this older one! It's done better than most in its class; it has performed better than most in bull markets but has been hit hard in bear markets. Annual fees are reasonable for this reasonably performing actively managed fund.

Royal Trust U.S. Money Market ($US) — This fund can be described as having dismal returns. Normally I'd say that this actively managed fund has reasonable expenses compared to its peers, but poor overall performance makes that argument weak.

RoyFund Bond Fund — Here is an older fund that has shown middle-of-the-road performance against similar funds with disappointing results in bull markets and top-notch performance in bear markets. Annual fees are reasonable for this reasonable performing closet indexer.

RoyFund Canadian Equity Fund — Here is an older fund that has shown middle-of-the-road performance against similar funds. As well as performing better than most in bull markets it's been a top-notch performer in bear markets. Annual fees are reasonable for this reasonably performing closet indexer.

RoyFund Canadian Money Market Fund — This well-established fund has been a dog. Normally I'd say that this actively managed fund has reasonable expenses compared to its peers, but poor overall performance makes that argument weak.

RoyFund Canadian T-Bill Fund — This fund has shown middle-of-the-road performance against similar funds. Annual fees are reasonable for this reasonably performing actively managed fund.

RoyFund Dividend Fund — This fund has done better than most in its class with top-notch performance in bull markets but has been hit hard in bear markets. Annual fees are reasonable for this reasonably performing actively managed fund.

Legend: ★ = overall past performance vs. similar funds (5 ★ max). Boxes show the quartile performance for a fund each calendar year vs. only similar funds (□ is the best score possible). ● = high; ◐ = average; and ◔ = a fund with low expenses.

Overall Past Performance (Consistency)	Fund Name	Type	Risk Up	Risk Down	% of Time Losing $	Biggest Drop	Date	No. of Mo's to Recover	MER (Efficiency)
★★★	RoyFund International Income Fund	FixInc	C	N/A	5%	-4%	1/1/96	9	2.06
★★★★	RoyFund Mortgage Fund	FixInc	A	A	2%	-5%	3/1/94	11	1.79
★	RoyFund U.S. Dollar Money ($US)	FixInc	N/A	N/A	0%	0%	N/A	N/A	1.20
★★★✦	RoyFund U.S. Equity Fund	USEq	A	N/A	0%	-8%	6/1/96	5	2.12
★★	Saxon Balanced Fund	Balan	D	D	25%	-26%	4/1/87	70	1.75
★★	Saxon Small Cap (Howson Tattersall)	CdnEq	D	B	29%	-28%	9/1/89	42	1.75
★★	Saxon Stock Fund	CdnEq	C	C	29%	-29%	4/1/87	71	1.75
★★★✦	Saxon World Growth	FgnEq	A	D	22%	-32%	6/1/89	31	1.78
★★★	Sceptre Asian Growth Fund	FgnEq	A	D	39%	-24%	1/1/94	N/A	2.40
★★★✦	Sceptre Balanced Growth Fund	Balan	A	B	10%	-10%	8/1/87	10	1.43
★★★	Sceptre Bond Fund	FixInc	B	B	6%	-11%	2/1/94	15	1.25
★★★	Sceptre Equity Growth Fund	CdnEq	A	B	23%	-19%	10/1/87	15	1.51

Fund descriptions:

RoyFund International Income Fund — This fund has shown middle-of-the-road performance against similar funds. Annual fees are reasonable for this reasonably performing actively managed fund.

RoyFund Mortgage Fund — This fund has impressive past performance characteristics overall vs. its peers with top-notch performance in all market conditions. This actively managed fund is expensive but well worth it.

RoyFund U.S. Dollar Money ($US) — This fund has been a dog. High expenses exacerbate the problem for this actively managed fund.

RoyFund U.S. Equity Fund — This fund has done better than most in its class. Annual fees are reasonable for this reasonably performing actively managed fund.

Saxon Balanced Fund — This well-established fund has been set apart from its peers by its weak returns; it's been hit hard in all market conditions. Low fees have not helped this actively managed fund.

Saxon Small Cap (Howson Tattersall) — This well-established fund has been set apart from its peers by its weak returns. Low fees have not helped this actively managed fund.

Saxon Stock Fund — This well-established fund has been set apart from its peers by its weak returns, with disappointing results in all market conditions. Normally I'd say this fund has reasonable fees, but poor overall performance makes that argument weak.

Saxon World Growth — This well-established fund has done better than most in its class with top-notch performance in bull markets but has been hit hard in bear markets. Lower annual expenses than most bode well for the future of this actively managed fund.

Sceptre Asian Growth Fund — This fund has shown middle-of-the-road performance against similar funds with top-notch performance in bull markets but has been hit hard in bear markets. Lower annual expenses than most bode well for the future of this actively managed fund.

Sceptre Balanced Growth Fund — You won't find many like this older one! It's done better than most in its class with top-notch performance in bull markets as well as performing better than most in bear markets. Lower annual expenses than most bode well for the future of this fund.

Sceptre Bond Fund — This well-established fund has shown middle-of-the-road performance against similar funds along with performing better than most in all market conditions. Lower annual expenses than most bode well for the future of this closet indexer.

Sceptre Equity Growth Fund — This well-established fund has impressive past performance characteristics overall vs. its peers with top-notch performance in bull markets as well as performing better than most in bear markets. No wonder performance has been so good for this actively managed fund, its fees are among the lowest in its group.

Legend: ★ = overall past performance vs. similar funds (5 ★ max). Boxes show the quartile performance for a fund each calendar year vs. only similar funds (□ is the best score possible). ● = high; ◐ = average; and ● = a fund with low expenses.

Overall Past Performance	Fund Name	Type	88	89	90	91	92	93	94	95	96	Sep-97	Risk Up	Risk Down	% of Time Losing $	Biggest Drop	Date	No. of Mo's to Recover	MER
★★★	**Sceptre International Fund**	FgnEq	□	□	□	□	□	□	□	□	□	□	A	N/A	19%	-25%	10/1/87	18	2.10
★★★★	**Sceptre Money Market Fund**	FixInc				□	□	□	□	□	□	□	N/A	N/A	0%	0%	N/A	N/A	0.75
★★★	**Scotia CanAm Growth Fund**	USEq							□	□	□	□	B	N/A	3%	-7%	2/1/94	12	1.34
★★★	**Scotia CanAm Income Fund**	FixInc						□	□	□	□	□	A	A	7%	-5%	3/1/94	10	1.60
★★★★	**Scotia CanAm Money Market Fund**	FixInc									□	□	N/A	N/A	0%	0%	N/A	N/A	1.00
★★	**Scotia Excelsior American Growth**	USEq	□	□	□	□	□	□	□	□	□	□	D	B	21%	-36%	9/1/87	68	2.19
★★★	**Scotia Excelsior Balanced Fund**	Balan							□	□	□	□	B	N/A	5%	-9%	2/1/94	15	2.01
★★	**Scotia Excelsior Cdn. Blue Chip**	CdnEq	□	□	□	□	□	□	□	□	□	□	D	C	24%	-28%	8/1/87	50	2.03
★★★	**Scotia Excelsior Cdn. Growth Fund**	CdnEq	□	□	□	□	□	□	□	□	□	□	C	A	25%	-30%	6/1/81	20	2.09
★★	**Scotia Excelsior Defensive Income**	FixInc	□	□	□	□	□	□	□	□	□	□	C	C	4%	-7%	2/1/94	14	1.37
★★★	**Scotia Excelsior Dividend Fund**	CdnEq	□	□	□	□	□	□	□	□	□	□	C	C	17%	-10%	8/1/87	11	1.07
½	**Scotia Excelsior European Growth**	FgnEq											N/A	N/A	0%	-4%	8/1/97	N/A	2.17
½	**Scotia Excelsior Global Bond Fund**	FixInc								□	□	□	N/A	N/A	33%	-7%	7/1/95	16	1.86

Fund descriptions:

Sceptre International Fund — This well-established fund has done better than most in its class with top-notch performance in all market conditions. Lower annual expenses than most bode well for the future of this actively managed fund.

Sceptre Money Market Fund — This fund has off-the-charts performance overall vs. its peers. No wonder performance has been so good for this actively managed fund, its fees are among the lowest in its group.

Scotia CanAm Growth Fund — This fund has shown middle-of-the-road performance against similar funds. Lower annual expenses than most bode well for the future of this fund.

Scotia CanAm Income Fund — This fund has shown middle-of-the-road performance against similar funds with top-notch performance in all market conditions. High expenses haven't been much of a problem for this actively managed fund.

Scotia CanAm Money Market Fund — This newer fund has off-the-charts performance overall vs. its peers. Reasonable fees represent bargains for this actively managed fund.

Scotia Excelsior American Growth — This well-established fund has been set apart from its peers by its weak returns. Normally I'd say this fund has reasonable fees, but poor overall performance makes that argument weak.

Scotia Excelsior Balanced Fund — This fund has shown middle-of-the-road performance against similar funds. Annual fees are reasonable for this reasonably performing actively managed fund.

Scotia Excelsior Cdn. Blue Chip — This well-established fund has been set apart from its peers by its weak returns, with disappointing results in bear markets. Normally I'd say that this closet indexer has reasonable expenses compared to its peers, but poor overall performance makes that argument weak.

Scotia Excelsior Cdn. Growth Fund — This well-established fund has shown middle-of-the-road performance against similar funds with disappointing results in bull markets and top-notch performance in bear markets. Annual fees are reasonable for this reasonably performing actively managed fund.

Scotia Excelsior Defensive Income — This fund has been set apart from its peers by its weak returns, with disappointing results in all market conditions. Normally I'd say this fund has reasonable fees, but poor overall performance makes that argument weak.

Scotia Excelsior Dividend Fund — Here is an older fund that has shown middle-of-the-road performance against similar funds with disappointing results in all market conditions. Lower annual expenses than most bode well for the future of this actively managed fund.

Scotia Excelsior European Growth — This newer fund has been a dog. Low fees have not helped this actively managed fund.

Scotia Excelsior Global Bond Fund — This fund has been a dog. Low fees have not helped this actively managed fund.

Legend: ★ = overall past performance vs. similar funds (5 ★ max). Boxes show the quartile performance for a fund each calendar year vs. only similar funds (□ is the best score possible). ● = high; ◐ = average; and ○ = a fund with low expenses.

Consistency	Fund Name	Type	Performance Trend										Risk		% of Time Losing $	Biggest Drop	Date	No. of Mo's to Recover	Efficiency MER
Overall Past Performance			88	89	90	91	92	93	94	95	96	Sep-97	Up	Down					
★★ʳ	**Scotia Excelsior Income Fund**	FixInc											C	A	7%	-10%	2/1/94	14	1.37
★★	**Scotia Excelsior International Fund**	FgnEq											C	D	16%	-27%	9/1/87	44	2.20
★★★★	**Scotia Excelsior Latin American**	FgnEq											N/A	N/A	10%	-12%	12/1/94	7	2.31
★	**Scotia Excelsior Money Market Fund**	FixInc											N/A	N/A	0%	0%	N/A	N/A	1.00
★★★★	**Scotia Excelsior Mortgage Fund**	FixInc											A	B	7%	-7%	3/1/94	12	1.56
★★ʳ	**Scotia Excelsior Pacific Rim Fund**	FgnEq											N/A	N/A	0%	-8%	8/1/97	N/A	2.36
★★★	**Scotia Excelsior Prec. Metals Fund**	CdnEq											B	C	42%	-32%	6/1/96	N/A	2.19
★★★★	**Scotia Excelsior Premium T-Bill**	FixInc											N/A	N/A	0%	0%	N/A	N/A	0.52
★	**Scotia Excelsior T-Bill Fund**	FixInc											N/A	N/A	0%	0%	N/A	N/A	1.00
★★★ʳ	**Scotia Excelsior Total Return Fund**	Balan											B	N/A	9%	-12%	2/1/94	17	2.27
★★★★	**Scudder Canadian Equity Fund**	CdnEq											N/A	N/A	0%	-4%	6/1/96	3	1.25
★★★★	**Scudder Canadian Short Term Bond**	FixInc											N/A	N/A	0%	-1%	3/1/97	2	0.50
★★★★	**Scudder Emerging Markets Fund**	FgnEq											N/A	N/A	0%	-5%	8/1/97	N/A	2.00

Scotia Excelsior Income Fund — This well-established fund has been unimpressive so far with disappointing results in a bullish environment. Normally I'd say that this closet indexer has reasonable expenses compared to its peers, but overall performance makes that argument weak.

Scotia Excelsior International Fund — This well-established fund has been set apart from its peers by its weak returns, with disappointing results in bull markets as well as in bear markets. Low fees have not helped this fund.

Scotia Excelsior Latin American — This fund has off-the-charts performance overall vs. its peers. No wonder performance has been so good for this actively managed fund, its fees are among the lowest in its group.

Scotia Excelsior Money Market Fund — This fund has been a dog. Normally I'd say that this actively managed fund has reasonable expenses compared to its peers, but poor overall performance makes that argument weak.

Scotia Excelsior Mortgage Fund — This fund has off-the-charts performance overall vs. its peers with top-notch performance in bull markets as well as performing better than most in bear markets. Reasonable fees represent bargains for this actively managed fund.

Scotia Excelsior Pacific Rim Fund — This fund is a super fund overall vs. its peers. No wonder performance has been so good for this actively managed fund, its fees are among the lowest in its group.

Scotia Excelsior Prec. Metals Fund — This fund has shown middle-of-the-road performance against similar funds. Along with performing better than most in bull markets it has been a disappointment in bear markets. Lower annual expenses than most bode well for the future of this actively managed fund.

Scotia Excelsior Premium T-Bill — This fund has off-the-charts performance overall vs. its peers. No wonder performance has been so good for this actively managed fund, its fees are among the lowest in its group.

Scotia Excelsior T-Bill Fund — This fund has been a dog. Normally I'd say that this actively managed fund has reasonable expenses compared to its peers, but poor overall performance makes that argument weak.

Scotia Excelsior Total Return Fund — You won't find many like this one! It's done better than most in its class. High expenses haven't been much of a problem for this actively managed fund.

Scudder Canadian Equity Fund — This newer fund has off-the-charts performance overall vs. its peers. No wonder performance has been so good for this actively managed fund, its fees are among the lowest in its group.

Scudder Canadian Short Term Bond — This newer fund has off-the-charts performance overall vs. its peers. No wonder performance has been so good for this actively managed fund, its fees are among the lowest in its group.

Scudder Emerging Markets Fund — This newer fund has off-the-charts performance overall vs. its peers. No wonder performance has been so good for this actively managed fund, its fees are among the lowest in its group.

Legend: ★ = overall past performance vs. similar funds (5 ★ max). Boxes show the quartile performance for a fund each calendar year vs. only similar funds. ■ is the best score possible. ● = high; ◐ = average; and ○ = a fund with low expenses.

Overall Past Performance	Fund Name	Type	Risk Up	Risk Down	% of Time Losing $	Biggest Drop	Date	No. of Mo's to Recover	MER
★★★★✓	**Scudder Global Fund**	FgnEq	N/A	N/A	0%	–5%	8/1/97	N/A	● 1.75
★★★✓	**Scudder Greater Europe Fund**	FgnEq	N/A	N/A	0%	–3%	8/1/97	N/A	● 1.75
★★★✓	**Scudder Pacific Fund**	FgnEq	N/A	N/A	13%	–14%	8/1/97	N/A	● 1.75
★★★✓	**Scudder U.S. Growth & Income Fund**	USEq	N/A	N/A	0%	–3%	8/1/97	N/A	● 1.25
★★	**Special Opportunities Fund**	FgnEq	D	N/A	19%	–23%	2/1/94	16	◐ 2.14
★★★	**Spectrum United American Equity**	USEq	B	C	17%	–28%	9/1/87	20	◐ 2.30
★★	**Spectrum United American Growth**	USEq	B	D	14%	–30%	9/1/87	23	◐ 2.35
★★★	**Spectrum United Asian Dynasty Fund**	FgnEq	A	D	57%	–19%	5/1/96	N/A	◐ 2.58
★★	**Spectrum United Asset Alloc. Fund**	Balan	D	N/A	59%	–10%	2/1/94	16	◐ 2.22
★★★✓	**Spectrum United Canadian Equity**	CdnEq	A	A	20%	–29%	7/1/81	20	● 2.35
★★★	**Spectrum United Canadian Growth**	CdnEq	B	B	26%	–43%	12/1/80	49	◐ 2.35
★	**Spectrum United Canadian Investment**	CdnEq	D	N/A	26%	–23%	8/1/87	23	◐ 2.33
★★★	**Spectrum United Canadian Portfolio**	Balan	A	N/A	14%	–10%	2/1/94	16	◐ 2.20

Scudder Global Fund — This newer fund is a super fund overall vs. its peers. No wonder performance has been so good for this actively managed fund, its fees are among the lowest in its group.

Scudder Greater Europe Fund — You won't find many new ones like this one! It's done better than most in its class. Lower annual expenses than most bode well for the future of this actively managed fund.

Scudder Pacific Fund — You won't find many new ones like this one! It's done better than most in its class. Lower annual expenses than most bode well for the future of this actively managed fund.

Scudder U.S. Growth & Income Fund — You won't find many new ones like this one! It's done better than most in its class. Lower annual expenses than most bode well for the future of this actively managed fund.

Special Opportunities Fund — This fund has been set apart from its peers by its weak returns. Normally I'd say that this actively managed fund has reasonable expenses compared to its peers, but poor overall performance makes that argument weak.

Spectrum United American Equity — This well-established fund has shown middle-of-the-road performance against similar funds. Along with performing better than most in bull markets it has been a disappointment in bear markets. Annual fees are reasonable for this reasonably performing actively managed fund.

Spectrum United American Growth — This well-established fund has shown middle-of-the-road performance against similar funds; it has performed better than most in bull markets but has been hit hard in bear markets. Annual fees are reasonable for this

Spectrum United Asian Dynasty Fund — This fund has shown middle-of-the-road performance against similar funds with top-notch performance in bull markets but has been hit hard in bear markets. Annual fees are reasonable for this reasonably performing actively managed fund.

Spectrum United Asset Alloc. Fund — This fund has been set apart from its peers by its weak returns. Normally I'd say that this fund has reasonable expenses compared to its peers, but poor overall performance makes that argument weak.

Spectrum United Canadian Equity — You won't find many like this older one! It's done better than most in its class with top-notch performance in all market conditions. High expenses haven't been much of a problem for this fund.

Spectrum United Canadian Growth — Here is an older fund that has shown middle-of-the-road performance against similar funds along with performing better than most in all market conditions. Lower annual expenses than most bode well for the future of this actively managed fund.

Spectrum United Canadian Investment — This well-established fund has been a dog. Normally I'd say that this fund has reasonable expenses compared to its peers, but poor overall performance makes that argument weak.

Spectrum United Canadian Portfolio — This fund has shown middle-of-the-road performance against similar funds. Annual fees are reasonable for this reasonably performing fund.

Legend: ★ = overall past performance vs. similar funds; similar funds (5 ★ max). Boxes show the quartile performance for a fund each calendar year vs. only similar funds (☐ is the best score possible). ● = high; ◐ = average; and ○ = a fund with low expenses.

Consistency			Performance Trend										Risk						Efficiency
Overall Past Performance	Fund Name	Type	88	89	90	91	92	93	94	95	96	Sep-97	Up	Down	% of Time Losing $	Biggest Drop	Date	No. of Mo's to Recover	MER
★★?	**Spectrum United Cdn. Resource Fund**	CdnEq											N/A	N/A	100%	−16%	2/1/97	N/A	2.35
	Check out how unimpressive this new fund has been. Normally I'd say that this fund has reasonable expenses compared to its peers, but poor overall performance makes that argument weak.																		
★★	**Spectrum United Canadian Stock Fund**	CdnEq											D	B	27%	−20%	8/1/87	22	2.33 ●
	This fund is not worth the extra bucks.																		
★★	**Spectrum United Canadian T-Bill**	FixInc											N/A	N/A	0%	0%	N/A	N/A	0.92
	This fund has been set apart from its peers by its weak returns. Normally I'd say that this actively managed fund has reasonable expenses compared to its peers, but poor overall performance makes that argument weak.																		
★★	**Spectrum United Diversified Fund**	Balan											D	B	17%	−12%	2/1/94	19	2.08
	This fund has been set apart from its peers by its weak returns. Normally I'd say this fund has reasonable fees, but poor overall performance makes that argument weak.																		
★★★	**Spectrum United Dividend Fund**	CdnEq											C	C	11%	−11%	2/1/94	18	1.61
	This fund has shown middle-of-the-road performance against similar funds with disappointing results in all market conditions. Lower annual expenses than most bode well for the future of this actively managed fund.																		
★★★★	**Spectrum United Emerging Markets**	FgnEq											A	N/A	43%	−28%	2/1/94	28	2.66
	This fund has off-the-charts performance overall vs. its peers. Reasonable fees represent bargains for this reasonably performing actively managed fund.																		
★★★?	**Spectrum United European Growth**	FgnEq											N/A	N/A	0%	−3%	6/1/96	3	2.60
	This fund has done better than most in its class. Annual fees are reasonable for this reasonably performing actively managed fund.																		
★★	**Spectrum United Global Bond Fund**	FixInc											D	N/A	17%	−6%	2/1/94	11	2.03
	This fund has been set apart from its peers by its weak returns. Normally I'd say that this actively managed fund has reasonable expenses compared to its peers, but poor overall performance makes that argument weak.																		
★★★	**Spectrum United Global Diversified**	Balan											B	N/A	11%	−10%	2/1/94	16	2.30
	This fund has shown middle-of-the-road performance against similar funds. Lower annual expenses than most bode well for the future of this actively managed fund.																		
★★	**Spectrum United Global Equity Fund**	FgnEq											D	N/A	15%	−11%	9/1/94	15	2.30
	This fund has been set apart from its peers by its weak returns. Low fees have not helped this fund.																		
★★	**Spectrum United Global Growth Fund**	FgnEq											D	D	36%	−40%	9/1/87	69	2.30
	This well-established fund has been set apart from its peers by its weak returns. It has been hit hard in all market conditions. Normally I'd say that this actively managed fund has reasonable expenses compared to its peers, but poor overall performance makes that argument weak.																		
★	**Spectrum United Global Telecomm.**	SpcIty											D	N/A	12%	−13%	6/1/96	11	2.55
	Here is one that is a dog. Normally I'd say that this actively managed fund has reasonable expenses compared to similar funds but has been hit hard in bull markets but has been hit hard in bull markets.																		
★★★	**Spectrum United Long-Term Bond Fund**	FixInc											A	D	13%	−17%	2/1/94	20	1.66
	This fund has shown middle-of-the-road performance against similar funds with top-notch performance in bull markets but has been hit hard in bear markets. Annual fees are reasonable for this reasonably performing fund.																		

Legend: ★ = overall past performance vs. similar funds (5 ★ max). Boxes show the quartile performance for a fund each calendar year vs. only similar funds (□ is the best score possible). ● = high; ⦿ = average; and ● = a fund with low expenses.

Overall Past Performance	Fund Name	Type	Risk Up	Risk Down	% of Time Losing $	Biggest Drop	Date	No. of Mo's to Recover	MER
★★	Spectrum United Mid-Term Bond Fund	FixInc	C	D	8%	-15%	2/1/94	19	1.59
★★★	Spectrum United Optimax USA Fund	USEq	C	N/A	0%	-7%	6/1/96	5	2.35
★★	Spectrum United RRSP Int'l Bond	FixInc	C	N/A	12%	-5%	1/1/96	10	1.98
★★★☆	Spectrum United Savings Fund	FixInc	N/A	N/A	0%	0%	N/A	N/A	1.00
★	Spectrum United Short-Term Bond	FixInc	D	D	3%	-8%	2/1/94	14	1.45
★★★	Spectrum United U.S. Dollar Money	FixInc	N/A	N/A	0%	0%	N/A	N/A	1.20
★	Sportfund Inc.	Labour	N/A	N/A	0%	-2%	2/1/97	N/A	5.54
★★★	Standard Life Balanced Mutual Fund	Balan	A	N/A	14%	-10%	2/1/94	15	2.00
★★★	Standard Life Bond Mutual Fund	FixInc	B	C	20%	-12%	2/1/94	15	1.50
★★★★	Standard Life Canadian Dividend	CdnEq	N/A	N/A	0%	-4%	8/1/97	N/A	1.50
★★★	Standard Life Equity Mutual Fund	CdnEq	B	D	4%	-8%	2/1/94	15	2.00
★★★	Standard Life Growth Equity Fund	CdnEq	N/A	N/A	0%	-7%	11/1/94	7	2.00
★★★	Standard Life Ideal Balanced Fund	Balan	B	D	17%	-12%	8/1/87	17	2.00

Spectrum United Mid-Term Bond Fund — This fund has been set apart from its peers by its weak returns, with disappointing results in bull markets as well as in bear markets. Normally I'd say that this closet indexer has reasonable fees vs. its peers, but its poor overall performance makes that argument weak.

Spectrum United Optimax USA Fund — This fund has shown middle-of-the-road performance against similar funds. High expenses haven't been much of a problem for this actively managed fund.

Spectrum United RRSP Int'l Bond — This fund has been set apart from its peers by its weak returns. Normally I'd say that this actively managed fund has reasonable expenses compared to its peers, but poor overall performance makes that argument weak.

Spectrum United Savings Fund — This fund has done better than most in its class. Annual fees are reasonable for this reasonably performing actively managed fund.

Spectrum United Short-Term Bond — This well-established fund can be described as having dismal returns; it's been hit hard in all market conditions. Low fees have not helped this actively managed fund.

Spectrum United U.S. Dollar Money — This fund has shown middle-of-the-road performance against similar funds. High expenses haven't been much of a problem for this actively managed fund.

Sportfund Inc. — This fund has been set apart from its peers by its weak returns. High expenses exacerbate the problem for this actively managed fund.

Standard Life Balanced Mutual Fund — This fund has shown middle-of-the-road performance against similar funds. Annual fees are reasonable for this reasonably performing fund.

Standard Life Bond Mutual Fund — This fund has shown middle-of-the-road performance against similar funds. Along with performing better than most in bull markets it has been a disappointment in bear markets. Annual fees are reasonable for this reasonable performing closet indexer.

Standard Life Canadian Dividend — This fund has off-the-charts performance overall vs. its peers. No wonder performance has been so good for this closet indexer, its fees are among the lowest in its group.

Standard Life Equity Mutual Fund — This fund has shown middle-of-the-road performance against similar funds; it has performed better than most in bear markets. Annual fees are reasonable for this reasonably performing fund.

Standard Life Growth Equity Fund — This fund has shown middle-of-the-road performance against similar funds. Annual fees are reasonable for this reasonably performing closet indexer.

Standard Life Ideal Balanced Fund — This well-established fund has shown middle-of-the-road performance against similar funds; it has performed better than most in bull markets but has been hit hard in bear markets. Annual fees are reasonable for this reasonably performing closet indexer.

Legend: ★ = overall past performance vs. similar funds (5 ★ max). Boxes show the quartile performance for a fund each calendar year vs. only similar funds (□ is the best score possible). ● = high; ◐ = average; and ◑ = a fund with low expenses.

Overall Past Performance	Fund Name	Type	Performance Trend (88–Sep-97)	Risk — Up	Down	% of Time Losing $	Biggest Drop	Date	No. of Mo's to Recover	MER
★★?	**Standard Life Ideal Bond Fund**	FixInc	□	C	C	9%	-12%	2/1/94	15	2.00 ●
	This well-established fund has been unimpressive so far with disappointing results in all market conditions. High expenses exacerbate the problem for this closet indexer.									
★★	**Standard Life Ideal Equity Fund**	CdnEq	□	C	B	18%	-26%	8/1/87	52	2.00 ◑
	This well-established fund has shown middle-of-the-road performance against similar funds with disappointing results in bull markets and better than average in bear markets. Annual fees are reasonable for this reasonable performing fund.									
★★★★	**Standard Life Ideal Money Market**	FixInc	□	N/A	N/A	0%	0%		N/A	1.00 ◐
	This fund has off-the-charts performance overall vs. its peers. Reasonable fees represent bargains for this actively managed fund.									
★★★	**Standard Life International Bond**	FixInc	□	N/A	N/A	10%	-7%	2/1/96	N/A	2.00 ◐
	This fund has shown middle-of-the-road performance against similar funds. Annual fees are reasonable for this reasonably performing closet indexer.									
★★★?	**Standard Life International Equity**	FgnEq	□	N/A	N/A	0%	-6%	8/1/97	N/A	2.00 ◐
	You won't find many like this one! It's done better than most in its class. Annual fees are reasonable for this reasonably performing closet indexer.									
★★★★★	**Standard Life Money Market Fund**	FixInc	□	N/A	N/A	0%	0%		1	0.90 ◐
	This fund has off-the-charts performance overall vs. its peers. Reasonable fees represent bargains for this actively managed fund.									
★★★	**Standard Life Natural Resources**	CdnEq	□	N/A	N/A	10%	-11%	11/1/94	7	2.00 ●
	This fund has shown middle-of-the-road performance against similar funds. Lower annual expenses than most bode well for the future of this closet indexer.									
★★★	**Standard Life U.S. Equity Fund**	USEq	□	N/A	N/A	0%	-4%	8/1/97	N/A	2.00 ●
	This fund has shown middle-of-the-road performance against similar funds. Lower annual expenses than most bode well for the future of this closet indexer.									
★★★	**STAR Cdn. Balanced Growth & Income**	Balan	□	N/A	N/A	0%	-2%	8/1/97	N/A	
★	**STAR Cdn. Conserv. Income & Growth**	Balan	□	N/A	N/A	0%	-2%	3/1/97	2	
★★★?	**STAR Cdn. Long-Term Growth**	Balan	□	N/A	N/A	0%	-2%	8/1/97	N/A	
★★★	**STAR Cdn. Maximum Equity Growth**	CdnEq	□	N/A	N/A	0%	-4%	6/1/96	3	
★★★?	**STAR Cdn. Maximum Long-Term Growth**	CdnEq	□	N/A	N/A	0%	-3%	8/1/97	N/A	
★★	**STAR For. Balanced Growth & Income**	Balan	□	N/A	N/A	0%	-4%	6/1/96	5	
★★★	**STAR For. Maximum Equity Growth**	FgnEq	□	N/A	N/A	0%	-6%	6/1/96	6	
★★?	**STAR For. Maximum Long-Term Growth**	Balan	□	N/A	N/A	0%	-6%	6/1/96	8	
★★	**STAR Inv. Balanced Growth & Income**	Balan	□	N/A	N/A	0%	-2%	8/1/97	N/A	

Legend: ★ = overall past performance vs. similar funds (5 ★ max). Boxes show the quartile performance for a fund each calendar year vs. only similar funds □ is the best score possible). ● = high; ◕ = average; and ● = a fund with low expenses.

	Consistency			Performance Trend										Risk						Efficiency
	Overall Past Performance	Fund Name	Type	88	89	90	91	92	93	94	95	96	Sep-97	Up	Down	% of Time Losing $	Biggest Drop	Date	No. of Mo's to Recover	MER
	★★★	STAR Inv. Conserv. Income & Growth	Balan											N/A	N/A	0%	-2%	3/1/97	2	
	★★	STAR Inv. Long-Term Growth	Balan											N/A	N/A	0%	-3%	8/1/97	N/A	
	★★	STAR Inv. Maximum Long-Term Growth	Balan											N/A	N/A	0%	-5%	6/1/96	5	
	★★	STAR Reg. Balanced Growth & Income	Balan											N/A	N/A	0%	-3%	8/1/97	N/A	
	★★	STAR Reg. Conserv. Income & Growth	Balan											N/A	N/A	0%	-2%	3/1/97	2	
	★★	STAR Reg. Long-Term Growth	Balan											N/A	N/A	0%	-3%	6/1/96	3	
	★★	STAR Reg. Maximum Equity Growth	CdnEq											N/A	N/A	0%	-5%	6/1/96	4	
	★★	STAR Reg. Maximum Long-Term Growth	Balan											N/A	N/A	0%	-5%	6/1/96	4	
	★	Stone & Co. Flagship Mny. Mkt. CAN	FixInc											N/A	N/A	0%	0%	N/A	N/A	◕ 1.00
		This newer fund has been a dog. Normally I'd say that this actively managed fund has reasonable expenses compared to its peers, but poor overall performance makes that argument weak.																			
	★★★	Stone & Co. Flagship Stock Fund	CdnEq											N/A	N/A	0%	-5%	2/1/97	3	● 2.85
		This newer fund has shown middle-of-the-road performance against similar funds. High expenses haven't been much of a problem for this actively managed fund.																			
	★	Stone & Co. Growth & Inc. Fund CAN	Balan											N/A	N/A	0%	-2%	8/1/97	N/A	● 2.85
		This newer fund has been a dog. High expenses exacerbate the problem for this fund.																			
	★	Strategic Value American Equity	USEq											N/A	N/A	0%	-7%	1/1/97	4	● 2.75
		This newer fund has been a dog. High expenses exacerbate the problem for this closet indexer.																			
	★★★★	Strategic Value Canadian Equity	CdnEq											N/A	N/A	0%	-2%	8/1/97	N/A	● 2.75
		This newer fund has off-the-charts performance overall vs. its peers. This closet indexer is expensive but well worth it.																			
	★	Strategic Value Cdn. Money Market	FixInc											N/A	N/A	0%	0%	N/A	N/A	
	★★	Strategic Value Fund	FgnEq											N/A	N/A	0%	-9%	6/1/96	2	● 3.00
		This newer fund can be described as having dismal returns. High expenses exacerbate the problem for this actively managed fund.																			
	★★	Strategic Value Global Balanced RSP	Balan											N/A	N/A	0%	-4%	2/1/97	3	● 2.75
		This newer fund has been set apart from its peers by its weak returns. High expenses exacerbate the problem for this closet indexer.																			
	★	Strategic Value Global Equity Fund	FgnEq											N/A	N/A	0%	-6%	8/1/97	N/A	● 2.75
		This newer fund has been a dog. High expenses exacerbate the problem for this closet indexer.																			

Legend: ★ = overall past performance vs. similar funds (5 ★ max). Boxes show the quartile performance for a fund each calendar year vs. only similar funds (□ is the best score possible). ● = high; ● = average; and ● = a fund with low expenses.

Overall Past Performance	Fund Name	Type	Up	Down	% of Time Losing $	Biggest Drop	Date	No. of Mo's to Recover	MER
★★★	Talvest Bond Fund	FixInc	B	C	9%	-12%	2/1/94	15	1.99
★★	Talvest Canadian Asset Allocation	Balan	D	B	8%	-9%	8/1/87	7	2.42
★★★	Talvest Canadian Equity Value Fund	CdnEq	C	A	22%	-30%	7/1/81	21	2.40
★	Talvest Dividend Fund	CdnEq	N/A	N/A	0%	-2%	2/1/96	2	1.99
★★★	Talvest Foreign Pay Canadian Bond	FixInc	B	N/A	14%	-7%	4/1/94	10	2.15
★★★	Talvest Global Asset Allocation	Balan	B	N/A	14%	-11%	8/1/90	16	2.75
★★	Talvest Global RRSP Fund Inc.	FgnEq	D	N/A	24%	-11%	9/1/94	16	2.50
★★★	Talvest Income Fund	FixInc	D	D	3%	-8%	2/1/94	14	1.50
★★★★	Talvest Money Fund	FixInc	N/A	N/A	0%	-3%	8/1/86	4	0.75
★	Talvest New Economy	CdnEq	D	C	21%	-13%	2/1/94	16	2.50
★★★	Teachers' RSP – Equity Section	CdnEq	A	A	17%	-33%	6/1/81	19	N/A
★★★	Templeton Balanced Fund	Balan	B	D	30%	-27%	8/1/87	72	2.34
★★	Templeton Canadian Asset Allocation	Balan	N/A	N/A	0%	-2%	8/1/97	N/A	2.15

Talvest Bond Fund — Here is an older fund that has shown middle-of-the-road performance against similar funds. Along with performing better than most in bull markets it has been a disappointment in bear markets. High expenses haven't been much of a problem for this closet indexer.

Talvest Canadian Asset Allocation — This well-established fund has been set apart from its peers by its weak returns. This actively managed fund is not worth the extra bucks.

Talvest Canadian Equity Value Fund — Here is an older fund that has shown middle-of-the-road performance against similar funds with disappointing results in bull markets and top-notch performance in bear markets. High expenses haven't been much of a problem for this fund.

Talvest Dividend Fund — This newer fund has been a dog. High expenses exacerbate the problem for this actively managed fund.

Talvest Foreign Pay Canadian Bond — This fund has shown middle-of-the-road performance against similar funds. Annual fees are reasonable for this reasonably performing actively managed fund.

Talvest Global Asset Allocation — This fund has shown middle-of-the-road performance against similar funds. High expenses haven't been much of a problem for this actively managed fund.

Talvest Global RRSP Fund Inc. — This fund has been set apart from its peers by its weak returns. High expenses exacerbate the problem for this actively managed fund.

Talvest Income Fund — This well-established fund has done better than most in its class, but has been hit hard in all market conditions. Annual fees are reasonable for this reasonably performing closet indexer.

Talvest Money Fund — This well-established fund has off-the-charts performance overall vs. its peers. No wonder performance has been so good for this actively managed fund, its fees are among the lowest in its group.

Talvest New Economy — This fund can be described as having dismal returns with disappointing results in all market conditions. Normally I'd say this fund has reasonable fees, but poor overall performance makes that argument weak.

Templeton Balanced Fund — This well-established fund has shown middle-of-the-road performance against similar funds; it has performed better than most in bull markets but has been hit hard in bear markets. This actively managed fund is expensive but worth it in rising market conditions.

Templeton Canadian Asset Allocation — This fund has been set apart from its peers by its weak returns. Normally I'd say that this actively managed fund has reasonable expenses compared to its peers, but poor overall performance makes that argument weak.

Legend: ★ = overall past performance vs. similar funds (5 ★ max). Boxes show the quartile performance for a fund each calendar year vs. only similar funds (□ is the best score possible). ● = high; ◐ = average; and ○ = a fund with low expenses.

Overall Past Performance	Fund Name	Type	Up	Down	% of Time Losing $	Biggest Drop	Date	No. of Mo's to Recover	MER
★	**Templeton Canadian Bond Fund**	FixInc	D	A	10%	-8%	2/1/94	19	1.65 ○
	This fund has been a dog, but it's been a top-notch performer in bear markets. Normally I'd say that this fund has reasonable expenses compared to its peers, but poor overall performance makes that argument weak.								
★★	**Templeton Canadian Stock Fund**	CdnEq	D	C	32%	-18%	9/1/89	47	2.44 ●
	This fund has been set apart from its peers by its weak returns, but it's been a top-notch performer in bear markets. High expenses exacerbate the problem for this actively managed fund.								
★★★	**Templeton Emerging Markets Fund**	FgnEq	B	N/A	30%	-18%	9/1/94	21	3.30 ●
	Lead Manager Dr. Mark Mobius escaped the worst of the Mexican peso meltdown. Mobius has been very consistent, beating most of his peers every year since inception.								
★★★	**Templeton Global Balanced Fund**	Balan	N/A	N/A	0%	-2%	8/1/95	3	2.55 ◐
	This fund has done better than most in its class. Annual fees are reasonable for this reasonably performing actively managed fund.								
★★★	**Templeton Global Bond Fund**	FixInc	C	N/A	9%	-6%	2/1/94	14	2.25 ●
	This fund has shown middle-of-the-road performance against similar funds. High expenses haven't been much of a problem for this actively managed fund.								
★★★	**Templeton Global Smaller Companies**	FgnEq	A	D	11%	-22%	10/1/89	19	2.55 ◐
	This fund has shown middle-of-the-road performance against similar funds with top-notch performance in bull markets but has been hit hard in bear markets. Annual fees are reasonable for this reasonably performing actively managed fund.								
★★★	**Templeton Growth Fund Ltd.**	FgnEq	A	C	15%	-27%	9/1/87	22	2.00 ◐
	A core global holding, this fund boasts one of the most consistent performance records around! It has managed above-average performance so far in '97, even with lower than usual US exposure and a pile of uninvested cash.								
★★★	**Templeton Int'l Balanced Fund**	Balan	N/A	N/A	0%	-4%	8/1/95	4	2.55 ◐
	This fund has shown middle-of-the-road performance against similar funds. Annual fees are reasonable for this reasonably performing actively managed fund.								
★★★★	**Templeton International Stock Fund**	FgnEq	A	C	13%	-15%	6/1/90	18	2.51 ●
	This fund has remarkably been able to make big profits without investing in the sizzling US market (by policy). This fund fits in nicely to a portfolio with heavy North American exposure.								
★	**Templeton Mutual Beacon Fund**	USEq	N/A	N/A	0%	-1%	3/1/97	1	N/A
	This newer fund has been a dog. Low fees have not helped this fund.								
★★★	**Templeton Treasury Bill Fund**	FixInc	N/A	N/A	0%	0%	N/A	N/A	0.75 ○
	This fund has shown middle-of-the-road performance against similar funds. Lower annual expenses than most bode well for the future of this actively managed fund.								
★	**The Goodwood Fund**	CdnEq	N/A	N/A	0%	-4%	2/1/97	3	N/A
	This newer fund has been a dog. Low fees have not helped this fund.								
★	**The McElvaine Investment Trust**	CdnEq	N/A	N/A	0%	0%	2/1/97	3	N/A
	This newer fund has been a dog. Low fees have not helped this fund.								

Legend: ★ = overall past performance vs. similar funds. Boxes show the quartile performance for a fund each calendar year vs. only similar funds (5 ★ max). (□ is the best score possible). ● = high; ○ = average; and ◐ = a fund with low expenses.

Consistency		Performance Trend			Risk					Efficiency
Overall Past Performance	Fund Name	Type	(88 89 90 91 92 93 94 95 96 Sep-97)		Up	Down	% of Time Losing $	Biggest Drop	Date	No. of Mo's to Recover	MER
★	**Tradex Bond Fund**	FixInc			D	D	11%	-13%	2/1/94	19	1.68
★★★	**Tradex Emerging Mkts Country Fund**	FgnEq			N/A	N/A	0%	-10%	3/1/96	11	3.72
★★★★	**Tradex Equity Fund Ltd.**	CdnEq			A	A	20%	-26%	6/1/81	19	1.35
★	**Trans-Canada Bond Fund (Sagit)**	FixInc			D	A	6%	-6%	2/1/94	14	2.38
★★	**Trans-Canada Dividend Fund (Sagit)**	CdnEq			C	A	20%	-14%	9/1/89	20	2.88
★★★★	**Trans-Canada Money Market (Sagit)**	FixInc			N/A	N/A	0%	0%	N/A	N/A	0.59
★★	**Trans-Canada Pension Fund (Sagit)**	Balan			D	D	28%	-26%	8/1/87	23	2.87
★	**Trans-Canada Value Fund (Sagit)**	CdnEq			D	A	28%	-28%	4/1/81	25	2.89
★★	**Transamerica Balanced Inv. Growth**	Balan			D	A	6%	-16%	6/1/96	2	2.00
★★★	**Triax Growth Fund Inc.**	Labour			N/A	N/A	50%	-3%	1/1/97	N/A	4.62
★	**Trillium Growth Capital Inc.**	Labour			N/A	N/A	53%	-8%	4/1/96	N/A	5.60
★★★★	**Trimark – The Americas Fund**	FgnEq			N/A	N/A	26%	-15%	9/1/94	16	2.53
★★★★★	**Trimark Advantage Bond Fund**	FixInc			N/A	N/A	0%	-2%	2/1/96	4	1.25

Tradex Bond Fund: This fund has been a dog, but it's been hit hard in all market conditions. Normally I'd say that this fund has reasonable expenses compared to its peers, but poor overall performance makes that argument weak.

Tradex Emerging Mkts Country Fund: This fund has shown middle-of-the-road performance against similar funds. High expenses haven't been much of a problem for this actively managed fund.

Tradex Equity Fund Ltd.: This well-established fund has done better than most in its class with top-notch performance in all market conditions. Lower annual expenses than most bode well for the future of this actively managed fund.

Trans-Canada Bond Fund (Sagit): This well-established fund has been a dog, but it's been a top-notch performer in bear markets. High fees exacerbate the problem for this fund, especially in bull markets.

Trans-Canada Dividend Fund (Sagit): This well-established fund has been set apart from its peers by its weak returns, with disappointing results in a bullish environment. High expenses exacerbate the problem for this actively managed fund.

Trans-Canada Money Market (Sagit): This fund has off-the-charts performance overall vs. its peers. No wonder performance has been so good for this actively managed fund, its fees are among the lowest in its group.

Trans-Canada Pension Fund (Sagit): This well-established fund has been set apart from its peers by its weak returns; it's been hit hard in all market conditions. High expenses exacerbate the problem for this actively managed fund.

Trans-Canada Value Fund (Sagit): This well-established fund can be described as having dismal returns, but it's been a top-notch performer in bear markets. High fees exacerbate the problem for this actively managed fund, especially in bull markets.

Transamerica Balanced Inv. Growth: This well-established fund has been set apart from its peers by its weak returns, but it's been a top-notch performer in bear markets. Normally I'd say That this actively managed fund has reasonable expenses compared to its peers, but poor overall performance makes that argument weak.

Triax Growth Fund Inc.: This newer fund has shown middle-of-the-road performance against similar funds. Annual fees are reasonable for this reasonably performing actively managed fund.

Trillium Growth Capital Inc.: This fund has been a dog. High expenses exacerbate the problem for this closet indexer.

Trimark – The Americas Fund: With something like 60% of its assets invested in the US, this fund escaped the peso crisis with minimal damage. For those who can't stomach the wild ride, this is a conservative way to play the Latin markets.

Trimark Advantage Bond Fund: Manager Patrick Farmer is a bond whiz on a team often overshadowed by its stock-picking prowess. A healthy serving of corporate bonds provides a good yield for income-starved investors.

Legend: ★ = overall past performance vs. similar funds (5 ★ max). Boxes show the quartile performance for a fund each calendar year vs. only similar funds [□] is the best score possible). ● = high; ◐ = average; and ○ = a fund with low expenses.

Overall Past Performance	Fund Name	Type	Risk Up	Risk Down	% of Time Losing $	Biggest Drop	Date	No. of Mo's to Recover	MER
★★★✦	**Trimark Canadian Bond Fund**	FixInc	N/A	N/A	0%	-2%	12/1/96	6	1.25 ◐
	A heavier focus on government bonds than the Advantage Bond fund. Don't expect the stellar double-digit bond returns of the last fifteen years. All bond funds will struggle to overcome their rising expenses.								
★★★★	**Trimark Canadian Fund**	CdnEq	A	A	11%	-24%	8/1/87	17	1.52 ●
	Relative performance has suffered recently. Trimark has been buying up an awful lot of the yellow stuff. Not because they are making a big call, but because they found gold to be an undervalued asset.								
★★★	**Trimark Discovery Fund**	SpcIty	N/A	N/A	0%	-11%	2/1/97	4	2.50 ◐
	This newer fund has shown middle-of-the-road performance against similar funds. Annual fees are reasonable for this reasonably performing actively managed fund.								
★★★✦	**Trimark Fund**	FgnEq	A	D	12%	-30%	9/1/87	18	1.52 ●
	This is a low-cost, top-notch global fund with an extra twist of US stocks. Bob Krembil has led this fund to the top of its class, beating 95% of its competition.								
★★★	**Trimark Government Income Fund**	FixInc	B	B	3%	-5%	2/1/94	12	1.25 ●
	This fund has shown middle-of-the-road performance against similar funds along with performing better than most in all market conditions. Lower annual expenses than most should bode well for the future of this closet indexer.								
★★★★	**Trimark Income Growth Fund**	Balan	A	A	9%	-12%	11/1/89	15	1.60 ●
	This fund beats three-quarters of all funds in its class in all market conditions. It has low expenses and has posted only one losing year (1990). What else could you ask for in a balanced fund?								
★★★★★	**Trimark Indo-Pacific Fund**	FgnEq	N/A	N/A	0%	-13%	8/1/97	N/A	2.74 ◐
	This is the only Trimark fund where you'll find an external manager (Lloyd George Management). A great performer so far, this is one of the few Asian funds that invests in Japan.								
★★★★	**Trimark Interest Fund**	FixInc	N/A	N/A	0%	0%	N/A	N/A	0.75 ●
	This well-established fund has impressive past performance characteristics overall vs. its peers. No wonder performance has been so good for this actively managed fund, its fees are among the lowest in its group.								
★★★	**Trimark RSP Equity Fund**	CdnEq	C	B	10%	-16%	10/1/89	17	2.00 ◐
	Low expenses, but still half a point higher than the Trimark Canadian. Has shown less than average returns in up markets, but solid in down times.								
★★★✦	**Trimark Select Balanced Fund**	Balan	A	N/A	4%	-8%	2/1/94	13	2.20 ◐
	A stellar performer but 0.60% more expensive per year compared to the Income & Growth fund. The fund has lost money in only 4% of all twelve-month periods since its inception.								
★★	**Trimark Select Canadian Growth Fund**	CdnEq	C	C	2%	-7%	11/1/94	6	2.25 ◐
	How big is too big? Sceptics have been asking this question for a few years. With somewhere around $10 billion in Canadian equities and a pile of cash yet to be invested, the team at Trimark is still confident that it can deliver.								
★★★	**Trimark Select Growth Fund**	FgnEq	A	C	6%	-24%	6/1/90	11	2.25 ●
	This fund is almost 0.75% more expensive annually than the Trimark fund. Good performance overall but weak during down markets.								
★★	**Trust Pret & Revenu American Fund**	USEq	D	B	25%	-30%	9/1/87	47	2.09 ◐
	This well-established fund has been set apart from its peers by its weak returns. Normally I'd say this fund has reasonable fees, but poor overall performance makes that argument weak.								
★★★	**Trust Pret & Revenu Bond Fund**	FixInc	B	B	8%	-12%	2/1/94	15	1.57 ◐
	This fund has shown middle-of-the-road performance against similar funds along with performing better than most in all market conditions. Annual fees are reasonable for this reasonably performing closet indexer.								

Legend: ★ = overall past performance vs. similar funds (5 ★ max). Boxes show the quartile performance for a fund each calendar year vs. only similar funds (□ is the best score possible). ● = high; ◐ = average; and ○ = a fund with low expenses.

Consistency — Overall Past Performance	Fund Name	Type	Risk Up	Risk Down	% of Time Losing $	Biggest Drop	Date	No. of Mo's to Recover	MER
★★	**Trust Pret & Revenu Canadian Fund**	CdnEq	D	B	25%	−37%	4/1/81	21	1.93
★★★★	**Trust Pret & Revenu Dividend Fund**	CdnEq	N/A	N/A	0%	−2%	12/1/94	3	1.63
★★	**Trust Pret & Revenu H Fund**	FixInc	D	D	1%	−6%	2/1/94	13	1.67
★★	**Trust Pret & Revenu International**	FgnEq	N/A	N/A	0%	−5%	6/1/96	5	2.13
★★	**Trust Pret & Revenu Money Market**	FixInc	N/A	N/A	0%	0%	N/A	N/A	1.10 ●
★★★	**Trust Pret & Revenu Retirement Fund**	Balan	C	D	16%	−16%	4/1/81	18	1.93
★	**Trust Pret & Revenu World Bond Fund**	FixInc	N/A	N/A	10%	−4%	1/1/97	N/A	1.90
★★★	**Universal Americas Fund**	FgnEq	N/A	N/A	17%	−27%	9/1/87	22	2.53
★★★★★	**Universal Canadian Balanced Fund**	Balan	N/A	N/A	0%	−1%	8/1/97	N/A	
★★	**Universal Canadian Growth Fund Ltd**	CdnEq	D	A	29%	−29%	9/1/89	45	2.41 ●
★★	**Universal Canadian Resource Fund**	CdnEq	B	D	46%	−55%	12/1/80	75	2.40
★★★★★	**Universal European Opportunities**	FgnEq	N/A	N/A	0%	−4%	8/1/95	1	2.48
★★	**Universal Far East Fund**	FgnEq	C	C	50%	−21%	1/1/94	41	2.60

Performance Trend columns (88, 89, 90, 91, 92, 93, 94, 95, 96, Sep-97) show quartile boxes for each fund.

Trust Pret & Revenu Canadian Fund: This well-established fund has been set apart from its peers by its weak returns. Normally I'd say this fund has reasonable fees, but poor overall performance makes that argument weak.

Trust Pret & Revenu Dividend Fund: This fund has off-the-charts performance overall vs. its peers. No wonder performance has been so good for this actively managed fund, its fees are among the lowest in its group.

Trust Pret & Revenu H Fund: This well-established fund can be described as having dismal returns; it has been hit hard in all market conditions. Normally I'd say that this actively managed fund has reasonable expenses compared to its peers, but poor overall performance makes that argument weak.

Trust Pret & Revenu International: This fund has been unimpressive so far. Low fees have not helped this actively managed fund.

Trust Pret & Revenu Money Market: This fund has been unimpressive so far. High expenses exacerbate the problem for this actively managed fund.

Trust Pret & Revenu Retirement Fund: This well-established fund has shown middle-of-the-road performance against similar funds with disappointing results in bull markets along with being hit hard in bear markets. Annual fees are reasonable for this reasonable performing fund.

Trust Pret & Revenu World Bond Fund: This fund has been a dog. Normally I'd say that this actively managed fund has reasonable expenses compared to its peers, but poor overall performance makes that argument weak.

Universal Americas Fund: This fund has done better than most in its class. Annual fees are reasonable for this reasonably performing actively managed fund.

Universal Canadian Balanced Fund: This newer fund has off-the-charts performance overall vs. its peers. No wonder performance has been so good for this closet indexer, its fees are among the lowest in its group.

Universal Canadian Growth Fund Ltd: This well-established fund has been unimpressive so far but it's been a top-notch performer in bear markets. High fees exacerbate the problem for this actively managed fund, especially in bull markets.

Universal Canadian Resource Fund: This well-established fund has been unimpressive so far; it's performed better than most in bull markets but it's been hit hard in bear markets. Normally I'd say that this actively managed fund has reasonable fees vs. its peers, but its poor overall performance makes that argument weak.

Universal European Opportunities: Stephen Peak of Henderson International Management has guided this fund to the top of its class! You'll find some emerging-markets exposure via Eastern European holdings.

Universal Far East Fund: This fund has been set apart from its peers by its weak returns, with disappointing results in all market conditions. Normally I'd say this fund has reasonable fees, but poor overall performance makes that argument weak.

Legend: ★= overall past performance vs. similar funds (5 ★ max). Boxes show the quartile performance for a fund each calendar year vs. only similar funds (□ is the best score possible). ● = high; ◐ = average; and ○ = a fund with low expenses.

Overall Past Performance	Fund Name	Type	Risk Up	Risk Down	% of Time Losing $	Biggest Drop	Date	No. of Mo's to Recover	MER
★★★	**Universal Growth Fund**	FgnEq	N/A	N/A	0%	-6%	6/1/96	5	2.39
★★★	**Universal Japan Fund**	FgnEq	B	C	70%	-31%	7/1/94	N/A	2.54
★★★	**Universal Precious Metals Fund**	CdnEq	C	D	23%	-38%	6/1/96	N/A	2.41
★★★↗	**Universal U.S. Emerging Growth Fund**	USEq	A	N/A	7%	-29%	6/1/96	N/A	2.40
★	**Universal U.S. Money Market ($US)**	FixInc	N/A	N/A	0%	0%	N/A	N/A	1.25
★★	**Universal World Asset Allocation**	Balan	D	N/A	41%	-13%	2/1/96	16	2.45
★★★★↗	**Universal World Balanced RRSP**	Balan	A	N/A	10%	-8%	9/1/94	10	2.43
★★★	**Universal World Emerging Growth**	FgnEq	B	N/A	44%	-22%	9/1/94	31	2.56
★★★	**Universal World Equity Fund**	FgnEq	B	C	30%	-19%	8/1/90	32	2.45
★★★	**Universal World Growth RRSP Fund**	FgnEq	N/A	N/A	0%	-8%	8/1/97	N/A	2.44
★★★↗	**Universal World Income RRSP Fund**	FixInc	N/A	N/A	0%	-3%	2/1/96	5	2.16
★★★	**Universal World Science & Tech.**	Spclty	N/A	N/A	0%	-7%	2/1/97	3	
★★	**Universal World Tactical Bond Fund**	FixInc	N/A	N/A	10%	-6%	2/1/96	14	2.62

Universal Growth Fund — This fund has shown middle-of-the-road performance against similar funds. Annual fees are reasonable for this reasonably performing actively managed fund.

Universal Japan Fund — This fund has shown middle-of-the-road performance against similar funds. Along with performing better than most in bull markets it has been a disappointment in bear markets. Annual fees are reasonable for this reasonable performing fund.

Universal Precious Metals Fund — This fund has shown middle-of-the-road performance against similar funds with disappointing results in bull markets along with being hit hard in bear markets. This actively managed fund is expensive but worth it in rising market conditions.

Universal U.S. Emerging Growth Fund — This fund has done better than most in its class. Annual fees are reasonable for this reasonably performing actively managed fund.

Universal U.S. Money Market ($US) — This fund has been a dog. High expenses exacerbate the problem for this actively managed fund.

Universal World Asset Allocation — This fund has been set apart from its peers by its weak returns. Low fees have not helped this actively managed fund.

Universal World Balanced RRSP — Who couldn't love this one! It's a super fund overall vs. its peers. Reasonable fees represent bargains for this actively managed fund.

Universal World Emerging Growth — This fund has shown middle-of-the-road performance against similar funds. Lower annual expenses than most bode well for the future of this actively managed fund.

Universal World Equity Fund — This well-established fund has shown middle-of-the-road performance against similar funds. Along with performing better than most in bull markets it has been a disappointment in bear markets. Annual fees are reasonable for this reasonably performing fund.

Universal World Growth RRSP Fund — This fund has impressive past performance characteristics overall vs. its peers. Reasonable fees represent bargains for this actively managed fund.

Universal World Income RRSP Fund — You won't find many like this one! It's done better than most in its class. High expenses haven't been much of a problem for this actively managed fund.

Universal World Science & Tech. — This newer fund has shown middle-of-the-road performance against similar funds. Lower annual expenses than most bode well for the future of this actively managed fund.

Universal World Tactical Bond Fund — This fund has been set apart from its peers by its weak returns. High expenses exacerbate the problem for this closet indexer.

Legend: ★ = overall past performance vs. similar funds (5 ★ max). Boxes show the quartile performance for a fund each calendar year vs. only similar funds (□ is the best score possible). ● = high; ◐ = average; and ○ = a fund with low expenses.

Overall Past Performance	Fund Name	Type	Up	Down	% of Time Losing $	Biggest Drop	Date	No. of Mo's to Recover	MER
★★★	**University Avenue Bond Fund**	FixInc	C	A	12%	−7%	2/1/94	12	1.99 ●
	This fund has shown middle-of-the-road performance against similar funds with disappointing results in bull markets and top-notch performance in bear markets. High expenses haven't been much of a problem for this fund.								
★★★	**University Avenue Canadian Fund**	CdnEq	A	D	19%	−19%	2/1/94	24	2.60 ●
	This fund has shown middle-of-the-road performance against similar funds with top-notch performance in bull markets but has been hit hard in bear markets. This actively managed fund is expensive but worth it in rising market conditions.								
★	**University Avenue Growth Fund**	USEq	D	C	41%	−33%	9/1/87	100	2.99 ●
	This well-established fund has been a dog, but it's been a top-notch performer in bear markets. High expenses exacerbate the problem for this actively managed fund, especially in declining markets.								
★★★	**Valorem Canadian Bond-Value**	FixInc	N/A	N/A	0%	−2%	3/1/97	1	
	This newer fund has impressive past performance characteristics overall vs. its peers. No wonder performance has been so good for this fund, its fees are among the lowest in its group.								
★★★★★	**Valorem Canadian Equity-Value**	CdnEq	N/A	N/A	0%	−5%	3/1/97	2	
	This newer fund has off-the-charts performance overall vs. its peers. No wonder performance has been so good for this fund, its fees are among the lowest in its group.								
★★★★★	**Valorem Demographic Trends Fund**	FgnEq	N/A	N/A	0%	−3%	8/1/97	N/A	
	This newer fund has off-the-charts performance overall vs. its peers. No wonder performance has been so good for this fund, its fees are among the lowest in its group.								
★★	**Valorem Diversified**	Balan	N/A	N/A	0%	−3%	3/1/97	2	
	This newer fund has been set apart from its peers by its weak returns. Low fees have not helped this fund.								
★★★	**Valorem U.S. Equity-Value**	USEq	N/A	N/A	0%	−4%	3/1/97	1	
	This newer fund has shown middle-of-the-road performance against similar funds. Lower annual expenses than most bode well for the future of this fund.								
★★★★★	**Value Contrarian Canadian Equity**	CdnEq	N/A	N/A	0%	−2%	3/1/97	2	2.00 ◐
	This newer fund has off-the-charts performance overall vs. its peers. Reasonable fees represent bargains for this fund.								
★★★	**VenGrowth Investment Fund Inc.**	Labour	N/A	N/A	0%	−2%	6/1/96	5	4.00 ○
	Earl Storie and his team do a good job of mitigating risk by investing only in "later stage" venture companies. This team has been managing venture capital for pension funds since the early '80s.								
★★★	**Vision Europe Fund**	FgnEq	A	N/A	4%	−11%	10/1/92	10	2.23 ●
	This fund has shown middle-of-the-road performance against similar funds. Lower annual expenses than most bode well for the future of this fund.								
★★	**Westbury Canadian Balanced Fund**	Balan	D	N/A	9%	−10%	2/1/94	15	2.42 ●
	This fund has been set apart from its peers by its weak returns. High expenses exacerbate the problem for this actively managed fund.								
★⯪	**Westbury Canadian Bond Fund**	FixInc	D	C	14%	−12%	2/1/94	19	2.08 ●
	This fund can be described as having dismal returns. High expenses exacerbate the problem for this fund, especially in declining markets.								

Legend: ★ = overall past performance vs. similar funds (5 ★ max). Boxes show the quartile performance for a fund each calendar year vs. only similar funds (□ is the best score possible). ● = high; ◐ = average; and ● = a fund with low expenses.

Consistency			Performance Trend										Risk						Efficiency
Overall Past Performance	Fund Name	Type	88	89	90	91	92	93	94	95	96	Sep-97	Up	Down	% of Time Losing $	Biggest Drop	Date	No. of Mo's to Recover	MER
★★	**Westbury Canadian Equity Fund**	CdnEq				N/A	□	□	□	□	□	□	C	N/A	32%	−14%	4/1/94	21	2.42 ●
	This fund has been set apart from its peers by its weak returns. High expenses exacerbate the problem for this actively managed fund.																		
★★★	**Working Opportunity Fund**	Labour						N/A	□	□	□	□	N/A	N/A	0%	−1%	4/1/94	5	4.00 ◐
	This fund has shown middle-of-the-road performance against similar funds. Annual fees are reasonable for this reasonably performing actively managed fund.																		
★★★★	**Working Ventures Canadian Fund Inc.**	Labour						N/A	□	□	□	□	N/A	N/A	8%	−4%	6/1/96	N/A	2.67 ●
	This fund has off-the-charts performance overall vs. its peers. No wonder performance has been so good for this actively managed fund, its fees are among the lowest in its group.																		
★★	**Zweig Global Managed Assets**	Balan								□	□	□	N/A	N/A	0%	−2%	8/1/95	3	2.99 ●
	This newer fund has been set apart from its peers by its weak returns. High expenses exacerbate the problem for this actively managed fund.																		
★★★	**Zweig Strategic Growth**	USEq							□	□	□	□	C	N/A	2%	−4%	6/1/96	5	2.59 ●
	This fund has shown middle-of-the-road performance against similar funds. High expenses haven't been much of a problem for this actively managed fund.																		

Glossary

AMR (Average Monthly Rankings)   A rating system based on a fund's monthly performance relative to other funds just like it. Monthly performance scores are averaged to provide a fund's ranking within its group.

Asset allocation   The relative weights of equities, bonds, cash, real estate, and other asset types held in a portfolio at a given time. In a tactical asset allocation mutual fund, the portfolio manager weights each type to maximize total return when economic conditions change.

Automatic Reinvestment   An option available to investors in a mutual fund or other investment whereby income (dividends, interest, or capital gains) distributions are used to purchase additional units of the fund.

Balanced portfolio   The distribution of investments into several asset categories to help increase returns and reduce risk. The basic components of a balanced portfolio are cash, bonds, and equities. The weighting of the different components varies depending on the age and risk tolerance of the investor.

Bear market   A stock market which is declining in value over an extended period (this is measured by an index of representative stocks, like the TSE300). A "bearish" investor believes share prices will fall.

Blue-chip stocks   Stocks with good investment qualities. They are usually common shares of well-established companies with good earning records and regular dividend payments that are known nationally for the quality and wide acceptance of their products and services. (Think "IBM.")

Bond A debt instrument issued by governments and corporations. A bond is a promise by the issuer to pay the full amount of the debt on maturity, plus interest payments at regular intervals.

Bottom-up A style of investing that places a priority on examining companies that may be appropriate for investment. Less emphasis is placed on macroeconomic considerations. A "bottom-up" investor makes buy and sell decisions based on close scrutiny of the financials of a company. See also Top-down.

Bull market A stock market whose index has been rising in value. A "bullish" investor believes share prices will rise.

Canada Deposit Insurance Corporation (CDIC) An agency of the Government of Canada that insures the deposits of Canadians in banks and trust companies up to $60 000.

Capital Cost Allowance (CCA) A tax deduction available to reflect the depreciation of various types of assets. Applied to buildings (either commercial or residential), CCA can be used to shelter rental income from real estate investment trusts (REITs).

Capital gain/loss A profit (or loss) made on the sale of an asset when the market price rises (or falls) above the purchase price — usually in real estate, stocks, bonds, or other capital assets.

Closed-end fund A mutual fund in which the total number of units is limited. If units are not purchased when the fund is initially offered, they can only be purchased from another owner. They often trade on stock exchanges.

Common share A class of stock that represents ownership, or equity, in a company. Common shares entitle the holder to a share in the company's profits, usually as a dividend. They may also carry a voting privilege.

Consumer Price Index (CPI) A statistical measure of the increase in the cost of living for consumers. Often used to demonstrate general increases in the level of inflation over a period of time.

Current yield   A term applied to money market funds, which refers to the actual rate of return over the past seven days, annualized.

Cyclical stock   A stock within a specific industry sector that is particularly sensitive to changes in economic conditions. The natural resources sector tends to be cyclical, as do particular stocks in the sector.

Deferred Sales Charge (DSC)   An increasingly popular alternative for mutual funds that charge front-end acquisition fees. Here, a fee is paid when the investor sells units in the fund. This usually begins at 4.5 percent of the unit's value in the first year and declines by 0.5 to one percent per year, eventually reaching zero percent several years into the future. Sometimes called an "exit fee."

Distribution fees   Fees levied by some mutual fund companies on the value of units purchased with a back-end load or deferred sales charge. While most funds have stopped charging these fees, a few hold-outs remain.

Distributions   The payments made by a mutual fund to its unitholders of the interest, dividends, and/or capital gains earned during the year. Shareholders may either take distributions in cash or reinvest them in additional shares of the fund.

Diversification   Spreading investment risk by investing in a variety of asset categories (stocks, bonds, gold) in different industries and/or countries.

Dividend tax credit   A special tax credit applied to reduce the effective rate of tax paid on Canadian dividend income.

Dividend   A portion of a company's profit paid out to common and preferred shareholders, the amount having been decided on by the company's board of directors. A dividend may be in the form of cash or additional stock. A preferred dividend is usually a fixed amount, while a common dividend may fluctuate with the earnings of the company.

Dollar-cost averaging   An investment program in which contributions are made at regular intervals with specific and equal dollar amounts

This often results in a lower average cost per unit because more units are purchased when the prices are depressed than when they are high.

Equity funds Mutual funds that invest in common and preferred shares.

Ex-dividend The date on which distributions that have been declared by a mutual fund are deducted from total net assets. The price of the fund's shares or units will be reduced by the amount of the distribution.

Fixed asset mix For balanced funds, an approach that fixes the asset mix to be maintained in the fund: often 50 to 60 percent equity and 40 to 50 percent fixed income. Compare to an asset allocation fund, where there is no pre-set fixed asset mix.

Fixed-income funds Mutual funds that invest in mortgages, bonds, or a combination of both. Mortgages and bonds are issued at a fixed rate of interest and are known as fixed-income securities.

Front-end commission charge An acquisition fee based on the total value of mutual fund units purchased. The fees can range from two to nine percent, but average four to five percent on most purchases.

GIC (Guaranteed Investment Certificate) A deposit certificate usually issued by a bank or trust company. An interest-bearing investment that matures after a specified term, usually anywhere from 30 days to five years. The interest remains fixed during this period.

Growth investing An approach to investing that places greater emphasis on a stock's future growth potential than on its current price. A growth manager may therefore be prepared to pay a higher price for a stock than a value manager would if he or she believes it has attractive future growth potential. It is viewed as a more aggressive style of management than value investing.

Growth stock Shares of a company whose earnings are expected to grow faster than average.

Hedging The strategy of taking positions in more than one commodity, security, or asset category in an attempt to reduce investment risk. An investment in gold or oil/natural gas, for example, is often seen as a hedge or protection against inflation.

Income splitting   The process of diverting taxable income from an individual in a high tax bracket to one in a lower tax bracket.

Index fund   A mutual fund designed to match the performance of a recognized group of publicly traded stocks, such as those represented by the TSE 300 Index or the Standard & Poor's 500 Index in the United States.

Index   For stocks, an indicator of broad market performance. The Dow Jones Industrial Average includes the shares of 30 large companies; the Toronto Stock Exchange's Composite Index includes 300 companies; the Standard & Poor's index contains 500 companies. These indices are developed from statistics that measure the state of the economy, based on the performance of stocks or other key indicators such as the Consumer Price Index.

Investment fund   See Mutual fund.

Leverage   Using borrowed funds to maximize the rate of return on investment. A potentially dangerous strategy if the investment declines in value.

Limited partnership   See Tax shelter.

Liquidity   The ease with which an asset can be sold and converted into cash at its full value.

Management Expense Ratio (MER)   The total of all management and other fees charged to the fund, shown as a percentage of the fund's total assets.

Management fee   The amount paid annually by a mutual fund to its managers. The average annual fee in Canada is between one and two percent of the value of the fund's assets.

Marginal tax rate   The rate at which tax is calculated on the next dollar of income earned. This rate steps up progressively as your income rises.

Market timing   The process of shifting from one type of investment to another with the intention of maximizing the return as market conditions change.

Money market fund   Fixed-income mutual funds that invest in short term securities (maturing within one year).

Mortgage A legal instrument given by a borrower to the lender entitling the lender to take over pledged property if conditions of the loan are not met.

Mortgage-Backed Securities (MBS) These invest in first mortgages on residential properties, and provide higher yields than many other savings options.

Mutual fund A professionally managed pool of assets, representing the contributions of many investors, which is used to purchase a portfolio of securities that meets specific investment objectives. See also Open-end fund and Closed-end fund.

Net Asset Value (NAV) The value of a fund's assets, less its liabilities. The NAV is used to calculate the buying or selling price of shares or units in a fund, usually expressed as the Net Asset Value Per Share (NAVPS).

Net Asset Value Per Share (NAVPS) The total market value of all securities owned by a mutual fund, less its liabilities, divided by the number of units outstanding.

No-load fund A mutual fund that does not charge a fee for buying or selling its units.

Open-end fund A mutual fund whose units are offered for sale on a continuous basis; the fund will also buy back units at their current price (net asset value per share). Sometimes called an investment fund. The most common type of mutual fund.

Portfolio A group of securities held or owned for investment purposes by an individual or institution. An investor's portfolio may contain common and preferred shares, bonds, options, and other types of securities.

Prospectus A thorough description of an investment vehicle offered to the public. A prospectus will describe the investment objective and style, and must also identify any investment restrictions, as well as the officers of the company.

Real Estate Investment Trust (REIT)   A form of real estate mutual fund with the difference that the REIT trades on a stock exchange. As a result, it provides greater liquidity than is usually available through a traditional real estate mutual fund. The units generally trade at a discount from Net Asset Value.

Real rate of return   The stated rate of return, less inflation and taxes.

Registered investment   A security held in a tax-sheltered plan — most often an RRSP or RRIF — that has been approved by Revenue Canada.

Risk tolerance   The ability of an individual investor to tolerate risk. Risk tolerance is a function of the individual's personality and other factors, and is an important element in determining investment strategy.

Risk-free return   The return available from securities that have no risk of loss. Short-term securities issued by the government (such as treasury bills) normally provide a risk-free return.

Risk   The possibility that some or all of the money put into an investment will be lost.

RRIF (Registered Retirement Income Fund)   A non-annuity investment vehicle for maturing RRSPs. One of the options available to RRSP holders upon cashing in their retirement funds at age 69 or sooner. RRIFs generally provide for a series of payments that increase each year.

RRSP (Registered Retirement Savings Plan)   A savings program approved by Revenue Canada that permits tax-deferred saving for retirement purposes. Contributions to an RRSP are tax-deductible. Earnings on contributions are sheltered from tax while they remain in the plan.

Sector rotation   A style of investing that identifies prospective investments (or the weighting of an investment portfolio) according to which sectors of the economy are poised to do well. Often associated with the "top-down" approach to investing.

Segregated funds   Funds sold and administered by life insurance companies.

Self-directed RRSP   RRSP whose investments are controlled by the plan holder. A self-directed RRSP may include stocks, bonds, residential mortgages, or other types of investments approved by Revenue Canada.

Systematic Withdrawal Plan (SWP)   A plan for withdrawing money from a mutual fund on a regular basis — monthly, quarterly, semi-annually, or annually. Used mostly by investors who require a steady stream of income from their investments.

Tax shelter   An investment that, by government regulation, can be made with untaxed or partly taxed dollars. The creation of tax losses in order to offset an individual's taxable income from other sources thereby reduces tax liability.

Taxable income   The amount of annual income that is used to calculate how much income tax must be paid: total earnings for the year, minus deductions.

Term deposit   Similar to a guaranteed investment certificate. An interest-bearing investment to which an investor commits funds for a specified term and rate of interest.

Top-down   A style of investing that considers the economic "big picture" to identify sectors of the economy that are expected to outperform. Less importance is attached to identifying individual companies that may do well. See also Bottom-up.

Total return   The amount of income earned from an investment, together with its capital appreciation, expressed as a percentage of the original amount invested. It indicates an investment's performance over a stated period.

Treasury bills   Short-term debt securities sold by governments, usually with maturities of three months to one year. They carry no stated interest rate, but trade at a discount to their face value. The discount represents the market's valuation of the future return at maturity.

Unit   In mutual funds, a unit represents a portion, or share, of the total value of the fund. Units are purchased by investors, and rise or fall proportionately with the net asset value of the fund.

Value investing   An approach to investing that attempts, through the use of various analytical models, to identify companies that are fundamentally strong but that may be out of favour in the marketplace and trading at prices that represent a good buy. This conservative approach is often associated with Sir John Templeton and is one that many investment managers claim to use.

Volatility   A measure of a mutual fund's tendency to fluctuate in value. More volatile funds are traditionally considered to have a greater degree of risk, although the fluctuation in value may, in fact, be either up or down.

Index